FOOD SECURITY GOVERNANCE

This book fills a gap in the literature by setting food security in the context of evolving global food governance.

Today's food system generates hunger alongside food waste, burgeoning health problems, and massive greenhouse gas emissions. Applying food system analysis to review how the international community has addressed food issues since World War II, this book proceeds to explain how actors link up in corporate global food chains and in the local food systems that feed most of the world's population. It unpacks relevant paradigms – from productivism to food sovereignty – and highlights the significance of adopting a rights-based approach to solving food problems. The author describes how communities around the world are protecting their access to resources and building better ways of producing and accessing food. She discusses the reformed Committee on World Food Security, a uniquely inclusive global policy forum, and how it could be supportive of efforts from the base. The book concludes by identifying terrains on which work is needed to adapt the practice of the democratic public sphere and accountable governance to a global dimension and extend its authority to the world of markets and corporations.

Food Security Governance will be of interest to students of food security, global governance, development studies, and critical security studies in general.

Nora McKeon is engaged in teaching, writing, and advocacy on food issues and social movements, following a career at the Food and Agriculture Organization (FAO) of the United Nations. She is the author of *Global Governance for World Food Security* (2011), *The United Nations and Civil Society* (2009), and *Peasant Organizations* (2004).

Routledge Critical Security Studies Series

"There are few people who have been involved in grassroots efforts to transform the global food system, been veterans of international organizations, and still been able to imagine compatibility between the two. Yet Nora McKeon's subtle analysis, with its centerpiece examination of the history and possibilities of the Committee on World Food Security, is required reading for those who feel the trenches dug by governments and civil society can never move. It's a wonderfully readable account of the world food crisis, distinguished by its grounded faith in the capacity of organizations – of people and governments – to prevent future hunger".

—*Raj Patel, University of Texas at Austin, USA, and author of*
Stuffed and Starved *and* The Value of Nothing

"Global food governance is at crossroads. The rich world is over-consuming; the poor continue to lose out; meanwhile global systems of governance have not fully risen to the challenge. This book is an overdue account of the fight over reform. It is a fine reminder that food democracy is the key to feeding everyone equitably, healthily, affordably, and sustainably."

—*Tim Lang, City University, London, UK*

"At such an uncertain time in global food provisioning, Nora McKeon's book offers an exceptional perspective. Not only does she evaluate the organization and politics of the world's food systems with erudition, but also she provides brilliant practitioner insights from within the UN Committee on World Food Security and the Food Sovereignty movement. The result is a lively account of food system crisis, competing paradigms and new questions of governance in an accessible and forward-looking analysis."

—*Philip McMichael, Cornell University, USA*

"Nora McKeon does a superb job at describing how governments have allowed markets and corporations to take control of food systems, and which tools could be used to provide healthier diets, ensure greater resilience, and empower communities. Building on her unmatched experience working both with farmers' organisations and with international institutions, she brings us into how global governance of food security is shaped, and why food democracy matters: an illuminating and eye-opening journey."

—*Olivier De Schutter, former UN Special Rapporteur on the Right to Food*

"Nora McKeon understands the Byzantine world of global food politics better than anyone I know – from inside the Rome-based agencies and from outside. She has put herself on the line time after time and has earned enormous respect for her intelligence and integrity. Everyone fighting for Food Sovereignty has to read this book."

—*Pat Mooney, ETC Group*

"Brilliant! An eye-opening tour of the march to democratize global food governance. Discover the other side of corporate globalization as social movements gain a voice at the table. With the eyes of a veteran insider and the mind of an astute analyst, McKeon offers powerful insights. A must-read for all who want to go beyond competing "issues" to governance itself – and real solutions."

—*Frances Moore Lappé, author of* Diet for a Small Planet

"The far-reaching implications of food governance – local and global – are trenchantly addressed in this impeccably researched book. Nora McKeon brings decades of engagement with farmers' movements, multilateral agencies, and academia to bear on the question of how the dysfunctional global food system can be transformed through citizens' concerted action. A must-read for food activists seeking to go beyond slogans, techno-administrative fixes, or business as usual into the realm of active, popular democracy."

—*Eric Holt-Giménez, Food First/Institute for Food and Development Policy*

"Nora McKeon, with her long professional experience and transdisciplinary approach, takes us admirably through the various components, contradictions, and controversies of food systems governance, both at global and local scale. This insightful book is an essential guide for anyone who wants to understand the social and political dynamics of the food systems in the contemporary capitalist world-economy."

—*Pasquale De Muro, Roma Tre University, Italy*

"Nora McKeon's book is a must-read for both social activists and academics involved in the realms of agriculture, food, justice, and social movements. But it is equally an accessible and highly informative source for interested members of the general public."

—*Jan Douwe van der Ploeg, Wageningen University, The Netherlands*

"The author weaves together a complex landscape of policies, activities, and levels of food security governance. Opinions differ because of the ideologies of the constituencies, but in all those controversies, small producers of food are pivotal to ending hunger, malnutrition, and extreme poverty. Nora, thank you for this effort."

—*Yaya Adissa Olaitan Olaniran, Former Chair, Committee on World Food Security (CFS), Permanent Representative of Nigeria to the UN Agencies of Food and Agriculture*

FOOD SECURITY GOVERNANCE

Empowering communities, regulating corporations

Nora McKeon

Routledge
Taylor & Francis Group

LONDON AND NEW YORK

First published 2015
by Routledge
2 Park Square, Milton Park, Abingdon, Oxon OX14 4RN

and by Routledge
711 Third Avenue, New York, NY 10017

Routledge is an imprint of the Taylor & Francis Group, an informa business

© 2015 Nora McKeon

British Library Cataloguing-in-Publication Data
A catalogue record for this book is available from the British Library

Library of Congress Cataloging-in-Publication Data
McKeon, Nora.
Food security governance : empowering communities, regulating corporations / Nora McKeon.
    pages cm.—(Routledge critical security studies series)
  Includes bibliographical references and index.
  1. Food security.   2. Food supply—International cooperation.   I. Title.
HD9000.5.M3695   2015
363.8—dc23   2014030092

ISBN: 978-0-415-52909-9 (hbk)
ISBN: 978-0-415-52910-5 (pbk)
ISBN: 978-1-315-88252-9 (ebk)

Typeset in Bembo
by Apex CoVantage, LLC

Printed and bound in the United States of America by Publishers Graphics, LLC on sustainably sourced paper.

To my families – original, created, extended – the premise for all I know about community and governance.

CONTENTS

FIGURES, TABLES, AND BOXES

Figures

ACRONYMS AND ABBREVIATIONS

AoA	Agreement on Agriculture
ANAP	National Association of Small Farmers of Cuba
ARPA	Agricultural Rehabilitation Program for Africa
AS-PTA	Family Farming and Agro-ecology
BRIC	Brazil, Russia, India, China
BTA	Bilateral trade agreement
CAADP	Comprehensive Africa Agriculture Development Program
CBD	Convention on Biodiversity
CBO	Community-based organization
CC	Coordinating Committee
CDM	Clean Development Mechanism
CETA	Canada-EU Trade Agreement
CFA	Comprehensive Framework for Action
CFS	Committee on World Food Security
CFTC	Commodities Futures Trading Commission
CGIAR	Consultative Group on International Agricultural Research
CIRAD	Agricultural Research for Development Center
CIW	Coalition of Immokalee Workers
CNCR	National Council for Dialogue and Cooperation of Rural People of Senegal
CNOP	National Coordination of Peasant Organizations of Mali
CNRS	National Center for Scientific Research of France
CONSEA	National Council of Food and Nutritional Security of Brazil
CSM	Civil Society Mechanism
CSO	Civil society organization
CSR	Corporate social responsibility
EAFF	East African Farmers Federation
ECOSOC	Economic and Social Council of the United Nations

ECOWAS	Economic Community of West African States
ESCR	Covenant on Economic, Social, and Cultural Rights
EPA	Economic Partnership Agreement
EU	European Union
FAC	Food Aid Convention
FAO	Food and Agriculture Organization of the United Nations
FFHC	Freedom from Hunger Campaign
FONGS	Federation of NGOs of Senegal
FPIC	Free Prior and Informed Consent
FTT	Financial transaction tax
G8	Group of 8
G20	Group of 20
G33	Group of 33
G77	Group of 77
GAFSP	Global Agriculture and Food Security Program
GATT	General Agreement on Tariffs and Trade
GDP	Gross Domestic Product
GMO	Genetically modified organism
GNP	Gross national product
GPAFS	Global Partnership for Agriculture and Food Security
GRET	Group for Technological Research and Exchanges
GSF	Global Strategic Framework
HLPE	High-Level Panel of Experts
HLTF	UN High-Level Task Force on the Food Security Crisis
HR	Human rights
IAASRD	International Assessment of Agricultural Knowledge, Science, and Technology for Development
IBGE	Brazilian Institute of Geography and Statistics
ICARRD	International Conference for Agrarian Reform and Rural Development
IFAD	International Fund for Agricultural Development
IFIs	International financial institutions
IFOAM	International Foundation for Organic Agriculture
IFSN	International Food Security Network
ILC	International Land Coalition
ILO	International Labor Organization
IMF	International Monetary Fund
INGO	International nongovernmental organization
IPC	International Civil Society Planning Committee for Food Sovereignty
IRAM	Institute for Research and Application of Development Methods
ITGRFA	International Treaty on Plant Genetic Resources for Food and Agriculture
LARR	Land Acquisition and Rehabilitation and Resettlement Bill

LSPPC	Local Solidarity Partnerships between Producers and Consumers
LVC	La Via Campesina
Mcal	Megacalorie
MDGs	Millennium Development Goals
MERCOSUR	Common Market of Southern America
MST	Landless Workers Movement
NAFTA	North American Free Trade Agreement
NEPAD	New Partnership for Africa's Development
NGO	Nongovernmental organization
NIEO	New International Economic Order
ODA	Official Development Assistance
OECD	Organization for Economic Cooperation and Development
ORSTOM	Office for Scientific and Technical Research Overseas
OTC	Over the counter
PAFO	Pan African Farmers Organization
PANAP	Pesticides Action Network – Asia and the Pacific
PO	Peoples' organization
PPP	Public–private partnership
PRA	Participatory rural appraisal
PRAI	Principles for Responsible Agricultural Investment
PROPAC	Regional Platform of Central African Peasant Organizations
REDD	Reducing Emissions from Deforestation and Forest Degradation
R&D	Research and development
RtFNW	Right to Food and Nutrition Watch
ROPPA	Network of West African Peasant and Agricultural Producers' Organizations
RRC	Relief and Rehabilitation Commission
SOFA	State of Agriculture
SOFI	State of Food Insecurity
SRI	System of rice intensification
TNC	Transnational corporation
TNI	Transnational Institute
TRIPS	Agreement on Trade-Related Aspects of Intellectual Property
T&V	Training and Visit
UEMOA	West African Economic and Monetary Union
UN	United Nations
UNCED	United Nations Conference on Environment and Development
UNICEF	United Nations Children's Fund
UNCTAD	United Nations Conference on Trade and Development
UNEP	United Nations Environment Program
UNFCCC	United Nations Framework Convention on Climate Change
UNHCR	United Nations Human Rights Council
UPOV	International Union for the Protection of New Varieties of Plants

WB	World Bank
WEF	World Economic Forum
WFC	World Food Conference
WFF	World Forum of Fish Harvesters and Fishworkers
WFFP	World Forum of Fisher Peoples
WFP	World Food Program
WFS	World Food Summit
WHO	World Health Organization
WIPO	World Intellectual Property Organization
WSF	World Social Forum
WTO	World Trade Organization
WWII	World War II

INTRODUCTION

It is not easy for us to conceive that there may have been a time, within a smaller and more integrated community, when it appeared to be "unnatural" that any man should profit from the necessities of others, and when it was assumed that, in time of dearth, prices of "necessities" should remain at a customary level, even though there might be less all round.

E. P. Thompson, "The Moral Economy of the English Crowd in the Eighteenth Century", pp. 252–253

"Prices are rising every day and people don't know what to do. It's like placing matches near cotton that can catch fire at any moment", warned the Secretary General of the National Confederation of Workers of Burkina Faso just before food riots broke out in the capital city of this West African country in February 2008 (Humanitarian News and Analysis 2008). In early April, crowds in Egypt protesting against the scarcity of bread tore down a billboard of President Hosni Mubarak and fought with police in clashes that forecast more to come. "The pot is empty, Garcia", women shouted on the streets of Lima later that month, pinning accountability for the food shortages that were tormenting them on an identifiable actor, the President of the Republic. "Without corn there is no country" was the protestors' slogan in Mexico on New Year's Day 2008 when final barriers to importing key commodities from the United States fell under the NAFTA agreement, destroying the local market for Mexico's staple food and a cornerstone of its rural economy (Schneider 2008). Whatever the level of political sophistication that people applied to understanding the situations they were experiencing, it was evident that something had gone dramatically wrong in countries around the world. That something had to do with food governance: decision making, rule setting, and authority wielding related to collective food security or, some would say, food sovereignty.

Food is the most basic of human needs. Maintaining a proper supply of it is essentially what food governance is about, and failure to do so provokes serious consequences. One to which governments are particularly sensitive is that of insurrection. The Roman historian Suetonius reports that it was the unpleasant experience of being pelted with bread crusts by an angry mob in the forum in 51 AD that prompted the Emperor Claudius to institute the most comprehensive food supply system the Roman empire ever knew, ranging from bread distribution to more complex measures like offering inducements to ship owners to fill their vessels with grain and planning a new port for Rome. Unsustainable – and often iniquitous – food systems are said to have contributed to the fall of a host of illustrious societies. The Sumerian civilization succumbed to a combination of technical problems (soil salinity caused by poorly drained irrigated soils) and political issues (the growing power of the priestly caste, who vested in themselves ownership of previously common land). The opening act of the uprisings that toppled the French Ancien Régime was the women's march on Versailles on 5 October 1789, sparked by the high prices of bread in the market places. In a positive vein, three centuries of stability in the far-flung Chinese empire of the Great Qing, embracing the same period as the French Revolution, can be attributed at least in part to deliberate policies aimed at keeping rural producers on the land and ensuring food distribution when needed through a vast network of locally supported granaries (Wong 1997 quoted in McDonald 2010, p. 44).

Today food security is without doubt a key component of governments' vision of their national security interests. The establishment of a United Nations Food and Agriculture Organization (FAO) was, as we shall see, a key piece of the post–World War II institutional strategy for guarding against a repeat of global conflict. In 1974 Henry Kissinger, then US Secretary of State, warned in a classified study that inadequate food supplies for growing populations in unstable developing countries, many of them recently independent and the object of Cold War attentions, could affect the security and national interests of the United States (Kissinger Report 1974). Forty years later the president of the Earth Policy Institute, Lester Brown,

FIGURE 0.1 Women marching on Versailles

Source: Bibliothèque Nationale de France. Reproduced with permission.

pleaded again for a redefinition of security, beyond concern for armed aggression. "The overriding threats in this century are climate change, population growth, spreading water shortages, rising food prices, and politically failing states" (Brown 2012, p. 121).

Despite this awareness of how much it matters, the history of post–WWII food governance is essentially one of selling out public responsibility to markets and corporations. It is one of progressive disempowerment of the primary food security actors: the small-scale producers and the family units in whom immediate concern for food provision is invested. Unprotected by state and intergovernmental directives, small-scale producers are being driven off their land and out of their markets with the allegation that they are inefficient and archaic, ignoring the fact that they are responsible for producing some 70 percent of the food consumed in the world. The capacity of families to ensure an adequate supply of food for their members is constrained by developments at all levels, from local to global. Increasingly, not only individual families but even nations have lost control over the aggregate body of factors that determine the food security of their populations. The range of imponderables has broadened from acts of God, like the droughts or locust attacks that form part of the earliest narratives of the human race, or coups inflicted by political or military powers, to the disembodied machinations of globalized economic forces. The food crisis is global, but it is rooted in local and national struggles against dispossession. Food riots are a declaration by urban and rural social classes that contest the ways in which their livelihoods have been disrupted for reasons that, as the examples in the opening paragraph suggest, most often escape them (Bush 2010).

Food governance has become an intricate web of often overlapping or contradictory formal policies and regulations, complicated by unwritten rules and practices. Increasingly, regulatory responsibilities are being shifted from the public sector to the very private sector interests who profit from the rules they put in place. Decisions that affect the food security of the population of a country or the world at large are open, in theory, for negotiation among a range of interest groups and social forces that bring different and conflicting objectives to the table. The problem is that most often the table is located behind closed doors, and the most affected and vulnerable are not welcome to sit at it. Even where anything that remotely resembles inclusive negotiation takes place, its dynamics are affected by the power relationships among interest groups and by the degree to which states successfully carry out their function of mediation in the common interest. The former are highly unequal, with private sector interests weighing in heavily, and the latter is most often insufficient (Lang et al. 2009, pp. 9, 23). The outcome is not subject to adequate political oversight. The market is taken to be a neutral and efficient arbitrator despite overwhelming evidence to the contrary. The global food system is largely orchestrated by corporate, financial, and powerful political actors to reflect their interests.

Fathoming the global governance of food, then, is by no means an easy task. But without a doubt now is the time to make the effort. Over the past few years a series of interrelated crises – food, energy, climate change, financial – has unequivocally unmasked the systemic flaws in the current world food system and turned a spotlight on its tendency to reward a small club of privileged economic actors and their political allies. These very crises have opened up a moment of unprecedented visibility and political opportunity for decisive reform. The unsustainability of a food system based on intensive use of petrol products and chemical inputs has been dramatically highlighted by climate change and the energy crisis. The conventional industrial agriculture model that prevails in the global food chain – and that is strongly subsidized by both the European Common Agricultural Policy and the US Farm Bill – accounts for at least 14 percent of the total annual greenhouse gas emissions, mostly due to the use of nitrogen fertilizers derived from rarifying petrol (UNEP 2010). And production is not the only link in the chain affected. The entire globalized distribution process of the currently dominant world food system is dependent on being able to ignore or externalize the energy, petrol, and emissions cost of whisking food around the world before it ends up on a supermarket shelf. The rapine that has come to be popularly termed "land grabbing" is converting large areas of land to the production of crops slated to be processed into agrifuels or food for export to rich, food-deficit countries, expelling local producers and pastoralists in the process (De Schutter 2010a, Margulis et al. 2013).

The impacts of this situation are felt in the Global North as well as in the Global South. The World Food Summit called by the UN Food and Agriculture Organization (FAO) in 1996 focused primarily on hunger in developing countries. Now it is recognized that the dysfunction of the food system affects the entire world and that under-nutrition isn't the only problem. Roughly one-third of the food produced is lost or wasted each year, much more in the industrialized world than in developing countries (Gustavsson et.al. 2011, p. v). More people globally suffer from overweight and obesity than hunger, and type 2 diabetes kills some 3.8 million people a year (Lang et al. 2009, p. 112; Nestle 2007, p. 7). Who is to blame? Consumer choice is the answer of those who profit from the way the system works today. When unhealthily overweight victims of fast food began to sue McDonald's, one of the chain's defense lawyers grumbled that "there is a concerted effort to move away from personal responsibility and shift the blame to industry" (Trent 2011). Lawsuits brought against McDonald's lost in courts in the United States, where personal responsibility is an enduring legacy of the founding fathers' defense of individual rights against encroaching government, the Protestant ethic, and the legend of the self-made man. They have triumphed, however, in courts in Brazil, where the right to food is enshrined in national legislation. Where does personal responsibility lose traction and collective responsibility to frame and enforce appropriate rules have to weigh in? At what levels does this broader responsibility need to be exercised, and how?

The financial crisis has given the final igniting touch to this already explosive mixture of trends. Indeed, a long-term part of what is wrong today has to do with the triumph of financial capital and speculation over good old capitalism that actually produced goods and services and distributable wealth. During 2008 many knowledgeable observers predicted that, like any self-respecting crisis, the food price peaks would simply melt away after enjoying a moment of visibility and cede space in the headlines to the next contender. Now, on the contrary, it

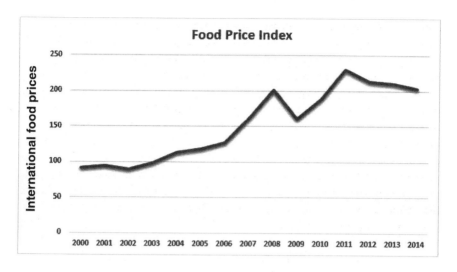

Food Price Index

FIGURE 0.2   Food price volatility – 2000–2014

Note: Based on data in FAO 2014a. The FAO Food Price Index is a measure of the changes in international prices of a basket of food commodities: cereals, vegetable oil, dairy, meat and sugar.

has become evident that price volatility is likely to be with us for the foreseeable future. Prices of major commodities soared in the last months of 2010, and the FAO Food Price Index for January 2011 was the highest it has been since it was initiated in 1990 (FAO 2011b). End-of-year data in 2013 was still alarming, as the graph in Figure 0.2 indicates. The World Bank has warned that high and volatile food prices risk becoming "the new 'normal'" (World Bank 2012). The role that financial speculation on food commodities has played in stimulating food price volatility has unveiled another important area related to food security governance in which current regulatory mechanisms are unsatisfactory if not nonexistent, and it has shed light on what can happen when the "necessities" referred to in our epigraph are transformed into commodities.

The accumulated evidence is becoming cohesive and incontrovertible. In reacting to the financial crisis even governments wedded to neoliberal policies showed themselves to be capable of controverting the dominant ideology in order to "save" banks and financial institutions. Is it inconceivable that these regulatory exceptions to the dominant mode of market governance could extend to the global governance of food if the stakes were high enough? Unaffordable food was a spark that helped to set off the popular revolts in the Maghreb in 2011 that unsettled important geo-political equilibriums. These are developments to which no government can be indifferent, as President Sarkozy underlined in 2011 in a press conference introducing the French Presidency of the G20 whose objectives included that of implementing efficient commodities market regulation (Sarkozy 2011). The *Wall Street Journal*'s "Market Watch" advised readers to "keep their money out of" countries like Algeria and Greece, or even Russia and China, which could be prone to food price–sparked revolutions in 2013 (Lynn 2013). *New Scientist* analysts suggested that severe food price volatility could be an underlying cause of the Brazilian rioting in the summer of 2013 that was apparently motivated by resentment of the substantial resources the government was investing in preparing to host the World Cup tournament (MacKenzie 2013). Concern to secure adequate food for their populations is pushing some governments who can afford it to defy the architecture of the WTO's free trade–based Agreement on Agriculture by outsourcing actual production to other countries where the necessary land can be "grabbed", rather than depending on the undependable marketplace (McMichael 2013b, p. 128). What would it take to tip the balance?

Now is the time to focus on food governance not only because we are getting very close to the absolute ecological, socio-economic, and political limits of today's unsustainable and inequitable food system, but also because there are alternatives out there. If we have the courage to say "no" to the dominant food system, we are not jumping off a cliff into a Pollyanna dream world of pre-capitalist pastoral utopia. Over the past three decades a robust, diversified, and increasingly articulated network of different ways of going about food provision have sprung up, rooted in territories and cultures throughout the world. Sometimes they are not "alternative" at all, since they constitute the main avenue through which peoples' food needs are met, as in the case of the "invisible" food webs composed of family farmers and local markets in Africa. These solutions are practiced and advocated by increasingly authoritative organizations of peasant farmers, artisanal fisher folk, pastoralists, indigenous peoples, urban poor, and other constituencies most affected by food insecurity. They are mobilizing around their experiences and their claims at all levels, up to the global. Many of them identify with what has become known as the food sovereignty movement. This book will tell their stories, along with that of the dominant food system.

The implications of this inquiry will reach beyond its immediate object, since the position of food at the very center of the workings of society and the economy makes it a propitious terrain for exploring more broadly what is happening today in our globalized world. But what lens to adopt? A review of the food security literature reveals multiple and quite diverse entry points: agricultural models and productivity, trade and markets, environmental impact and services, socio-cultural significances, corporate concentration along the food chain, nutrition and health, human rights and entitlements, agrarian transformation and dispossession, and economic justice. And all of these factors interact at multiple levels and involve different actors with different interests.

Recognizing these complexities, the exploration of food governance conducted in this book will be guided by three questions that have to do with power, who wields it, to what effect, and to whose benefit. The first concerns who frames the food agenda—who establishes the "facts" of the situation and the meanings of the terms adopted. This is what is known as discursive power, and it plays an important role in food governance because it determines what issues are brought to the table and in what terms they are debated (Clapp and Fuchs 2009). The second question has to do with who decides in cases of conflict of interests and how. What actors weigh in when decisions about food are being made, with what relative weights? What possibilities do we have to address imbalances of power and give more voice *power* and leverage to the majority of the world's population, who are now in the camp of the hungry, the food insecure, the dispossessed? What possibilities are there to identify common goods and public interests that are fundamental to the well-being of today's and future generations? And finally, assuming that they can be identified, what prospects are there to defend these goods and interests in a globalized world? What is underway today, locally and globally, that leads in that direction? What are the challenges, and how might they be addressed? The aim here will be to look behind the commonplace, the "taken for granted", and equip readers to be better situated to understand the issues and examine the evidence. We will seek to liberate terms and trends from an oversimplified "good/bad" logic that impedes discussion and to see instead how they may be viewed dialectically, in interaction and evolution.

This is not to say that I don't have my own lens and my own views, shaped by my life's trajectory, and it is proper to state them. I was born in an academic home steeped in the discourse of human rights in mid-America during World War II. Among my earliest memories are those of my father leaving for an unimaginably far-off Paris and his later accounts of what was involved in drafting and negotiating the Universal Declaration of Human Rights around a table fractured by the Cold War. At university I chose history first and then political science as a methodological formation, and I continue to have a propensity for retracing how we have gotten where we are and what it looks like in terms of power relations. I chose to turn aside from academia, although I now teach at a university in Rome and have published a number of books and papers. I preferred engagement in "real life" food problems, on the interface between institutions and civil society, between villages and global policy forums. I elected to work alongside those who have most to lose by faulty governance, most to contribute to solving the food problem, and yet are most marginalized in decision-making processes: small-scale food producers themselves. Despite (or perhaps because of) this commitment I hope that this book will do a better job of equipping readers to make independent choices than many others that purport to communicate "the objective truth". I have been directly involved in many of the processes described in this book and will share with readers the results of my often painful efforts to make sense of what I was experiencing.

The first chapter provides a rapid broad-brush historical review of how the international community has defined and addressed the issues of food security since the end of World War II. In doing so it highlights the dynamic interrelations that obtain between evolutions in the overall geo-political and economic context, developments in the institutional settings for debate on food issues and the paradigms adopted to make decisions and develop strategies and, finally, the actors who have intervened directly and indirectly in weighting the decisions and the interests they have represented. Food-related actors, paradigms, and institutions, briefly presented in this chapter, are examined in greater detail in successive ones. The chapter presents the concept of "food regimes" as key to understanding the evolution, over the past decades, of the complex global relations within which food is produced and distributed. It closes by introducing the food price crisis that erupted on the world scene in late 2007/2008 and the effect it has had in terms of unveiling the deficiencies of current food security strategies and governance and opening a window of opportunity for change.

The second chapter focuses on the actors and interests that are involved in food provision. It illustrates how producers, processors, distributors, retailers, and consumers can be related to each other in different ways according to the context and the policy environment in which they are located. It discusses a range of terms whose meanings are often taken for granted but shouldn't be, like "progress", "modern", "traditional", "the market", and "value addition". It contrasts the way different actors are linked in the global corporate food chains that have been consolidated over the past decade with the informal food "webs" that connect producers and consumers in many countries of the Global South and, increasingly, the Global North. It examines the comparative effects of these differentiated food systems regarding important challenges such as maintaining dwindling biodiversity, addressing climate change, dealing with the energy crisis, ensuring environmental sustainability, protecting the health of the world's population, halting the phenomenon of land and water grabbing, and combatting waste. The chapter ends by posing the possibility that decision making on food policies could be based on – or at least more decisively influenced by – not the foregone outcome of unequal battles about interests but inclusive, informed political process.

Chapter 3 considers an important aspect of what would be required for such an approach to decision making to prevail by looking at how facts are ordered and how evidence is assembled and made available to those responsible for policy. It reviews paradigms that impact on food and agriculture, starting with the paired concepts of "modernization" and "productivism", enduringly installed at the heart of development discourse. It describes the instructive evolution of the term "food security" from its first appearance in official discourse at the World Food Congress in 1974 and the grounds on which it has been critiqued over the years. It contrasts the institutionally grounded concept of food security and that of "food sovereignty", which has emerged more recently from the practice and engagement of social movements and civil society. The chapter illustrates how food security can accommodate strategies based on trade liberalization and increased production through the application of Green Revolution–type technology. Food sovereignty, instead, draws on agro-ecological approaches to production; concentrates on local, national, and regional markets; and emphasizes ensuring access to and control of natural resources by local populations. Views of those who feel that the two concepts could be complementary are also examined. The evolution of the "right to adequate food", a component of both food security and food sovereignty, is given particular attention in this regard. The chapter touches on other more general paradigm shifts underway in a world in which the finite nature of resources has become evident, such as "sufficiency economy" and "de-growth" as opposed to growth theory, and "gross national happiness" as contrasted with gross national product.

It looks at issues connected with what is behind paradigms: what constitutes "evidence-based policy", how food insecurity is measured, how data is collected and packaged, whose evidence counts, what is the demarcation between evidence provision and political decision making. It closes by noting the importance of taking on board evidence from those most affected by the outcomes of decision making, opening the way to the presentation of the 2009 reform of the Committee on World Food Security in the following chapter.

Chapter 4 opens with a brief review of how intergovernmental process evolved into a broader approach to multi-actor governance in the period from the founding of the United Nations through the global summits of the 1990s. It focuses on the World Food Summits and parallel civil society forums in Rome in 1996 and 2002, which were characterized by an unprecedented engagement of rural social movements and led to the adoption of a food sovereignty platform and the establishment of a global network to take it forward. It reviews the reactions of members of the international community to the food crisis of 2007–2008 and the very different causes to which they attributed it. It discusses the deficiencies of the global system for food governance to which the crisis drew attention and presents three categories of institutional initiatives, illustrative of the range of responses to such situations. The establishment of a High-Level Task Force on the Global Food Security Crisis by the UN Secretary-General falls into the technical/administrative category. The launching of the Global Partnership for Agriculture and Food Security by the G8 exemplifies the smoke screen, or *plus ça change plus c'est la même chose*, approach. The rarer category of political response is illustrated by the reform of the Committee on World Food Security (CFS) undertaken in 2009 with strong participation by social movements and civil society. The chapter describes that reform process and its outcome, a precedent-setting exercise in opening up intergovernmental process to participation by other actors with particular emphasis on those representing the sectors of the population most affected by food insecurity and most active in developing solutions: small-scale food producers and poor urban consumers.

With a promising global forum like the CFS in place, it is instructive to assess the degree to which the potential of better global food governance is being fulfilled and the challenges that are being encountered along the way. The following two chapters address this question from both a local and a global perspective. Chapter 5 reviews some of the countless ways in which food sovereignty is being built up from the local level, starting with the household and the community. It presents examples of innovative approaches that are being developed around the world in four key areas: ensuring peoples' access to and control of resources, developing sustainable agro-ecological models of production, building and defending markets that are beneficial to small-scale producers and compatible with local food systems, and developing approaches to research that valorize local indigenous knowledge. The chapter examines some of the measures that could help this myriad of local peoples' practices to coalesce and reinforce its political clout: capacity building, networking and alliances within single societies and transnationally, and strengthening interaction between citizens' movements and governance spaces from the bottom up.

Exemplary forums at local, national, and regional levels are cited – like the Toronto Food Policy Council, the Brazilian "Zero Hunger" program, and the interaction between the West African peasant network ROPPA and the Economic Community of West African States. Implementation of the guidelines adopted by the FAO in 2004 on the application at the national level of the right to adequate food is highlighted as one way of tracking progress in establishing national and regional frameworks and legislation that are supportive of equitable food governance.

Chapter 6 picks up the story of the CFS where Chapter 4 left off. It attempts a very initial assessment of the degree to which the reformed CFS's operations over the first five years of its existence are moving in a direction of better global governance that promises support for the kind of citizens' movements encountered in the previous chapter. It focuses on two interconnected issues that are at the center of the powerful geo-political and economic interests discussed in earlier chapters and that have significant impacts on the food security of the disempowered: land grabbing and investments in agriculture. Initiatives underway in the reformed CFS are examined, along with the implications they could have for local and national peoples' struggles to defend their right to food: the negotiation and implementation of the first ever global guidelines on tenure of land and other natural resources and the adoption of principles to guide investment in agriculture so that it promotes food security and supports small-scale producers. The chapter closes by looking at how effectively civil society is occupying the global political space it helped to create and how the CFS as a whole is progressing in putting into operation the generous and innovative mandate with which the reform endowed it.

The final chapter of this book gathers together the reflections undertaken and the ground covered in the preceding chapters, setting them in a framework of discourse on public spheres and governance. It returns to a question posed at the outset – what prospects are there to define and defend common goods and interests in a globalized world? – and points to both challenges that need to be addressed and assets and alternatives that can be drawn on in doing so. While acknowledging capitalism's remarkable power to turn crises to its advantage, the concluding section seeks to convince readers that this time may be different. Productive capital has been supplanted by financial. Boundless hunger for profits is running up against the finite resources of the planet. The alternatives emerging in reaction to the global corporate food regime may succeed in liberating the dialectic of different ways of approaching food provision from the homogenizing tyranny of the market. The concluding section revisits the paradoxical situation of states – currently among the worst offenders in promoting narrow and short-sighted objectives, and yet a basic building block for accountability and defense of citizens' collective rights. Better world food governance, it concludes, can only be the outcome of political will generated by mobilization in which social and citizen movements – all of us – are the prime movers.

1

FOOD GOVERNANCE

A rapid historical review

The levels of decision making seem to be jumping around like frogs, from the national scene on up. The temptation of just huckling down to work in one's own field is strong. But it is no longer an option.

Interview with Ndiogou Fall, West African farmer leader, 2002

Reviewing the experience of the post–World War II decades in addressing food issues is a fruitful prelude to reflecting on the present. This chapter will trace simultaneously the evolution of three strongly interconnected elements: the institutions and the informal spaces in which global decision making has been exercised, the paradigms on which strategies and actions have been based, and the actors and interests that have played a significant role in the governance game. Placing trends and ideas in the historical contexts in which they have developed helps to guard against their "naturalization", their widespread acceptance as "just the way things are" rather than as products of specific time-bound social, economic, cultural, and political conjunctures.

The concept of food regimes is an effective tool for contextualization since it situates food within global power systems as they evolve over time. As described by one of its original framers, the food regime concept refers to "the political structuring of world capitalism, and its organization of agricultures to provision labor and/or consumers in such a way as to reduce wage costs and enhance commercial profits" (McMichael 2013b, p. 8). The rule setting involved is legitimated by ideologies such as "free" trade, free enterprise, and development aid aimed at achieving "modernization". Thanks to these discursive justifications, the way in which the regime operates appears not to be an imposition but just the natural state of affairs, until such time as the equilibrium that has allowed it to function breaks down. "Food regimes emerge out of contests among social movements and powerful institutions, and reflect a negotiated frame for instituting new rules. The relationships and practices of a regime soon come to seem natural. When the regime works really well, the consequences of actions are predictable and it appears to work without rules"

(Friedmann 2005, p. 234). Three successive food regimes have been identified. These correspond to geo-political-economic conjunctures of which the first two were state dominated, first by the British state in the 1870s–1930s and then the US state in the 1950s–1970s. These two regimes were succeeded by a third one dominated by corporate-financial power in the 1980s–2000s that is currently undergoing a period of crisis (McMichael 2013b, p. 8). We will refer to these regimes as we conduct our review. The survey will be a cursory one, intended to provide an illustrative historical overview. The food-related actors and interests, paradigms and institutions, and governance processes briefly presented here will be examined in greater detail in successive chapters, respectively in Chapters 2, 3, and 4. The composite timeline at the close of the chapter illustrates the evolution of these three components of food governance, with no pretense to being comprehensive, along with the flow of successive food regimes. The box below provides a brief introduction to food regime analysis.

BOX 1.1
FOOD REGIME ANALYSIS

The food regime project is an ongoing analysis by scholars and activists of the political geography of the global food system. It emerged in the 1980s as a methodological initiative to specify relations between world ordering and agro food trade. It claimed that episodes of restructuring and transition are bounded by periods of stable patterns of capital accumulation. It is an intrinsically *comparative* approach to recent world history, insofar as food regimes come and go with political reordering, in a mutually conditioning dynamic. The distinctiveness of the first two food regimes lay in the instrumental role of food in securing global hegemony – in the first, Britain's "workshop of the world" project linked the fortunes of an emergent industrial capitalism to expanding cheap food supply zones across the world; in the second, the United States deployed food aid to create alliances, markets, and opportunities for its intensive agro-industrial model. Market hegemony defines the third food regime and its role in a broad neoliberal project dedicated to securing transnational circuits of money and commodities (including food) – displacing smallholders into a casual global labor force for capital. Each period, and the transitions between them, have reframed the politics of development and the scope and significance of agricultural and food technologies. In this sense, the food regime concept offers a unique comparative-historical lens on the political and ecological relations of modern capitalism writ large. The food regime conceptualizes how particular food complexes (from seed technologies through cropping systems to food processing/manufacturing) and food circuits in each regime support the exercise of particular forms of power in expanding and sustaining fields of market and ideological dominance.

Adapted from McMichael (2013b). pp. 1–12

The 1940s and 1950s: a new multilateral architecture and a bottomless faith in science and technology

Food policy was the purview of institutions located essentially at national or local level before World War II. The coexistence in the world of widespread malnutrition and global over-availability of food had, indeed, become evident by the 1930s, and the League of Nations had entertained acrimonious debate about how to address it. However, war broke out before remedial measures could be taken (McKeon 2009a, p. 17; Shaw 2007, pp. 7–8).

This global unbalance was a sign of the breakdown of what has been termed the first truly integrated world food regime (1870–1930s). Centered on Britain and its empire, it involved imports to Europe of colonial tropical products along with basic grains and livestock imports, which provided cheap food for the emerging European industrial classes. The benefits that accrued to the West were achieved at the cost of famines and disruption of local economies and societies in other parts of the world (Davis 2001). This operation was legitimized by the "civilizing narrative" that accompanied empire and colonization. It was justified also by the free trade ideology ushered in with the repeal in 1846 of the Corn Laws that had protected British agriculture but hampered the rising industrial class's need to provision cheap food for its workers. The balance of interests that had sustained this food regime broke down in the early 20th century due to a combination of factors. These included anti-imperial counter-movements on the part of the colonized; interstate rivalry among European states; and the collapse of the gold standard, which had acted as the foundation for a world wheat price. Economic nationalism in Europe, post–WWI depression, and the ecological disaster of the U.S. Dust Bowl rang down the curtain on the first food regime as the winds of WWII began to blow (McMichael *op.cit.*, p. 32).

The establishment of the Food and Agriculture Organization (FAO) in 1944 was an institutional watershed so far as global interstate food governance was concerned. Situated within the emerging UN system, it was heralded as a contribution to building a better post-war society and guarding against another global conflict. The founding members of FAO shared the objective of combating hunger as both a moral and a security imperative. Consensus broke down, however, on the role of international institutions in this regard, especially where food security impinged on trade and what were seen to be "national interests" (McKeon 2009a, pp. 17–18; FAO 1970, p. 11; Gustafson and Markie 2009, p. 181). The fate of the proposed World Food Board was exemplary in this regard. The establishment of this mechanism was championed by FAO's first Director-General, Lord Boyd Orr, as a means of accomplishing some of the governance functions that are recognized as crucial today. These include stabilizing world agricultural prices, managing an international cereal reserve, and cooperating with the organizations responsible for agricultural development loans and international trade policy to ensure that the measures they took were coherent with food security goals (Shaw *op.cit.*, p. 24). Strongly opposed by the grain trade – which had no desire to be regulated – with the backing of some powerful governments, the World Food Board never got off the starting blocks. FAO was pushed into a more narrowly technical track, and Boyd Orr resigned. His parting shots – "food is more than a commodity" and "the world requires a food policy based on human needs" – are just as pertinent today as they were seventy years ago (McKeon 2009a, p. 192; Cépède 1984).

Conflict between political commitment to long-term public collective goals and contrasting short-term particular national or private interests is a constant in the history of global food governance and a leit-motif of this book. A reaction of moral indignation to such incoherence may well be justified but does not suffice. It is necessary to read beneath the rhetoric and understand the interests at play. In Boyd Orr's own assessment, "Britain and America were not prepared to give either funds or authority to an organization over which they had not got full control. Britain might have lost her advantage of cheap food imports, while the US thought that she could do better for herself as a world power through bilateral aid to other countries" as an outlet for its recurrent surplus stimulated by post-depression policies and WWII production efforts (Boyd Orr and Lubbock 1953, quoted in Shaw *op.cit.*, p. 27). Opposition by these two governments was all it took. Global food governance decision making in this period was dominated by a few powerful Western countries. Much of the South, of course, was still under colonial rule. The purview of global rule making was limited. State sovereignty was defended against global encroachment and within national boundaries the state's role in stabilizing prices and ensuring food supplies was acknowledged. Although governments were the formal decision makers, commodity traders were a strong lobby force and, as we have seen, contributed significantly to US-Great Britain opposition to the World Food Board's potential interference in their commercial interests.

Scientists were playing an important role in building the paradigms on which decision making was based. Foundations entered the scene as actors with the start-up of the Green Revolution when the Norman Borlaug–Rockefeller Foundation partnership was established in 1944. The challenge of fighting hunger in the post–World War II period was framed essentially as one of growing more food by applying an agricultural productivism approach based on science and technology (Lang et al. 2009, pp. 27–29). This, indeed, was the era in which President Truman pronounced his Point Four inaugural speech: "Greater production is the key to prosperity and peace. And the key to greater production is a wider and more vigorous application of modern scientific and technical knowledge" (Truman 1949). In two short sentences this speech enunciates several of the key terms and concepts that we will be critiquing in this book: the cause-effect link postulated between "greater production" and "prosperity and peace", the uncomfortably undefined term "modern", and the implication that science and technology can be viewed as objective givens that are not subject to conditioning by mindsets or economic incentives. Truman's Point Four speech has also been identified as the launch of "the age of development" (Sachs 1992, p. 2). This much unpacked concept is viewed by many critics, beyond its declared humanitarian objectives, as part of the post-war reaction to the security threat of Third World poverty and the rising influence of the Soviet Union, the first country that had industrialized outside of capitalism.

Discourse lauding the push for the "development" of those countries deemed to be losers in the race, rooted in the "idea of progress" (Bury 1960) that has played such a foundational role in the West, has served to sanctify the role of the "developers" and to legitimate their often self-serving recipes for addressing the problems of the "developing world" (Cush 1995, p. xiii; Escobar 1995, p. 5).

This complex of institutions, actors, interests, and paradigms is understood in food regime analysis as constituting the second regime, centered around the United States. The US government had reacted to the combined adversities of the Depression and the Dust Bowl disaster with a program of state-subsidized, input- and energy-heavy stimulation of agricultural commodity production complemented by food aid as an outlet for the resulting surplus production. Food aid was used ostensibly to fight world hunger. In fact it served to contain communist overtures to countries of the South as they attained independence and to open up their markets to American agro-exports while promoting the dispossession of their patently "unmodern" peasantry (Patel and McMichael 2010, p. 15). As candidly described by President Eisenhower when he signed the bill first establishing it into law in 1954, food aid was intended to "lay the basis for a permanent expansion of our exports of agricultural products with lasting benefits to ourselves and peoples of other lands" (US Food Aid and Security n.d.). As such it has been a successful instrument. By 1986, seven of the ten leading importers of US farm goods were previous Food for Peace recipients (Hancock 1989, quoted in Schanbacher 2010, p. 33).[2] In parallel, developing countries were encouraged to adopt the Green Revolution technical package of high-yielding hybrid seed dependent on agrochemicals and irrigation, touted as key to agricultural productivism (Patel 2012). At the same time they were induced to profit from the easy credit available at that time to engage in capital- and technology-intensive development schemes parroting the West's agricultural modernization and industrialization-based path to development. This bubble burst in the late 1970s when interest rates rose sharply, leaving the countries that had taken the bait saddled with debt as well as inappropriate and un–utilizable industrial complexes.

The 1960s and 1970s: institutional global food governance vacillates in the face of a global crisis . . . and corporations pick up the slack

The balance of power within the United Nations was revolutionized by the coming to independence of a host of former colonies in the early 1960s. The group of developing countries – G77 – was established in 1964, introducing North-South rivalry alongside East-West. The G77, numerically superior in the United Nations, championed a more equitable New International Economic Order (NIEO) of which the UN Conference on Trade and Development (UNCTAD) and the UN Center on Transnational Corporations[3] were two of the institutional centerpieces. The NIEO sought to move toward more symmetrical world trade and finance arrangements involving measures such as improved terms of trade, particularly for the commodities that the developing world exported, and greater control over the operations of multinational corporations in their territories. These objectives clearly clashed with US and European efforts to keep raw material prices low and to maintain developing country dependence on imports of food and manufactures. In this conjuncture FAO was an agency to which the developing countries attached importance as an instrument that could help them valorize their agricultural commodities and achieve food security.

A world food crisis in the mid-1970s turned the spotlight on the FAO, under fire from the powerful economies of the West.[4] Pulling in the opposite direction to the G77, the OECD countries reacted to the crisis by dismantling the various functions that FAO exercised as the UN's "Ministry of Agriculture" (ETC 2009). The establishment in 1971 of the Consultative Group on International Agricultural Research (CGIAR) had already excised agricultural science from the UN family and headquartered it at the World Bank. A World Food Conference was held in 1974 to address the crisis, under the auspices of the UN rather than the FAO. This represented a big power gesture of lack of confidence in the capacity for effective action of the agency that they themselves had castrated at its foundation. The Conference failed once again to address the real issues, such as the need for a global system of food reserves and regulation of agricultural trade in the name of food security (Aziz 1975). It proposed instead the creation of a top-heavy policy body – the World Food Council – that had no authority over the myriad of UN system bodies concerned in some way with food, but which nonetheless eroded FAO's normative power until it was discontinued in 1993 (Shaw 2007). As for the financing of agriculture, it was hived off from FAO and entrusted to the newly established International Fund for Agricultural Development (IFAD). Finally, the World Food Program with its responsibilities for reacting to food emergencies, a strategic area for the United States given its surplus production, was progressively separated out from its original home in FAO and established as an independent UN agency.

In paradigmatic terms, the optimistic post-war phase was shaken by famines that hit the Sahel and Ethiopia in the 1970s and by the rise in the cost of oil leading to escalating fuel and food prices. The food crisis heralded the breakdown of the equilibrium on which the food regime centered on the United States had been based and opened the way to the progressive emergence of a third regime, led by corporations. The US hegemony had prepared the way for this handover by facilitating the international reorganization of agricultural provisioning around transnational commodity complexes covering the entire chain from production to consumption. The freedom of enterprise that the US regime touted set the scene for an increasingly private regime of global trade managed by transnational corporations (McMichael op.cit., p. 40). The crisis was seized by the growing body of neoliberal advocates as an occasion to argue that the world's food system was overly dependent on subsidies and states and to push for market liberalization and privatization as the way forward.

BOX 1.2
NEOLIBERALISM

Neoliberalism advocates freer movement of goods, resources, and enterprises and reduction of the policy role of the state and its interventions in the economic sphere. To achieve this involves removing controls deemed to hamper free trade, such as tariffs, regulations, certain standards and legislation (including those protecting workers and the environment), and restrictions on capital flows and investment. Guiding principles behind this ideology include:

- Sustained economic growth is the way to human progress.
- "Free" markets without government "interference" would ensure the most efficient and socially optimal allocation of resources.
- Economic globalization would be beneficial to everyone.
- Privatization is a more efficient way of providing services (water, education, research, etc.) than through the public sector.

Adapted from Shah (2010)

At the same time, the Green Revolution narrative reached its apex in this period with its emphasis on a particular technical package as the solution to hunger. Synergetic with the political and economic interests of its promoters and supported by foreign aid and policy advice, the Green Revolution proved to be an effective means for exporting the industrial agricultural model to countries in Asia and Latin America and for seeking to contain agrarian unrest that might otherwise have taken a more revolutionary turn (Clapp 2012, p. 33). The paradigm of productivism was just as comfortable with a market-led orientation as it had been with Truman's vision of a greater role for state-led development programs.

The Western powers' fear of rural uprising was not paranoiac. This period was one in which popular mobilization for agrarian reform was strong in Latin America and in Asian countries like the Philippines. Occupations of land that would lead to the establishment of the Brazilian Landless Workers Movement (MST) in 1984 got underway already during the 1970s. Independence struggles in some African countries, like Mozambique and Algeria, had agrarian reform and support for peasant agriculture as basic planks in their platforms. In post–WWII Italy, peasants in Sicily and other regions began to occupy and cultivate land left fallow by absentee landlords, setting off what would become a major land reform program. In all regions, national struggles and organization laid the foundations for what would become global mobilization in the 1980s.

In terms of dominant actors, despite the rise of market liberalization solutions a considerable role continued to be recognized for the state in regulating and supporting agriculture at the national level through mechanisms such as food stocks, supply management, commodity boards, and price support. However, urban bias – then as now – pushed developing country governments to favor cheap food for the urban population over the interests of the scattered rural producers who were much less likely to rise up in protest. Alongside of governments, commercial interests became increasingly strong contenders on the global scene in this period. "Upstream" agribusiness profited from the Green Revolution–promoted seed varieties and related input packages thanks to corporation-promoted initiatives to protect intellectual property rights. The first international treaty introducing intellectual property into agriculture – the International Union for the Protection of New Varieties of Plants (UPOV) – entered into force in 1968 and inaugurated the protection of the products of corporate investments over the eons-old right of farmers to plant their own harvested seeds (Tansey and Rajotte 2008, pp. 32–34).[5]

From the 1980s up to 2005: triumph of economic globalization and the "free" market . . . and the emergence of alternatives

From the early 1980s on the global governance of food has been dominated, in formal institutional terms, by the international financial organizations – the World Bank (WB) and the International Monetary Fund (IMF) – and successively the World Trade Organization (WTO). Developing countries that had been strangled by debt with the credit crunch of the 1970s were obliged to turn to the WB and the IMF for bailout loans. These came accompanied by neoliberal structural adjustment regimes, which drastically reduced the policy space of national governments, opened developing country markets to unfair competition with subsidized products from abroad, and cut back severely on state support to and regulation of agriculture. Developing countries were encouraged to abandon their national and regional grain reserves on the grounds that integrated global markets would provide stability (Lawrence et al. 2010, p. 232). Here too, as in the case of the push for "development", we find a marriage between sincere conviction of the well-foundedness of the neoliberal recipe, on the one hand, and adherence to the particular interests it promoted, on the other. This increasingly unconvincing union has endured in the face of growing evidence of structural adjustment's negative impacts on poverty and food security.[6]

The establishment of the World Trade Organization (WTO) in 1995 and the promulgation of global trade regulations regarding agriculture did the rest (Weis 2007; FAO 2006, pp. 75–76). The call for freer trade in agriculture – previously excluded from global liberalization negotiations – was supported by the United States as a way of reducing the costs of its agricultural support system and pushing its main competitor, Europe, to cut back its export subsidies. It was also promoted by a group of other agro-exporting countries, including some emerging economies like Brazil, that have a strong comparative advantage in the sector based on their commercialized farming classes (Weis 2007, p. 131; Clapp 2012, p. 66). Other developing countries were totally unprepared to understand what they were getting themselves into when they signed onto the complex WTO Agreement on Agriculture (AoA). The negotiated text made it possible for developed countries to maintain their support for and protection of their agricultural sectors in a disguised fashion, while developing countries were obliged to further open their markets. It is worth noting that the AoA was framed without even a rhetorical nod toward the interests of the peasant producers who constituted the majority of the world's population.

The Doha Round of WTO negotiations, launched in 2001, was declaredly intended to cater to the concerns of developing countries but failed to do so. It progressively ground to a halt until a very minimal agreement was finally reached in December 2013. The space has been filled by a myriad of bilateral trade agreements like the US-Canada-Mexico North American Free Trade Agreement (NAFTA) denounced by Mexican demonstrators in our opening paragraph and the fraught Economic Partnership Agreements (EPAs) that the European Union has been attempting to negotiate with the ex-colonies of European countries since 2002. These agreements have gone even further than the WTO in prying open markets in the Global South to foreign corporate investment and enterprise and reducing national government capacity to regulate them.

A parallel result of this takeover by the financial institutions was the reduction of the policy weight of the UN system, concentrated on "soft" policies such as peace and human rights in contrast to the "hard" economic realms in which liberalization prevailed. "Corporations are left free to profit from the production of food, leaving the governance structure to feed those that the market bypasses" (Rosin and Martinez-Torres 2012, p. 6). The end of the Cold War marked by the fall of the Berlin wall in 1989 gave rise to hopes that the resources that had been invested in armaments could be reallocated to constitute a "development dividend" and that the attention that had been focused on bi-power competition might be recast into collective attention to emerging global problems. The 1990s were the decade of UN global summits and of reflection on global governance, to which we will return in Chapter 2. However, this same period, during which the UN sought to recuperate authority, saw a multiplication and further fragmentation of negotiation forums impacting on food security. Some of these were situated within the UN family – such as the multitude of conventions stemming from the 1992 Rio Conference on environment and development. Others were outside. In the latter category, the G7/8 constituted itself in this period as a powerful and exclusive alternative forum for addressing world problems, championed by its advocates as a more effective alternative to what they viewed as a cumbersome and argumentative UN.

One of the most significant phenomena impinging on food governance in this period took place outside of the world of intergovernmental institutions. It was the galloping growth of corporate ownership, concentration, and integration in the food system that translated into a disproportional corporate impact on global food decision making (ETC 2008; McMichael 2005; MacMillan 2005; Clapp and Fuchs 2009). The Agreement on Trade-Related Aspects of Intellectual Property

(TRIPS), adopted in 1994 as part of the establishment of the WTO, a key factor in stimulating corporate control of the food system, was pushed by the United States under pressure from a group of large corporation lobbyists against the wishes of the developing countries (Roffe 2008, pp. 50–51). If states had managed markets in the context of the development vision announced by Truman in 1949, the tables were now turned and states were put at the service of markets. The resulting "corporate food regime" has been described in the terms reproduced in the box below.

BOX 1.3
THE CORPORATE FOOD REGIME

Under the corporate food regime cheap food depends on the union of North Atlantic grains and southern fruits, vegetables, and seafood in an international division of agricultural labor coordinated by transnational corporate supply chains, with trade relations governed by International Financial Institutions (IFIs), structural adjustment policies, and WTO protocols. With the combined effect of intellectual property protection, agribusiness centralization and subsidization, and private quality standards for global retailing, the agro-export model fostered a "world farm" phenomenon, demanding standardization from producers for world supermarkets. Farmers unable to meet certification requirements or compete with cheap grain flows face displacement and dispossession, exacerbating world hunger. It is this fundamental contradiction, in a now *global* food regime, that defines the corporate food regime.

McMichael (2013). p. 60

The institutionalization of structural adjustment and free trade was accompanied by the pervasive neoliberal thesis that economic growth and global market integration constitutes the infallible recipe for addressing all the world's ills, including food insecurity. The term "Washington Consensus" coined in 1989 was shorthand for the standard package of market-based reforms prescribed for debt-ridden developing countries by major Washington-based institutions like the IMF, the WB, and the US Treasury Department. Within this paradigm, hunger eradication was downplayed as a specific global objective, despite the declarations of the World Food Summits (WFS) convened by FAO in 1996 and 2002 (McKeon 2009a). It took a determined lobby effort led by FAO to get a "hunger" objective incorporated into the Millennium Development Goals that emerged in 2000 from the UN decade of global summits. Alongside the dominant neoliberal economic recipe, the indefatigable productivist paradigm continued to dominate so far as discourse regarding food supply was concerned.

At the same time, however, the sustainability of industrial agriculture was progressively called into question throughout this period, and the negative impacts of structural adjustment and market liberalization on poverty and hunger also became increasingly evident. Alternatives to the dominant neoliberal, productivist paradigm began to emerge. In 1981 Nobel prize–winning economist Amartya Sen published his influential essay *Poverty and Famines*, which introduced the idea that what counts is not so much the supply of food as peoples' "entitlements" to obtain access to it (Sen 1981). The concept of food as an undeniable human right, not as a possible side effect of increased production and free trade, had already been enshrined in the 1948 Universal Declaration of Human Rights and the 1966 Covenant on Economic, Social, and Cultural Rights (ESCR). It received renewed attention, however, thanks to the 1996 and 2002 World Food Summits. On another front, the damage inflicted on the environment by the chemical input–intensive agriculture of the Green Revolution – of which Rachel Carson's *Silent Spring* (1962) had been an early and explosively controversial herald – prompted increasing attention to the relation between agriculture and ecology.

Contestation of the dominant regime and the paradigms that accompanied it was far from being exclusively a matter for intellectuals. On the contrary, the increasingly devastating impact of globally determined structural adjustment policies, trade rules, and market flows on the small-scale producers of the world stimulated a progressively articulated movement of resistance, denunciation, and alternative proposals. The right to food, food sovereignty, and agro-ecology were championed by civil society actors who entered the global governance scene for the first time. Among these the most politically significant were the rural social movements – the majority of the population in many countries of the Global South – that mobilized in reaction to the effects of neoliberal policies on agricultural production and rural livelihoods (McKeon 2012). The birth of the WTO gave an additional stimulus to networking among the primary victims of economic globalization and liberalization. The decision to set up the global peasant network La Via Campesina (LVC) in 1993 was triggered by the Uruguay Round of the GATT and the realization, in the words of a LVC leader, that "agricultural policies would henceforth be determined globally and it was essential for small farmers to be able to defend their interests at that level" (McKeon and Kalafatic 2009, p. 3; Desmarais 2007). The regional Network of West African Peasant and Agricultural Producers' Organizations (ROPPA) was established in 2000 with similar motivations (McKeon et al. 2004). Evolutions along the same lines have taken place in other regions both in the Global South and in the North (Edelman 2003). We will hear more about these actors in Chapter 2 when we analyze the local food systems of which they are proponents, in Chapter 3 when we discuss the origin and development of the food sovereignty paradigm they espouse, and in Chapter 5 when we review concrete alternatives to the corporate-led food regime that they are developing. Mobilization by rural actors, along with mounting indignation on the part of a broad range of civil society, was expressed in the Seattle demonstration against the WTO ministerial meeting in 1999 and in the World Social Forums inaugurated in January 2001 as a counter-meeting to the World Economic Forum, which brings the cream of the financial actors together in Davos each year.

The civil society forums held in parallel to the two World Food Summits convened by FAO in 1996 and 2002 gave a strong impetus to global networking by rural social movements. The organizers of these forums made a deliberate effort to ensure that small-scale food producers and indigenous peoples were in the majority by applying a quota system for delegates and mobilizing resources to cover their travel costs. Introduced by LVC in 1996, the principle of food sovereignty – "the right of peoples to healthy and culturally appropriate food produced through eco-logically sound and sustainable methods, and their right to define their own food and agriculture systems" – had become the forum's rallying point by 2002. The Forum mandated the network that had emerged from the preparatory work, the International Civil Society Planning Committee for Food Sovereignty (IPC),[7] to carry forward the Action Agenda it adopted, based on four pillars: the right to food and food sovereignty, mainstreaming agro-ecological family farming, defending people's access to and control of natural resources, and trade and food sovereignty. This mounting movement – the other side of the globalization coin – expressed a politici-zation and deep questioning of the dominant food regime and, progressively, a capac-ity to propose alternative approaches to addressing the food needs of the world.[8] It signaled a contestation of the corporate food regime, which was clamorously proving incapable of ensuring world food security in a sustainable and equitable fashion.

From 2005 on: systemic failure is exposed and the international community faces the food crisis

From 2005 on, three of the major agricultural institutions – IFAD, FAO, and CGIAR – underwent external evaluations that exposed serious institutional failures and, successively, entered into reform processes (ETC 2009). For its part, the World Bank devoted its 2008 World Development Report to Agriculture and Develop-ment for the first time in twenty-five years and recognized that it had made a strate-gic error in neglecting agriculture as a motor of growth (World Bank (2007b). The independent evaluation of the Bank's assistance to agriculture in Africa published the same year acknowledged the negative impacts of two decades of structural adjustment policies (World Bank 2007a, p. 67). It was also in 2005 that the WTO Doha Round ground to a resounding halt in Hong Kong on agricultural issues. The Food Aid Convention (FAC), due to expire in 2007, was under redefinition with a view to shifting the emphasis from food as an instrument to the problems that food assistance is expected to address (Hoddinott and Cohen 2007). Intergovernmental institution instability has been accentuated by the contestation of long-standing equilibria on the international scene on the part of the so-called emerging powers. The BRIC (Brazil, Russia, India, and China) held their first formal forum in 2009, and South Africa joined the group in 2010. In food regime terms, the arrival on the scene of new major food exporters has consecrated a polycentric food regime, which has destabilized previous equilibria.

In this atmosphere of institutional rethinking, the eruption in late 2007–2008 of the food price crisis with which this book opened unveiled a vacuum in global governance, to which we will return in Chapter 4. The food crisis – and concomitant attention to energy, environment, health, and climate change – has jolted dominant paradigms as well as the governance system. There is now widespread recognition that the world market has failed to ensure the food security of the developing countries. The World Bank and the International Monetary Fund – international institutional kingpins of the neoliberal, "free" market–based approach to solving whatever ails society – have been under pressure to admit that they made a bad mistake in counseling African governments to exploit their "comparative advantage" by exporting raw commodities and purchasing food for their populations on the world market. This advice, accompanied by heavy conditionalities and WTO regulations, transformed African countries from net food exporters to net food importers in the space of a decade, leaving them out on a limb when food prices shot up and started to fluctuate wildly. Concepts that had been considered taboo or laughable over the past two decades are now being seriously entertained in policy discussions: protection for developing country markets, food reserves and supply management, and agro-ecology as a climate-friendly approach to agricultural production.

Civil society organizations and people's movements promoting these alternative paradigms have come into their own and have built up their outreach and their capacity for proposals. Small-scale food producer organizations' networks are engaging governments and intergovernmental forums at national, regional, and global levels and building alliances with other sectors of civil society. They are impacting on government policy and gaining accreditation and credibility in global institutions like FAO and IFAD.[9] Locally, alternative food networks and fair trade movements are conducting concrete experiences at community level, proposing agro-ecological production and food webs as an alternative to the industrial food chain, as we will see in Chapter 5. The transnationalization of civil society movements has facilitated the emergence of alternative paradigms and brought pressure "from below" on governments at all levels, empowering groups that would have been much weaker if they had remained isolated. The International Assessment of Agricultural Knowledge, Science, and Technology for Development (IAASTD) study published in 2008[10] has provided significant scientific support for alternative paradigms, although it is not receiving the recognition it merits.

At the same time, however, the promoters of the agro-industrial global food system are positioned to turn the food and climate crises to their advantage by

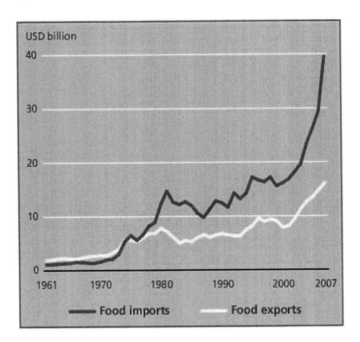

FIGURE 1.1 Africa's food import and export trends

Source: Food and Agriculture Organization of the United Nations (2011). "Why Has Africa Become a Net Food Importer?", www.fao.org/docrep/015/i2497e/i2497e00.pdf. Reproduced with permission. FAO.

advocating solutions led by technology, capital, and market liberalization. It is reported that "the six largest agrochemical and seed corporations are filing sweeping, multigenome patents in pursuit of exclusive monopoly over plant gene sequences that could lead to control of most of the world's plant biomass . . . under the guise of developing 'climate ready' crops" (ETC 2010). The UN Environment Program (UNEP) suggests that the "green economy" will "result in improved human well-being and social equity, while significantly reducing environmental risks and ecological scarcities" (UNEP n.d.). Critics argue, however, that in the absence of effective and socially responsive governance the green economy will spur even greater convergence of corporate power and unleash the most massive resource grab in more than five hundred years (ETC 2011a). The corporations' investment in agriculture in the developing world has been marginal up to now, and their approaches to agricultural production and food system are in crisis. Yet they have been able to normalize themselves as aid actors thanks to both their structural and their discursive power. The financial crisis and the downward turn in Official Development Assistance has given them a hand in this. Failure of G8 governments to meet the aid commitments they had made at the 2009 G8 Summit at L'Aquila was one factor that induced them to open their arms to the private sector to pick up the slack.

Corporate sector interests and paradigms have received support from a major new entry in the cast of actors in this latest period, a category of foundations with unprecedented financial power to shape the agricultural development agenda. The Bill & Melinda Gates Foundation made its first grant in the field of agriculture in 2006. By the end of 2009, it had invested more than $1.4 billion in promoting a "new green revolution" strategy whose implementation is accountable solely to its two co-chairs. This compares – in terms of democracy and transparency – with FAO's regular budget of $1 billion for the 2010–2011 biennium, which is debated, approved, and monitored by its 192 member governments. The box below presents a recent statement of the technology-led productivist paradigm by an academic who is associated with the Gates Foundation's work on the politics of winning acceptance for corporation-produced bio fortified food crops in developing countries.

BOX 1.4
WHAT KIND OF FARMING IS ENVIRONMENTALLY SUSTAINABLE?

Agricultural scientists often believe there will be less harm done to nature overall by highly capitalized and specialized high-yield farming systems employing the latest technology. Increasing the yield on lands already farmed would allow more of the remaining land to be saved for nature. Environmentalists invoke the damage done by modern farming, whereas agricultural scientists invoke the greater damage that would be done if the same production volume had to come from less productive low-yield farming systems.

Paalberg (2010). p. 112

This excerpt is illustrative of the need to read carefully between the lines of what purports to represent solid academic reasoning. Questionable assumptions on which this argument is based include dividing agricultural scientists and environmentalists into two separate categories with unanimous and opposed views, equating low-tech farming systems with low yields, and taking it for granted that land not put under agricultural production will be "saved for nature".

A thoughtful analysis of who wields power in the food system published almost on the eve of the eruption of the food price crisis argued that the three most significant evolutions over the past few decades had been the hollowing out of the state

TABLE 1.1 Indicative timeline of food governance: institutions/paradigms/actors/food regimes

	Global institutions/processes	Paradigms	Non-global actors/ processes (state, civil society, private sector)	Food regimes
1940s	-end WWII (1945) -FAO established (1945) but . . . -World Food Board defeated -Universal Declaration of Human Rights (1948) -GATT takes effect (1948)	-modernization of agriculture/productivism (Truman Pt 4 speech 1949)	-Rockefeller-Borlag partnership founded (1944) -Int. Federation Agricultural Producers founded (1946)	-Breakdown of 1st food regime (UK-centered)
1950s	-FAO's Freedom from Hunger Campaign (1959)	-...modernization/ productivism... -development planning + food self-sufficiency	-US food aid act (1954) -Bandung Conference (1955)	- 2nd food regime (US-centered)
1960s	-1st Development Decade -World Food Program (1961) -World Food Congress (1963) -Codex Alimentarius (1963) -G77 born (1964) -World Conference on Agrarian Reform (1966) -UPOV (1968)	-green revolution (1968) -Rostow, *Stages of Development* (1960) -Carson, *Silent Spring* (1962)	-decolonization in Africa -EU Common Agriculture Policy (1962) -Walmart incorporated (1969)	-... 2nd food regime ...
1970s	-CGIAR established (1971) -UN Conference on the Human Environment (1972) -Food crisis (1971–1974) -World Food Conference (1974) -Oil crisis/easy credit (1973–1974) -Declaration New Intl Economic Order (1974) -Covenant Economic, Social and Cultural Rights (1976) -World Conference Agrarian Reform and Rural Development (1979)	-...modernization/ productivism... -food security	-World Economic Forum born (1971)	-Breakdown of 2nd food regime

1980s	-end Cold War (1989) -WB/IMF structural adjustment regimes imposed	-...modernization/productivism... -...food security... -Sen on assets (1981) -"free" market–neoliberalism (Washington Consensus 1989)	-Brazilian MST (1984)	-3rd food regime (corporate)
1990s	-Rio Conference (1992) -Intl Conf. on Nutrition (1992) -TRIPS (1994) -WTO (1995) -World Food Summit (1996) -Kyoto Protocol adopted (1997)	-...modernization/productivism... -...food security... -...neoliberalism... -"good governance" -food sovereignty (1995) -IAASTD (2009)	-McDonald's opens in Beijing (1992) -La Via Campesina (1993) -Monsant Bt cotton approved for marketing (1994) -NAFTA (1994) -Intl Agrifood Network (1996) -Seattle WTO protest (1999)	-...3rd food regime
2000s	-UN Global Compact (2000) -MDGs (2000) -Special Rapporteur on Right to Food (2000) -ITPGRFA adopted (2001) -WTO Doha Round (2001) -World Food Summit (2002) -VGs on Right to Food (2004) -Kyoto Protocol enters into force (2005) -WB WDR on agriculture (2007) -Food price crisis (2007–2008) -UN HLTF (2008) -G8 L'Aquila (2009) -World Summit on Food Security (2009) -CFS reform (2009) -First BRIC meeting	-...modernization/productivism/sustainable intensification... -...food security... -...neoliberalism... -..good governance... -..food sovereignty... -growing attention to buen vivir, degrowth	-ROPPA (2000) -US Congress dismantles regulation of derivatives (2000) -IPC for Food Sovereignty (2002) -Negotiation of EPAs launched (2003) -1st World Social Forum (2001) -Gates enters agriculture (2006) -AGRA founded (2006) -Nyéléni (2007)	-breakdown 3rd food regime

(Continued)

TABLE 1.1 (Continued)

	Global institutions/processes	Paradigms	Non-global actors/ processes (state, civil society, private sector)	Food regimes
			-GRAIN denounces land grabbing (2008) -Goldman Sachs earns c.$1billion from food speculation (2009) -People's Food Sovereignty Forum (2009)	
2010s	-GAFSP (2010) -Civil Society Mechanism/CFS (2010) -Scaling Up Nutrition framework (2010) -CFS Tenure Guidelines and Global Strategic Framework(2012) -G8 New Alliance for Food Security and Nutrition (2012) -Mini-agreement WTO Doha (2013) -ICN2 (2014)	-...modernization/ productivism/sustainable intensification -green economy/climate smart agriculture -...food security -...neoliberalism -...good governance -...food sovereignty -...buen vivir, degrowth	-Pan African Farmers Organization (2010) -IFAP dissolved, World Farmers' Organization established -US Dodd-Frank Financial Regulation Act (2010) -EU Financial Instruments Act (2014)	???

by globalization and devolution, the growing power of transnational corporations in the world food system accompanied by the prospect that "private global regulation" may weigh in more strongly than public regulation, and the emergence of new food movements presenting alternative visions of the food system (MacMillan 2005, pp. 2–5). The brief historical review we have conducted above corroborates this view. The tensions among these evolutions have been highlighted by the explosion of the food price crisis. In food regime analysis, the food price spikes in 2007–2008 and the resulting riots could be read as an externalization of the crisis of the corp-orate food regime. Following the introduction of structural adjustment policies and WTO regulations that denied states the right to pursue food self-reliance objec-tives, the fulfillment of "food security" had been entrusted to corporations on the grounds of their presumed capacity to organize global relations of food production and circulation of food (McMichael 2013b, pp. 110–111). Their ability to do so, and the WTO's capacity to manage global markets, is now in doubt. At the same time, there are legitimate suspicions that the expansion of a market-based solution to global food provision may be reaching its absolute limits in ecological terms. The ensuing shakeup of the global food system and of its governance framework opens up both threats and opportunities. We will explore them further in Chapters 4–6, after first becoming more closely acquainted with the actors, interests, and para-digms to which this chapter has provided a first introduction.

Notes

1. Parts of this chapter and of Chapter 4 draw on an earlier paper published by the Hein-rich Boll Foundation (McKeon 2011a).
2. Food aid aligned progressively with the increased corporate concentration in the food chain that developed over the succeeding years. Two-thirds of food for the billion-dollar US food aid program in 2010 was bought from just three US-based multinationals (*Guardian*, 18 July 2012).
3. Established in 1974 and shut down in 1992 under pressure from the United States and lobbying organizations like the International Chamber of Commerce.
4. See Chapter 3, p. 73, for a brief discussion of the causes of the crisis.
5. See Chapter 2, p. 37, and Chapter 5, p. 123–125, for fuller discussions of intellectual property rights.
6. More on structural adjustment, the WTO, and corporate concentration and financializa-tion in Chapter 2, p. 36–48.
7. The IPC is an autonomous, self-managed global network of some forty-five people's movements and NGOs involved with at least eight hundred organizations throughout the world. Its membership includes constituency focal points (organizations represent-ing small-scale farmers, fisher folk, pastoralists, indigenous peoples, agricultural work-ers), regional focal points, and thematic focal points (NGO networks with particular expertise on priority issues). It is not a centralized structure and does not claim to represent its members. It is rather a space for self-selected CSOs that identify with the food sovereignty agenda adopted at the 2002 forum.
8. More on food security, food sovereignty, and the right to food in Chapter 3, p. 73–83.

9. IFAD established a Farmers' Forum in 2005 to dialogue with its Governing Council and enhance farmer organization involvement in the formulation and implementation of national strategies and programs. See McKeon and Kalafatic (2009, pp. 18–20).

10. The IAASTD was a four-year process involving four hundred experts from all regions, sponsored by the World Bank, FAO, UNEP, and UNDP. Its report, published in 2008, called for a fundamental paradigm shift in agricultural development and advocated strengthening agro-ecological science and practice. See www.agassessment.org.

2
FOOD PROVISION IN A GLOBALIZED WORLD

In the preceding chapter we conducted a rapid historical review of the evolution of global food governance during the past decades and identified the actors, interests, and concepts that have animated the scene over time. This chapter will take a horizontal look at how the different players involved with food are linked with one another. Keeping in mind the basic questions raised in the introduction, we will seek to understand what determines the way in which the pieces are joined up and who benefits from the resulting assemblage.

Food systems, chains and webs: terms and the meanings behind them

Over the first eons of humanity's existence producers and consumers were a single category, although different food-related roles were played by different members of the family unit with men doing the hunting, women and children most of the gathering, and women the food preparation. The development of sedentary agriculture based on domestication of wild plants in the Fertile Crescent some 10,000–12,000 years ago furnished the basis for further differentiation of roles (Mazoyer and Roudart 2002, pp. 63–65). The agricultural surpluses produced by concentrated investment of labor, the introduction of water control, and breeding of species for desired traits made it possible for some people to specialize in nonagricultural artisanal activities and, progressively, for warrior and priest classes to be formed. Since then the cast of characters in what is commonly called a "food system"[1] has multiplied and become more complex. Producers are always still consumers, of course, but consumers are often not direct producers. A host of other actors have inserted themselves upstream and downstream of production and interact with each other in arenas that range from the local to the global.

A food system includes at a minimum the set of activities involved in producing food, processing and packaging it, distributing and retailing it, and consuming it. In order to be able to analyze the dynamics of how the system functions, it is also necessary to consider the "drivers", or factors that provide impetus for these activities and their social, environmental, and food security outcomes (Ingram et al. 2010, p. 27). A recent FAO report on food systems groups their different components into three phases: i) production "up to the farm gate" (R&D, inputs, production, farm management), ii) postharvest supply chain "from the farm gate to the retailer" (marketing, storage, trade, processing, retailing), and iii) consumers (advertising, labeling, education, safety nets). It warns against thinking of these elements in linear fashion and emphasizes, instead, that the actors responsible for them interact and influence each other and that they function within broader economic, social, cultural, environmental, and policy contexts (FAO 2013b, pp. 7–8). The graph below, taken from an earlier FAO publication, is a good starting point since it provides a rather elementary but clear depiction of different aspects of food systems. We will encounter more complex representations further along in this chapter.

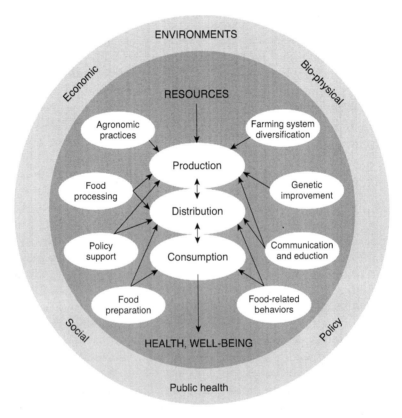

FIGURE 2.1 A food system

Source: Food and Agriculture Organization of the United Nations, 1997, 'Agriculture, Food and Nutrition for Africa', www.fao.org/docrep/w0078e/w0078e04.htm. Reproduced with permission. FAO.

The comprehensive concept of food systems is compatible with the broad brush of food regime analysis as we encountered it in the last chapter. Food regime analysis describes the big picture of how global food provisioning is organized in political economy terms. "Food system" addresses how food-related functions and actors link up one with another in operational terms within a global economic and geo-political context. A globalized food system may be essentially coterminous with a particular food regime. As we will see, however, there is also a vast and rich variety of forms of food provisioning, or food systems, that are not integrated into global flows and hence cannot be subsumed into food regimes, although they are impacted by them.

Other terms that are adopted to talk about food as it moves from producers to consumers are more limited than that of food systems in their purview and tend to concentrate on the aspects of food provision to which those who use them attach greatest importance. "Economists will value markets as key to food security, climate scientists will worry about greenhouse gas emissions from intensive agriculture, agronomists emphasize yields, and political scientists focus on governance arrangements as the solution to undesirable outcomes" (Ingram et al. 2010, p. 30). Terms that involve the word "chain" tend to conceive of food provision as a kind of highway or pipeline between the first link on the chain and the ultimate consumer. They often explicitly or implicitly view the market and its mechanisms of supply and demand as the main regulator of flows along the highway. Reasoning primarily in quantitative terms, they may consider that "if supply grows more rapidly than demand, average quality of life in the world will almost certainly improve" (Leathers and Foster 2009, p. 3). Food chain analysis focuses essentially on yields and flows and can tend to exclude broader consideration of drivers and outcomes. Often this kind of approach to viewing how actors relate to one another concentrates on a single product or commodity and analyzes its flow through a "commodity chain". In this vision a commodity starts off its life not as a particular product of a particular territory incorporating qualities that its producer's skills have given it, but as a basic good that is interchangeable with others of the same type in a standardized manner. The distinguishing characteristics of the products are added during the later processing and retailing phases of the chain. The concept of "food supply chains", a term also widely used, is closer to that of food systems, so much so that use of the term "chain" can appear inappropriate. As one food policy analyst puts it, "[M]odels of food-supply chains that start off looking very neat and simple on paper can quickly start to look like a bowl of spaghetti or noodles! Economic and physical connections weave everywhere, with health, social and environmental outputs added as well" (Lang et al. 2009, p. 145).

The term "value chain" places emphasis on how each step or link in the chain adds "value" to the product. The World Bank defines a value chain as a "sequence of production, processing and marketing activities: products pass through all activities of the chain in a certain order and, with each activity, the product gains value" (World Bank 2008, p. 1). A fundamental question left unasked and unanswered here, but to which we will return, is that of what is being "valued" in a value chain. Who decides, and on the basis of what criteria? The linear highway or pipeline image dominates in discussions of value chains, as with other related terms. Insufficient attention is often paid to power differentials among actors along the chain. In reality, profits from progressive "value addition" accrue disproportionately to actors situated further along the chain – transporters, processors, retailers – as compared with the primary producers without whom there would be nothing to which value could be added. Interestingly enough, consumers tend to disappear as a category of actors in graphic representations since they are not value adders in the economic sense but simply ingest the final product. The terminology that contrasts most strongly with the food and value chain imagery is that of food networks or food webs (Cranbrook 2006). These terms highlight the multiple and crisscrossing links – many of which are not market led – among people involved with food in different ways within a particular territory. We will return to these two images later in this chapter when we contrast the "conventional" global food regime with more local "alternative" food networks.

Our progress-indoctrinated culture tends to view the developments that have led to an ever more differentiated food system as an unmitigated evolution for the better. It is good to keep in mind that dynamics of this kind are never linear and one-sided. The advent of sedentary agriculture, for example, is associated with the very birth of civilization, yet it had some effects on the well-being of the populations concerned that were clearly negative. The increasing reliance on a few plants entailed poorer nutrition than did the more varied diets afforded by pastoralism and hunting and gathering (Leathers and Foster 2009, p. 75), and the concentrated living conditions introduced a propensity to disease epidemics. Other impacts, such as the social and economic differentiations attendant on sedentary agriculture, are the object of contested interpretations. More recent evolutions in food systems are also subject to different assessments. The premises on which interpretations are based are not always declared, and it is important to seek them between the lines. An FAO publication on "the transformation of agri-food systems", edited by two former FAO staff who moved on to the Agricultural Development Division of the Bill and Melinda Gates Foundation, frames the process in the following manner:

> We lay out three different typologies for food systems that correspond roughly with the development process. The first is a traditional food system, characterized by a dominance of traditional, unorganized supply chains and limited market infrastructure. The second is a structured food system, still characterized by traditional actors but with more rules and regulations applied to marketplaces and more market infrastructure. . . . The third type is an industrialized food system, as observed throughout the developed world, with strong perceptions of safety, a high degree of coordination, a large and consolidated processing sector and organized retailers.
>
> (McCullough et al. 2008, p. 4)

Productivity

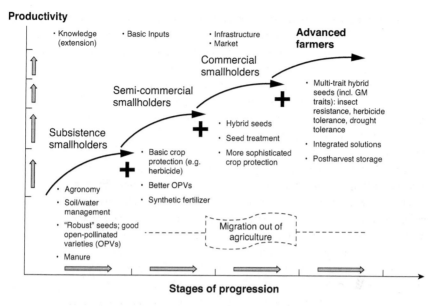

Stages of progression

FIGURE 2.2   Agricultural intensification and migration out of agriculture

Source: Zhou, Y. (2010). *Smallholder Agriculture, Sustainability and the Syngenta Foundation.* Syngenta Foundation for Sustainable Development. Reproduced with permission. Syngenta Foundation.

Although this is not explicitly stated, the use of terms like "development" and the contrast posited between "traditional, unorganized" and "coordination, consolidated, organized" convey the view that we are talking about a process of evolution from the less good through the better to the best. Indeed, although the book does document how difficult it is for smallholders in developing countries to keep pace with the industrialized food system, it conveys the message that the future lies in linking up with it – for those who can manage to do so – while "exit strategies" from agriculture and "safety nets" will have to be put in place for the rest. It is assumed that the path of progress leads through the phase of "modernizing" economies to industrialized ones and that this will inevitably entail a progressive drastic reduction of the number of farmers on the land, while agribusiness will step in to provide employment and ecosystem services (*ibid.*, p. 11). Figure 2.2 illustrates this vision as set forward in a publication of the Syngenta Foundation, established by one of the world-leading agribusinesses.

Let us contrast this upbeat framing of the volatilization of the farming population with the following text that seeks to get at the structural conditions behind the trend toward migration out of agriculture:

> Worldwide, agricultural development has been premised on de-peasantization in the global South and the continued corporatization of agriculture in both the global North and the global South – with the two outcomes

> underpinned by the dynamic of the concentration and centralization of capital. De-peasantization occurs when small, previously self-sufficient farmers . . . are literally forced off their farms as an inevitable consequence of having attempted to move to a more "advanced" form of agriculture. . . . Meanwhile, other farmers are "structurally adjusted" out of agriculture to enable the consolidation of larger units of production. The consequence is that people who once had direct access to food are no longer connected to the land and the food that it produces.
>
> (Lawrence et al. 2010, p. 4)

The way reality is evolving today, however, is pretty much the opposite of the scenario projected in the modernization narrative according to rural sociologist Jan Douwe van der Ploeg. The current economic and financial crises to which we alluded in the introduction are driving entrepreneurial industrialized farming into debt, whereas the far more autonomous and multifunctional logic of peasant farming is experiencing a renaissance (van der Ploeg 2010 p. 105). So much for linear progression. We will return to these alternative scenarios at the end of this chapter.

The corporate-led global food system

Corporate concentration in the food chain

Assessments of the impacts of how the world food system has evolved over the past few decades differ. Two incontrovertible and worrisome facts, however, are the astounding concentration of the power of transnational agrifood corporations that characterizes the global food chain today and, more recently, the rise of financial speculation on food and agriculture by economic actors who have no interest whatsoever in the actual products from which they profit.[2] Transnational corporations (TNCs) dominate three strategic segments of the world food economy – provision of inputs, trade in agricultural commodities and food processing, and food retailing – and impinge on production as well. The trade and processing companies have been on the scene for over a century. As we saw in the previous chapter, their operations were favored by the big powers who stood to benefit by importing cheap food (United Kingdom) or exporting agricultural surpluses (United States). The fact that the grains in which they deal can be served up as food, animal feed, or – most recently – fuel according to how the market fluctuates has further enhanced their ability to operate flexibly and massively. Since the mid-1990s, there has been an acceleration of the tendency toward concentration of market activity in an increasingly small number of increasingly powerful commodity conglomerates. Horizontal coordination involves the merging of businesses involved in the same stage of the food chain. The five largest traders in grains (Cargill, Bunge, Archer Daniels Midland [ADM], Gencore, and Dreyfus) are estimated to control 75 percent of international trade in grains – dominantly corn, soy, and wheat (De Schutter and Cordes 2011, p. 7). At the same time, these economic actors may seek to ensure that they have unfailing access to the commodities in which they deal at prices favorable to them by practicing vertical integration with enterprises operating at other stages of the production cycle. Vertically integrated companies can control portions of the food system virtually from "field to fork". Multinationals like Cargill buy, ship, and mill grain; feed it to livestock; and then supply the supermarkets with meat products. In a production system of this nature price is internal to the company's operation rather than being negotiated by different actors who meet in the marketplace, as the "free" market narrative would have it (Corporate Watch 2004, p. 28). Already a decade ago ConAgra distributed seed, fertilizer, and pesticides; owned and operated grain elevators, barges, and railroad cars; manufactured animal feed; and produced chickens and processed them for sale in meat cases and for frozen dinners (Howard 2006).

Compared to grain traders and processers, the multinational input industry is a relative newcomer on the scene. It received a first boost with the development of the Green Revolution technology package in the 1960s, which promoted the use of hybrid seeds, synthetic nitrogen fertilizer, and pesticides. As we have seen in Chapter 1, an even bigger leg up came with the extension of "intellectual property", originally conceived of as applying to "creations of the mind", to cover "industrial property" including the products of corporation laboratories. The segment of the input industry that has received most attention are the seed companies – rightly so since seeds are the very basis of food and of life itself. Up until not more than a few decades ago, seeds were overwhelmingly in the hands of the farmers who had been breeding them since the days of the Fertile Crescent, with public sector plant breeders joining them in the 20th century. In just a short time span the major private sector seed breeders have operated a massive takeover of the world's commercial seed supply. Brand-name seeds subject to exclusive monopoly under intellectual property rights (proprietary seeds) accounted for 82 percent of the market worldwide by 2007 (ETC 2008, p. 11), with the top three companies alone (Monsanto, DuPont, and Syngenta) claiming almost 50 percent of the global proprietary seed market. Intellectual property rights (IPRs) are justified on the grounds that they are a necessary compensation for the resources invested in research and innovation by private companies, who have increasingly supplanted public sector research activities in agriculture. This patently ignores the far more justifiable need to protect the rights of farmers themselves to save and exchange their own seeds, developed through centuries of anonymous effort and local knowledge. It also fails to take into account the negative impacts of massive market control by a few corporations operating on a profit motive in this vital area. Displacing traditional plants and livestock and promoting industrial monocultures with reduction of biodiversity and increase in environmental pollution is high on this list. Others include orienting research to commercially valuable products rather than to meeting the needs of small-scale producers in developing countries, restricting farmers' access to seeds, and provoking debt on the part of small-scale producers who previously had cost-free access to productive resources.

Genetically modified organisms (GMOs) are the most contentious aspect of the corporate seed market because of their impact on the world's biogenetic and germplasm reserves. GMOs are touted by their manufacturers as a solution to hunger since they are claimed to increase crop yields. However, mounting evidence indicates that GM crops are not higher yielding than traditional seeds in the long run and are not the best way of addressing hunger for other reasons as well (IAASTD 2009; De Schutter and Cordes 2011, pp. 53–55). Considering the fact that they are complex operations that go beyond the bounds of natural processes, it is not surprising that transgenic insertions can have unanticipated consequences that can depress productivity. An example is the reduced uptake of the vital nutrient manganese reported for Monsanto's Roundup Ready soya, which was genetically modified to be resistant to glyphosate, the active ingredient in the Monsanto herbicide with which it is marketed (Latham and Wilson 2008). Recent research is also questioning claims that genetically engineered crops reduce the use of environmentally damaging chemical inputs. On the contrary, the spread of GM-based herbicide-resistant weed management systems in the United States over the past decade and a half has led to the development of glyphosate-resistant weeds and, as a result, to substantial increases in the number and volume of herbicides that need to be applied (Benbrook 2012; Friends of the Earth 2014, pp. 32–35). Finally, on the human health front a link has been suggested between the increase in glyphosate use in the United States and the rise in celiac disease or gluten intolerance in the same period (Samsel and Seneff 2013). On the other side of the GM fence, scientists of the US Department of Agriculture, using conventional breeding, have recently produced a variety of rice that provides good grain quality and high yields while outcompeting weeds and weeds and reducing herbicide use (Farming Online 2014). Despite this debunking, the seed corporations are now proposing to meet the challenge of climate change by producing "climate-ready" genetically modified crops designed to grow on poor soils with less rain. Of the 1,663 patent documents claiming stress tolerance in plants that were published between June 2008 and June 2010, just six corporations (including Monsanto, DuPont, and Syngenta) accounted for 77 percent (ETC Group 2011b). Many of the gene sequences that they were seeking to patent had been excised by corporation "biopirates" from African staple crops like millets and sorghums that local farmers have been breeding for years because of their tolerance to drought (African Centre for Biosafety 2009).

Genetic modification of seeds has had an energizing effect on other areas of the corporate input business. As we have seen in the case of Monsanto's Roundup Ready crops, GMOs are the glue that allows corporations to market packages combining seeds with other inputs to which they have been artificially rendered synergetic, mostly environment-damaging herbicides and pesticides. This genetic "triumph" has revitalized flagging chemical input sales. It has been accompanied by mergers in the previously separate chemical and seed industries: the top three seed firms are among the top six pesticide firms. The oligopoly paradigm already characterized individual sectors, with not more than four firms controlling 58.2 percent of seeds; 61.9 percent of agrochemicals; 24.3 percent of fertilizers; 53.4 percent of animal pharmaceuticals; and, in live-stock genetics, 97 percent of poultry and two-thirds of swine and cattle research. Now it has spread to the entire food system. The same six multinationals – Monsanto, DuPont, Syngenta, Bayer, Dow, and BASF – control 75 percent of all private sector plant breeding research, 60 percent of the commercial seed market and 76 percent of global agrochemical sales. Some also have links to animal pharmaceuticals (ETC Group 2011a). Multinational fertilizer companies are more of a separate set, but some firms primarily known for their grain trade activities, like Cargill, also have a big stake in some of the fertilizer industries, and fertilizer king Yara has branched out into mineral additives for animal feeds.

The retail market, the latest arrival in the corporate-controlled global food chain, has become the tail that wags the dog. The spread and the concentration of today's ubiquitous supermarket chains are phenomena of the last few decades. The giant in the field, Walmart, was incorporated only in 1969. Today it is the second largest public corporation in the world, the largest retailer, and the biggest private employer with over 2 million employees. Runner-up Carrefour opened its first hyper-market in 1963. By 2007 the top one hundred global food retailers had combined sales of $1.8 trillion, representing 35 percent of all grocery retail sales worldwide (ETC 2008). The top three – Walmart, Carrefour, and Tesco – accounted for 50 percent of the top ten's revenues. Supermarket chains have moved into the Global South, aided by structural adjustment policies and WTO regulations that have opened up these economies to foreign direct investment. In Latin America the top five chains control 65 percent of the food retail market, up from just 10–20 percent in the 1990s (Clapp 2012, p. 110). A combination of the NAFTA and an aggressive expansion campaign, allegedly including political bribes, has pushed the number of Walmart stores in Mexico from 14 in 1994 to 1,724 in 2012 (Rojo and Perez-Roche 2013). Global supermarket presence is also growing in Asia and in Africa, where in 2011 Walmart acquired a 51 percent interest in the South African firm Massmart, which operates in twelve sub-Saharan African countries. The other form of emerging global giant reaching out to consumers is the food-service companies of which the fast food servers like McDonald's and KFC are the best known. The rapid multiplication of McDonald's arches in China starting in 1992, including one near the Forbidden City in Beijing, was so strong a culturally invasive image as to evoke – for people like me with an historical bent – a pacific re-edition of the opium wars. This was just one particularly visible step in the evolution from 1963, when McDonald's opened its five hundredth restaurant in the United States, to the present, when its 34,000 local restaurants serve 69 million people in 118 countries around the world each day.

In the competition among different actors along the global industrialized food chain, retailers played a minor role as compared with traders and processors up until the 1960s. By the turn of this century, they were in poll position (Lang et al. 2009, p. 166). Several factors help to account for their exceptionally rapid concentration. Sometimes companies have been able to purchase or enter into joint ventures with existing firms, as in the South African case cited above. The fact that supermarket chains handle such vast amounts of products through global supply chains makes it possible for them to practice economies of scale and offer lower prices than smaller competitors (Clapp 2012, p. 111). The supply-chain management they have introduced allows them to control the product chain from farm to

FIGURE 2.3 McDonald's in Schenzhen, China

Source: Bob He (2011). Reproduced with permission.

shelf and to dictate supply conditions and prices (Fuchs 2006). The push for profits at the last link of the food supply chain drives down prices, wages, and working conditions throughout the industrial food system (ETC 2008). Disputes between retailers – closer to pressure from consumers – and input manufacturers on issues like GMO food have developed over the past few years, a phenomenon that some feel may be opening up a chink in corporate hegemony between "Big Food" and "Big Agriculture".

Corporations exercise their power and influence over the industrialized global food system not only by their sheer size and their capacity to set prices but also by the ways in which they shape the rules of the game and the choices of consumers. They would not be able to rule the global roost as they do if they did not have the support of public policies. Corporations have come to play an increasingly important role in regulation of the food system through the rise of private standards and the decline of the state's regulatory role (Clapp 2012, p. 117; Lang et al. 2009, p. 169), an issue to which the concluding section of this book will return. They also weigh in through participation in governmental delegations in intergovernmental regulatory bodies like the Commission of the joint FAO-WHO Codex Alimentarius, which sets the standards applied by the WTO for international trade in food products. Of the nine-person US delegation to the thirty-sixth session of the Commission in 2013, five were from the food industry and only four from government, while there were no representatives of consumer or farmer organizations. The more informal lobbying activities of agrifood corporations and practices like contributions to election campaigns or the "revolving door", whereby corporation executives move in and out of government regulatory positions, are well documented (Nestle 2007). The biotech industry discussed above would not have been as successful as it has been in pursuing its agenda without the support of the US State Department, which has lobbied foreign governments to adopt pro-agricultural biotechnology policies and laws, conducted multifaceted public relations campaigns to improve the image of biotechnology, opposed genetic engineering labeling efforts, and exercised economic and political conditionalities on developing countries (Food & Water Watch 2013).

Finally, the agrifood businesses expend enormous amounts of resources in seeking to influence public opinion, particularly on contentious issues like GMO foods. An incident in the United States in 2012 that received considerable publicity was the massive last-minute investment of $44 million in "voter education" by corporations to win a Californian referendum decision that threatened to introduce food labeling showing the presence of GMOs.[3] It has been alleged (Nestle 2013) that Coca Cola was financing scientific research aimed at casting doubt on science linking soda consumption to health problems. Other activities seeking to frame the terms of the debate are less obvious but, by the same token, more insidious. These include the Gates Foundation's apparently harmless or even laudable support for research and education on food and agriculture in prestigious, opinion-making institutions. A deeper examination of this philanthropic gesture reveals that Gates holds 500,000 shares in Monsanto (Buczynski 2010) and that the programs in question are pro-GMO. Gates grants to Harvard University have produced such products as Robert Paarlberg's (2008) passionate plea for allowing Africa to profit from biotechnology and the pro-GMO work of Harvard Professor Calestous Juma in the context of the Agricultural Innovation in Africa program (Juma 2011). We are treading here on the treacherous terrain, to which we will return in the next chapter, of the degree to which science is "objective" and enables "evidence-based" policy decisions. For the moment, let us take a look at the following statement about GMOs and food production. Although it presents itself as grounded in science, it takes several undemonstrated logical leaps, which end up by implicitly characterizing opposition to the introduction of GMOs as misguided and not terribly rational attacks against efforts to end hunger:

> While GM crops have the potential to greatly increase crop and livestock productivity and nutrition, a popular backlash against GM foods has created a stringent political atmosphere under which tight regulations are being developed. . . . The cost of implementing these regulations could be beyond the reach of most African countries . . . and tends to conflict with the great need for increased food production.
>
> (Juma 2011, pp. 38–39)

Financial speculation and price volatility

Up until now we have spoken about the power and the effects of multinational corporations and conglomerates that are actually involved in producing, trading, processing, and retailing food. Another class of actors without functional links to food has entered into the globalized food system more recently, along with the phenomenon of increasingly strong and complex linkages between the world of finance and the world food economy.[4] This trend is known as "financialization", defined in broad terms as "the increasing role of financial motives, financial markets, financial actors and financial institutions in the operation of the domestic and international economies" (Epstein 2005, p. 3). It translates into an effort to transform all value that is exchanged into either a financial instrument – an easily tradable package of capital – or a "derivative", deriving its value from the performance of a financial instrument. Financial capital has replaced productive capital in the quest for new profits (Clapp 2013, p. 3), hence downgrading the importance of what has come to be referred to nostalgically as "the real economy" of actually producing goods and services. In the context of the global food regime, financialization has had the result of exacerbating the separation between decisions related to production and to consumption. It contributes to this "distancing" both by increasing the number of actors involved in global agrifood commodity chains and by "abstracting food from its physical form into highly complex agricultural commodity derivatives that are difficult to understand for all but seasoned financial traders" (Clapp 2013, p. 2). By the same token, it is increasingly difficult to establish cause-and-effect relationships and to hold investors accountable for the results of their action.

Trading in financial products based on agricultural commodities, or "agricultural derivatives", is not new. "Futures contracts", specifying amounts of grain to be sold or purchased at a given date and a given price, have traditionally been purchased and sold on exchange markets as a way for farmers, grain companies, and processers to insulate themselves against future price shifts. Most of this trading takes place on US markets. In 1936 federal regulators were empowered to impose "position limits" on the number of contracts that could be held by traders not involved in the "real economy" of commodities in order to guard against "excessive" speculation. Since 1974 the Commodities Futures Trading Commission (CFTC) has been entrusted with the regulatory role of monitoring position limits and other aspects of commodity futures markets in the United States.

During the 1980s and 1990s, however, US banks began to bundle agricultural derivatives together with other commodities into a single financial instrument, "commodity index funds" (CIFs), that are sold "over the counter" (OTC) rather than being directly traded on the regulated commodity futures exchanges. The Commodities Futures Modernization Act adopted by the US Congress in 2000 dismantled the regulation of financial derivatives, a step decried by financier Warren Buffet himself, who defined them as "weapons of mass destruction" (Buffet 2002, p. 15). The ruling was very heavily determined by Wall Street lobbying. It has been reported that during the decade from 1998–2008, the major Wall Street banks directly contributed over $1.7 billion to the campaigns of US Congress representatives and senators and spent a further $3.4 billion on lobbyists charged with promoting deregulation (Essential Information and Community Education Foundation 2009). Deregulation has run in parallel to the drying up of other opportunities for speculation, like the housing market, and to the advent of biofuels operations as an attractive investment opportunity. Together these trends pushed the level of investments in commodities from $65 billion in 2006 to $126 billion in 2011, causing fluctuations unrelated to actual supply of food and allowing Goldman Sachs to earn close to $1 billion from food speculation in 2009 alone (World Development Movement 2011). The categories of financial speculators and agribusiness corporations are not necessarily separate ones. The key agricultural trading and processing firms are also engaged in financial services, including agricultural commodities futures trading, and have made significant profits from the rising prices stimulated by speculative investment. Cargill saw an 86 percent increase in its annual profits in the first quarter of 2008, "which it openly attributed to its commodity futures trading business" (Clapp 2012, p. 145). Large-scale institutional investors like insurance companies, pension funds, and university endowments have also been increasingly attracted to including agriculture-based financial investment products in their portfolios as the value of food and energy commodities – intertwined and linked to purchase of farmland thanks to the biofuels boom – began to rise significantly (Daniel 2010; McMichael 2012b).

That this explosion of financial speculation in food and land has had an impact on the sharp upward turn and subsequent volatility of food prices shown in the chart in the introduction and on the phenomenon of land grabbing is hard to deny. Because of the complexity and lack of transparency of the financialized economy, however, it is difficult to document precise cause-and-effect relations. Voices like the World Bank and the OECD have pooh-poohed the arguments advanced somewhat timidly by the FAO (FAO 2008b) and more assuredly by a range of civil society actors. The financial crisis of 2008 prompted the G20 to turn its attention to the issue of food price volatility in 2011 under the French Presidency as recalled in the introduction, but without effective results. In the United States the Dodd-Frank Wall Street Reform and Consumer Protection Act, signed into law by President Obama on 21 July 2010, was hailed as bringing the most sweeping changes to the financial regulation system since the regulatory reform that followed the Great Depression. Three years later, however, over 60 percent of the deadlines set for turning the act's provisions into rules had been missed, thanks in good part to the determined and well-funded opposition of the finance industry lobby (McCoy 2013). The Markets in Financial Instruments Directive adopted by European Union negotiators during the night between 14 and 15 January 2014 seeks to curb speculation on food prices by placing a limit on the number of food contracts that banks and other finance companies can hold and by forcing traders to open their activities to greater public scrutiny. Civil society lobbying played a significant role in getting this provision through, but industry pressure was expected as the regional regulations moved on to application at national level.

The global market

The corporate-led food regime would not be able to function without a global market organized in a way that favors its operations. Only some 10 percent of all food produced in the world transits through the global market. Most food is consumed in the country or region in which it originates. Yet the impacts of the way the global market is organized and the speculation it permits are visited on the local food systems of countries whose share in the global market is minimal. These countries, in Africa above all, have been sucked into the global market first through structural adjustment and then by adhering to regulations of the WTO and bilateral trade agreements.[5] A cornerstone of the structural adjustment policies imposed on indebted developing countries by the IMF and the World Bank in the 1980s/1990s was that the countries receiving loans were obliged to open their markets to importations from abroad essentially by lowering or eliminating tariffs. The result of this reduction of barriers was to put into direct competition the products of industrialized agriculture with those of peasant agriculture and family farming in the Global South. The subsidies that the industrialized agriculture products receive enable them to be put on the global market at prices that do not need to cover the actual costs of production. Additionally, the technological evolution of the industrialized model during the 20th century targeted increased productivity without regard for other benefits that agriculture could provide or for the negative impacts of productivist agriculture, which were visited on the environment and local societies and economies as "externalities". This had led to an increase in the relation of productivity between the two agricultures from 1 to 10 at the beginning of the century to 1 to 500 by the end (Mazoyer and Roudart, p. 455). The competition, clearly unfair, was devastating for the small-scale producers particularly in the Global South.

It was exacerbated by the WTO and its Agreement on Agriculture (AoA).[6] The AoA represents the first ever set of multilaterally agreed-upon rules that restrict the policy space of national governments in the area of agriculture. Its objective, as stated in the Preamble to the Agreement, is to establish a "fair and market-oriented agricultural trading system" (WTO n.d.), although critics question the validity of coupling the two adjectives. As indicated in the previous chapter, there were clear interests in liberalizing global agricultural trade on the part of several groups of actors. The United States and the European Union wanted to lighten the heavy financial burden of their agricultural support systems. The Cairns Group of countries[7] with a commodity export vocation based on their relatively unsubsidized large-scale commercial farmers was seeking liberalized market access and reductions in domestic support and export subsidies. Agribusiness TNCs wanted to increase their flexibility to sell and source their products and to move regulation on delicate issues like GMOs beyond the reach of national governments.

The expected benefits to developing countries were predicated on classic comparative advantage theory, whereby developing countries were better off exporting tropical commodities and importing (artificially) cheap food from the global market, and the neoliberal assumption that an unencumbered world market would set fair prices, fluidify exchanges, and stimulate greater growth for all participants. Developing countries were expected to benefit from a reduction of the high levels of protectionism practiced by OECD countries and to increase their share in the world market. The neoliberal vision sees the market as a "level playing field" but in reality, of course, it is far from that. Lowering of governments' capacity to protect their markets was supposed to be compensated by reduction of the subsidies that led to cheap surpluses flooding the world market and pushing down prices. But even before the AoA was negotiated, the United States and the European Union had conducted a bilateral deal, the Blair House Accord, which introduced exceptions to liberalization designed to maintain the advantages of their farm sectors. As a result, the OECD countries have actually increased their subsidies in absolute terms since the AoA went into effect while the developing countries' share of world agricultural trade has remained steady (Clapp 2012, pp. 72–73). What's more, they have been locked into the role of exporting essential commodities, without profiting from value addition, by the WTO regulation that allows importing countries to practice "tariff escalation", whereby higher tariffs are applied on processed products than on raw commodities.

The unequal effects of the AoA became increasingly evident as the agreement was implemented, as did the unequal capacity of developing countries to defend their interests in the WTO arena. In the run-up to the WTO Ministerial meeting in Seattle in 1999, the Senegalese government delegation was so disoriented by the mass of complicated texts on the table that they asked to be briefed by the Senegalese peasant movement, which was benefiting from an FAO training program on WTO challenges that my colleagues and I had managed to arrange for them. An unexpected mass of civil society protesters took to the streets in Seattle, contesting both the content of the negotiations and its undemocratic, closed-door nature. Over the following years an increasingly strong network of social movement advocacy developed in opposition to "free" trade in agriculture, led by the world peasant movement La Via Campesina. An effort was made to address developing countries' concerns by launching a "development round" of WTO negotiations at Doha in 2001. The Doha Ministerial Declaration made it clear that, in the WTO cosmos, "development" was equated with economic development, and participation in global trade was considered to be the privileged highway to attain it (WTO 2001). Even in these terms, however, the round did not take off. The United States and the European Union continued to face each other off, with the United States being urged to reduce its domestic support and the European Union to lower its tariffs and other forms of market protection. Opposition to OECD pretensions built up progressively within the groups of developing and emerging countries, leading to a stalemate in the negotiations in Cancun in 2003 and repeated failures to conclude the round. A major bone of contention was the design of "special safeguard mechanisms" intended to allow governments to protect poor farmers by imposing a special tariff on certain agricultural goods in the case of a price fall and/or a rapid increase in importations. As the Indian trade minister Kamal Nath put it after the talks broke down in July 2008, "I can negotiate commerce but I cannot negotiate livelihood security" (Thakurta 2008).

The agreement that was finally adopted at the WTO Ministerial meeting in Bali in December 2013 saved the WTO's skin but was strongly criticized by social movements and civil society organizations. At the heart of the negotiations was the clash between global trade regulations biased in favor of developed countries and the right of developing and emergent countries to promote the food security of their citizens. Once again India was on the frontline, defending its recently adopted national food security program. This scheme foresees public action to buy small-scale producers' crops at supported levels, stock them, and release them to poor consumers at affordable prices when needed. Such measures have been unsuccessfully pushed by the G33 group since 2006 on the grounds that they address domestic food security and are incommensurably less trade distorting than the agricultural support for export crops and the export subsidies that the United States and the European Union continue to practice (Wise 2013b). The compromise adopted at Bali shields countries like India that have already adopted such programs from WTO sanctions for a four-year period. However, it slams the door shut against poor countries that have not yet been able to enact them, although they arguably need them even more than emergent countries like India (Africa Trade Network 2013). The plum that the rich countries sought and obtained was a "trade facilitation" agreement, heralded as a measure that would add $1 trillion to the global economy by simplifying trade procedures and reducing the cost of doing business at the border (Ramdoo 2013). The main beneficiaries of this agreement, however, are transnational firms that already control the sphere of export and import and are looking for improved access to developing country markets (Wise, *op.cit.*). As La Via Campesina points out, the 2013 World Trade Report data shows that "80 percent of US exports are handled by 1 percent of large exporters, 85 percent of European exports are in the hands of 10 percent of big exporters and 81 percent of exports are concentrated in the top 5 largest exporting firms in developing countries" (LVC 2013b).

The long stall in the WTO negotiations left a vacuum that has been filled by bilateral free trade negotiations, which are even more damaging to developing country interests than the multilateral talks in which these countries can bind together. The North American Free Trade Agreement (NAFTA) negotiated between Mexico, the United States, and Canada in 1994, to which a quote in the opening paragraph of this book refers, is a good illustration. It obliged Mexico to lower its tariff protection against imported maize, its staple crop and source of the livelihoods of most Mexican peasants, while the United States was free to increase its domestic subsidies and provide export credit encouraging Mexico to import more US maize (Clapp 2012, p. 85). Bilateral trade agreements have mushroomed since the NAFTA, as has opposition by civil society and social movements. In the case of the Economic Partnership Agreements (EPAs), which the European Union has been negotiating with regional groupings of its ex-colonies since 2003, this opposition, particularly by small-scale producers' organizations themselves, has played an important role in pushing the regional organizations to stand up to EU pressure and insist on terms beneficial to the rural producers who constitute the majority of their populations (McKeon 2008). Whether or not the final results will be up to civil society expectations, there has undoubtedly been a significant impact in terms of opening up intergovernmental negotiations to organizations representing those most affected (ECOWAS Peoples' Summit 2013). The issue of transparency is particularly important given the closed-door nature of the latest generation of free trade agreements now under negotiation. The Trans-Pacific Partnership, the Canada-European Union Free Trade Agreement, and the Transatlantic Trade and Investment Partnership have been labelled "corporate bills of rights" (Engler 2013) for the way in which they favor TNCs on delicate issues like investor-state dispute settlements, intellectual property rights, public procurement, and GMOs. Equally dangerous is the way in which they override the capacity of national parliaments, courts, and municipal governments to defend citizens' interests. We will come back to the issue of corporate and financial regulation in subsequent chapters, since it is one of the greatest food governance challenges we face today.

BOX 2.1
ASKING THE QUESTION: WHO BENEFITS?

"Promoting global and regional trade in agriculture is essential to enhancing food security and to sustainably meeting the demand of a growing, increasingly affluent population, projected to surpass 9 billion by mid-century" (Global Harvest 2011).

"The poorest developing countries are net losers under most trade liberalization scenarios" (IAASTD Synthesis Report 2008, p. 65.)

"The most likely groups to benefit from the reduction of trade barriers in foreign markets and the expansion of exports are commercial producers. Small farmers may not be able to participate in growing export-oriented crops and may experience greater competition in accessing resources, including land, marginalizing their position even further. The winners and losers of open trade policies are likely to be different, and it is feared that it is often the poor who are hurt most" (FAO 2003).

As the UN Special Rapporteur on the Right to Food points out,

> Increased cross-border trade in agricultural products implies that . . . the role of transnational corporations increases. . . . Since these corporations have activities in different countries and can chose the country from which they source, they may be difficult to regulate, particularly as regards their buying policies. This constitutes a source of dependency for the farmers who supply

them. It also encourages the segmentation of the farming sector, increasingly divided between one segment which has access to high-value markets . . . and another which is left to serve only the low-value domestic markets, and is comparatively neglected and marginalized.

(De Schutter 2009c, pp. 29–30)

In short, undoubted beneficiaries of trade liberalization are the transnational corporations, who state their case in the first quote in the Box 2.1, while undoubted losers are the small-scale farmers.

The corporate food system's impact on food producers

Although the corporations that control the global food system deal essentially in upstream and downstream products and the process of channeling them through global markets, they also impact heavily on the heart of the food story: production itself. They do so by influencing both the models of production farmers adopt and the ways in which they are linked to markets. Because of the logic and the scale on which it operates and the economic interests that drive it, the global food chain is intimately connected to an industrialized model of agricultural production. This model is characterized by intensive monoculture cultivation on large extensions of land, adopting capital and technology rather than labor-intensive farming methods. Its objective is to increase productivity in the short run. In doing so it relies largely on chemical inputs and fossil fuels and their derivatives and promotes standardization and homogenization of crops and agricultural methods. It draws heavily on increasingly scarce water. Industrialized agriculture as introduced in developing countries has tended to be oriented toward export crops, with the bulk of value addition through successive steps of processing and packaging taking place outside the country of origin. Intensive industrial production is often conducted on corporate-owned plantations in which rural people are employed as workers, most often under precarious and health-threatening conditions (PANAP 2010, Banana Link). Small-scale producers are being pushed off the land to make room for corporation-controlled plantations, which may be dedicated to agrifuel crops rather than food, or to what have been termed "flex crops", which can be marketed as food, feed, or fuel (Borras, Franco and Wang 2013).

Corporate external input-oriented production is important in the industrial food chain logic, but concepts and approaches linked to the marketing side of the equation are equally significant. As a result of market concentration, farmers in the Global North often find themselves confronted with a small number of oligarchic buyers with whom they are obliged to enter into contractual arrangements in which the corporations set the conditions. Contract farming is being promoted in the Global South, as well, as an allegedly more inclusive way of linking small-scale producers into value chains than plantation farming. This trend is in part a reaction to public concern about the phenomenon of land grabbing. Despite the aura of social responsibility with which it is framed, however, contract farming may actually enhance the benefits of the corporate players on the chain by leaving small-scale producers on their land and shouldering climatic and other risks, while at the same time subjecting them to corporate control over what they plant, when and how, and what price they receive. The problem is not with the concept and practice of contractual arrangements as such, but with the partners in the contracts, their respective interests and power, and the regulatory frameworks within which they operate.

BOX 2.2
CONTRACT FARMING

Contract farming can be defined as "a condition in which a buyer of agricultural products (e.g. an agri-processor, an export firm, a specialized wholesaler or a supermarket, or agents working on their behalf) establishes a contract or a quasi-contract with one agricultural producer or with an informal or formal organization of producers, to purchase a given volume, at an estimated date, under a set of conditions (typically including product quality standards), for a pre-set price or a price that will vary within a more or less fixed range. . . . These contractual arrangements can include the provision by the buyer to the producer of credit, agricultural inputs, technical advice, machinery services, transportation and so on; the cost of these goods and services is deducted from the final payment to the producer".

HLPE (2013). pp. 75–76

Over the past years contract farming linked to value chains has become one of the main models of agricultural production and a key sourcing mechanism for agribusiness corporations operating in 110 countries around the world (Kay 2012, pp. 18–19). Its promoters hold that this arrangement offers small-scale producers improved incomes and other benefits like access to markets, credit, and inputs. Contract farming has been adopted by the development establishment as a winning strategy for reaching and benefitting the rural poor and, as such, worthy of public support through aid programs and from national budgets. The World Bank states the case in terms that merit deconstructing: "with its focus on competitiveness globalization favors larger-scale operations in the quest for increasingly higher trade volumes to counter ever tighter margins." Large companies, which dominate international agricultural trade, prefer large suppliers, the argument continues. "Thus, the challenge facing small farmers is how to gain greater access to markets, enhance their value chain position and increase their value-added so as to boost incomes and reduce poverty" (World Bank 2008, p. 1). The terms "thus" or "therefore" are often signposts of illogical syllogisms such as that of the Cheshire cat in *Alice in Wonderland*: "[D]ogs are not mad; dogs growl when they are angry and wag their tails when they are pleased while cats do the opposite; therefore cats are mad". In this case the unquestioned assumptions that render the argument illogical are that competition-oriented globalization is ineluctable and beneficial, that it is in the interest of small farmers to gain access to international markets, and that this step will increase their capacity to capture value added and will reduce poverty.

The evidence does not substantiate these assumptions. Contract farming schemes often tend to exacerbate the gap between the better-off producers who are able to participate in these schemes and the more marginalized farmers, including women, who are not (Oya 2012, p. 28). Value chain linkages have been found to work for only the top 2–20 percent of small-scale producers, mostly men (Vorley et al. 2012, p. 6). The poorest farmers, women in particular, tend to be excluded (FAO Investment Centre 2012, p. 10), and expected benefits are not forthcoming unless a rather formidable range of preconditions are met (Kay *op.cit.*; Oya *op.cit.*; HLPE *op. cit.*; pp. 75–78). As a recent FAO publication recognizes, "[I]f the conditions that are stipulated in a contract farming agreement are detrimental to the interests of either partner, be it for reasons of imbalances in market power, opportunistic behavior or other unfair practices . . . contract farming operations will not be successful" (FAO Rural Infrastructure and Agro-industries Division 2012, p. 1). Yet imbalances in market power are inevitably present, by definition, when contractual relations are forged between large corporations and small-scale producers (De Schutter 2011b, p. 12).

Some analysts take the critique further. Incorporating smallholders into international value chains through contract farming, they hold, draws them into markets over which they have no ultimate control, thereby threatening their autonomy, while monoculture destroys the capacity for diversified farming on which their resilience depends. Agro-inputs replace peasant farmers' former sustainable practices and capital appropriates their labor. "By subordinating farming to price relations it is transformed, with agricultural resources converted into values that can be *redistributed* along the chain as profits for processors, retailers, agro-dealers and traders" (McMichael 2013a, p. 674). Whatever benefits in terms of enhanced income may be accruing at the outset are often short lasting due to a series of factors beyond the control of farmers, like fluctuations of commodity prices, leaving farmers in debt (*ibid.*; De Schutter 2011b, p. 12).

And all of this with the bonus for corporations of providing them with access to subsidized credit and other benefits in the name of their contribution to "feeding the world". The reasoning as expressed in a recent FAO publication is as follows:

> By their nature inclusive models involve more stakeholders, hence building consensus on the project requires time and decision-making is slower. Transaction costs are high, especially in the initial phase. They should be viewed as a necessary investment that will enable higher returns in the longer term. However, most companies need relatively rapid returns to their investment and their time frame is not compatible with that of local economic development. There is a need for "patient capital" provided by investors with a longer

time horizon initially to ensure that the expected benefits materialize. Such investors are usually from the public sector (e.g. governments, development banks and sovereign-wealth funds).

(FAO 2012b, p. 336)

The publication recognizes that far more research into the impacts of foreign direct investment in developing country agriculture is required, particularly regarding its impacts on food security (*ibid.*, pp. 338–339). Yet despite this gap in the evidence it is simply taken for granted that foreign direct investment is beneficial and hence ways of making it work must be sought. Another way to look at the question would be to reflect on whether the public sector resources used as "patient capital" to reduce corporations' transaction costs could be better employed to directly support the investments of small-scale farmers themselves in other ways that would be more beneficial to food security and local economic development. These can involve contractual arrangements. As we will see in Chapter 5, there are many forms, both in the Global South and in the Global North, of contractual producer-to-consumer marketing and of public sector contractual arrangements with small-scale producers to provision schools and hospitals that are beneficial to all parties – except corporations.

Local food webs

So what exists apart from the global corporate-controlled food chains we have been looking at thus far? Are there systems in which small-scale producers fare better? In the official narrative, other forms of food procurement in the Global South are commonly characterized as "traditional" or "indigenous". As indicated in the quotation on p. 34, terminology like this can be not simply descriptive but also judgmental. It often implies that these food systems are inferior to "modern" ones, that they are locked into time and incapable of evolution. A different adjective often used by those who value food provisioning that operates by logics other than that of the global corporate system is "local". This is what the report of the 2007 international Nyéléni Forum for Food Sovereignty had to say, in terms that straddle the descriptive and the aspirational:

> Food Sovereignty Localises Food Systems: Food sovereignty brings food providers and consumers closer together; puts providers and consumers at the centre of decision-making on food issues; protects food providers from the dumping of food and food aid in local markets; protects consumers from poor quality and unhealthy food, inappropriate food aid and food tainted with genetically modified organisms; and resists governance structures, agreements and practices that depend on and promote unsustainable and inequitable international trade and give power to remote and unaccountable corporations.

(Nyéléni 2007, p. 1)

Some authors couple the two terms "traditional and local" in describing how indigenous peoples and pastoralists source what they consume, in contrast to market-controlled supply systems. Whereas the latter, they argue, are dominated by supply and demand logic to the exclusion of other considerations, traditional and local food systems take into account not only economic factors but also environmental, social, and cultural factors. They tend to be characterized by nutritional diversity and balance, a biodiverse ecosystem focus, and social and cultural rootedness. Their economy is based on reciprocity, complementarity, risk aversion, and giving priority to subsistence. They owe these features precisely to the fact that they are "traditional", that is they are maintained by people who retain knowledge of the land and food resources rooted in historical continuity within their region of residence (Johns 2012). In this case "traditional" is assigned a positive connotation.

The term "local" merits attention as well, since it can signify different things according to who uses it and in what context. To some it can mean whatever takes place within a day's back-and-forth walking distance from the living place. In other cases it refers to the national or the regional economy as contrasted with the international marketplace. It often includes linkages between the household, nearby villages and marketplaces, even if these may be across the border in a neighboring country. Referred to food systems, it is never a purely geographic term but includes economic, social, and cultural dimensions as well. It highlights the dimension of control by people of a region over a series of factors that globalization tends to remove from their reach. In narratives that belittle the quality of being local, on the contrary, it is equated with an isolationist approach, hostile to urban and global markets, hopelessly outdated and autarkic. To overcome this kind of sterile opposition, it is useful to build awareness of how words are used and what is behind the different meanings they are given, with a view to putting them into communication rather than simplistic polarity.

Chapter 5 will illustrate in greater detail key components of an emerging worldwide movement for food sovereignty that crosses North/South and rural/urban boundaries. For now we will limit ourselves to identifying some of the major characteristics of local food systems in contrast to the corporate-controlled food regime discussed above and to illustrating peoples' motivations for engaging in them. In the Global North, initiatives to defend or reconstruct alternatives to the global food chains are proliferating, although the corporate system's steamroller effect has flattened much more of the diversity here than in the South. In some cases these local initiatives represent in the first instance a reaction to poverty combined with the negative impacts of the conventional food system on the access to food and the health of groups of disadvantaged citizens. In the United States, for example, close to 15 percent of all households were food insecure in 2011, that is they did not have access to enough food for an active, healthy life at all times throughout the year. Ethnic minorities are disproportionately poor and face additional barriers of structural racism whereby combined policies, programs, and institutions effectively wall off resources and opportunities (Anderson 2013). In urban "food desert"[8] communities like Oakland, Detroit, and Brooklyn, where affordable and healthy food is difficult to obtain, food justice advocates are building practical solutions to their problems through activities like local gardening, locally owned processing and retail operations, and community controlled school feeding programs. The Detroit Food Justice Movement seeks to turn ghettoization to the advantage of residents: "While abandoned by major supermarket chains, Detroit, like many inner city communities, has rich social and environmental capital that has been largely untapped or under-utilized in addressing food security for the people in our communities." The movement brings together local growers, social justice organizations, schools, churches, food educators, restaurants, caterers and restaurant suppliers, residents, and stakeholders, along with local government, "to expand urban agriculture production, improve food access and security, create jobs and contribute to community sustainability" (Detroit Black Community Food Security Network n.d.).

Where economic disadvantage is less severe, other reasons for engagement in local food provision initiatives may be predominant. A study conducted by the US Department of Agriculture in 2010 found that motives for "buying local" included "perceived quality and freshness of local food and support for the local economy" as well as concern for the methods of production and their impacts on the environment. Local food markets accounted for a small but growing share of total US agricultural sales, up to $1.2 billion in 2007, according to the 2007 Agricultural Census, as compared with $551 million in 1997 (USDA 2010). The evocative term "food web" was used in the report of an eight-year study conducted in East Suffolk, United Kingdom, to describe local food networks that link people and businesses that grow, process, sell, and buy food within a delimited area. The report documents the multiple benefits that the local food economy brings. It provides fresh, healthy food and allows for genuine consumer choice. It supports farming, rural communities, and the sustainable management of local landscapes. It leads to long-term reductions in energy use and promotes the development of associated industries, such as tourism and countryside recreation. "These findings reinforce the conclusion that, far from being a marginal and declining element of modern life, local food economies are integral to it" (Cranbrook 2006).

Reconnecting consumers to the source of their food and supporting small-scale local farmers – and hence overcoming the phenomenon of "distancing" referred to above – is a strong element in initiatives like these. The international network of Local Solidarity Partnerships between Producers and Consumers (LSPPC), Urgenci, established in 2006, now brings together LSPPC groups in the United States, United Kingdom, France, Belgium, Italy, Canada, Portugal, and Japan. Similar initiatives exist in many other countries (FANN 2010). The Hansalim movement in South Korea is one of the oldest and largest. Launched in 1986, it now brings its 2,000 producers and 380,000 consumers together in a cooperative that supports local agriculture, produces healthy food, and sustains an alternative local economy in a country where official policy is staunchly neoliberal (Ahn and Muller 2013). It is not a coincidence that Slow Food, founded in 1989 "to counter the rise of fast food and fast life, the disappearance of local food traditions and people's dwindling interest in the food they eat, where it comes from, how it tastes and how our food choices affect the rest of the world", was born in Italy, one of the Western countries whose food traditions are most solidly anchored in the hearts of its citizens and its economy (Slow Food n.d.).

In the Global South the dominance of small-scale family farming and local food webs is overwhelming. Family farms produce over 70 percent of Brazil's food supplies on much less land than the "modern" agribusinesses.[9] This includes 70 percent of the beans consumed in the country, 87 percent of the manioc, 58 percent of the milk, and 59 percent of the pork. Family farms employ 75 percent of the workers in the agricultural sector although they occupy only 24 percent of the agricultural land (IBGE 2006). In India smallholder family farmers contribute more than 50 percent of total farm output although they cultivate only 44 percent of the land. Many studies have confirmed the inverse relationship between farm size and productivity per hectare (Thapa and Gaiha 2011, p. 5). Awareness of the need to protect local food systems and small-scale farmers from the negative impacts of the globalization of agriculture is growing in Asia and the Pacific (FFTC 2011). Worldwide the "peasant food web" produces more than 70 percent of the total food eaten by people: 15–12 percent via urban agriculture, 10–15 percent from hunting and gathering; 5–10 percent fishing, and 30–50 percent from farms. It is the major provider of the food that reaches the world's 2 billion hungry and undernourished (ETC 2013). Family farmers are also responsible for the bulk of the investment made in agriculture, on their

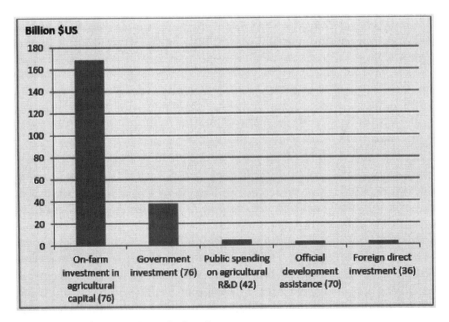

FIGURE 2.4 Who invests in agriculture?

Source: Lowder et al., (2012). "Who Invests in Agriculture and How Much?", p. 14, www.fao.org/docrep/017/ap854e/ap854e.pdf. Reproduced with permission. FAO.

Note: The number of countries covered is shown in parenthesis next to the relevant type of flow.

farms on a day-to-day basis. Public sector support is relatively minimal, and invest-ment from abroad – both from aid programs and from enterprises – is marginal.

Nowhere is this reality more evident than in Africa, where agriculture, the rural economy, social security, and natural resource management are all based on family farming and food webs substantially feed the continent. FAO statistics peg the num-ber of family farms in Africa at 33 million, or 80 percent of all farms in the conti-nent (FAO 2009a, p. 2). Africa's family farmers are responsible for up to 90 percent of all agricultural production in some countries (Livingston et al. 2011, p. 13) and meet up to 80 percent of the food needs of the population. Research undertaken by the national producers' platform in Senegal, the CNCR, demonstrates with facts and figures that family farms produce two-thirds of all of the food consumed in Senegal today and practically all of the dry cereals that constitute the staple food of more than 60 percent of the population (CNCR 2010b; SOS Faim 2014).

BOX 2.3
FAMILY FARMS, AUTONOMY, AND RESILIENCE

The family farm can be described as an association composed of two or more members united by family or customary ties, which exploits production factors in common – in rural or urban areas – in order to generate resources for social reproduction as well as for financial, material, moral benefits. (EAFF, PROPAC and ROPPA 2011, p. 6). A key distinction between family farmers and entre-preneurial and capitalist farmers who are fully embedded within the market is that the resource base for the family farmers' systems of production is largely uncommodified and hence not dependent on market transactions. This base includes land, seeds, livestock, water, and of course labor, but also knowledge, skills, social networks, and institutions. Control of their resource base enhances the autonomy and resilience of family farmers and is essential to the viability of the family farming system of production (EAFF, PROPAC, ROPPA 2103, p. 7).

The need to "link smallholder farmers to markets" is a buzz word of today, but African farmers point out that "all family farmers are in markets of various types. What counts is the nature of these markets and the terms in which they participate in them" (*ibid.*, p. 12). Much of the food consumed in Africa reaches those who consume it through "informal" or "invisible" markets based not only on economic transactions but also on social institutions, shared cultures, and values and regula-tion enforced by social custom and social sanctions. These trading practices include efforts by producers or groups of producers to add value to their products by storing or processing them before marketing them, activities often conducted by women. The "invisible" market channels are largely ignored by official programs and statis-tics, which tend to concentrate on the commercial commodity value chains (*ibid.*, p. 9). It is more difficult for family farmers to benefit from the "formal" markets, however, since "all the players on the value chain compete to capture as much value as possible. Each player's chances of succeeding depend upon their market power – their ability to determine prices through their control of supply and demand" – and that of family farmers is small as compared with the market power of the agribusiness suppliers, traders, processors, and retailers (*ibid.*, p. 8).

As suggested earlier in this chapter, the dominant conception of value chains does not "value" the noneconomic benefits that family farming and local food webs provide. African family farmer organizations describe them in these terms:

> Family farming is the basis for modern food provision in Africa. Its multi-functionality and sustainable productive potential is confirmed by extensive research evidence. Family farms generate food and well-being for the major-ity of the population and the wealth of the region, and conserve its natural resources. It can ensure employment for young people, thus promoting so-cial peace and attenuating migration. Innovative family farming, backed by appropriate research, supportive investments and adequate protection, can out-perform industrial commodity production.
>
> (EAFF, PROPAC, ROPPA 2013, p. i).

The formal market system's organization around single commodity value chains is at odds with the diversified nature and overall logic of the family farm. In contrast to entrepreneurial or capitalistic modes of production, the family farm cannot be considered simply as an economic enterprise since it is diversified in all senses: its actors, its products, its activities, its objectives (ROPPA 2012a, p. 13–14; EAFF, PROPAC, ROPPA 2011, pp. 5–6). African small-scale producers do not reject the idea of value addition. On the contrary they advocate stronger efforts to add value to agricultural products so long as much of the benefit is retained by the produc-ers and in the rural areas. What they object to is when donors impose on African regions their own concepts of value chain organization. USAID's purely economic version – contrasting sharply with that of the African small-scale producers – is aimed at promoting "competitive operations" led by "catalyst firms", targeting "high potential areas" and operating under conditions in which "the target food staple crop can be produced, distributed and marketed in greater volumes, with higher quality and for lower cost, thereby contributing to increased food security and higher rural incomes" (USAID 2009, pp. 6–7). As always the word "thereby" is an invitation to close examination of assumptions.

Family farms and local food webs are vitally important to the food security and the livelihoods of the majority of African citizens, yet they have been undersup-ported for decades. Starting under colonialism, continuing after independence, and exacerbated by structural adjustment, official policies and programs have drained wealth from the rural areas to feed urban development, the central administration, and elite interests (McKeon, Watts, and Wolford 2004, pp. 8–12). Producer prices have been kept low to ensure cheap food in urban centers, where protesting crowds are more likely to hit the streets than in the rural areas. Until recently what support there has been for agriculture has concentrated on male-managed export crops, leaving women largely in charge of handling the "invisible" task of producing food for the sustenance of the family. In 2003 at a Summit of the African Union, African heads of state recognized that they had neglected agriculture and pledged to dedicate at least 10 percent of the national budget to this fundamental sector, but ten years later only nine of the fifty-four countries had fulfilled this commitment. African government representatives can be capable of recognizing that "it is Africa's smallholder family farmers – women in particular – who produce Africa's food, create jobs for the majority of the population, and maintain the social peace" and of recognizing that "if the cost of these services were factored into the economic calculations there would be no doubt about what model of agriculture should receive the lion's share of investment" (Africa Group and PAFO, 2011). Indeed, if you ask any tie-and-suited person on the streets of Nairobi where he sources the staple maize that his household consumes, he will answer without hesitation, "from the family shamba [farm] up-country". Despite this reality many African governments seem to be convinced that "traditional" family farming is not capable of ensuring agricultural development and might, at the most, be maintained for social reasons alongside a "modern" "business-oriented" agriculture based on large-scale capitalistic farming. This conception may be partially the result of cultural acclimatization in Western institutions and a real conviction that this approach to modernization is best for the nation. However, the pressure exercised by the proponents of the corporate-led food regime, and the benefits they afford to national elite and capital, also weigh in very strongly.

Confronting today's challenges: which way wins out?

The above presentation of the industrial, corporate global food system as contrasted with local food networks or webs could well be criticized for being partisan. The fact is, however, that the discourse of the proponents of the global food system is just as partisan if not more so, although they don't admit it. It is also backed by infinitely more economic and political clout. It ought to be self-evident that a system whose motor is the quest for profits for shareholders and speculators cannot be entrusted with promoting the common good in a world in which inequalities and unsustainable practices of all sorts are as pronounced as they are in ours. This recognition ought to be seen as an acknowledgment of reality rather than an ideological judgment. It should be taken as the foundation for any reasonable discussion of the conditions under which for-profit private sector and financial actors might contribute to the fight against hunger and of the kind of dialectic relations that might obtain between the two approaches. Since this is not the case, the first step toward reasonable discussion can only be to debunk the myths that the discursive power of the corporations has propagated in its effort to demonstrate that only industrial agricultural and global food chains can feed the world. We will close this chapter by looking at how the two contrasting food systems measure up to some of the most important challenges we face today. We will continue in the following chapter to de-colonize words over whose meanings the dominant development discourse has established ownership.[10]

Comparing how the two food systems address today's challenges raises the issue of which parameters to adopt in the assessment. There is a good deal of often facile talk among policymakers today about the inevitability of "trade-offs" on the grounds that no policy decision can provide all benefits desired by all parties. This ignores the fact that some benefits are unnegotiable, as the example of the Indian trade minister cited on p. 46 recalls. Economists commonly translate costs and benefits into monetary terms in order to compare them (Leathers and Foster 2009, p. 264). This, however, is obviously tricky where nonmaterial parameters are concerned, as it is for goods that are not traded in formal markets and in the (universal) case of imperfect markets. The problem is complicated by the fact that the prices assigned to goods and transactions in formal markets, and most related policymaking, do not take into account the cost of their "externalities", that is the consequences that are experienced by third parties not directly involved in the economic activity. Pollution of the environment by factories and industrial farming is perhaps the most obvious example, but there are many others. This said, we will look briefly at how the two contrasting food systems impact on seven major global challenges: maintaining dwindling biodiversity, addressing climate change, dealing with the energy crisis, ensuring the sustainability of the environment, protecting the health of the world's population, halting the phenomenon of land and water grabbing, and combatting food waste.

Even without considering the fraught issue of GMOs, the diversified, localized model of family farming and local food systems is without doubt a friendlier custodian of the world's priceless and irreplaceable stock of *biodiversity* than the industrial food chain. The latter grows 150 crops but focuses on only a dozen species, while the former has bred 2.1 million varieties of 70,000 species since the 1960s. For livestock, only five species and one hundred breeds have been developed by less than a dozen corporate breeders as compared with 40 species and 7,000 local breeds under the care of 640 million peasant farmers and 190 million pastoralists (ETC 2013). All industrial seeds are grown from farmers' seeds that have been bred and stored by hundreds of generations of farmers. The industry has only standardized the seeds, cross-bred them, or manipulated them genetically, but it is still unable to create new seeds without using these "old" seeds. Bred and preserved on the farms where they are used, farmers' seeds are essential in order to constantly renew local adaptation, diversity, and variability, which are the only ways to promote their resilience under increasingly changing conditions (Kastler et al. 2013, p. 47). The strategic importance of maintaining a widely diversified supply of our basic stock of life is evident. In the 1970s the staple crop in South Asia, rice, was threatened by a virus, but the availability of more than 17,000 species conserved by communities put researchers in a position to identify a single variety that was resistant to the virus (Food Think Tank 2014, p. 6). Yet already two decades ago FAO estimated that since the 1900s, some 75 percent of plant genetic diversity had been lost, due principally to the rapid expansion of industrial agriculture and the globalization of the food system and marketing (FAO 2004). An additional third of the biodiversity that exists today could disappear by 2050 if current trends are not reversed (FAO 2011a). In Chapter 5 we will hear more about how small-scale producers are defending this fundamental common good.

Where *climate change* is concerned, as indicated in the introduction to this book, the conventional agriculture production model accounts for at least 14 percent of the total annual greenhouse gas emissions, mostly due to use of nitrogen fertilizers. Yet the agricultural sector could be largely carbon neutral by 2030 and produce enough food for a growing population if localized agro-ecologic systems proven to reduce emissions were widely adopted (UNEP 2010; Lin et al. 2011). When emissions from land use change and deforestation – most of which are due to large-scale agriculture – and from food-related transport, process storage, and consumption are factored in, the global food chain's contribution to greenhouse gas emissions rises to 50 percent.

"Climate-ready" GMOs favorable to the industrial food chain have been critiqued for proposing more of the same medicine that caused the illness and for distracting attention from the real priority of reducing emissions (Paul 2010). Market-based solutions like the UN REDD (Reducing Emissions from Deforestation and Forest Degradation), publicized as "win-win" solutions that benefit communities using the land as well as companies and governments that pollute, have been denounced by civil society groups and indigenous peoples as a new form of expropriation and enclosure (No REDD 2010). Carbon trading, introduced under the Kyoto Protocol, has been defined in simple terms as the process of buying and selling permissions to pollute. Supposed benefits to communities in the Global South are difficult to document. In 2009, 71 percent of the "Clean Development

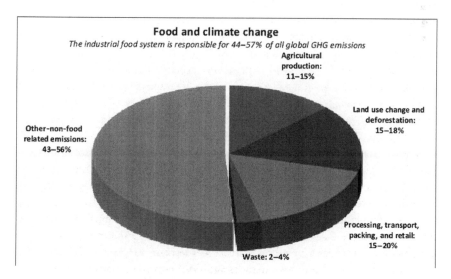

FIGURE 2.5   Food and climate change

Source: GRAIN (2011). Reproduced with permission.

Mechanism" (CDM) projects under the Kyoto Protocol were reported to be located not in poor countries but in emerging giants like China, India, and Brazil. Even here most projects benefitted multinationals and were contested by the local populations (Fern 2010). Carbon trade has led to a phenomenon baptized "green grabbing" that is stimulating the industrial system to convert farmland into carbon sinks in the form of tree farms (McMichael 2014, p. 18). In a further leap of financialization, it has also given rise to a florid financial market for investors and speculators interested in "profiting today from an increasingly diverse range of carbon related investment opportunities" (Fern, *op.cit.*) – about as far away from the original problem as one can imagine.

Where dealing with the *energy* crisis is concerned, it has been demonstrated that peasants are vastly more efficient than the industrial food chain. It takes the latter 2.7 Mcal of external energy to produce a kilogram of rice but only 0.03 Mcal for local food webs (ETC 2013). The difference in the energy cost of transportation in the context of global food chains as compared with that of local food webs is self-evident. As the corporate system butts up against the finite nature of our planet's resources, one consequence has been the controversial promotion of agrifuels as a way of maintaining current levels of energy availability and avoiding consideration of more nature-friendly lifestyles. Even apart from their negative effects in terms of promoting land grabbing and contributing to the rise and volatility of food prices, agrifuels are failing to offer an adequate solution to the energy crisis and can actually contribute to climate warming due to the nitrous oxide emissions from the nitrogen fertilizers used to produce the crops (Brown 2012).

The contested nature of the concept of *environmental sustainability* elects it to serve as a privileged terrain for corporate efforts to play a role in "setting the parameter and tone of debates about the sustainability implications of various models of organization for global food and agriculture" (Clapp and Fuchs 2009, p. 13). Different interpretations of the 1930s Dust Bowl in the United States, a veritable icon of unsustainability, are illustrative here. One view holds that "it came about because Americans blazed their way across a richly endowed continent with a ruthless devastating efficiency" exploiting technological developments like mechanization with the sole aim of increasing production (Macdonald 2010, pp. 50–51). Another maintains that the disastrous phenomenon was the result of "low-yield wheat farming" and recommends addressing environmental concerns in farming with a high-tech "precision farming" approach whose ultimate vision includes "small solar-powered robots working farm fields in groups, hoeing weeds and picking off bugs 24 hours a day without any polluting chemicals or fossil fuels at all, and then harvesting the crops with almost no human supervision required" (Paalberg 2010, pp. 113 and 116–117). Even the most dedicated proponent of dialogue would be challenged by the task of putting these two visions into communication.

Increasing attention has been paid over the past few years to the links between food security and environmental sustainability (Millennium Ecosystem Assessment 2005; Lawrence et al. 2010; IAASTD 2009; FAO 2011a; Lang et al. 2009). The environmental dimension of food security includes both the resource base that directly supports food production and the more basic functions that nature performs for the ecosystem, like soil formation and maintenance of nutrients, biodiversity, and climatic processes. Both of these elements are under severe stress according to a recent UN report (UNEP 2012). The monocultures and intensive farming systems of industrial or "conventional" agriculture are major culprits due to their substitution of external chemical inputs for natural processes, the use of mechanized tillage provoking soil erosion, and increasing reliance on nonrenewable resources. Traditional smallholder farming systems, characterized by year-round vegetation cover, low level of inputs, and maximization of energy yields, are found to be more environmentally friendly than conventional agriculture. They are also far more suited to adopting agro-ecological practices that can intensify production by enhancing natural supporting processes (*ibid.*, p. 8). Additionally, "productivist" industrial farming generates wastes that are not reused, causing environmental pollution. It also reduces food crop diversification, which, in turn, attracts pests, triggering toxic doses of pesticides and fostering pest resistance (Lawrence et al. 2010, p. 11). As one succinct assessment states it, "[S]ustainability is not what the food system has been aiming for since the mid-20th century" (Lang et al. 2009, p. 144).

Some students of global food systems note that industrial farming and the global corporate food regime have introduced a separation between social reproduction and its natural biological base (McMichael 2009, p. 284) and point to what they feel is an irresolvable contradiction between "capitalism's insatiable hunger for profit and accumulation and a planet composed of finite resources" (Rosin et al. 2012, p. 8). The technology and market-based proposal to address this challenge, the "Green Economy", assumes that benefits will derive from the quantification and commodification of the Earth's natural processes, a hypothesis with which the global peasant movement takes issue. "We cannot afford, nor can this planet sustain, a growth path that is still driven by the same economic imperatives of profit maximization. To do so would mean to continue on a path towards collective suicide imposed by those that profit from our current economic system's industrial model of production and consumption, and who are now seeking to gain from the ongoing environmental collapse which they have caused" (LVC 2011).

Differential impacts of food systems on *human health* have received more attention as awareness about food-related health problems has increased and the nutritional dimension has been better integrated into debates on food security. The dominant discourse takes it for granted that the industrialized food system will be accompanied by an increase in safety, as the quote on p. 34 illustrates. This, however, is not necessarily the case. Burgeoning problems of obesity and unsafe food are sensitizing public opinion and policymakers to the fact that the malfunctioning of the food system impacts the North as well as the South. One in three adults in the world (1.46 billion) were overweight or obese in 2008, up by 23 percent since 1980 (Keats and Wiggins 2014). Mad cow disease in the United Kingdom, salmonella in US eggs, and dioxin-affected Belgian chickens are just some of the recent examples of the food risks engendered by insufficiently and inappropriately regulated industrial food production and processing systems in the North. Indeed, "the eco-health nexus poses immense challenges and has considerable implications for defining what is meant by progress" (Lang et al. 2009, p. 8).

In low-income countries, traditional market outlets have been found to be the primary point of purchase for foods rich in micronutrients, as well as the staples that contribute a large part of energy requirements (FAO 2013b, pp. 40–41). A comprehensive study led by the International Center for Tropical Agriculture and recently published in the Proceedings of the US National Academy of Sciences documents the homogenization of the world food diet over the past five decades and the threats that this trend poses for public health (Kouras et al. 2014). As we have seen, health benefits are among those sought by communities in the Global North that have engaged in building local food webs. On the contrary, the shift in national food distribution systems toward supermarkets and food service chains has been found to increase consumption of energy-dense foods with increases in fat intake both in developed and transition countries (Lawrence et al. 2010, p. 121). Advertising and "eat more than you need" approaches to packaging and retailing contribute to these negative health outcomes. Industrial food is bred and processed to last during transit and on the shelf and to appeal to the "educated" consumer eye. In contrast, a "not so pretty" peasant-bred Peruvian potato has twenty-eight times more cancer-fighting phytonutrients than its industrial cousin (ETC 2013). Industrial agriculture has negative impacts on the health of agricultural workers, as well, particularly through the use of hazardous pesticides in plantations and out grower schemes (PANAP 2010).

Yet, at the same time, there is evidence that corporations and global retailers are seeking to cash in on consumers' search for solutions to the health problems they have helped to create. Giant supermarket chains like Walmart are building up their offerings of organic foods, stimulating agrifood corporations like Kellogg's to produce "natural" versions of their staple products like Rice Crispies and Raisin Bran. This development is widely criticized as a co-optation of technicalities that ignores organic agriculture's broader identity as "an alternative way of producing and consuming food that benefits not only the environment and human health but encourages a deeper understanding of the social and ethical aspects of food production" (Corporate Watch 2011). An equally worrisome aspect of the "wellness phenomenon" is the appearance on the market of new food products that have been manipulated in order to deliver perceived health benefits to consumers, in a growing convergence between the food and the pharmaceutical sectors (Lawrence et al. 2010, pp. 176 and 179). Corporation-created fortified foods are given a boost in the developing world and an enhanced image by public–private partnerships like the Global Alliance for Improved Nutrition and the Scaling Up Nutrition (SUN) initiative. Yet, critics note, these approaches cannot substitute for the broader nutritional benefits offered by a well-functioning food system (FAO 2103b, p. x). They risk detracting resources and attention from the long-term solutions to malnutrition like diversification of agriculture and diets and support for family farms (RtFNW 2012, p. 24). The case of the genetically modified Golden Rice is emblematic in this regard.

BOX 2.4
GOLDEN RICE

Golden Rice has been fitted with genes that produce carotene, which is the precursor of vitamin A. Worldwide, approximately 5 million pre-school aged children and 10 million pregnant women suffer significant Vitamin A deficiency. . . . By such statistics a vitamin A-rich rice seems eminently justified.

Yet the case for Golden Rice is pure hype. For Golden Rice is not particularly rich in carotene and in any case, rice is not, and never will be, the best way to deliver it. Carotene is one of the commonest organic molecules in nature. It is the yellow pigment that accompanies chlorophyll in all dark green leaves (the many different kinds known as "spinach" are a great source) and is clearly on show in yellow roots such as carrots and some varieties of cassava, and in fruits like papaya and mangoes that in the tropics can grow like weeds.

So the best way by far to supply carotene (and thus vitamin A) is by horticulture – which traditionally was at the core of all agriculture. Vitamin A deficiency is now a huge and horrible issue primarily because horticulture has been squeezed out by monocultural big-scale agriculture – the kind that produces nothing but rice or wheat or maize as far as the eye can see; and by insouciant urbanization that leaves no room for gardens. Well-planned cities could always be self-sufficient in fruit and veg. Golden Rice is not the answer to the world's vitamin A problem. As a scion of monocultural agriculture, it is part of the cause.

Tudge, Colin (2013). "The Founding Fables of Industrialized Agriculture". *Independent Science News*, 30 October 2013. Reproduced with permission

---

One of the most visible and intolerable negative trends linked to food and agriculture over the past few years is the phenomenon of *land and water grabbing*. Throughout the world, but in Africa above all, small-scale producers and communities are being displaced from their territories to make way for large-scale industrial production of food, animal feed, or agrifuel crops, or simply to hold the land for speculative purposes. Rural dispossession has a long historical pedigree, and the drivers behind the form that it is taking currently are complex, but there is no doubt that today's phenomenon is closely related to the financialization of food and land that has accompanied the recent evolution of the global corporate food regime (Margulis, McKeon, and Borras 2013). The complicity of the governments and elite of the countries in which land grabbing occurs is also evident. The dimensions of this trend and the concrete and violently destructive impacts it is having on the livelihoods and well-being of the local people involved have made it the object of worldwide mobilization by social movements and of concern on the part of the international community. We will return to land grabbing in Chapter 6 when we look at efforts underway globally to regulate these abuses. For now we can limit ourselves to noting it down in the negative column of the corporate industrial food system's score card. Grabbing of land goes hand in hand with grabbing of water, when powerful actors are able to take control of or divert valuable water resources and watersheds for their own benefit, depriving local communities whose livelihoods often depend on these resources and ecosystems (Kay and Franco 2012). The quantities involved are considerable: an estimated 454 billion cubic meters per year, or about 5 percent of the water that the world uses annually (Rulli et al. 2013). Chapter 5 will report on peoples' movements around the world to counter the privatization of this common good.

The issue of *waste* is also not a newcomer to the food scene but has received considerable publicity in recent years. We referred in the introduction to an FAO study published in 2011 that hit the headlines by announcing that "roughly one-third of food produced for human consumption is lost or wasted globally" and noting that "much more food is wasted in the industrialized world than in developing countries" (Gustavsson et al. 2011, p. v). The recipes for addressing food waste in the developing world have to do supporting smallholder family famers to diversify their production and strengthening local food networks by overcoming constraints like storage and transport. In the industrialized world, instead, the problems to be tackled have to do above all with consumer behavior, itself often influenced by advertising geared more toward increasing purchases than to making best use of food supplies. Dysfunctions in the "modern" supply chain also play an important role, particularly during the retail phase, which "views waste as part of doing business" (Gunders 2012 p. 10). The British supermarket giant Tesco acknowledged recently that 28,500 tons of food waste had been generated in Tesco stores and distribution centers in the first six months of 2013, and that 68 percent of the salad it sold in bags is thrown out in stores or consumers' homes (*The Guardian* 2013). A recent report published by the UK House of Lords found that waste in the industrialized countries amounted to almost as much food as the entire net food production of sub-Saharan Africa. The report argued that retailers lie at the heart of the problem because of the influence they have on the behavior of producers, manufacturers, and consumers, but "thus far [they] have failed to take their responsibilities sufficiently seriously" (House of Lords 2014, p. 5).

The fallback argument for supporters of the global corporate food chain is that – whether we like it or not – only industrial agriculture can double food production by 2050 to feed the world's growing population. This thesis rests on several questionable assumptions. The first is that the world's population will inevitably soar beyond 9 billion by 2050, ignoring the fact that the average family size worldwide has dropped by about half over the last four decades. This trend is due in large part to women's increased educational and economic opportunities and access to contraception and healthcare and could be reinforced by strengthened investment in empowering women (Food Mythbusters 2013). Even at current levels of gender justice, although human numbers are rising, the percentage rise is going down and should reach zero by 2050, so the numbers should level out (Tudge 2013).

The second assumption is that it will be indispensable to double food production. The arguments to the contrary are multiple. On the one hand, these estimates are flawed by misconceptions about the nature and the validity of the modeling on which they claim to be based (Wise 2013a). There is overwhelming evidence that the present food supply is more than adequate already today and will be tomorrow. The problem is one of unequal and iniquitous access to food and unsustainable use of the calories produced, and its solution requires political will and not technical attention to productivity (Leather and Foster 2009, p. 133; Sen 2013; Bittman 2013; De Schutter 2014b).

If any further rebuttal to the production imperative were required, it could come from considering how much food supply would be liberated if waste was reduced and if incentives were introduced to promote use of land for production of food crops rather than to fuel engines. Finally, the corporate narrative assumes that industrial, high-tech agriculture is, indeed, more productive than agro-ecological family farming, a false thesis that we have addressed earlier in this chapter and that has been controverted by a host of authoritative studies (Pretty et al. 2006; Badgley et al. 2007; IAASTD 2009; De Schutter 2010d; De Schutter and Vanloqueren 2011; UNCTAD 2013). We will return to it in Chapter 5. The poster on the next page visually sums up the evidence regarding the two competing food systems.

So what happens in a world in which two so strongly contrasting systems of food provision are present? Is it possible to imagine that they can coexist peacefully, at least at national level, or even establish synergetic relations? This is the approach taken by some countries, like Brazil, which are trying to manage a strongly rooted dualism in their agriculture between large, industrial export-oriented enterprises and the small-scale family farming that occupies the majority of the population and produces most of the food consumed. This thesis is questioned by many observers of what happens when textbook theory encounters reality. The UN Special Rapporteur on the Right to Food, Olivier De Schutter, notes that the new wave of investments in large-scale, highly capitalized plantations has created a situation in which industrial agriculture competes with smallholders on an unequal footing both for land and for markets, given the economies of scale they can practice and the externalities they are allowed to ignore (De Schutter 2011a, p. 540). While some argue that arrangements like contract farming and out grower schemes can create win–win situations for corporate agriculture and smallholders, there is much evidence that questions this thesis, as we have seen in this chapter. Family farmers themselves note that when they become part of a commodified chain, they hand over to agribusiness the control of their resource base, their production choices, and the prices they receive, losing the autonomy on which their resilience is founded (EAFF, ROPPA, PROPAC 2013).

There is a long tradition of analysis of processes of structural transformation of agriculture over time (HLPE 2013, p. 55). The "classic" evolution is considered to be one in which the shares of agriculture in gross domestic product (GDP) and in the labor force decrease with time and development, marking a shift from agricultural and rural societies to urban societies. This trajectory was followed in the

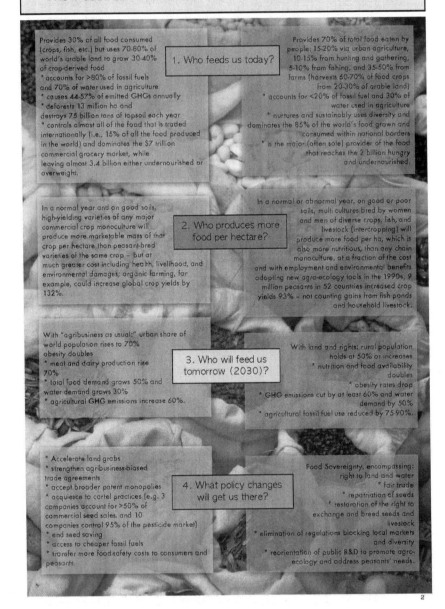

FIGURE 2.6 Who will feed us?

Source: ETC Group (2013). Reproduced with permission.

European countries starting at the time of their industrial revolutions in the late 18th century, and by many Latin American and Asian countries over the past forty years. Higher productivity in agriculture was achieved by higher use of inputs, often combined with irrigation, supported by public and private investments. Impacts on the environment were most often ignored, and implications for employment could be disregarded since the growth of employment in nonagricultural sectors was expected to pick up the slack. Labor-saving technologies in agriculture induced a process of technical change, of concentration, standardization, and specialization of the production process that favored the most productive units. The option for smallholders was to "get big or get out". There is a persistent school of thought that holds that this trajectory is a universal destiny applicable to agricultural development today as in the past (Collier 2008).

This viewpoint ignores some important facts. First, the ineluctability of the exit from farming is far from evident. Some key countries like China and India are departing from the classic pathway by opting to maintain a substantial share of employment in agriculture. In many other countries in the Global South (and not only there) the assumption that employment opportunities for ex-farmers will be available in nonagricultural sectors can be questioned, as can the desirability of an unmanaged shift of the population from rural areas to urban slums (Davis 2006). In some countries in the Global North agriculture is proving to be an exception to the general gloomy employment possibilities offered to young people in a period of crisis. In Italy in 2013 employment in agriculture rose by 3.8 percent, in contrast with the rest of the economy, and one-third of the farms in the country were managed by people younger than forty (Mastrandrea 2013). Secondly, as we have seen earlier in the chapter, the technical and agronomic model that underlies the classical transformation pathway is being critiqued both for its negative environmental externalities and for its unsustainability in the face of the rising cost of rarifying energy-intensive inputs like fertilizers. Some analysts who read the evolution of agriculture and food systems through a dialectic lens highlight the unlikelihood that the corporate-led global system can continue its triumphant control indefinitely. "Food regimes have so far privileged power and profit by distancing ecological effects; as self-organizing spaces reach the limits of their ability to absorb shocks, something truly new under the sun becomes necessary" (Friedmann 2009, p. 341). The destruction of ecological, social, and cultural capital that the industrialized food system entails and the temporal, spatial, and contextual disconnections between production and consumption of food that it introduces in the situation of globalization and liberalization lead to the emergence of deep contradictions that are increasingly difficult to paper over (van der Ploeg 2008, pp. 4 and 9).

A recent authoritative UN study identifies a series of different and sometimes contrasting trajectories for the role of smallholder agriculture that are being followed today. These include managed decline of the smallholder sector in favor of emergence of a highly modern medium farm sector (as in Chile); managed dualism between large and small farms (Brazil, Mexico); support for long-term peasant agriculture in the crowded countries of Asia and Africa; and promotion of environmental services and high-quality foods by smallholders in Europe, North America, and some countries in Latin America and Asia (HLPE 2013, p. 57). The study makes the important point that transformations in agriculture and food systems are not a matter of destiny or accident but the result of explicit or implicit political choices (*ibid.*, p. 14). The rest of this book will explore various dimensions of what needs to happen for these choices to become increasingly explicit and inclusive.

Notes

1. This term has been critiqued by some peasant movement activists, in discussions in which I have participated, as a Western concept that does not sufficiently render the central role of small-scale producers.
2. For a comprehensive and accessible account of the world food economy, see Clapp 2012.
3. The "no" voters won by a small margin in the Californian referendum, but the outcome was judged a success by the pro-labelers since it stimulated interest in the issue and initiatives in a number of other states. In April 2014 Vermont became the first state in the United States to require labeling showing GMO presence.
4. Clapp 2012, pp. 125–157 provides a clear summary of this phenomenon.
5. For a succinct and accessible discussion of the theory and practice of agricultural structural adjustment, see Weis 2007, pp. 116–125.
6. See Weis 2007, pp. 128–160 and Clapp 2012, pp. 57–89 for detailed but accessible accounts.
7. Including Argentina, Australia, Brazil, Canada, Malaysia, South Africa, and thirteen other countries.
8. The term refers to geographic areas, most often low-income, where residents' access to affordable, healthy food options is restricted due to absence of grocery stores at convenient traveling distances.
9. Presentation by Francesco Maria Pierri, Brazilian Ministry of Agrarian Development, at the FAO Conference, 20 June 2013.
10. Four excellent and quite different debunking efforts are two by North American non-profits (ETC 2013 and Food Myth Busters 2013), one by a British science writer (Tudge 2013), and one by the West African networks of small-scale producers (ROPPA 2012a).

3

WHAT'S IN A PARADIGM?

Food security, food sovereignty,
and evidence-based
decision making

In the last chapter we reviewed two quite different ways in which food provision is ensured in today's world and discussed the interests and realities they represent. In the process we highlighted the disputed meanings of a number of key concepts – like progress, development, modernity, growth, and sustainability – and the contested interpretations of phenomena like the Green Revolution, the Dust Bowl, and the advent of industrialized supply chains. The chapter ended by evoking the desirability of basing food policy decision making not on the outcome of unequal battles about words and interests but on inclusive, informed political process defending common goods. In this chapter we will look at one important aspect of what would be required for such a style of decision making to prevail: how facts are ordered and how evidence is assembled and made available to those responsible for policy.

Ordering facts

Since the dawn of civilization people have conceived explanations and visions of the "how" and the "why" of life and the universe in order to interpret and give meaning to the phenomena that impinge on them. In ways ranging from the respectful to the aggressive, they have also sought to propitiate, to influence, or to master these phenomena. In the West, philosophy, religion, and scientific method vie for pole position in this interpretative effort. An entire branch of philosophy – epistemology – is devoted to studying the nature and scope of knowledge, while cognitive psychology tells us that we would drown in the multiple information stimuli we receive from the outside world if we didn't have schema with which to filter them.

Various terms are used to refer to the frameworks according to which we order the facts and experiences we encounter. "Worldview", or "*Weltanschauung*" in the terminology of Kant and Hegel who popularized it, refers to the all-encompassing framework of ideas, beliefs, and values through which an individual, a group, or an entire culture interprets the world and interacts with it. The term *episteme* was equated with knowledge in the original Greek use. The influential French social theorist Michel Foucault used it to refer to "the apparatus which makes possible the separation, not of the true from the false but of what may from what may not be characterized as scientific" or may be entertained within the historical context of discourse in a particular epoch (Foucault 1980 p. 197). An episteme is not an innocuous and value-free tool. On the contrary, it can be viewed as "an approach to knowledge about the world based on a core set of assumptions that seem like common sense" but are not necessarily so. "The market has come to represent the central episteme in the modern enterprise of development and as a consequence other such *epistemes* (views of the world) are rendered unviable, invisible, or unthinkable" (McMichael 2010, p. 3). Episteme is sometimes equated with "paradigm", a term that began life in the 15th century meaning "an example". The historian of science Thomas Kuhn popularized it with specific reference to the set of practices that define a scientific discipline. He also introduced the notion of "paradigm shifts", like Einstein's theory of relativity that transformed the field of physics, which has subsequently been extended to refer to theoretical frameworks more broadly. Finally, the term "ideology", to which the Oxford Dictionary confers rather noble connotations as "a system of ideas and ideals", has somehow come to acquire negative implications in policy deliberation spaces as implicitly constituting the opposite of factual or scientific.

Whatever we call them, worldviews and paradigms are the tools with which we shape our proposals for governing human communities, from the family on up, and regulate their relations with each other and with the natural environment. As such, they can operate under cover by filtering the ideas, evidence, and prospects that we are able to entertain given our "mindset". An objective of this book is to contribute to opening up windows in the "food mindsets" of policymakers and public opinion so that ideas and evidence that might otherwise be rejected can instead be given a fair audience. Worldviews and paradigms, however, can also be used explicitly to further the interests of actors or groups of actors. The Italian Marxist thinker Antonio Gramsci made an important contribution to understanding how this comes about with his reflections about the ways in which the capitalist state solidifies its hegemony by "manufacturing" consensus in society (Gramsci 1971).

The introduction made reference to the notion of discursive power popularized by Foucault, which highlights the relations between knowledge and the legitimation of power. In the contemporary sphere of food and agriculture and their governance, the discursive power of corporations and finance merits particular attention given the resources that they muster, their capacity to forge alliances with or condition political actors, and the efforts they make to influence the public debate through the framing of policy issues and underlying societal norms (Clapp and Fuchs 2009, p. 11). Corporations, of course, are not the only actors that wield discursive power. Albeit with less material resources and political alliances to count on than their adversaries, social movements adopt it as an important instrument in their efforts to bring about substantive and substantial changes in social, economic, and political orders. By influencing the way issues are framed, they seek to transform the terms and the nature of the debate. They may try to broaden the scope of practices that existing norms engender to the point where the norms themselves are transformed and "what was once unthinkable becomes obvious" (Keck and Sikkink 1998, p. 211). We will see a prime example of such use of discursive power by social movements when we discuss the concept of food sovereignty later in this chapter.

Paradigms in food and agriculture

Productivism

We have encountered in previous chapters one of the enduring paradigms that impact on food and agriculture policies – productivism – and made acquaintance with the interests and actors behind it. We have seen in Chapter 1 how the term has accompanied all of the post–WWII discourse about development starting with the famous line from Truman's 1949 inaugural address. We have run into it again in Chapter 2 as the quantitative, economized approach to measuring value that characterizes industrial agriculture and commodity chains. It is useful now to take a step back and look more systematically at how this term has evolved and what its use implies. "Production" derives from the Latin verb *producere*, referring evocatively to the bringing forth of something that is hidden. Up to the end of the 18th century it designated essentially an emanation of nature, in the form of the livelihoods that people could "produce" by husbanding nature. Production became an economic concept when it was posited as the source of value. With Adam Smith first and Ricardo next, the earth's generative powers were reduced to inputs of productive labor, and welfare and wealth were equated with exchange value. Progressively, labor too became just another input to the production of commodities uprooted from any specific context, and the gap between the spheres of production and consumption was sanctified.

More broadly, production became the yardstick for measuring welfare, as in the gross national product indexes. Development – based on the assumption that more production is necessarily a good thing – became the central concept mediating between the industrialized North and the South. It was framed in economic and monetary terms and conceived as a single, linear journey of progress, theorized as a process of "modernization" (Rostow 1960). The passage led from rural, agrarian societies to urban, industrialized ones and to greater integration into global markets. Peasants were clearly slated for scrapping in this scenario. The longevity of this vision, despite increasingly vociferous and documented contestation, is remarkable. Like the favored horses in the Palio race, which enflames the neighborhoods of Siena each summer – whose victory is independent of the fate of their more or less fortunate jockeys – modernization, development, and productivity seem to keep leading the pack whatever the circumstances. Those of us who sit today in negotiations about how to solve the world's food problems with a memory that stretches back to the 1970s could doze off and wake up to think we were listening to McNamara's famous Nairobi speech in 1973 when he introduced the basis of the World Bank's Integrated Rural Development strategy: "The question is what can the developing countries do to increase the productivity of the small farmer . . . so as to stimulate agricultural growth and combat rural poverty on a broad scale" (McNamara 1973)? The answer – in productivist-framed discourse – has to do with transiting smallholders from the traditional to the modern and linking them to the commodity markets that are considered to be the pulsing engine of the latter. It involves ignoring the many forms of social and ecological wealth, other than monetary, that sustain smallholders' livelihoods. It transforms the characteristics of the agricultural practices and livelihood strategies of smallholders from strengths on which to build into constraints that need to be overcome. A textbook example of this process was Gören Hydén's thesis that the underdevelopment of Tanzania was to be attributed to the existence of an "uncaptured peasantry" that still adopted the moral economy as its reference point rather than the monetized capitalist economy (Hydén 1980). Fifteen years later, when people woke up to how structural adjustment was assisting the market economy to wreak its damage on peasant communities, the World Bank discovered that there was something to say for human interrelatedness after all and began to invest in research on "social capital" (World Bank 1998).

An assessment of the paradigm of productivism that many would judge to be excessively charitable characterizes it as a "judicious mix of State support + Capital + Science" pitted against the Malthusian scenario of population growth exceeding growth of agricultural output. The package, in this vision, had some successes but ran into difficulties when the oil crisis of the early 1970s exposed how much it depended on nonrenewable resources. It was saved in the corner by the Green Revolution, which, however, has subsequently been critiqued on environmental, energetic, and nutritional grounds (Lang 2011, p. 272). Today's food and energy crises and the attendant financialization of food and land, however, risk revitalizing once again "a long-standing modernization trope, namely that modernization of agriculture is necessary to development" (McMichael 2012b, p. 69). The current version of the productivist narrative has been revised and corrected to take into account criticism of industrial agriculture's impact on the environment and on climate change. It has reemerged from the spin doctor's bag as "sustainable intensification", opportunely opening a big window for GMOs and disguising chemical fertilizers and other inputs under epithets like "sustainable crop nutrition". Productivism is still very much with us, as this recent, facile explanation of poverty in Africa illustrates:

> The metrics here are pretty simple. About three-quarters of the poor who live on these farms need greater productivity, and if they get that productivity we'll see the benefits in income, we'll see it in health, we'll see it in the percentage of their kids who are going off to school. These are incredibly measurable things. The great thing about agriculture is that once you get a bootstrap – once you get the right seeds and information – a lot of it can be left to the marketplace.
>
> (Gates 2013)

The point is not that Africa's small-scale producers don't need and want improved productivity. They do. The problems arise when the question of how to measure productivity is not addressed. "Performance criteria must go beyond classical agronomical measures, such as yield, and economic measures, such as productivity per unit of labor. In a world of finite resources and in a time of widespread rural unemployment, productivity per unit of land or water is a vital indicator of success" (De Schutter and Vanloqueren 2011, p. 41). And they arise when productivity is excised from the political, economic, and policy context in which it is situated and is simplistically assumed to be promotable by providing farmers with "the right seeds and information", the kind of things that corporations and foundations think they do so well, without concern for the multiple factors that have worked against smallholder production, productivity, and livelihoods over the past decades.

Food security

If productivism is the path, according to dominant discourse about the fight against hunger, then "food security" is the destination. It is legitimate to ask why we have waited until midway through Chapter 3 before delving deeper into the meaning of a term that graces the title of this book. The answer is that we needed to cover a certain amount of terrain in order to give it a more than superficial examination. Given that concern about ensuring an adequate supply of food has been a constant in human history, what is it that put the concept of "food security" into current parlance? How has it evolved since it began to be used, and what does it represent today?

Freedom from hunger, an integral part of the post–WWII human rights agenda, was included in the mission of the FAO from the very outset (Shaw 2007; Jarosz 2009; Edelman 2013). Use of the term "food security" as a formal concept came a bit later. It had its roots in the intensification of global concern for food supplies in the early 1970s described in Chapter 1. Then, as in the case of the 2007/2008 food crisis, the sudden shift from the situation of global food surpluses and low prices that had prevailed for over two decades to one of scarcity and rising prices was provoking consequences that could not be ignored (Friedmann, 1993, p. 31). A proximate cause of the scarcity was a significant reduction in available stocks due to massive purchase of US grain by the USSR following a crop failure in 1972. Another was the devaluation of the US dollar subsequent to its delinking from the gold standard the previous year. This step impacted on food prices both directly – by increasing the dollar price of grain – and via the retaliatory increase it provoked in the price of oil, which was visited on the already energy-intensive dominant food production systems (Heady and Fan 2010, p. 87). Poor people and poor countries were the major victims, with famines raging in Bangladesh, Ethiopia (where they contributed to the fall of the imperial government), and the Sahel. The international community judged inadequate food supply and price fluctuations to be the problem. Other more structural causes of the kind uncovered by food regime analysis were not contemplated. The report of the World Food Conference called by the United Nations in 1974 to address the crisis contains the first official mention of the term "food security", defined in "supply-side" terms as *availability at all times of adequate world supplies of basic food-stuffs to sustain a steady expansion of food consumption and to offset fluctuations in production and prices*" (UN 1975, p. 6, italics added).

The hypothesized causal link between food supply and food security, however, did not hold up under more sustained analysis over the following years. It became increasingly evident that other factors intervene in determining whether or not people were able to access available food. Amartya Sen's study, *Poverty and Famines*, published in 1981, to which we referred in Chapter 1, introduced the concept of "entitlements". Drawing on case studies of famines in different parts of the world, he highlighted the fact that what counts is not simply the supply of food but whether or not people are able to access it either by producing it themselves, or by drawing on assets that they can sell or trade in order to purchase food, or thanks to entitlements vis-à-vis the state. This growing concern with access constraints was reflected in a 1983 report by the Director-General of FAO, which proposed that "*the ultimate objective of world food security should be ensuring that all people at all times have both physical and economic access to the basic food that they need*" (italics added). Attainment of this objective should be sought by a balanced combination of "ensuring production of adequate food supplies; maximizing stability in the flow of supplies; and securing access to available supplies on the part of those who need them" (FAO 1983, para. 60). At the same time the frame of reference shifted from the global and national levels to encompass that of needy households as well. Field research increasingly drew attention to the impact on food security of social norms and conventions of sharing and to issues of differential levels of access to food by individuals even within disadvantaged households.

Heightened awareness of the social costs of structural adjustment compounded by the African famine in 1984–1985 prompted the World Bank to enter the debate on its own terms. Its 1986 report, *Poverty and Hunger*, drew attention to the distinction between chronic and transitory food insecurity by defining food security as "*access by all peoples at all times to enough food for an active healthy life*". (World Bank 1986, p. 1, italics added). It acknowledged the problematic nature of "the present distribution of assets and opportunities" whereby poor people "suffered from a lack of purchasing power". It proposed to address this issue by enacting measures to accelerate growth – the Bank's core business – along with short- and medium-term safety nets for the most stubbornly vulnerable. The 1990 World Development Report ushered in a decade of concentration on poverty reduction strategies on the part of the Bank and sidelined food security as a distinct goal. This vigorous proclamation of the unsubstantiated assumption that economic growth automatically engenders poverty reduction, which, in turn, reduces food insecurity, has had unfortunate consequences that continue to weigh today on the international community's reaction to the food crisis and the formulation of the post-2015 development goals.

While the World Bank sought to headline poverty, developments in other arenas contributed to reducing the saliency of food security. Work on livelihood strategies during the late 1980s and the 1990s cast food as just one of a number of goals, resources, and outcomes that poor and vulnerable households need to balance in order to subsist in the short and longer term (Maxwell and Smith 1992). For its part, the publication of UNDP's influential Human Development Report in 1994 introduced the concept of human security, of which food security was only one aspect. The downsizing of the food security focus to the household level, on the one hand, and its incorporation into broader frameworks, on the other, seemed to put into question the capacity of the concept to serve as an organizing framework for action.

The World Food Summit (WFS) called by FAO in 1996 – in the midst of a decade of UN conferences on major global problems – sought to put food security back on the international agenda. As often happens, behind this effort there was a good dose of institutional and personal protagonism on the part of the newly elected Director-General of FAO, as well as a sincere conviction that the UN should not ignore hunger in identifying its priorities (McKeon 2009, pp. 23–24). The run-up to the WFS witnessed a surge of febrile normative activity within FAO. A visit I arranged in early 1996 for a group of civil society leaders seeking to grasp just what the Summit would be debating uncovered as many different understandings of what food security entailed as technical units interviewed, with the agriculture and the nutrition divisions sharpening their figurative knives in a particularly vigorous manner. Position taking and mediation were rife in the outside world as well. The definition of food security that the WFS finally adopted incorporated both livelihood approaches and the concern for nutrition that had developed during the first half of the 1990s, speared by the International Conference on Nutrition co-organized by FAO and WHO in 1992. This brought the pillars of food security to four: availability, access, stability, and – finally – utilization, incorporating the idea of food quality. The Action Plan adopted by the Summit took poverty reduction as an overarching objective and extended the purview of food security action to the new frontier of a "fair and market-oriented world trade system" opened up by the establishment of the WTO a year earlier. Despite this effort to accommodate the concerns of all parties, it took strong lobbying by FAO to ensure that food security was included as a component of the first Millennium Development Goal adopted by the United Nations in 2000: "Halve, between 1990 and 2015, the proportion of people who suffer from hunger". Finally, in 2001 FAO added the idea of "social access" alongside physical and economic, establishing the definition used today by the Committee on World Food Security: "*Food security exists when all people, at all times, have physical, social and economic access to sufficient safe and nutritious food that meets their dietary needs and food preferences for an active and healthy life.*"

The evolution of "food security" over the years has been accompanied by criticism, coming particularly from civil society. From the outset, the concept was judged to pay insufficient attention to issues of power and conflicting interests. Already in 1974 the NGO observers to the World Food Conference criticized the official declaration for its failure to recognize that the causes of the food crisis were predominantly political and structural (McKeon 2009, p. 19). A decade later civil society voices in Africa voiced a lucid critique of the response of the international community to the devastating 1984–1985 drought and famine. In their view, what had been labeled a sudden crisis was, instead, a long-term process that had unfolded within given economic, political, and social power structures and had laid the basis for famine by inducing dependence on foreign models, economic extroversion, "mining agriculture", and loss of power by the peasantry. Ignoring the long-term causes of the crisis, the international response also ignored, or even undermined, the ways in which the people directly affected were seeking solutions to their own problems (McKeon, 1988, p. 3). In the run-up to the 1996 World Food Summit, an African regional civil society consultation championed food self-sufficiency over food security, urging countries to refuse to implement the newly adopted WTO Agreement on Agriculture if it entailed competition with local products. A diplomatic incident was narrowly averted when a Sahelian peasant leader entered into acrimonious dispute with a USAID observer engaged in extolling the virtues of accessing cheap food from the world market, who was clearly not accustomed to encountering disagreement from such quarters. A few months later, the civil society forum held in parallel to the WFS adopted a statement that unequivocally identified as causes of food insecurity "those tendencies which the official declaration presents as solutions: liberalization of agricultural trade, concentration of farms and capitalistic intensification of production, strengthened role of transnational corporations in the food chain" (McKeon 2009, p. 37). In short, food security as an approach might address issues of access, civil society commentators maintained, but it failed to answer the extremely important questions of where food should be produced, how, by whom, under what conditions, for whose benefit, and under whose control.

These main messages remain dominant today among the critical voices and have been enriched over the years. Food security as a concept has been censored for offering a context in which hunger can be decontextualized and depoliticized by applying growth-oriented discourse. It also lends itself to perpetuating the militaristic component of traditional security discourse by brandishing notions of risk, threat, and permanent emergency (Alcock 2009, pp. 14 and 30). Others feel that the concept is inherently too narrow to be useful and that "food security can only come from making food systems sustainable, locally, nationally and globally" (Lang 2011, p. 279). Still others, applying an ethical perspective, note that "ultimately the food security model is founded on and reinforces a model of globalization that reduces human relationships to their economic value" and looks to "economic growth, competition, efficiency and profiteering" for solutions (Schanbacher 2010, pp. ix and 9). The concept has been critiqued most substantially from a political economy viewpoint. Evolving from a tool initially adopted by state-led efforts to curb social unrest under cover of "development", food security has subsequently accompanied the corporate takeover of the global food system under a neoliberal regime that has installed "a privatized system of international 'food security' institutionalized in WTO protocols under the discourse of 'comparative advantage'" (McMichael 2009, p. 288). According to these analysts, the neoliberal concept of food security has run its historical course. "The modern food system has eaten itself out of a home. It has become the architect not of a solution to 'food insecurity' but of an edifice that makes poverty and hunger more likely" (Patel and McMichael, 2010 p. 24). Both the damage wreaked by a neoliberal reading of food security and the contradictions within it, in their analysis, have stimulated the development of the other paradigm we will explore, that of food sovereignty.

Food sovereignty

The appearance on the scene of the term "food sovereignty" is associated with the birth of La Via Campesina (LVC) in the mid-1990s, but its "take" on food and agriculture issues and the aspirations it expresses are shared by a large and growing range of social movements in different parts of the world. Earlier use of the word by actors such as the governments of Mexico and of Canada has been documented (Edelman 2013), however, and the concept as such is said to have emerged in Central America already in the mid-1980s in response to the combined impacts of structural adjustment programs and food imports from the United States (Claeys 2013, p. 2). For LVC in the 1990s a key issue was to obtain recognition for peasant-based food production and to develop a "vehicle" around which peasant movements could organize and build up their strength. Food security was seen as being framed in neoliberal terms of increasing productivity per plant/animal, making food available through formal markets and imports, counting on economic growth to improve incomes and employment, and – along the way – reducing pressure for agrarian reform. In this logic peasant-based production was backward and inefficient. Food sovereignty emerged as a counter-concept to combat the neoliberal frame.[1] The term appears in the declaration of LVC's second International Conference held in Mexico in April 1996 (LVC 1996a). Seven months later it debuted on the world scene at the NGO Forum held in parallel to the FAO World Food Summit in Rome, in a position paper entitled "Food Sovereignty: A Future without Hunger". Although at that time few civil society organizations were familiar with the concept, it made its way into the Forum's Final Statement thanks to strong advocacy by LVC (NGO Forum 1996).

By the time of the 2002 World Food Summit, food sovereignty was brandished by the civil society assembly as an alternative paradigm to the neoliberal, technology-driven analysis that had dominated development discourse and action for over two decades. It overarched the Action Agenda the Forum adopted, unifying its four pillars: the right to food and food sovereignty, mainstreaming agroecological family farming, defending people's access to and control of natural resources, and trade and food sovereignty. The Political Statement delivered to the plenary of the official Summit spelled out the ground that the paradigm was understood to cover in terms that contrasted strongly with the Summit's weak reiteration of food security objectives and that are fully pertinent over a decade later:

Food sovereignty requires:

- *Placing priority on food production for domestic and local markets* based on peasant and family farmer diversified and agro-ecologically based production systems.

- *Ensuring fair prices for farmers*, which means the power to protect internal markets from low-priced, dumped imports.
- *Access to land, water, forests, fishing areas* and other productive resources through genuine redistribution, not by market forces and World Bank–sponsored "market-assisted land reforms".
- *Recognition and promotion of women's role* in food production and equitable access and control over productive resources.
- *Community control over productive resources*, as opposed to corporate ownership of land, water, and genetic and other resources.
- *Protecting seeds*, the basis of food and life itself, for the free exchange and use of farmers, which means no patents on life and a moratorium on the genetically modified crops that lead to the genetic pollution of essential genetic diversity of plants and animals.
- *Public investment in support for the productive activities of families and communities* geared toward empowerment, local control, and production of food for people and local markets.

Food sovereignty means the primacy of peoples' and communities' rights to food and food production, over trade concerns. This entails the support and promotion of local markets and producers over production for export and food imports (IPC 2002).

In February 2007 a global encounter on food sovereignty held in Mali brought together more than five hundred delegates from local movements and struggles in all regions and deepened the common understanding of what food sovereignty means (Mulvany 2007; Pimbert 2009).

BOX 3.1
SIX PILLARS OF FOOD SOVEREIGNTY

Focuses on food for people, putting the right to food at the center of food, agriculture, livestock, and fisheries policies; and *rejects* the proposition that food is just another commodity or component for international agribusiness.

Values food providers and respects their rights; and *rejects* those policies, actions, and programs that undervalue them, threaten their livelihoods, and eliminate them.

Localizes food systems, bringing food providers and consumers closer together; and *rejects* governance structures, agreements, and practices that depend on and promote unsustainable and inequitable international trade and give power to remote and unaccountable corporations.

Puts control locally over territory, land, grazing, water, seeds, livestock, and fish populations; and *rejects* the privatization of natural resources through laws, commercial contracts, and intellectual property rights regimes.

Builds knowledge and skills that conserve, develop, and manage localized food production and harvesting systems; and *rejects* technologies that undermine, threaten, or contaminate these, e.g. genetic engineering.

Works with nature in diverse, agro-ecological production and harvesting methods that maximize ecosystem functions and improve resilience and adaptation, especially in the face of climate change; and *rejects* energy-intensive industrialized methods that damage the environment and contribute to global warming.

Nyéléni (2007). www.nyeleni.org/IMG/pdf/31Mar2007NyeleniSynthesisReport-en.pdf

Food sovereignty has been described by an historical leader of LVC as "a vision for changing society and, from a broad social and community perspective, an alternative to the neoliberal policies. It is the right of citizens to determine food and agricultural policies and to decide what and how to produce and who produces" (Nicholson 2011, p. 11). This political dimension of choice, a reaction to the limitations imposed by structural adjustment policies and international trade regimes, is one feature that distinguishes it from food security. Food sovereignty addresses the unanswered questions of food security to which we referred earlier and reclaims "a peoples' possibility to master the necessary choices that enable it to ensure its own food security with its own resources" (Coulibaly 2006, p. 3). Food security – even with its contemporary emphasis on access – fiddles with technicalities but leaves the door wide open for trade liberalization and corporate concentration along globalized food chains. Food sovereignty, instead, aims at "changing the existing, inequitable, social, political and economic structures and politics that peasant movements believe are the very cause of the social and environmental destruction in the countryside in both the North and the South" (Wittman, Desmarais and Wiebe 2010, p. 3).

Food sovereignty rejects the annihilation of cultural diversity and the distancing that the globalized food system introduces among territories, producers, and consumers and re-places food provision in local contexts. This involves recognizing something else to which food security gives only a nod – the social relations that are inherent in producing food, consuming food, and sharing food. The gender dimension, expressed in food security forums in anodyne resolutions that generically recognize women as central actors in food provision, becomes, in the relations-sensitive universe of LVC, a campaign launched with a slogan that penetrates to the heart of the household: "food sovereignty means stopping violence against women". While food security has evolved over the years essentially as a concept developed by technicians and discussed and adopted in intergovernmental forums, food sovereignty is rooted in local resistance and invention of solutions to concretely lived problems. This divergence in process engenders a difference in the very nature of the resulting concept that cannot be overestimated. In strategic terms, the challenge of bridging the global–local gap is turned on its head in the vision of food sovereignty. "We have to construct our own realities now. We cannot wait for them to arrive from above. Transformation comes from the power of a process from below" (Nicholson 2011, p. 17).

The scope of food sovereignty as an alternative paradigm was sketched out in broad strokes from the outset. Over the past fifteen years greater detail has been painted in as pieces of the movement have dedicated attention to different issues. The trade plank was understandably an early focus given its topicality in the mid-1990s. Campaigns targeting the WTO and bilateral trade agreements have been conducted globally and in all regions, condemning the liberalization of agricultural trade on the grounds that food cannot be treated as just another commodity. The food sovereignty platform advocates the right of countries to protect their domestic small-scale producers and food systems against unfair competition from artificially underpriced products on the world market and to prioritize the food security of their citizens. The plank of protecting local peoples' access to and control of productive resources has expressed itself in struggles for agrarian and land tenure reform and against land grabbing, but also in a strong focus on farmers' seeds – and their right to save, multiply, and exchange them – as the very basis of locally rooted, people-centered food systems. The movement's mode of addressing the issue of *how* food is produced has evolved from a progressively more serious interest in agro-ecological models of production, as contrasted with industrial agriculture, to encompass a broader look at what happens to food in the other links of the industrialized, corporate chain. Concern for the issue of the nutritional value of food is starting to grow along with awareness of how closely it is linked to the models of production and food provision adopted and how it can be used to counter productivism, since large quantities of food and calories do not add up to adequate diets in qualitative terms. In the process, an understanding has emerged that the underpinning of all that the food sovereignty movement is fighting against is the corporate-controlled globalized food system. This system is defended by some intergovernmental institutions – with the World Bank, the IMF, and the WTO on the frontline – and by an array of governments whose lineup has expanded from the G8 core to include a number of emerging economies. Experience has confirmed the original intuition that the battle is not between Northern and Southern agriculture but between proponents and opponents of a global system that impacts negatively on small-scale producers and consumers in all parts of the world.

The contrasts between the concepts of food security and food sovereignty seem clear. Potential complementarities between the two, however, have also been explored. For some, food security defines a goal without automatically recommending a specific program to achieve it, whereas "food sovereignty is a more precise policy proposal, with proponents challenging political inactivity or other failures to pursue appropriate policies" (Windfuhr and Jonsén 2005, p. 23). It has been suggested that the essential components of food sovereignty are either broader than the concept of food security (the idea of sovereignty, seen as an essential attribute of a modern state) or more specific (priority to family farming as a model of production) but not conflicting (Gordillo 2013, p. 6). Attention has been drawn to the fact that the two terms were used practically interchangeably in Central America in the late 1980s and early 1990s (Edelman 2013, pp. 4–5). The problem, obviously, is not with the term itself but with the productivist and neoliberal incrustations it has accumulated over years of intergovernmental debate and corporate discursive flourishes. Should it be jettisoned along with the food system with which it has come to be identified, or should it be reappropriated and put to work within a food sovereignty framework? In any event, as we will see in the following chapters, the global policy space that the food sovereignty movement has helped to construct and in which it feels most at home is the Committee on World Food Security, suggesting that there is scope for dialectic exchange between the two terms.

The right to food

The "right to adequate food" provides an interesting perspective on the relation between food security and food sovereignty since it is a component of both concepts. It was first recognized as a basic human right in the Universal Declaration of Human Rights in 1948, as part of the right to a decent standard of living. It became legally binding when the International Covenant on Economic, Social, and Cultural Rights (ICESCR) entered into force in 1976. States who ratified it (the United States is not among them) committed to "recognize the right of everyone to an adequate standard of living for himself and his family, including adequate food" and affirming the existence of "the fundamental right of everyone to be free from hunger". In 1999 the UN Committee on Economic, Social, and Cultural Rights specified that "the right to adequate food is realized when every man, woman and child, alone or in community with others, has physical and economic access at all times to adequate food or means for its procurement" (UNCESCR 1999, para. 6). As in the case of other international human rights, the primary responsibility for the realization of the right to food lies with the state, which is expected to "respect, protect and fulfill" it. In contrast with poverty reduction or other developmental goals, the right to food is not a desirable possible outcome of policies and programs but an unassailable entitlement for rights-holders and an obligation for duty-bearers. It is rooted in the rule of law and hence has a potential dimension of enforceability, despite all the caveats accompanying "soft" law, which is totally absent from the development world. It is not by chance that the Millennium Development Goals adopted by the UN in 2000 accurately avoided any reference to human rights.

The first paragraph of the declaration adopted by the World Food Conference in 1974 referred to "the inalienable right to be free from hunger and malnutrition" of all individuals. The right to food was subsequently reaffirmed in a number of international agreements, but not much was done to put it into practice. In 1996, thanks essentially to civil society lobbying, rights related to food finally made it beyond the preamble of the World Food Summit declaration into the operative action plan, where the UN High Commissioner for Human Rights was invited "to propose ways to implement and realize these rights" (FAO 1996, para. 61. Objective 7.4[e]).

Following up on this invitation, the Committee on Economic, Social, and Cultural Rights formulated General Comment No. 12, which elaborated on the content of the right to food and defined the corresponding state obligations as those of respecting, promoting, and fulfilling it. The 2002 World Food Summit, again under pressure from civil society, went so far as to adopt a time-bound commitment that left nothing to chance. In its final Declaration it called on the FAO Council to establish an Intergovernmental Working Group, with the participation of nonstate actors, "to elaborate a set of voluntary guidelines to support Member States' efforts to achieve the progressive realization of the right to adequate food in the context of national food security" in a period of two years (FAO 2002, para. 10). The commitment was implemented and civil society actors had a significant impact on the text that was finally adopted. Working explicitly under the banner of food sovereignty and ably coordinated by the international NGO FIAN, they managed to strengthen the legal interpretation of the right to food by extending it beyond simple access to food to include access to productive resources, and beyond individuals to collectivities. Governments were enjoined to adopt national strategies to respect, protect, and fulfill their citizens' right to food, and to take responsibility for the impact of their policies on other countries (McKeon 2009, p. 76).

The establishment of a post of UN Special Rapporteur on the Right to Food by the UN Commission on Human Rights in 2000 and of a Right to Food Unit in FAO gave impetus to action and strengthened the basis for alliance between the growing food sovereignty movement and some like-minded pieces of the institutional architecture. The language of the official representatives of the right to food evolved toward a potent statement of the structural and political issues that institutions often seek to avoid, as demonstrated by this analysis penned by the Special Rapporteur on the Right to Food in the midst of the food price crisis:

> The arrival of investors can, if it goes unchecked, destroy livelihoods. . . . The push towards large-scale, highly mechanized farms . . . can produce huge negative externalities that are not accounted for in the price of food – and either push smallholders onto marginal lands and the low segments of the market or displace them entirely. Each of these developments is sometimes encouraged in the name of producing more. But we must be guided, not only by the need to increase yields, but also by the imperative to do so sustainably – by improving the livelihoods of small farmers and by limiting the ecological footprint of agriculture. The human right to adequate food provides a signpost. It obliges us to pay attention to the situation of the most vulnerable. It requires participation and accountability. It asks questions that are political and not merely technical.
>
> (De Schutter 2009d, p. 13)

The food sovereignty movement has sought over time to take the right to food on board not only as a principle but as a tool to support its objectives. Internalization and application of a human rights approach is an important work in progress. It is moving ahead on various terrains, some of which we will examine in Chapter 6 when we discuss negotiations underway in the Committee on World Food Security on issues like land tenure and agricultural investments. There are important potential benefits at stake. A human rights approach links policy decisions regarding food to legally binding obligations to which states have committed and for which they can be held accountable. It underlines the fact that access to food alone is not enough if human dignity and the right of access to productive resources are not respected (Winfuhr and Jonsén 2005, pp. 22–23). It focuses attention on the most vulnerable and marginalized populations and requires states to support them. While the state is the primary duty-bearer toward its population, other entities like corporations and international institutions also have human rights responsibilities (Claeys and Lambert 2014, p. 10). Looking inward, rights-based language can provide a way to address the disparities of views that gather under the food sovereignty "big tent" in a manner that highlights issues of power inequalities and privilege. "To talk of a *right* to shape food policy is to contrast it with a *privilege.* . . . By summoning this language, food sovereignty demands that such rights be respected, protected and fulfilled" (Patel 2009, pp. 666–667). But an appeal to rights-based language is not without problematic aspects that need to be considered. The human rights framework is associated with strong and responsible national institutional and legal frameworks, which do not exist in many of the countries where they are most needed. The defense of human rights requires the expertise of informed and committed lawyers and judges, beyond the realm of ordinary citizens (Claeys 2013, p. 6). On the contrary, the kind of social change that food sovereignty is all about requires a democratic, egalitarian approach to shaping food policy at all levels (Patel 2009, p. 670).

A sensitive review of ways in which the actors of contemporary agrarian struggles are using the human rights framework points out that law is a major means of exercising power. Consequently, any people's movement that challenges existing power relations cannot avoid dealing with legal issues. A legal strategy based on human rights can contribute to transforming the framing of conflicts from private/ civil law to a collective/social conflict involving the public interest and constitutional principles. It can facilitate opening the door to complementing macroeconomic data with case-based empirical evidence drawn from the experiences of communities. Access to the monitoring and claims-making system of the human rights bodies is also an important benefit (Monsalve Suárez 2012).

"Unity in diversity" is an often evoked slogan of the food sovereignty movement. There is a tension between the effort to reach critical mass by building alliances among groups that come at food issues from different perspectives and the need for a core set of principles and practices that distinguish food sovereignty as a radically different approach to meeting the most basic human need and right. There is tension between the multiple levels at which the concept is brought to play and the relative priorities to be given to local level action-oriented approaches as compared with efforts to influence policies. There is tension between the no-nonsense language of social movement claims-making and the need to develop nuanced answers to difficult questions like how markets would work, in a food sovereignty regime, to meet the needs of both small farmers and food consumers (Bernstein 2013, p. 25). There are also many open questions. One of these is the term "sovereignty" – which might seem to evoke nostalgia for a Westphalian[2] world – and the role that is foreseen as bulwarks against globalization for states whose track record of defending their citizens' interests is often hardly enthusing. A response from within the food sovereignty movement is to speak in terms of "peoples' food sovereignty", grounding the concept in the centrality of peoples or communities, whose right to choice can then be supported by policies adopted at higher governance levels.

"Who is the sovereign in food sovereignty?" was a topic of debate at a stimulating two-part encounter held in at Yale University in 2013 and the Institute of Social Studies in the Netherlands in 2014. These symposia consecrated food sovereignty as an object of serious academic inquiry and sought to build collaboration between those who study and those who practice it (Critical Agrarian Studies 2014). Some 360 scholars and activists, the majority young and enthusiastic, came together at The Hague to discuss a dizzying array of issues and field experiences in the domain of food sovereignty, which the colloquium website described as "a political project and campaign, an alternative, a social movement, and an analytical framework". One tacit conclusion of the discussions was that the idea of applying food sovereignty as a tightly coherent analytic framework was an academic hallucination rather than an activist concern. We will respect this reasonable conclusion by ending our descriptive and definitional discussion of food sovereignty here. We will come back to its internal tensions and open questions in more concrete, experiential terms in Chapter 5.

For now, we can close this discussion of food paradigms by noting that the emergence of the concept of food sovereignty is situated in a context in which other more general paradigm shifts are underway as the finite nature of the world's resources and the limitations of economic measurement have become increasingly evident. Efforts to dethrone gross national product (GNP) as the dominant measure of countries' progress and replace it with a gross national happiness index, as championed by Bhutan and inspired by Buddhist values of spirituality, is one example. In late 2013, as a contribution to defining the post-2015 global development vision, the Government of Bhutan submitted to the UN a report proposing a new development paradigm that adopts "a holistic view of development [which] has the potential to transform humanity's relationship with nature, restructure our economies, change our attitudes to food and wealth, and promote caring, altruism, inclusiveness and cooperation". The concept of "buen vivir", or good living, is another alternative paradigmatic proposal that focuses on the attainment of "the good life" not as measured in economic terms but in accordance with the common interests of a community that includes nature. Rooted in values of Andean indigenous peoples, it is now spreading to other areas of the world (Focus on the Global South 2013). In the Western world the de-growth movement, an explicit critique of productivism, also decouples consumption from happiness and seeks to create a different ranking of values between goods that accents relational and public goods over economic value (Lawrence et al. 2010, p. 51; Latouche 2009). Food sovereignty is not an odd man out. It is part of a general and growing movement to imagine and build a more equitable and welcoming world for today's and tomorrow's inhabitants.

Gathering and analyzing evidence

Paradigms are frameworks for ordering facts on the basis of which policy decisions are taken. But what about the facts themselves? The distinction between objective, technical, scientific evidence on the one hand and strategic, political choice on the other is a pillar of today's approach to decision making. Where the Greeks called on oracles to complement philosophical reasoning and Egyptian divinatory expertise lives on in tarot cards, contemporary decision makers consider that they can count on scientific information, incontrovertible baseline studies, statistical data, and solid technical monitoring to provide them with "objective" grounds for what is termed "evidence-based policy". To what degree is this assumption founded? Disputes between climate change skeptics and believers surrounding the existence and causes of global warming offers a concrete example of how "objective" scientific data can be served up in wildly different sauces by different cooks. We will close this chapter by taking a look at what constitutes "evidence-based policy", how food insecurity is measured, how data is collected and packaged, whose evidence counts, and to what degree there is a clear demarcation between evidence provision and political decision making.

Evidence is framed by the assumptions made, the questions asked, the data that is looked for and that can be found. A recent review of a range of assessments of the implications of global environmental change for food security concluded that they had fallen short of providing comprehensive and balanced evidence and were limited in their ability to shape food system strategies and policies. Their major weakness was the fact that the dominant food system component treated across all assessments was that of producing food, and the metric of food production that was most commonly cited was change in crop yields. A risk of such a productivist approach to measurement, the review points out, is that it could induce the policy outcome of a relative overinvestment in boosting production potential (Ingram et al. 2010, pp. 58 and 60). But even if one's explicit objective were to measure productivity increases, there are different ways to go about it, as suggested earlier in this chapter. Emphasis on output per plant sets the stage for advocating more use of chemical inputs and "improved" seeds. Measuring the total productivity of a given parcel of land, on the contrary, exalts the virtues of agro-ecological production that avoids use of environment-damaging inputs by adopting practices in synergy with natural processes and ensuring that the various components of the farm contribute to the overall output.

Applied to entire food systems, this kind of selective blindness can be even more striking and damaging. The recent study on sustainable food systems in Africa cited in Chapter 2 had this to say about how data is collected:

> Throughout the research and preparation of this study the problem was en-
> countered that . . . statistics only exist about the commercial commodity and
> export markets and large scale traders, but not about the forms of market and
> structures of exchange and trade which are the most important for family
> farmers and small-scale producers and processors providing food for most
> people in the region. . . . The commodity market is bound up in the same
> systems of governance, finance and commerce from which official statistics
> are derived, while informal trade is not. It is "invisible". Information derives
> from what is recorded. However it also embodies an assumption by those
> who administer agriculture and data collection about what is important and
> worthy of study and research. If they prioritise the industrialised, commodi-
> fied food system, small-scale, food systems will be relegated to studies about
> food *in*security, completely blind to the many vibrant food systems that pro-
> duce healthy, nutritious and tasty food, support livelihoods and sustain the
> environment. The economic force and value of such systems is ignored and
> its specific, autonomous mode of functioning is essentially unknown.
>
> (EAFF, PROPAC, ROPPA 2013, p. 5)

This kind of state of affairs leads to the "naturalization" of phenomena and tendencies that are not "natural" or inevitable at all but are, on the contrary, the direct
result of specific policies and economic forces often dressed up with selectively
gathered evidence.

More often than we suspect, apparently impeccable technical evidence can hide
a mismatch between the reality of what is being measured, the indicators adopted,
and the messages that are communicated. *Framing Hunger* was the title of a reaction
by civil society organizations and academics to the 2012 edition of the authoritative
State of Food Insecurity in the World (SOFI) published by FAO, IFAD, and WFP. The
authors of the critique argued that the primary hunger indicator adopted by the
UN to measure progress toward attainment of the Millennium Development Goal
(MDG) of halving the number of the hungry by 2015 is too narrow since it cap-
tures only severe, chronic undernourishment as measured in caloric terms without
attention to food quality. The implication conveyed by the data is that the world
is on track to meet the MDG 1 and that all that is needed is more of the same.
Aggregation of data at global and regional levels masks important variations within
regions and the potential impact of anti-hunger policies adopted by single governments. Finally, the authors take issue with the headline message of *SOFI 2012*:
"Economic growth is necessary but not sufficient to accelerate reduction of hunger
and malnutrition" since it relegates to a back row policy objectives that could arguably do more to reduce hunger than the pursuit of economic growth, and might
even be at odds with it. "The report's emphasis on growth can distract readers from
realizing how much economic growth and progress against hunger are the results of
equity-and-inclusion-promoting public policies" (Lappe et al. 2013, p. 12). In this
virtuous case the critique led to constructive dialogue with FAO and some significant changes in the presentation of the subsequent 2013 edition of *SOFI*.

Even when respectable evidence does exist, does it reach policy decision makers, and is it acted on? In *Food Wars* Lang and Heasmann ask themselves, "[W]hy does the Productionist paradigm have such a grip in the face of increasing weight of 'evidence' as to its shortcomings?" "Food policies and processes tend to be developed not by evidence but by political expediency and much more" is their answer. They serve the reader up with an amusing list of the possible relationships between food policy and evidence to highlight their point, ranging from the exceptional case of policy with evidence, to policy without evidence, policy despite evidence, policy burying evidence, policy (falsely) claiming evidence, all the way to evidence in the face of policy. Evidence is too often a tool – if not also a product – of lobbies, of which the commercial ones headed by corporations are the most powerful. "The benchmark" they conclude "must be policy's impact upon positive human and environmental health outcomes", and this will also require institutional reform (Lang and Heasmann 2004, pp. 42 and 44).

One of the reasons decision makers are so hungry for "objective evidence" is that it lets them off the political hook of deciding and taking responsibility for the results. Accountability is a victim of overuse or misuse of evidence. Another victim is value-based political debate, debate that allows collectivities to make decisions based on what they feel to be just, important, and desirable. The "precautionary principle" is an excellent example of why value-based policy formulation is needed. This principle was developed in the context of the Convention on Biodiversity precisely to address situations where there is a lack of scientific proof of potentially serious – even irreversible – harm in the event that a given measure is applied, but there are serious reasons to suspect that this could indeed be the case. "The precautionary principle is not a matter for science alone, as it is a political and value-laden statement expressing a fundamental shift in the attitude of the general public to the environment and risk" (Lang et al. 2009, p. 206). Another example is the fraught assessment of the widely documented negative impact of the EU biofuels policy in terms of promoting land grabbing and food insecurity in Africa. The Energy Direction of the European Commission, responsible for the policy, steadfastly refused to entertain anything but quantitative data that directly and univocally linked a specific negative impact solely to the European policy. A chink in the Commission's armor was breached when the officers responsible for the assessment were brought face-to-face with the testimony of representatives of African smallholder farmers' organizations during a seminar in February 2012 and recognized that the experiences and the mobilization the farmers were recounting came from another planet than the statistics with which they were used to dealing and could not be ignored (EuropAfrica 2012).

This brings us to a final issue we need to examine: that of the actors of evidence gathering. First of all, whose evidence is listened to and how? One way in which official data collectors react when their quantitative analyses are called into question for ignoring the perspective of those whose lives are most directly affected by the phenomena being studied is to "scientifically" collect the testimony of the affected. The World Bank's massive program of poverty reduction launched after stringent criticism of structural adjustment policies was accompanied at the turn of the millennium by a large-scale evidence-gathering and public relations effort entitled "Voices of the Poor". In this exercise thousands of the objects of poverty reduction were interviewed using "participatory" techniques, and what they had to say was then systematized, analyzed, and served up under piteous titles like "Can Anyone Hear Us?" by a team of consultants. Not surprisingly, although poor rural people had been building up their own organizations and advocacy capacity for over a decade at that time, no effort was made to listen to what these organizations had to say. Similarly, the increasingly evident inadequacies of quantitative measurement of hunger has led FAO to launch a "Voices of the Hungry" project. "Direct collection of information on peoples' experience of food insecurity using statistically sound survey methods will provide the data needed to more comprehensively assess the extent of food insecurity at various levels of severity throughout the world", says the description, illustrated by a logo in which FAO acts as a megaphone channeling the voices of depressed individual hungry people to the global level (FAO n.d.).

These examples lead into the second question regarding the actors of evidence gathering: who analyzes the information collected and serves it up to policy decision makers? Like the early World Bank initiative, the FAO project is undertaken by FAO statisticians advised by a team of what are qualified as "distinguished experts". Well-meaning people who are concerned about the gap between evidence and policy speak of the bridging role of "knowledge brokers" and "boundary organizations", who can "facilitate interactions between research, policy and stakeholder communities" (Ingram et al. 2010, p. 161). They too underestimate the fact that "affected sectors" of the population have very often established their own organizations that are mandated to speak for them, without intermediation. The demarcation between evidence and policy is, in the best of circumstances, a contested one. The most legitimate way to bridge it is to ensure that what are politely known as "stakeholders" are part of the process, with emphasis on those who have the most to lose by decision making that ignores their evidence. This is also the best way to guard against the fact that what Lang and Heasman discretely call "key established interests" are often the best placed to move with changes in admitted evidence and policies in order to keep the paradigms they champion in place whatever the new trends may be. The technology- and market-based solutions that corporations are offering to address climate change and environmental damage illustrate this capacity. Taking on board the evidence of those most affected is the most effective way to build and enforce the accountability of those who hold the power to make decisions. It is what the reformed Committee on World Food Security, to which we will turn in the next chapter, is all about.

Notes

1. Interview with a LVC support staff person, June 2014.
2. "Westphalian" designates the concept of the sovereignty nation-states exercise on their territory. The term derives from the Peace of Westphalia (1648), which ended the Thirty Years' War with an agreement by the major European continental states to respect each other's territorial integrity.

4

REACTIONS TO THE FOOD PRICE CRISIS AND THE CHALLENGE OF RETHINKING GLOBAL FOOD GOVERNANCE

This book opened with a series of dramatic flashes from the riots that erupted around the world in late 2007/2008, prompted by a food price crisis that was only symptomatic of deep structural problems that are with us still. In Chapter 1 we traced how the international community has – or has not – addressed the issue of governing food since WWII in an increasing globalized world. Chapter 2 introduced us to the social, economic, and political actors and the interests at play in the chains and webs through which food wends its way from the field to the consumer. In Chapter 3 we discussed paradigms that different groups employ to express their views about solutions to food problems, and we considered the perils of "evidence-based policy". We were on the track of modalities of deliberation and decision making that could respect the common interests of the majority of the world's population rather than the particular interests of a powerful few. We closed with a suggestion that the reform of the Committee on World Food Security in reaction to the 2007–2008 food crisis might have taken us some steps in the right direction, a hypothesis that we will explore further in this chapter. To set the scene we will first briefly review how the quest for what has come to be termed "global governance" has evolved over the past years with a focus on the space reserved for interaction with intergovernmental process by civil society actors, particularly those most affected by the impacts of food policies.

From intergovernmental process to global governance

The multilateral governance system established in the immediate post–WWII era, based on institutions in which collective decision making was negotiated among sovereign states alone, had become somewhat the worse for wear by the time the food price crisis erupted in 2007/2008. "There is a common thread running through the different themes explored in this report", the Special Rapporteur for the Right to Food commented in introducing his second report on the food crisis. "It is the need to strengthen multilateralism in order to address effectively the structural causes of the global food crisis" (De Schutter 2009a, p. 32). This was not, of course, the first shakeup the multilateral system had undergone since the founding of the UN. As we noted in Chapter 1, a major transformation had come about following the wave of de-colonization in the 1960s that multiplied and diversified the membership of the UN and shifted problems of development and North–South inequalities from the dockets of individual metropolitan powers to the heart of the world agenda. The notion of global governance – something that would somehow move beyond international diplomacy of the Westphalian nation-state variety – is rooted in this era. Explicitly political in its essence, it represented a rallying cry for a radical transformation of world order. "The world was just becoming aware that natural resources were finite, revolutionary regimes in the Third World were organizing solidarity in pursuit of a new international economic order, the United States were forced to withdraw from Vietnam just as the Portuguese were abandoning their latter-day colonial empire in Africa. Global governance would deliver humane and democratic institutions geared toward the management of humanity's common affairs" (Overbeek et al. 2010, p. 679).

Some twenty-five years later, the end of the Cold War provoked another transformation of quite a different nature. This profound recasting of the dynamics that had governed global politics for decades, occurring concurrently with rapid economic globalization and the need to address its social and environmental impacts, opened the door to a rethinking of how to deal with global concerns (McKeon 2009, pp. 5–6). The triumph of privatization and de-regulation that was ushered in from the 1980s on contributed to divesting governments and investing private actors with governance responsibilities (Avant et al. 2010, p. 4). The technological revolution in the area of communications and information opened up unprecedented possibilities for civil society actors to enter the stage of world politics directly, as in the case of the "anti-MAI campaign" in the mid-1990s in which a broad network of CSOs used Internet successfully to block behind-doors negotiations of a Multilateral Agreement on Investment.

An authoritative locus for reflecting on these trends was the Commission on Global Governance, an independent group of twenty-eight eminent individuals that stared its work in 1992 with the endorsement of the then UN Secretary-General Boutros-Ghali. The Commission's aspiration, as stated in the report it released in 1995, was for a world order in which Cold War politics would be replaced by "a set of core values that can unite people of all cultural, political, religious or philosophical backgrounds" (Commission on Global Governance 1995, pp. 26–27). Some read this as a generous effort whose implementation encountered the opposition of defenders of unbridled state sovereignty or, at most, of state-based world federalism. For others, instead, the Commission's work represented a post–Cold War de-radicalization of the earlier global governance vision, a managerial rather than a political approach to conducting the world's affairs (Overbeek et al. *op.cit.*, p. 698). We will return to the implications of these different assessments in the concluding chapter of this book.

Bringing civil society into the room

Whatever the reading, an important part of the revisiting of the architecture of world governance that took place in the 1990s was a search for ways of opening it up to actors other than sovereign states alone. The Commission stated the case in these terms:

> When the United Nations system was created, nation-states, some of them imperial powers, were dominant. . . . Thus the establishment of a set of international, intergovernmental institutions to ensure peace and prosperity was a logical, welcome development. . . .
>
> Moreover, the state had few rivals. The world economy was not as closely integrated as it is today. The vast array of global firms and corporate alliances that has emerged was just beginning to develop. The huge global capital market, which today dwarfs even the largest national capital markets, was not foreseen. The enormous growth in people's concern for human rights, equity, democracy, meeting basic material needs, environmental protection, and demilitarization has today produced a multitude of new actors who can contribute to governance.
>
> (Commission on Global Governance 1995, pp. 26–7)

Up until then the UN's regulations regarding civil society participation in policy debate had remained frozen in Article 77 of the Charter adopted in 1945, whose provisions enabled the Economic and Social Council (ECOSOC) to "make suitable arrangements for consultation with non-governmental organizations which are concerned with matters within its competence". This rather indeterminate provision had been refined in practice when the UN set up shop. Clearer limits were set for the involvement of nongovernmental organizations (NGOs) – the term adopted at that time to indicate this category of actors. They were excluded from the General Assembly, denied voting rights and equal status with governments, and divided into three categories with differentiated privileges. Although the Charter did not exclude extending consultative arrangements to national NGOs with the agreement of the concerned members of the UN, in practice formal status was confined to international NGOs (INGOs). The organizations on which status was conferred included bodies such as the international trade unions, faith-based organizations, international councils of women and of youth, and a range of professional and business associations. Their interaction with the United Nations was highly formal, and their possibilities of intervening in policy debate were limited and strictly regulated (McKeon 2009, p. 8).

Over the succeeding years some UN programs and specialized agencies developed more dynamic interaction with civil society than the central UN bodies. The ILO, founded before the UN itself, is a case apart with its tripartite statute involving employers' and workers' organizations as well as governments. UNICEF attached importance to public outreach from the outset and invested time and resources in it. FAO's Freedom from Hunger Campaign (FFHC), with its national committees, and UNESCO, with its national commissions and international scientific councils, also sought the engagement of sectors of civil society relevant to their work and tried to bring their concerns to bear on the governing bodies of the two agencies, which are separate from those of the UN secretariat. The FFHC is of particular interest in the context of our review due to the close and supportive relations it developed with emerging civil society networking and peasant movements in the Global South in the 1970s and 1980s (McKeon 2009, pp. 18–23). In quite a different logic, the advent of structural adjustment regimes during the 1980s and the consequent cut-back in the role of states provoked a blossoming of UN-family cooperation with Northern NGOs as operational partners in development and humanitarian programs. But policy dialogue forums remained the privileged space of governments throughout the UN system.

The changing political context in the 1990s helped to open them up to what was progressively being termed "civil society". The contribution that these actors could make to solving world problems was increasingly recognized in a paradigm of structural adjustment and redefinition of public/private spheres and responsibilities. As a study of NGOs, the UN and global governance conducted in the mid-1990s put it, "NGOs are emerging as a special set of organizations that are private in their form but public in their purpose" (Weiss and Gordenker 1996, p. 364). The global summits of the 1990s were unprecedented experiments in letting these actors into the room. A multitude of civil society organizations of all shapes and sizes – 1,378 in all – attended the UN Conference on Environment and Development (UNCED) in 1992, and most of them did not have formal accreditation to the UN (McKeon 2009, p. 10). Although UNCED has been critiqued for taking a giant step toward turning the environment into a global marketable commodity (McMichael 2014, pp. 2–3), it did give significant impetus to civil society networking and interaction with global decision making (Pianta 2005). The world conferences that the UN convened during the 1990s – on issues ranging from environment and development to human rights, population, social development, women, human settlements, and food – sidestepped the stifling institutional setting of UN deliberations. They provided an opportunity to break loose from heavy intergovernmental procedures in which only accredited INGOs could read prepared statements as observers at the end of each agenda item, when governments had already debated and decided. Parallel forums, caucusing, and happenings exploded before the bewildered eyes of official delegates. The one with the greatest shock effect that I myself witnessed was undoubtedly the performance of three young women who disrupted the press conference of the US Secretary of Agriculture at the World Food Summit in 1996 by stripping to reveal the body paint slogan "free trade = hunger" while their companions launched fistfuls of organic soya onto the astonished public.

The 1990s was a decade of fantasy, innovation, and idealism, but it closed with a sense of frustration on the part of many of the civil society organizations that had invested energy and enthusiasm in global engagement. The open-door policy that applied during the summits tended to slam shut when the UN got back to normal business. The Millennium Development Goals (MDGs) formulated behind closed doors in a UN committee and adopted at a Millennium Conference in 2000 to which civil society was not allowed access were felt to be a pallid reflection of the ardor of the summits. The gap between the high rhetoric of the resolutions adopted by governments globally and the low level of national implementation was unacceptable. The principles and values that civil society had defended in UN settings seemed to be no match for the neoliberal agenda promoted by the international financial institutions, global economic actors, and some powerful governments. As the decade advanced, civil society actors felt increasingly that they were in serious and growing danger of being co-opted to serve watered-down intergovernmental agendas rather than advancing their own visions and objectives (McKeon 2009, pp. 10–11). The attention of many shifted from UN-convened assemblies to the undoubtedly more powerful WTO, World Bank, and International Monetary Fund, most often in a mode of contestation rather than dialogue, and to the autonomous World Social Forum whose first session took place in Porto Alegre in 2001.

The food sovereignty movement and FAO

Engagement with the global food and agriculture agenda centered in Rome, however, was something of an exception to the general picture. As we have seen in Chapter 1, civil society interaction with the World Food Summits (WFS) of 1996 and 2002 had purposefully been handled in such a way that rural peoples' organizations were in command, in contrast to other global summits where NGOs tended to dominate the scene. If the rural movements bothered to congregate around FAO, it was because they felt it could constitute a politically interesting intergovernmental policy forum, an alternative to the Bretton Woods institutions and the WTO. There were several reasons for this: more democratic governance with universal membership and a one-county/one-vote decision-making process, specific focus on food and agriculture and a mission to eliminate hunger, a mandate that includes a strong normative role, and relative openness to engagement with civil society and rural people's organizations.

The network established by the rural social movements that participated in the World Food Summits, the International Civil Society Planning Committee for Food Sovereignty (IPC), proved to be an appropriate instrument for testing this hypothesis. Unlike the majority of the civil society mechanisms that interface with global policy forums, it is one in which social movements feel at home. Strongly rooted in rural and community movements in all regions, the IPC has combined the political legitimacy and mobilization capacity of people's organizations with the analytic and advocacy skills of NGOs in a mutually reinforcing relationship. It has been careful to distinguish between the political role of people's movements and the supportive stance of NGOs, an issue to which people's organizations are highly sensitive. The IPC and its rural social movement members have invested considerable energy in opening up meaningful political space within FAO. From 2003 to 2007, more than 2,000 representatives of small-scale food producers' organizations participated in FAO policy forums where they had never set foot before, championing the right to food, food sovereignty, and agro-ecological food production as an alternative paradigm to free trade and Green Revolution technology. The thematic advocacy work was underpinned by an insistence on recognition of civil society's right to autonomy and self-organization in its interaction with intergovernmental policy forums (McKeon 2009a, pp. 50–120; McKeon and Kalafatic 2009, pp. 17–18; see www.foodsovereignty.org). This global policy space, and almost a decade of experience in occupying it, was ready to be exploited by the food sovereignty movement when the food crisis hit the headlines in late 2007. It is worth underlining the fact that meaningful and effective participation by peoples' organizations in global governance requires a long-term vision and strategy. It does not just happen at the drop of a hat and the purchase of a few airline tickets.

BOX 4.1
CIVIL SOCIETY AND GLOBAL FOOD GOVERNANCE: WHO HAS THE RIGHT TO SPEAK FOR WHOM?

Nongovernmental organizations (NGOs) are voluntary, nonprofit, "intermediate" organizations. This means that they provide often valuable services of various kinds to disadvantaged sectors of the population and conduct advocacy on issues that concern them, but they have not been established by these sectors, do not represent them, and are not accountable to them. NGOs are the category of CSOs with most presence in UN system policy forums. Well-known examples of large international NGOs are OXFAM, Action Aid, and in the humanitarian field Save the Children Fund. Many NGOs have a habit of explicitly or implicitly speaking for "the hungry" or "the rural poor" although they have no mandate to do so. Others – most often smaller organizations with a more political analysis of their issues and their role – are close allies of people's organizations and respect their right to speak for themselves.

People's organizations (POs) are established by and represent disadvantaged sectors of the population like peasant farmers, artisanal fisherfolk, and slum dwellers. This basic characteristic makes them different from NGOs. POs take a wide variety of forms and exist at various levels.

Community-based organizations (CBOs) mobilize and represent grassroots populations in both rural and urban areas and directly address their immediate concerns. Examples include neighborhood associations, water-users groups, rural women's credit associations.

People's organization platforms structured above the local community level have been established by marginalized sectors of population at national, regional, and global levels to mobilize, build capacity, and participate in policy discussions and program negotiations. Examples referred to in this book include the regional West African Network of Peasant and Agricultural Producers' Organizations (ROPPA) and the two global fisherfolk organizations, World Forum of Fisher Peoples (WFFP) and World Forum of Fish Harvesters and Fishworkers (WFF). Peoples' platforms are most often less recognized by the UN system than are NGOs. The reformed Committee on World Food Security is an exception to this general trend.

Social movements are broad social alliances of people, organizations, networks, and communities who are connected through their shared interest in affecting social, economic, and/or political change in directions that are felt to be desirable. Social movements do not have to be formally organized, although they may include structured networks. Examples that are relevant to our exploration of food governance include La Via Campesina (LVC) and the food sovereignty movement to which LVC, ROPPA, WFFP, and many others adhere. The IPC for Food Sovereignty facilitates their interaction with international institutions like the FAO.

The food price crisis jolts dominant food paradigms . . .

The food crisis – and concomitant attention to energy, climate change, the environment, and the fragilities of the financial system – jolted dominant food paradigms as we saw in Chapter 1. Although their defenders resisted deep questioning, it was difficult to deny that the world market had failed to ensure the food security of the developing countries. This was particularly so for those whose governments had succumbed to World Bank advice to sell their commodities on the world market and purchase "cheap" food in exchange. The need, instead, was clearly to promote smallholder food production for domestic consumption, as the Sahelian peasants we encountered in Chapter 3 had tried to impress on the USAID observer a decade earlier. Yet discussion of what lay behind the crisis was far from consensual (McKeon 2009, pp. 110–112). The Declaration of a High-Level Conference on World Food Security that FAO called in June 2008, undersigned by representatives of 180 countries, skipped straight to remedies without bothering to analyze the causes of the crisis. The short-term measures recommended took the form of food assistance and safety nets and "immediate support for agricultural production and trade" (FAO 2008a). Medium- and longer-term measures placed the accent on investment in technology and trade liberalization as improbable instruments for promoting resilient food production systems. It all sounded uncomfortably like more of the same.

A "Comprehensive Framework for Action" (CFA) put together by a team of UN system secretariats during the same period went further in discussing the trends that had led to the crisis, citing factors such as supply and demand dynamics, declining investment in agriculture, rapid urbanization, low producer prices, and unstable land and resource use. However, it avoided reference to the policies that had determined these trends. The key components that could be expected to contribute to global food security in the longer term, in the CFA analysis, were an investment-led menu of social protection systems, sustained smallholder-led food availability growth (although "the majority of agricultural production will continue to come from larger farms"), improved international food markets, and an international biofuel consensus (United Nations High Level Task Force 2008, pp. 5 and 10). As Clapp notes in a balanced discussion published four years later, "[M]any official analyses of the crisis that emerged at the height of the price rises pointed the finger of blame at market fundamentals: supply was simply insufficient to meet demand" (Clapp 2012, p. 129). Changes of diet in emerging economies (with better-off Chinese eating more meat and hence diverting grain to animal feed), weather-caused supply shocks, and low stocks of grain were the favorite culprits. Somewhat more controversial was the issue of biofuels, despite the evidence that already in 2007 some 12 percent of the world maize production was being used to produce ethanol rather than to feed people. At the 2008 Rome Conference, biofuel production – which President Lula of Brazil had traveled to Rome to defend in an unholy alliance with the United States – got off the hook with a call for in-depth studies and exchange of experiences, standard intergovernmental language for "take no action". The "new entry" that official explanations tried hardest to avoid acknowledging was the role of financial speculation, along with that of the multinational grain traders who controlled the market. It was simply omitted from the early official accounts of the crisis and was minimized successively, when the issue had been brought to public attention and could not be ignored. An interagency report commissioned by the G20 in 2011 tight-roped the issue with the skill of a spider monkey navigating the Amazonian tree tops:

> The debate on whether speculation stabilizes or destabilizes prices resumes with renewed interest and urgency during high price episodes. Some analysts purport that the influx of financial investors in commodity futures markets has scant impact on market prices. Other analysts stress that the large amount of money invested in commodity futures by financial investors has amplified price movements to an extent which cannot be explained by market fundamentals. More research is needed to clarify these questions and in so doing to assist regulators in their reflections about whether regulatory responses are needed and the nature and scale of those responses.
>
> (FAO et al. 2011, p. 22)

In contrast, civil society organizations and social movements adopting a food sovereignty lens minced no words when they traced the roots of the crisis to three decades of wrong policies: "No More 'Failures-as-Usual'!" was the title of a civil society statement drafted by IPC members and signed onto by some nine hundred CSOs in the run-up to the FAO High-Level Conference (www.foodsovereignty. org). As at the time of the African famine of the mid-1980s that we encountered in Chapter 3, those who were most directly experiencing the effects of the "crisis" rejected the idea that it had unexpectedly fallen on the world out of the blue.

BOX 4.2
THE FOOD PRICE CRISIS THROUGH THE EYES OF PEASANT MOVEMENTS, INTERGOVERNMENTAL FORUMS, AND CORPORATIONS

"For over 30 years policy makers, national governments and international institutions like the World Bank, the International Monetary Fund and the World Trade Organization pushed the fundamental restructuring of national economies while chanting the mantra of liberalization, privatization and deregulation. In agriculture this led to dramatic shifts from production for domestic consumption to production for export . . . . The restructuring of agriculture also facilitated the corporatization of agriculture. While peasants and small-scale farmers have been systematically driven from the land in the North and the South, corporations increased their control over the food chain . . . . Agriculture has moved away from its primary function – that of feeding humans. Today less than half of the world's grains are eaten by humans. Instead, grains are used primarily to feed animals, and more recently, these grains are now being converted into agro-fuels to feed cars. This is manufactured scarcity par excellence" (La Via Campesina 2008).

***

"We are convinced that the international community needs to take urgent and coordinated action to combat the negative impacts of soaring food prices on the world's most vulnerable countries and populations. We are further convinced that actions by national governments, with the support of the international community, are required in the short, medium-and long-term, to meet global and household food security needs. There is therefore an urgent need to help developing countries and countries in transition expand agriculture and food production, and to increase investment in agriculture, agribusiness and rural development, from both public and private sources" (FAO High Level Conference on World Food Security 2008, para. 3)

***

"*The Challenge*. Undernourishment, population growth, agricultural production and changing consumption trends pose significant challenges to achieving global food security.

Solutions & Responses. Cargill believes food security can be improved by honoring comparative advantage, enabling open markets, supporting smallholder farmers, fostering cooperation between public and private sectors, encouraging agricultural investment and reforming biofuels mandates." (Cargill, n.d.)

Civil society was not totally alone in its analysis. The Special Rapporteur on the Right to Food's list of what contributes to hunger painted a similar picture in less fiery tonalities. It included increasingly dualistic farming systems in which smallholders find it difficult to survive, insecure land tenure and unequal access to resources, failure to adequately regulate the food chain, inequitable international trade regulations, unregulated markets that do not guarantee remunerative prices, and speculation in future markets on agricultural commodities. In his view these trends pointed to the need for appropriate mechanisms to ensure compliance with the right to food. He was hopeful that the crisis could stimulate action to address the deficiencies in global governance that had blocked process in overcoming the causes of hunger (De Schutter 2009f, p. 2).

. . . and unveils the deficiencies of global food governance

And, indeed, the eruption of the food crisis not only put dominant paradigms into question; it also unveiled a vacuum in global governance. In the absence of an authoritative and inclusive global body deliberating on food issues, decision making in this vital field was being carried out – by default – by international institutions like the WTO and the World Bank for whom food security is hardly core business, by groups of the most powerful economies like the G8/G20, and by economic actors like transnational corporations and financial speculators subject to no political oversight whatsoever. What's more, as we noted at the end of Chapter 1, the corporate food regime that had implicitly been entrusted with responsibility for food security was itself in a state of vacillation.

What were the major governance deficiencies that needed to be attended to? Fragmentation was one about which there could be little dispute. As we saw in Chapter 1, it was the cumulative result of a process that began with a contestation of FAO's governance authority from the very outset by powers and interests that sought to avoid ceding authority over what could narrowly be considered national interests. The architecture of food security governance – in 2008 and today – is piecemeal, incoherent, opaque, and unaccountable. On the multilateral scene the Bretton Woods Institutions and the WTO are strongly market oriented and dominated by rich countries (Clapp and Cohen 2009, p. 6). The recent reform of the CGIAR has strengthened the role of its funders and Board members – including the Gates Foundation and agribusiness corporations – in determining the agricultural research agenda to the detriment of representatives of non-OECD countries, not to mention the farmers who are presumably expected to apply the results of research (ETC 2012). The UN system agencies are more inclusive and more balanced in terms of North/South weight. Institutions like FAO, IFAD,[1] and the UN Human Rights Council's Special Rapporteur on the Right to Food temper neoliberal approaches with an emphasis on food security, rural poverty, and a rights-based orientation, but they wield less power than their BWI sisters. To further embroil the lineup, aside from what could be called the core global food governance agencies – like FAO, WFP, IFAD, WB, CGIAR, and WTO – a host of other international institutions and negotiating forums impact on food security directly or through entry points such as genetic resources for food and agriculture. These include the World Intellectual Property Organization (WIPO), the

World Trade Organization-Trade-Related Aspects of Intellectual Property Rights (WTO-TRIPS), the Convention on Biological Diversity (CBD), and the International Treaty on Plant Genetic Resources for Food and Agriculture (ITGRFA) to cite just a few examples (Tansey and Rajotte 2008). Agencies dealing with nutrition/health aspects of food security (WHO, UNICEF) and with employment/workers' rights (ILO) have not been sufficiently integrated into food security discussions. Intergovernmental organizations are often overlapping in their mandates. They also exercise these mandates through procedures that vary considerably in terms of formality, responsiveness to stronger and weaker members, staff discretion in formulating policies, openness to nonstate actors, and other variables (Held and Koenig-Archibugi 2005; McKeon 2009).

The institutional fragmentation initiated in the 1970s has thus been compounded, creating difficulties particularly for overburdened and under-resourced developing countries and civil society. More resourced actors take advantage of opportunities to attain their objectives through "forum shifting", a practice that involves moving from one negotiation table where the desired outcome is blocked to another more amenable one. Powerful economies have forum-shifted with aplomb when they have pushed through issues vetoed by developing countries in the WTO negotiations – like opening up government procurement to foreign bidders – in the context of bilateral free trade agreements. UN member countries are co-responsible for the multilateral confusion. Different ministries of the same government attend different global forums with different positions, and those responsible for food security tend to be less powerful than those dealing with finance and trade. Within the UN system itself, relations between the UN Headquarters and the Rome-based food agencies are far from transparent in terms of their respective responsibilities for global food governance, and institutional and personal tugs of war are not unknown.

The architecture of food governance suffers also from inadequate and top-down articulation among different levels of public authority. Differential attribution of decision making over food security–related policy issues at global, regional, national, and local levels is a maze. Developing country governments have not recuperated the national and regional policy space they lost with structural adjustment and the WTO. On the contrary, the multiplication of bilateral trade and investment agreements is whittling it away still further, as we have seen in Chapter 2. "Agriculture and food policies are now controlled only by a faceless international market. National polices, such as price controls, tariffs, and marketing boards, designed to ensure the viability of small-scale farmers and an adequate supply of culturally appropriate food through support for domestic agriculture, have been replaced by the voracious demands of the 'market'" (La Via Campesina 2008). Even where regions and countries formally retain decision making power, there are often problems of insufficient accountability of governments to citizens and failure to involve them adequately in policy formulation. We will return to these issues in the next chapter when we look at how better food governance could be built from the bottom up.

Conditionalities wielded by those who hold the checkbooks continue to weigh heavily, despite the commitment to support "country-owned programs" that the donor community undertook by adhering to the Paris Declaration on Aid Effectiveness (2005) and the Accra Plan of Action (2008). This OECD-led initiative has created what its promoters describe as an idyllic situation whereby "it is now the norm for aid recipients to forge their own national development strategies with their parliaments and electorates (ownership); for donors to support these strategies (alignment) and work to streamline their efforts in-country (harmonisation); for development policies to be directed to achieving clear goals and for progress towards these goals to be monitored (results); and for donors and recipients alike to be jointly responsible for achieving these goals (mutual accountability)" (OECD n.d.). It sounds like the paradise side of medieval representations of the Last Judgment, but anyone who has witnessed development program negotiations in capital cities knows the kind of elaborate window dressing that is often orchestrated to honor these principles in the breach. Those who haven't can use their imagination. The tendency to equate "country-owned" with "government-owned", leaving other actors out in the cold, is worth underlining in this context. Donors have a remarkable capacity to apply conditionalities when it suits their interests and to self-righteously refrain from doing so when it's a question of urging national governments to respect their commitments to stakeholder involvement. In defense of the concept of human agency, this is not to suggest that anyone who wears a World Bank or a USAID hat is automatically tarred with a neoliberal, neo-imperial brush. In Senegal in the early 1990s it was the head of the World Bank country office who supported the nascent peasant platform in its walk-out of negotiations on the Agricultural Structural Adjustment Program when the government refused to listen to its claims. Generally speaking, however, it is safe to say that short-term visions of national (or ruling-party or individual) interests – in countries in both the Global North and the Global South – continue to compound the difficulties of defending long-term global public interests. The scandal of state and elite complicity in land grabbing provides an unwelcome confirmation of this affirmation.

To further complicate matters, the web of global food governance includes components that are even more difficult to decipher and to hold accountable than the diffuse institutional architecture outlined above. Apart from the traditional intergovernmental organizations that operate through state-based ministers and diplomats supported by a permanent supra-state secretariat, like the UN, the WTO and the World Bank, Scholte (2011, pp. 11–12) identifies five types of global institutional mechanisms that need to be taken into account. One of these is transgovernmental networks in which civil servants from multiple states jointly pursue governance of common concerns by preparing conferences, declarations, or memoranda of understanding, without having a permanent institutional basis. In the case of the G8 and the G20, the best known, the decisions do require approval by the heads of state concerned, albeit a restricted club considering that the impact of their deliberations affects the world at large. Beyond these, however, there are thousands of less visible transnational networks in which it is essentially unelected technicians – ministry officials, regulating agencies, courts – from different governments who interact and decide on a multitude of regulatory issues without political oversight (Slaughter 2004). This is the managerial approach to global governance taken to the extreme, a vision of world order whose building blocks would be not states, but pieces of states reaching out to fold each other in functional embraces out of the sight of designated policymakers.

Interregional arrangements, in which one regional grouping of states comes to agreements with another, are a second variety of global governance mechanism. The EU has played a leading role in this field, interacting with other regional institutions like MERCOSUR or negotiating highly contested Economic Partnership Agreements with the regional configurations of former colonies in Africa, the Caribbean, and the Pacific. Interregional agreements are reaching new heights of gigantism, opacity, and neoliberal destructiveness with the corporation-friendly Transatlantic Trade and Investment Partnership and the Trans Pacific Partnership (Seattle to Brussels 2013). A third type of mechanism, that Scholte calls translocalism, involves direct networking by substate authorities, without the mediation of nation-states, in the regulation of common problems in areas like environmental conditions. We will see some examples of this kind of governance cooperation in the next chapter.

A fourth trend, arguably the most extensive and the most preoccupying, is the proliferation of private global governance mechanisms. These may be operated by civil society organizations, as in the case of the World Fair Trade Organization, but they are more often private sector instruments. The latter can target social and environmental corporate responsibility but often have aims that have little to do with anything other than profit motives. The East India Company that gave the British empire a startup in the centuries before the government took over could be considered an instance of private transnational governance. Today's credit rating agencies, capable of making elected heads of state and government shake in their boots, provide a highly visible and particularly controversial example of the application of private judgment to the public domain. In addition to the lack of accountability of this kind of "quasi-regulation", its development in global governance tends to depoliticize controversial issues and remove them from public debate (Sinclair 2012, p. 29). A final category of global governance in Scholte's list are the hybrid arrangements that combine public, business, and civil society elements, sometimes termed public–private partnerships or PPPs. This category has expanded enormously over the past few years as the corporate private sector has been enrolled to serve as the Saint Louis of the latter-day development crusade. Examples of these mixed mechanisms are the UN's Global Compact or the Roundtable on Sustainable Palm Oil but also the corporation-led food security programs promoted by the World Economic Forum and the G8 New Alliance for Food Security and Nutrition that we will encounter in Chapter 6. We will return to the exceedingly important questions of who regulates whom for what purpose in the concluding chapter of this book.

In short, assigning responsibility for decision making and its consequences has become highly problematic. Within this apparent chaos, however, there are some important demarcations that condition food governance. A significant distinction is between what happens when food is conceived as a global commodity, on the one hand, or as a human right, on the other. Institutionally speaking, at the level of global governance this translates into pitting the WTO, backed up by the IFIs and a whole system of regulation rooted in the free market paradigm, against the FAO (and now the reformed Committee on World Food Security) and the Human Rights Council with its Special Rapporteur on the Right to Food. The WTO's concerns interact with those of food security and right-to-food advocates solely on the supply-side of the question without any concern for issues of access and entitlement. It is "ideologically subsumed within the overarching premise that trade liberalization per se improves resource efficiency, which in turn aids economic growth and improved living standards. Hence, the goal of improving global food security is best pursued by implementing freer world trade" (Rosin et al. eds. 2012, p. 55). There is thus an institutional disconnect between multilateral rule setting for food trade and promoting food security (De Schutter 2008). Free trade proponents in the reformed Committee on World Food Security have gone so far as to refuse to let the CFS even consider placing discussion of the food security implications of trade on its agenda. Interestingly enough, the domination of trade rules is now being subjected to a novel threat from an unexpected quarter by the current trend for states and sovereign wealth funds to override WTO rules by grabbing agricultural land abroad to ensure non-trade-based access to food and fuel for the investing country (McMichael 2014).

A more recently perceived but equally important delimitation, fruit of increased concern for climate change and the environment, is that between food considered as a global commodity and food conceived as one product of processes that also provide multiple benefits to the environment. The concept of environmental services, formalized by the 2005 Millennium Ecosystem Assessment, views natural ecosystems as performing fundamental functions upon which human life depends. These include provisioning water and energy as well as food, supporting the nutrient cycle (whereby nutrients move from the physical environment into living organisms and are subsequently recycled back to the physical environment), and regulating pests and diseases (Millennium Ecosystem Assessment, 2005). As we have seen in Chapter 2, the environmental conditions under which food is produced impact on the quality of these services. The globalization of food understood as simply a commodity privileges use of production models and technology that are at odds with ecological perspectives on resources management. Moreover, environmental concerns in general, including ecosystem services, are themselves subject to being (mis) appropriated by market-based approaches. For some "the lack of market prices for ecosystem services and biodiversity means that the benefits we derive from these goods (often public in nature) are usually neglected or under-valued in decision-making" (TEEB 2009, p. 2). Our discussion in Chapter 2, however, suggested that transforming nature into an economy-serving adjective – as in the term "natural capital" – amounts to commodifying it so that it can be exchanged for cash, and this can open the way to ever more destructive enclosures of the finite bases of life

(Monbiot 2012). Food viewed through an environmental lens is institutionalized in a set of organizations and international agreements, principally those born from the 1992 Rio Conference, which do not interact adequately with the others (Ingram et al. 2010, pp. 254–255). The difficulties encountered in harmonizing the development of post-2015 Millennium Development Goals and that of the Sustainable Development Goals emerging from Rio+20, taking place in different rooms in UN Headquarters, is illustrative of this divide (Sustainable Development 2015).

Behind these institutional and discursive aspects of the fragmentation of authority lie structural issues of power relationships. Different governments have different weights in institutions like the Bretton Woods Institutions where voting is proportionate to the size of contributions to the budget. Most are excluded from limited membership clubs like the G8/G20 and from the inner circle negotiation rooms of the WTO. This compares with the universal membership, one-country/one-vote regime of the UN, where everyone is in the room although some votes count more than others. At the same time, while global *political* authority has been increasingly fragmented with the proliferation of institutions and mandates, *economic* power has become increasingly concentrated in the hands of increasingly larger and fewer corporations, which are not subject to global regulation. Within the labyrinth of unaccountable governance, private sector actors have carved out an unacceptably determinant and unregulated space. Of all of the deficiencies of the current food governance regime this is the most harmful and outrageous. As we illustrated in Chapter 2, horizontal and vertical integration in the food chain has led to intense corporate concentration with significant political impact (ETC 2008; Lang et.al. 2009, pp. 164–169; MacMillan 2005, pp. 10–13; Clapp and Fuchs 2009). The annual turnover of the largest food companies exceeds the GDP of many developing countries, giving them considerable influence in international regulatory processes (MacMillan *op.cit.*, p. 11). Regulatory capacity has not kept pace with global integration of markets (Clapp and Cohen 2009, pp. 6–7; Ghosh 2010, pp. 77–79; ETC 2008), and corporations often play a key role in establishing the very rules that seek to govern their activities (Clapp and Fuchs *op.cit.*, p. 1). The Codex Alimentarius is just one example of forums in which TNCs attempt to shape regulations to their advantage (Weis 2007, p. 133).

No international body mandated to monitor global corporate activity has existed since the UN Center for Transnational Corporations was closed down in 1992, and no UN body has the capacity to monitor and evaluate the global technologies they devise (ETC 2008, p. 46). In the absence of global regulation and accountable national governance, private sector corporations have almost untrammeled capacity to attain their objectives at country level to the detriment of citizens' rights and interests, as the current land grab phenomenon demonstrates. The phenomenon of financial speculation in food commodities has added a new twist to private sector impact on food security. So, in a different form, has the emergence of philanthrocapitalists like the Bill & Melinda Gates Foundation that we encountered in Chapter 1, which has more financial clout to orient agricultural policy than the multilateral FAO. Private sector forms of food governance that have emerged in the existing policy vacuum and "public–private partnerships" are no substitute for authoritative and accountable multilateral food governance. The fault is not to be laid so much at the door of the corporate private sector, which is simply seeking to realize its mission of earning profits for stockholders, as at that of governments, who are failing to fulfill their mission of defending common interests and public goods.

International community reactions to the food crisis

The food crisis turned a spotlight on this situation. It sparked a range of international institutional initiatives to address the food governance vacuum – or at least to create the appearance of addressing it. The most significant were the UN High-Level Task Force on the Food Security Crisis (HLTF), the Global Partnership for Agriculture and Food Security (GPAFS), and the reform of the Committee on World Food Security (CFS). It is interesting to contrast them since they iconically represent the panoply of ways in which the international community can respond to challenges, ranging from the technical/administrative mode, to the bombastically *plus ça change plus c'est la même chose*, to the political. The first to act, in technical/administrative fashion, was the Secretary General of the UN. In April 2008 he established a High-Level Task Force for the Global Food Security Crisis (HLTF) composed of secretariat heads and technical staff of twenty-two UN specialized agencies, funds, programs, Bretton Woods institutions, and relevant parts of the UN Secretariat, as well as the OECD. This initiative was welcomed by many who criticized the UN system's institutional dispersion and uncoordinated responses to global problems. In the words of the Secretary-General, the Task Force's objective was "to ensure that the UN system, international financial institutions and the WTO are ready to provide robust and consistent support to countries struggling to cope with food insecurity." To this end it produced the Comprehensive Framework of Action on Food Security (CFA) referred to on pp. 95–96. The HLTF is a technical secretariat-led initiative and does not entail any form of political oversight. The CFA was not submitted to governments for discussion and approval. There was, however, a real danger that its existence would be taken – by those who preferred a notional approach to global governance – as an excuse for avoiding the negotiation of a more political intergovernmental strategic commitment based on critical reflection on the deficiencies of the dominant strategies of the past two decades. It is an excellent illustration of how apparent concern for functional efficiency can annul the political dimension of decision making.

In July 2008 the G8, under the leadership of France and Britain, proposed the creation of a Global Partnership on Agriculture, Food Security, and Nutrition (GPAFS) with three pillars: increased investment in agriculture, enhanced expertise brought to bear on food security issues, and a global policy forum for decision making. Where to locate this third pillar was not specified, a remarkable omission given the FAO's recognized mandate for food and agriculture within the UN system. This proposal was justified in the eyes of its proponents by lack of confidence in the capacity of FAO to respond effectively to the crisis. In the eyes of many civil society actors, however, the underlying motivation was a desire on the part of the

G8 governments and private sector interests to bypass the UN multilateral system and strengthen their hold on the world's food system.[2] The GPAFS's promoters expected to obtain endorsement for the Partnership at a High-Level Meeting on "Food Security for All" convened in Madrid in January 2009 by the Government of Spain with the support of the HLTF, the UN Secretary-General, and the G8. This did not transpire due to the combined opposition of several forces. FAO argued for building on existing institutions rather than creating new ones. A number of G77 countries objected to an initiative that concerned them in the first instance yet in whose design they had not been involved. Small-scale food producer and civil society organizations motivated their rejection of the GPAFS in their final declaration:

> We need one single space in the UN system that acts in total independence of the international financial and trade institutions, with a clear mandate from governments, decisive participation by peasant, fisher-folk and other small scale food producers, and a transparent and democratic process of decision making. . . . We see the proposed Global Partnership as just another move to give the big corporations and their foundations a formal place at the table, despite all the rhetoric about the "inclusiveness" of this initiative.
>
> (*Surprise Ending in Madrid!* 2009)

The Partnership's evolution following the Madrid meeting was patchy. The investment pillar was tabled again at the 2009 meeting of the G8. It was adopted in the form of the "L'Aquila Food Security Initiative" (AFSI) with pledges of $20 billion. Of these, however, only some $6 billion represented fresh funding, and only $4.2 billion had actually been disbursed by the time of a subsequent AFSI meeting in February 2011. Agreement was not reached on establishing a dedicated "silo" fund to which all would contribute, although some donors subsequently came together to channel funds through a World Bank–administered Global Agriculture and Food Security Program (GAFSP) and the New Alliance for Food Security and Nutrition. The two other pillars of the Partnership – expertise and the global policy forum – have come together in the context of the reformed Committee on World Food Security in terms that are described in the next section. Although the GPAFS never achieved real existence, it continued to crop up in UN resolutions for several years with an ethereal longevity worthy of the indeterminate Parallel Campaign that animates 1,000 pages of the Viennese novelist Robert Musil's masterpiece, *The Man without Qualities*, without ever revealing its substance. The GPAFS was finally retired from active service when UN Secretary-General launched the "Zero Hunger Challenge" in June 2012 (UN n.d.).

The reformed Committee on World Food Security (CFS)

The only international reaction to the food crisis with explicit global political significance was an audacious effort to transform the FAO Committee on World Food Security from the ineffectual talk shop it had become into an authoritative global policy forum. The CFS had been established by the World Food Conference in

1974 as an intergovernmental body housed in FAO to serve as a forum for review and follow-up of policies concerning world food security. It was the body tasked with preparation of and follow-up to the two World Food Summits of 1996 and 2002, and for negotiating the Voluntary Guidelines to Support the Progressive Realization of the Right to Food at National Level in 2003–2004. Over the years, however, apart from these high points of international activity, it had failed to establish itself as an effective forum for negotiating policy and monitoring its application and was targeted for review. Following the debacle of the Madrid conference it was agreed to give the reform process a chance, although many felt it would fail. Discussions in the CFS got underway in April 2009. The then CFS Bureau Chair, the Argentinian Permanent Representative to FAO, Maria del Carmel Squeff, took the unusual step of opening them up to all concerned stakeholders. This departure from UN practice was intended to forecast the more open nature that was felt to be one of the necessary qualities of a reformed committee, an intelligent application of the interactive relation that obtains between process and product.

Organizations of small-scale food producers facilitated by the IPC, along with some international NGOs, were enabled to interact with governments on an equal basis and made a fundamental contribution to the reform. An innovative practice of posting all written inputs by delegations in a common space was adopted, which introduced a strong element of transparency. The regular face-to-face meetings provided a propitious opportunity for promoting mutual understanding of the positions of different actors. The fact that the IPC was speaking on behalf of small-scale food producers around the world strengthened the legitimacy and impact of its positions, which were often the most cogent on the table. In the end, despite their diversity, the majority of the participants came to feel a sense of ownership of the core proposal to the point of collectively resisting a last-minute effort on the part of the United States and a few other developed country delegations to downplay the political significance of the new forum. When the US delegation arrived with last-minute alternative text seeking to reduce the mandate of the CFS to serving as a platform for exchanging "good practices", they were voted out of order. A conciliatory speech just before the final vote by the new US Ambassador to the Rome-based UN agencies, a nominee of newly elected Obama, gave a clear indication that the message had gotten through (McKeon 2009b).

The final reform proposal was adopted by acclamation on 17 October 2009 during the thirty-fifth session of the CFS. It includes important points that civil society fought hard to defend against the attacks of some governments who wanted to keep the new CFS as toothless as possible. One of the most contested is the definition of the CFS as the foremost international platform for food security, unequivocally occupying the global policy space of what some hoped would still see the light of day as an overriding and unaccountable global partnership. Another is the inclusion in the CFS's mandate of working toward realization of the right to adequate food. This was opposed by countries that are allergic to collective economic rights and by those who preferred that the CFS's pronouncements not be grounded in international human rights legislation, which is binding on those countries that have adhered to it. Exactly what would be the CFS's policy role was the subject of great debate. In the end the conflict was addressed by dividing the assumption of different roles into two notional phases. In the first the CFS would start off with harmless activities with which no one would disagree, like serving as a platform for discussion and coordination at the global level or giving advice to countries and regions. In the second phase, whose kick-off date was not specified, the CFS would "gradually take on additional roles" such as monitoring and promoting accountability, a perennial red flag for governments, and developing its own policy guidelines. The CFS's "Global Strategic Framework" for food security and nutrition, unlike the HLTF's Comprehensive Framework for Action, would be negotiated and adopted by governments. The thorny terrain of evidence-based policy, which we explored in the last chapter, is addressed in the reform document by establishing a High-Level Panel of Experts, which supports the decision making of the CFS by undertaking autonomous reviews of contentious or complicated issues. A civil society victory is the recognition that expertise is not vested solely in academics and scientists and that a goal of the HLPE should be to "help create synergies between world class academic/scientific knowledge, field experience, knowledge from social actors and practical application" (CFS 2009, para. 36).

The reform document's provisions governing the inclusion of and participation by actors other than governments are unprecedented in the history of UN intergovernmental forums. Civil society's autonomy and right to self-organize is recognized, overcoming the resistance of governments who would have felt more comfortable if they had been able to maintain control over which potentially divergent voices would be allowed into the room. It also recognizes that organizations representing those directly affected by food security issues should have pride of place. The other categories of nonstate actor participants in the CFS are UN agencies and bodies whose activities are relevant to food security, international agricultural research systems, international and regional financial institutions and the WTO, and private sector associations and philanthropic foundations. Ultimate decision making power is vested in the member governments, the only ones who vote if comes to that. Social movements supported this provision in order to reinforce the accountability of governments as the ultimate decision makers. The other categories of participants, however, are enabled to take part in the discussions on the same footing as governments up to the final decision making moment, rather than intervening only as observers. They also accompany the work of the intergovernmental Bureau of the CFS by participating in an Advisory Group that works alongside of the Bureau throughout the year, from one plenary session to the next.

Finally, the CFS reform document is attentive to the need to respect the principle of subsidiarity (whereby decisions should be made at the lowest appropriate level) and to build links between policy forums and action at all levels. It enjoins governments and regional institutions to respect the open door approach of the CFS and "to constitute or strengthen multi-disciplinary national mechanisms (e.g. food security networks, national alliances, national CFS) including all key stakeholders dedicated to advance food security at national and local levels" (CFS

2009, para. 24). This is a point that was strongly defended by social movements which are interested above all in having more influence over policy decision making close to home.

BOX 4.3
THE REFORM DOCUMENT OF THE COMMITTEE ON
WORLD FOOD SECURITY: SOME IMPORTANT FEATURES

- Recognizes the structural nature of the causes of the food crisis and acknowledges that the primary victims are small-scale food producers.
- Defines the CFS as "the foremost inclusive international and intergovernmental platform" for food security, based in the UN system.
- Explicitly includes defending the right to adequate food in the CFS's mission.
- Recognizes civil society organizations – small-scale food producers and urban movements especially – as full participants, for the first time in UN history. Authorizes them to intervene in debate on the same footing as governments and affirms their right to autonomously self-organize to relate to the CFS through a Civil Society Mechanism.
- Enjoins the CFS to negotiate and adopt a Global Strategic Framework (GSF) for a food strategy providing guidance for national food security action plans as well as agricultural investment and trade regulations.
- Empowers the CFS to make decisions on key food policy issues, and promotes accountability by governments and other actors through an "innovative" monitoring mechanism.
- Arranges for CFS policy work to be supported by a High-Level Panel of Experts in which the expertise of farmers, indigenous peoples and practitioners is acknowledged alongside that of academics and researchers.
- Recognizes the principle of subsidiarity and urges that strong linkages be built between the global meetings of the CFS and regional and country levels. Governments commit to establishing national multi-stakeholder policy spaces in the image of the global CFS.

CFS (2009)

On paper there had never been anything like this in global food governance. High on the list of innovations is that of the Civil Society Mechanism (CSM). Obtaining approval that it be autonomously designed by civil society and not dictated by governments or the secretariat was a triumph in the name of treating interaction with civil society as political process rather than window-dressing (McKeon 2009, pp. 173–176). Translating this victory into concrete terms was, however, a major challenge. Thanks to the IPC's experience and outreach to rural social movements it proved possible to consult with networks in all regions over an eight-month period and to clarify ideas about what the mechanism would look like and how it would work. The resulting proposal was validated at a civil society forum in October 2010. It was presented the following week to the CFS plenary, which, in a departure from normal intergovernmental prerogatives, was called on not to approve it but simply to acknowledge it (CFS 2010a). The design of the CSM sought to put into practice the principle of awarding greatest voice to organizations directly representing sectors of the population most affected by food insecurity. Of the list of eleven civil society constituencies proposed by the IPC and included in the reform document and the CSM statute, ten refer to different kinds of small-scale food producers (peasants, fisherfolk, pastoralists, indigenous peoples, agricultural workers, the landless, rural women, and youth), consumers, and the urban poor. Only one is reserved for NGOs, normally the most numerous and vocal component of civil society interaction with intergovernmental processes.

The CSM is open to membership by all civil society organizations concerned with food issues, at all levels and in all regions. Governance is assured by a Coordinating Committee (CC) of forty-one focal points designated by the eleven constituencies and by thirty subregions throughout the world, in order to root the Mechanism in regional realities. A target of 50 percent female participation was set. The logic of "representation" was studiously avoided, since peoples' organizations cannot and will not delegate their self-representation. The CSM was designed as a space for information and exchange, for seeking consensus but not necessarily finding it given the diversity of views and the determination of social movements to avoid letting their positions be watered down. The intention was to ally the political leadership and legitimacy of social movements with the technical, analytic, and communications capacity necessary to develop proposals on complex issues, drawing on capacities of NGOs and engaged academics. To make this work is no easy task. It requires a deliberate strategy and methodologies; resources; and constant self-monitoring to avoid falling into a mode of operations conditioned by the rhythms, language, and practices of intergovernmental negotiations. In the words of a brief on the reformed CFS that La Via Campesina prepared for its members, "[T]he participation of representatives of small food producers is certainly a huge challenge for them and their movements. Effective and productive involvement requires continuous preparation, technical support and organizational skills, especially when it comes to negotiating in a multilateral system, responding to the increasing pressure of lobbyists, or coping with the monopoly of the English language" (LVC 2012, p. 1). Figure 4.1 presents the CSM and its relations with the CFS as visualized in the La Via Campesina document.

The reformed CFS has a number of features that could equip it to pick up the challenge of acting as centerpiece for a better global governance system. Its inclusiveness and the fact that it has been recognized as the foremost global food forum equip it to act against institutional fragmentation and sectoral silos. Incorporation

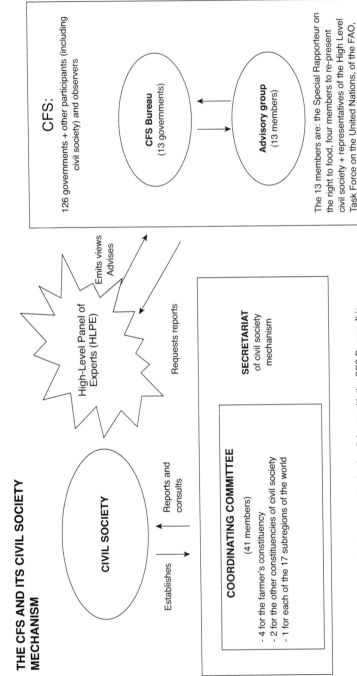

FIGURE 4.1 The Committee on World Food Security and the Civil Society Mechanism

Source: LaVia Campesina (2012). www.viacampesina.org. Reproduced with permission.

of defense of the right to food in its mission roots it in values, gives it a strong normative role, and inserts it into the corpus of international human rights legislation. The injunction to formulate and adopt a Global Strategic Framework and the establishment of an innovative High-Level Panel of Experts address the problems of paradigm change and of evidence-based policy deliberations. Its multi-actor design moves in the direction of democratizing global governance and rendering its operations more transparent. Although the CFS does not have the capacity of the WTO or the Security Council to enforce its decisions, its "soft" power is bolstered by its functions of monitoring and promoting accountability and its attention to building links between global and local levels. We will return to the CFS in Chapter 6 to review its first five years of life and assess the degree to which it is proving capable of addressing the deficiencies we discussed earlier in this chapter. Our assessment will be influenced by the conviction that no significant changes can be made in global food governance unless they are built up from the base. We will therefore turn in the next chapter to taking a look at what is happening in the world that can contribute to building better food governance from the local level on up.

Notes

1. Not a UN agency in the strict sense of the term but closer in its mission to the other Rome-based agencies than to the family of multilateral banks.
2. See discussion paper for working group on "Who Decides?" at the CSO Forum, "Peoples' Food Sovereignty Now!" held in parallel to the FAO World Summit on Food Security, 13–17 November 2009. A report on the discussions can be found in Swanston et al. 2009.

5

LOCAL–GLOBAL

Building food governance from the bottom up

The last chapter reviewed encouraging developments in food governance at the global level. We will now shift our perspective to look at how better food systems and more legitimate decision making about food are being built up starting from the level closest to home. The purpose of this chapter is to achieve a better understanding of the kinds of people-driven dynamics that are underway of which global governance could, in the best of circumstances, be supportive. We will profit from some of the terrain we have covered earlier in this book. In Chapter 2 we encountered the coupled terms "global" and "local" when we contrasted two very different types of food systems. Here we will come at them from the broader perspective of how different levels of experience can interact with and affect each other. Chapter 2 also acquainted us with the actors and the practices of local food systems. Building on that, and on the introduction we had to food sovereignty in Chapter 3, we will conduct an at least cursory review of concrete local experiences of equitable and sustainable ways of meeting food needs that are being conducted today throughout the world. We will start with the basic household unit and then move on to some of the key terrains on which the food battle is being waged, from access to resources to models of production, markets, and people-centered research. We will try to identify factors that come to play in determining whether or not these myriad Davids are able to collect the necessary strength to take on the Goliath of the global corporate-controlled food regime. To what degree is alternative local experience being networked horizontally and vertically? What supportive alliances are being constructed with other social actors and with concerned academics who could provide analytic insights on alternative practice? How are people-promoted initiatives interacting with subglobal governance, and under what circumstances are these interrelations producing supportive results? In essence, we will be looking at the opportunities, the challenges, and the tensions the food sovereignty movement faces today, which were evoked in Chapter 3, and at how they are being addressed in practice.

Of global and local

We have run into global–local dynamics on other occasions in previous parts of this book. Many of these encounters have had nation-states as their protagonists and global intergovernmental organizations as their sites. But the cast of characters in such interaction has broadened as the globalization of the food system, the implementation of a worldwide "free" trade agenda, and the exacerbation of global phenomena like climate change have intensified global impacts on local people. The capacity of national governments to mediate negative effects of global policies and trends on their citizens, assuming they would like to do so, has been reduced with structural adjustment and trade regulations. Top-down efforts to address worldwide problems by adopting global goals to be translated into national action – most visibly the Millennium Development Goals to which we referred in Chapter 4 – have failed to turn the trick, not surprisingly. They certainly have not inspired the peoples' movements that have mobilized autonomously to contest the effects of globalized neoliberalism on their own lives.

"Think globally – act locally" was a rallying cry that reached its apex in the 1970s and early 1980s, when the potential virulence of the impact of globalization on local possibilities was less evident than it is today. It suggested the need to take global phenomena into account but implicitly postulated a fairly autonomous sphere for local action to improve peoples' lives. The more recently coined "glocalization" collapses the global and the local into a single word, with the effect of freezing the dialectic relation that connected the terms in the earlier slogan. A product of the business world, its original significance had to do with binding local markets more closely into global ones by adapting products or services specifically to each locality in which they are sold, such as the "bulgogi" burgers introduced by McDonald's in an effort to seduce Korean consumers. Thinkers like the sociologist Zygmunt Bauman have adopted the neologism to discuss global–local relations in less cozy terms:

> Glocalization is a name for a hate-love relationship, mixing attraction with repulsion: love that lusts proximity, mixed with hate that yearns for distance. Such a relationship would have perhaps collapsed under the burden of its own incongruity, if not for the pincers-like duo of inevitabilities: if cut off from the global supply routes the "place" would lack the stuff of which autonomous identities, and contraptions keeping them alive, are nowadays made; and if not for the locally improvised and serviced airfields, global forces would have nowhere to land, re-staff, replenish and refuel.
>
> (Bauman 2011)

Many feel that the local–global coupling is too rigidly hierarchical and that the relationship should, at the very least, be considered as dialectic rather than unidirectional and causal. There are various other ways of thinking about interactions between what happens at the multiple levels and places in our globalized world. The term "transcalarity" highlights the fact that actors nowadays no longer remain docilely in their assigned positions but hop over boundaries from one level to another. "Cross-local" points to the horizontal nature of some of the most dynamic exchanges taking place today.

What interests us, beyond theory and terminology, are the ways in which transformational links among different sites are actually being constructed. In the area of food, local systems and movements are the place to start. It is difficult to conceive how accountable and legitimate global food governance and a better food system could be built without such a foundation. But how and where to proceed from there is not self-evident. Institutionally embedded food governance wends its way through bodies that take food-related decisions from the local community level (like town or village councils) up through the subnational (regional elected assemblies and administrative authorities), the national (parliaments, ministries, judicial systems), the regional (regional economic communities), on up to the global (UN, WTO). And, as we have seen in the previous chapter, institutional governance is only a part of the picture. An authoritative treatment of food policy features a table of no less than seven pages grouping a whole host of local, national, regional, and international food policy actors, organizations, and institutions into four categories with different and sometimes overlapping functions: state and public sector, private and corporate sector, civil society, and the consuming public (Lang et al. 2009, pp. 88–94). Finally, local scales are not inevitably part of nested hierarchies. The politics of the local can be multiscalar, involving local actors in direct local–global transactions or a multiplication of local transactions as part of global networks (Sassans 2003, p. 11).

People who write about food issues generally have their preferred strategies for making the system work better. Most of these have something to say about the global–local nexus, and many reflect on what might operate between or outside of these two extremes. Neoliberals, of course, advocate removing the remaining limitations on global "free" trade and letting the unencumbered market do its magic. An excellent account of the global food system that we have cited on several occasions talks about the "middle spaces" of the world food economy that have been opened up by governments, private foundations, TNCs, and financial actors, shifting control away from farmers and consumers, and postulates the need for the latter to reassert themselves (Clapp 2012). An analyst who uses the concept of food regime as a reference point speculates about the possible future development of regionally organized, ecologically resilient agro-food systems nested into global systems equipped to monitor multiple ecological dimensions and to blow the whistle if necessary. Such a development, the author hypothesizes, could be dialectically spurred by the lack of ecological resilience of the corporate food regime (Campbell 2009).

In the end it is an issue of what needs to happen at what level to build a better food system, and who needs to support and protect whom. In the logic of food sovereignty, the answer is straightforward. Initiatives are rooted in local communities and need to be able to count on support from higher levels. Instead, international and regional levels are now the source of policies that restrict national and local choice by imposing trade regulations, investment agreements, and intellectual property regimes. The actors of the global corporate food system are able to shift the entry point for decision making and action from level to level – international, regional, national – according to where they encounter least resistance in any particular case or moment in time. This capacity to play a multilevel game makes regulation more difficult. We will return to reflections of this nature in the concluding chapter of this book.

Standardized modernization or diversified local transformation?

It is clearly not enough to build multilevel links within the global food system as it is now conceived if substantial transformation is what we are after. The tyranny of imposition of meaning from above needs to be overcome for local meanings and movements to have a fighting chance. James Scott has written effectively about the violence that official programs and prescriptions operate on complex social and natural realities when, "seeing like a state", they simplify and standardize them in order to control them from above (Scott 1998). Like most practitioners, I have witnessed operations of this nature countless times in my field experience. The effect is destructive of peoples' agency even in relatively benign instances in which the administrators' motivations are not horrendous. This was the case, for example, in Tanzania in the mid-1980s, where district development officers triumphantly told me that the villages in the Dodoma area I was about to visit had uniformly elected building a school as their top development priority, just as the National Development Plan had prescribed. When I spoke on my own with the local village councils, it transpired that water supply was really at the top of their list, but they had acceded to the officials' prompting and had served them up with what they wanted to hear in order to comply with their superiors' instructions.

I found myself in an infinitely worse universe in Menghistu's Ethiopia during the famine of the mid-1980s. The only channel for outside assistance to those suffering from the drought was through the Relief and Rehabilitation Commission (RRC) responsible for the forced resettlement programs that were being imposed on communities, whereby they were moved hundreds or thousands of miles from their homes and installed in state farmlike enterprises. As FAO's civil society office we managed to wiggle our way through the government bureaucracy and develop an approach that involved helping communities that were likely objects of resettlement to plan their own integrated programs that would allow them to weather the drought and stay on their land. To our surprise, one of the biggest obstacles we encountered came from within FAO's own Development Department. In response to the drought FAO had formulated an Agricultural Rehabilitation Program for Africa (ARPA) composed of a series of separate sectoral components for seeds, fertilizers, irrigation, and livestock. When I brought our integrated community-based proposal to the office of the director, a dour Dutchman, he waved his ARPA bible at me and said, "Now what do you expect me to do with a program that has a bit of everything in it, all mixed up? It doesn't fit in the ARPA framework!" In the end, the proposal was saved only because we raised over $5 million for it, including a hefty contribution from Bob Geldorf's high-visibility Band Aid fund.

"Effective social formations of resistance, redistribution or transformation cannot be theoretically prescribed or academically engineered", socio-economist Fantu Cheru remarks. "Instead of focusing on a unifying conception of society and transformation we must look for a workable sense of cohesion to emerge out of the seemingly irreconcilable modes of resistance waged from below" (2000, p. 119). On similar lines, the upbeat concluding message of Tony Weis's account of the global food economy paraphrases the Zapatista slogan "one no and many yeses". "While we need to uniformly oppose the universalizing system of corporate-driven market integration", he suggests, "alternatives will materialize in diverse ways as struggles to democratize and localize control play out within different environments, histories and cultural traditions" (Weis 2007, p. 177).

We live in an age in which overtly politically inspired exercises in centralized planning have become history, ceding the way to the perhaps even more effective homogenizing operations of the globalized "free" market. In this context an enduring rhetorical force for standardization is the market-driven modernization theory discussed in Chapter 3, which continues to frame talk about development and is liberally extended to all emerging challenges, from food insecurity to climate change. Breaking this hold by politicizing market culture is what a collective of activists-scholars is aiming at in a collection of local experiences that refutes the vision of the local as a hierarchically subordinated counterpart of the global (McMichael 2010). Instead, "local actors are represented as they engage critically with their relations of subjection, in order to transcend the terms of their subjection". This does not involve repudiating universals like citizenship, democracy, development, rights, sovereignty, property, even markets – which development discourse has appropriated and to which it has assigned standardized meanings. On the contrary, these categories and values are reappropriated through place-based struggles that encourage us to think in terms of diversities and alternatives (*ibid.*, pp. 3 and 10). Essentially the same message, in somewhat more complicated language, that we have encountered in the words of activists when we discussed the food sovereignty paradigm in Chapter 3: "We have to construct our own realities now. We cannot wait for them to arrive from above. Transformation comes from the power of a process from below" (Nicholson 2011, p. 17).

Modernization development discourse has a way of taking what makes local people resilient and retooling it as symptoms of their backwardness and causes of their vulnerability. In his classic work on Tanzania to which we referred in Chapter 3, Göran Hydén spoke of an "uncaptured peasantry", which took as its reference point an "economy of affection" based on kinship and family that offered opportunities for social and economic action outside of the formal market and state control (Hydén 1980, p. 28). Hydén correctly diagnosed the fact that peasants were able to "escape" from the monetized market because of the control they possessed over their own means of production and subsistence. But he – in the name of socialist development – and countless others in the name of capitalist development judged this strength to be a weakness, a hindrance to development. Three decades later African peasant producers, who in the meantime have acquired the capacity to represent themselves and their ideas, hold that it is precisely this factor of control that constitutes the basis of their resilience (EAFF, PROPAC, ROPPA 2013, p. 23). In contrast to the characterization of the economy of affection as "pre-modern", they point out that the solidarity and capacity to maintain social peace that it incarnates represent precious values in the strife-ridden "modern" world we live in (ROPPA 2004, p. 2).

So what do peoples' own local strategies of resistance and alternative building look like, and how might they be supported at other levels? A rich pool of experience of different forms of "micro-resistance" to globalized food systems in all regions of the world is there to be built upon. The examples given here are in no way intended to furnish a comprehensive survey of what exists, nor to simplistically wish away the power of the adversary forces. Rather, they serve to document the fact that the call for other ways of conceiving and doing food provision is not simply a slogan but a reality in the making.

Reasserting the household and the family farm

The household is the most basic space in which people seek solutions to food problems. As pointed out in Chapter 3, during the 1980s researchers and policymakers began to turn to this level when the limitations of aggregate national statistics as a basis for decision making on food problems became increasingly evident. Initially this testified to a recognition that not all households have the same access to food or, in Sen's terminology, to assets that can translate into food. Progressively, however, it became apparent that households themselves are not unitary, and that intra-household issues of power and decision making need to be addressed. In particular women, although they are the key actors in ensuring the food security of the family as a whole, almost universally have less power and less access to resources than do men. Peoples' resistance and transformation strategies at the household level, correspondingly, aim both at strengthening the basic family unit's capacity to function and to meet the food needs of its members, on the one hand, and at seeking to resolve internal dysfunctions and inequalities, on the other.

The family has taken a real bashing under just about all of the "isms" that the last century has served up, from colonialism to Marxism to capitalism – so much so that in the "developed world" it almost seems that "right to lifers" and the Catholic Church have been able to stake out a claim to what is the basic unit of social organization. In the Global South, the family's capacity to function as the source of adequate food for its members was debilitated by the introduction of a dualistic male-centered export economy divorced from the invisible domestic food provision economy that was left in the hands of the women. This distortion was successively aggravated by all of the other stresses that have accompanied the buildup of a capitalist market economy serving interests other than those of the primary producers. Insertion into the commodity-centered market economy had such an effect on the economic organization of rural life that it took the nascent Senegalese peasant movement some time to realize that what was common to all its diverse sectors – peasant farmers, fisherfolk, pastoralists – was the fact of belonging to an "exploitation familiale" ("family farm" in English), the basis of both production and reproduction for practically all rural people. It wasn't until 1999, five years after its foundation, that the national peasant platform (Conseil National de Concertation des Ruraux [CNCR]) published a groundbreaking strategy paper that established defense of family farming as the basic plank of their platform of claims. The document denounced the fact that the government's agricultural policy attached too much importance to commodity chains and not enough to the family farming mode of production despite the fact that it was by far the dominant reality in the country (Faye 1999). Since then the Senegalese peasant movement has continued to track family-based agriculture, its state of health, the benefits it provides to the country, and what would be required for it to be able to do a better job of what it is already doing without support (CNCR 2010). The regional peasant network ROPPA has taken on defense of family farming as its primary claim and is now extending what it calls a "family farm observatory" throughout West Africa. This initiative aims at addressing the issue of lack of data on the dominant but invisible mode of production and consumption and at bolstering the peasant movement's strategic reflection and advocacy platform with locally generated facts.

Chapter 2 documented the continued dominance of family-based agriculture in food production. According to FAO, "Both in developing and developed countries, family farming is the predominant form of agriculture in the food production sector" (FAO 2014b). The declaration of the International Year of Family Farming in 2014 by the UN General Assembly could be considered a celebration of what, up until recently, was considered to be a museum piece. The term can be ambiguous, however, if it is not qualified:

> The term "family farming" is vast, and may include almost any agricultural model or method whose direct beneficiaries are not corporations or investors. It includes both small-scale and large-scale producers (with farms covering thousands of hectares), as well as small-scale producers who are entirely dependent on the private sector, through contract farming or other forms of economic exploitation, promoted though concepts such as "The value chain". This is why La Vía Campesina defends family farming in terms of peasant based ecological Farming, as opposed to the large-scale, industrial, toxic farming of agribusinesses, which expel peasants and small farmers and grab the world's lands.
>
> (La Via Campesina 2014)

In all regions of the world, members of La Via Campesina's network are reasserting the basic vocation of family farming and the dignity of what is disparagingly and erroneously referred to in dominant development discourse as "subsistence agriculture". In the words of a US former member of the La Via Campesina International Coordination Committee, Dena Hoff, "My first rule of farming is to feed yourself and your family. Forget national production, forget about export production. All that means nothing if you can't feed yourself and help feed your neighbors" (National Family Farm Coalition n.d., p. 3). Contrary to the logic of capitalism, production and reproduction are not separate universes.

However, the fact that family farms are the dominant source of food for the majority of the world's population does not mean that they are flourishing. On the contrary, as we have seen in Chapter 2, they have suffered from decades of neglect and exploitation. The drudgery of the work involved and the lack of amenities in rural areas in the Global South, along with the universally poor prospects for decent livelihoods in the face of low and volatile prices and punishing policies, are pushing young people, in particular, to abandon farming. One understandable but pernicious reaction to these external threats is to think in terms of making family farming more "entrepreneurial" and "business-like". We will meet up again in the next chapter with these siren calls, launched by agribusinesses, G8 governments, and the World Bank in the name of "modernizing agriculture". In reality, the shift toward entrepreneurial farming turns the family farm – in whatever part of the world it is located – into a mere supplier of labor at the expense of the

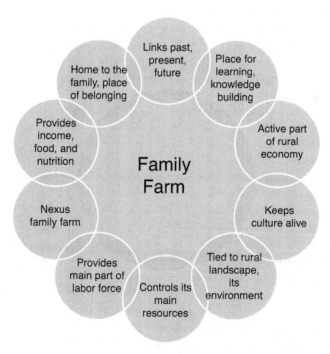

FIGURE 5.1   A family farm

Source: van der Ploeg (2013). "Ten Qualities of Family Farming". *Farming Matters.* AgriCultures Network. Reproduced with permission.

other features we discussed in Chapter 2, which constitute its identity and are well represented in Figure 5.1 (van der Ploeg 2013). "Modernization" need not take the form of "graduating" to entrepreneurial farming. Farmer-led research conducted in Senegal demonstrates that family farms are modernizing their collective decision-making processes and management of production, marketing, and consumption choices while maintaining their multifunctional character and their social capital (SOS Faim 2014).

Threats to family farming do not all come from the outside environment. The inner-looking dimension of constructing alternatives from the very base up is equally important and perhaps even more insidious. It involves fighting against gender and age inequalities internal to the household that are often deeply rooted in cultural and social practices and norms. A key challenge identified by the Senegalese peasant movement already in 1999 was that of addressing, within the family framework, the needs and desires of women and young people, traditionally under the domination of the male head of the family. Many of the answers are external – access to land, training, credit – but others have to do with the management of power relations within the family. Family assemblies launched by the Senegalese peasant federation FONGS constitute an innovative forum for bringing frustrations out into the open and helping stressed family units reconstruct overall strategies that reconcile the interests of all of their members (McKeon 2005, p. 194). In Uganda the male-centered approach to extension introduced with colonialism is being countered by family farm learning groups in which the whole family participates. They are proving to be effective in building trust and solidarity within and among families hand in hand with material benefits, starting with improved food security within the family (FAO 2013a, pp. 162–177). With its campaign "stop violence against women" and by enforcing the rule that 50 percent of the members of all its decision making mechanisms should be women, LVC has acted more decisively than most movements to address the gender issue. There is much more to be done.

It is a testimony to the resilience of family farms that they not only continue to operate in such an unfavorable environment and under stresses of all kinds but also generate a dynamic of renaissance that is a driving force in the food sovereignty movement. Building blocks of alternative food systems are being put in place locally throughout the world in areas where the household unit intersects with the community and the outside world. Four key domains, essentially those that have been identified as pillars of food sovereignty, are peoples' access to and control over resources, sustainable models of production, markets that are coherent with a logic of food sovereignty, and people-centered research and knowledge. These areas were referred to in Chapter 2 while contrasting local food systems with corporate industrialized food chains and in Chapter 3 when the planks of the food sovereignty platform were sketched out. The following sections will provide illustrations of how local people are addressing them in concrete terms and of how these experiences are coalescing.

Peoples' access to and control over resources

We will return to the issue of access to land in the next chapter when we look at how peoples' movements have promoted negotiation of global guidelines on tenure in the context of the reformed CFS. Land, however, is far from the only resource to which local people are defending their access. Increasingly scarce water is another. Water governance is dominated by the World Water Council and its triennial World Water Forums, an example of the hybrid variety of quasi-regulation discussed in the last chapter, in which corporations have a strong voice and express it in favor of privatization. In opposition, a "global water justice movement" has built up over the past decade, networking myriad local popular resistance struggles like the "Cochabamba water war".

BOX 5.1
THE COCHABAMBA WATER WAR

In Cochabamba in Bolivia popular mobilization was sparked in 2000 by a 35 percent increase in water tariffs when the government granted a concession to a private enterprise to run the city's water system. The Cochabamba "water war" drew on resistance of small farmers' organizations who perceived that the monopoly provisions of the water privatization law passed by the Bolivian government threatened their traditional water rights. In the Cochabamba Valley agricultural production is dependent on irrigation, a technology introduced by the Inca more than five hundred years ago. Water resources are managed collectively by associations of small farmers who had formed a Federation of Small Farmers and Community Systems of Potable Water of Cochabamba (FEDECOR) a few years before the law was passed. Thousands of members of the FEDECOR joined the urban protests demanding the modification of the new water law to recognize their traditional "uses and customs". The mobilization was successful and in October 2004 the Bolivian government approved a new irrigation law, which grants indigenous communities, small farmers, and landholders the right to continue with their "customary uses" of the water sources (wells, dams, rivers, and rainwater). Most of the communities in the poor barrios of the southern zone of the city of Cochabamba have built their own independent water systems provisioned by wells that are managed by independent cooperatives, informal committees, or neighborhood councils elected by the residents. Since 2004, many of these community-run water systems have been organized in the Association of Community Water Systems of the South (ASICA-Sur), which has given a collective voice to the citizens who lack public water services. The installation of Evo Morales's government in 2006 has opened the way to public support for these local peoples' initiatives.

Adapted from Our Water Commons (n.d.)

The combative Ghanaian National Coalition against the Privatization of Water drew inspiration from exchanges with Bolivia's Cochabamba experience and the South African Anti-Privatization Forum. Resistance to privatization of water in Vancouver, British Columbia, is judged to owe much of its success to the links activists built up between local and international concerns and coalitions (Robinson 2013). A first global alternative water forum took place in Florence in 2003. The movement's advocacy won an important victory in 2010 when the UN declared water to be a human right. The 2012 Alternative World Water Forum held in Marseille brought together more than 4,000 people around the slogan "Water is life. Not for Profit". Its declaration embraced the agricultural side of the movement alongside the urban:

> We support small-scale, family-run agriculture and demand food sovereignty that allows people to feed themselves, and access to water and land. We want agro-ecological production, which is adapted to climate change, respectful towards the environment, less water-intensive, and less polluting, to become a priority in industrialized and developing countries. We want agro-ecological farmers to be guaranteed their right to use water for agriculture to feed the cities and villages with quality food, by giving them adequate financing, and investing in smart rainwater collection techniques and water usage techniques, that are adapted to local capacities and take traditional practices into account.
>
> (Alternative World Water Forum 2012, p. 3)

Large-scale "water grabbing", often associated with land grabbing, is not easy to fight since it is at the heart of the neoliberal agenda of commodification of resources. Nonetheless, a recent collection of case studies of water grabbing concludes that "even though many of the dynamic protests around the world have not succeeded in reversing the trends of neo-liberal environmental governance and capitalist accumulation, alternatives at the margins are being proposed. . . . Movements protesting grabbing processes are providing us with new tools to counter some of the mechanisms of grabbing processes. Engaged scholars are also helping to create new vocabularies and imaginaries that can challenge dominant narratives that justify such appropriations" (Mehta et al. 2012, p. 204). Such academic validation of people-centered collective approaches to management of common resources has a solid pedigree. It is rooted in Nobel Prize winner Elinor Ostrom's work *Governing the Commons* (1990) in which she argues that voluntary organization by the people directly concerned can be a far more effective approach than that of coercive government or exploitative private enterprise, be it a question of irrigation systems, pastures, or fishing areas.

Biodiversity is another key natural resource that peoples' movements around the world are defending. Seeds are central to peasant farming and food sovereignty for a range of reasons. "At an emotional or spiritual level, seeds are life. When peasants hold them in their hands they feel like gods".[1] It is not by chance that it is women who are their custodians in cultures around the world. But farmers' seeds are also a key element in maintaining their autonomy from the market economy, their capacity to keep production costs down, and their adaptation to specific and changing environments. As we have seen in Chapter 2, farmers' rights to conserve, improve, multiply, exchange, and use their own seeds are threatened by the growing hegemony of corporate seeds. The multifaceted impoverishment this determines is imprinted in my memory as a young practitioner of watching an elderly Togolese peasant as she deftly sorted maize seeds that all looked pretty much the same to me into different piles to be used in different plots where different conditions obtained. In all regions farmers and rural communities are mobilizing to ensure that this richness is not lost. A recent La Via Campesina publication documents the fact that "despite the industry's dominance and continuing efforts to marginalize and even criminalize small-scale peasant and family farming, we find that our seeds have deeper roots. Everywhere, seeds are being reclaimed and brought back as a central part of life in communities, even in cities" (LVC, 2013a, p. i).

In reaction to the government's decision in 2008 to start importing GMO maize, the Korean Women Peasant Association has established native seed farms, which plant and distribute dozens of varieties of threatened native seeds and, in the process, ensure that the knowledge of elderly peasants is available for future generations. In marginalized Northern Uganda, Acheoli peasants have been able to maintain their livelihoods thanks largely to their success in protecting their capacity to produce and reproduce seeds in the face of "both corporate appropriation of genetic resources and seeds patenting and NGOs' attempts at promoting hybrid seed varieties among farmers" (Martiniello 2014, p. 26). In Mozambique the peasant movement is recuperating a culture of reproducing and exchanging seeds damaged by the plantation economy introduced with colonialism and the conflict of the civil war period. In Germany collective resistance is being mobilized against efforts by the seed industry to restrict farmers' rights to exchange and use their own seeds. In Indonesia peasants have been jailed for such "offenses", but peasant and civil society mobilization has obtained their release. Here as elsewhere traditional varieties suited to climate change are coming into their own. In Southern Brazil the Movement of Small Farmers launched a seed recovery campaign in 1996 and since then has saved some fifty-eight varieties of seventeen crop species that risked extinction. In Canada and the United Kingdom "seedy Sundays" bring thousands of small-scale farmers to exchange and enjoy. In France the movement to multiply the number of peasants growing their own seeds is supported by the civic disobedience of "Voluntary Reapers" who destroy GMO fields.

Industry efforts to control the seed market are redoubtable. The virulence of the battle is illustrated by the conflict around "suicide seeds", genetically modified to die after one season to the joy and profit of the multinational seed companies. Determined civil society advocacy slipped a moratorium against this technology into the UN Convention on Biological Diversity (CBD) signed on to by 193 countries in 2000. Brazil was one of the countries that passed a national law outlawing terminator seeds, but strong pressure from powerful landowners backed by corporations has recently led to a reconsideration. In October 2013 a civil society coalition successfully fought the adoption of a pro-terminator technology bill in Congress by collecting over 34,000 signatures on a petition in a matter of days and raising the issue in a national conference on rural development and in CBD and CFS meetings (ETC 2013). There is still a possibility, however, that the Brazilian Congress may cave in to the pressure. In Europe a private sector–promoted proposed reform of seeds regulations is seeking to introduce barriers to market access that would exclude small seed companies and small farmers from producing, exchanging, or marketing their seeds (Kastler et al. 2013, p. 48). One of the latest corporation-friendly measures is a new and more restrictive regulation of the UPOV (International Union for the Protection of New Varieties of Plants), which many countries of the Global South are being pushed to adopt in the context of bilateral trade agreements or "aid" programs like the G8's New Alliance for Food Security and Nutrition. Battles against the application of this latest version of UPOV are underway in Latin America (GRAIN 2013) and Africa (Saez 2013), in some cases with success. Popular mobilization against a GMO-friendly seed bill in Venezuela in October 2013 opened the discussion up to small-scale producers' organizations, winning points both for farmers' seeds and for democracy (Mills and Camacaro 2013). Mexico is the "center of origin" for maize, home to the sixty-five distinct landraces and thousands of varieties that are consumed by people throughout the world. On 21 April 2014, a Mexican judge ruled in favor of a class action suit filed by fifty-three citizen plaintiffs seeking a halt to further testing or commercial planting of GM maize by Monsanto on the grounds that it could put this precious biodiversity into peril (Wise 2014).

BOX 5.2
WHAT IS UPOV?

The International Union for the Protection of New Varieties of Plants (UPOV) is an intergovernmental organization based in Geneva, Switzerland, that was established in 1961. Its mission is "to provide and promote an effective system of plant variety protection, with the aim of encouraging the development of new varieties of plants, for the benefit of society". In UPOV-speak, "protection" means privatization.

The history of UPOV is that of an ongoing expansion of seed company rights along with a concomitant shrinkage of farmers' rights and freedoms. The original convention granted little more than an exclusive right to market a private variety and did not establish specific sanctions. With its subsequent revisions, UPOV now grants monopoly rights over varieties that corporations "discover" and the production, marketing, export, and import thereof. It allows property owners to apply for the confiscation of crops, plantations, harvests, and products derived from the harvest. It even allows companies to file criminal complaints, which can lead to prison terms for farmers.

UPOV 91 is the version of the convention now being imposed around the world. UPOV 91 violates farmers' individual and collective right to save seeds for replanting and allows corporations to monopolize biodiversity. These provisions give the corporations total commercial control over seeds and knowledge that were once owned collectively by whole communities. UPOV accelerates the erosion of biodiversity by promoting varietal uniformity. This is tremendously risky because uniformity can lead to crop loss and greater food insecurity. Finally, seed privatization hinders research and the free flow of knowledge.

Adapted from GRAIN (2013)

Worldwide the resistance to corporate control of biodiversity is increasingly linked and articulated (LVC 2013a). The Peasant Seeds Network founded in France in 2003 now counts over seventy organizations as members. It connects region-ally with the European "Let's Liberate Diversity" coalition. European advocacy has contributed to the adoption of a strategy on biodiversity for 2020 (EC 2012) that dethrones efforts to increase agricultural productivity through the use of "improved varieties" as the sole driver of agricultural policy. Here, as elsewhere in the world, gains made in policy decisions are rooted in activities in the field that put farmers' rights into practice (ACRA 2013). Internationally the Network connects with the IPC, which is advocating for better global governance of biodiversity across the range of international organizations that have some say in the matter. Globally, under pressure from farmers' organizations and other civil society participants, the Governing Body of the International Seed Treaty (ITPGRFA) meeting in September 2013 adopted a resolution renewing governments' commitment to implement the "Farmers Rights" provisions introduced into the treaty negotiations in 1986 thanks to determined civil society advocacy. The resolution calls for the defense of farmers' rights to save, use, exchange, and sell farm-saved seed; to be recognized and rewarded for their contribution to the global pool of genetic resources; and to participate in decision making on issues related to crop genetic resources (Mulvany 2013).

Corporate seeds are at the heart of the industrial mode of agriculture. This is why the battle over their control is so strong. But seeds are also one of the terrains where the peasant, food sovereignty approach is the most indisputably superior to the industrial, as we have seen in Chapter 2. The industrial seed system depends on access to the genetic resources of which peasants are the custodians in order to "discover" the varieties which it then privatizes. Yet its ability to make profits depends on destroying the very basis of its business by "banning the collective rights of farmers to use, exchange, sell and protect their seeds, and by confiscating and subsequently eradicating traditional seeds to the benefit of new industrial varieties controlled by Plant Breeders' Rights" through regimes like UPOV (Kastler et al. 2013, p. 48). These conflictual characteristics, accompanied by the fragmentation and incoherence of the international mechanisms that impact on seeds in one way or another, make seeds and genetic resources a prime – and contested – candidate for attention by the CFS.

Sustainable models of production

Defending peoples' access to resources is intimately connected with using them judiciously. Awareness has progressively spread, among rural social movements, of the need to combine three elements: people's access to land and other resources, defense of small-scale peasant family farming as a mode of production, and sustainable production models. We have spoken in Chapters 2 and 3 about the agro-ecological approaches that rural social movements and their civil society allies oppose to industrial agriculture. Local experimentation in this area often includes recuperating and building on traditional practices, many of which were frowned upon by Western agronomists or pushed into a corner by large-scale industrial farming. Among the myriad examples, we can cite intercropping, whereby different crops are planted in the same plot at the same time to protect against pests (since different plants are subject to attacks by different insects) and to ensure ground cover and fight against soil erosion (since different plants are harvested at different times). Intercropping is highly adapted to difficult environments like the Sahel, yet it was denounced under colonialism as an illustration of the lazy and messy farming habits of the "natives".

"Truly sustainable peasant agriculture", in LVC's terms, "comes from a combination of the recovery and revalorization of traditional peasant farming methods, and the innovation of new ecological practices." Simply substituting "good" inputs or practices for "bad" ones does not suffice. "The application of these principles in the complex and diverse realities of peasant agriculture requires the active appropriation of farming systems by peasants ourselves, using our local knowledge, ingenuity, and ability to innovate" (Rosset and Martinez-Torres 2012, p. 2). African small-scale producers adopt similar language when they define family farming as a mode of production "that allows for working in harmony with the environment by respecting the principles of sustainability based on agro-ecological methods of production" (EAFF, PROPAC, ROPPA 2011 p. 6).

Such synergy between peasant family farming as a *mode* of production and sustainable *methods* of production is not automatic, particularly when peasant farmers are operating under the pressure of poverty and insecure access to resources. Rural social movements are placing increased emphasis on ensuring that they move together. Case studies document how this is taking place in countries around the world (Ecumenical Advocacy Alliance 2012; FAO 2013a). Attention is moving to look not only at how to apply sustainable approaches in specific sites but also at how to promote their scaling-up and broad-based transitions from unsustainable to sustainable agriculture and food production (www.ag-transition.org). The experience of the National Association of Small Farmers (ANAP) in Cuba, stimulated by the US blockade that restricted availability of chemical inputs, constitutes one of the most extensive examples of this kind of process. In the decade from 1997 to

2007, ANAP promoted a grassroots movement that extended agro-ecological integrated and diversified farming systems to about one-third of the peasant families of the country. By 2008 peasants applying agro-ecological approaches produced more than 50 percent of the major food items while holding just 27 percent of the farmland. The greater the level of agro-ecological integration on farms, data demonstrated, the greater the total value of production both per worker and per hectare (Rosset et al. 2011, p. 177). Brazil has a long and solid experience in agro-ecology launched in the 1980s by committed researchers and NGOs like AS-PTA and progressively adopted by rural social movements. Here the government has adopted a National Policy and a $4 billion National Plan for Agroecology and Organic Production with the participation of peasant family farm organizations, the landless movement, agricultural workers, and other sectors of civil society (Agricultures 2012; Petersen et al. 2013). In Asia Bhutan is getting set to beat Cuba to it and become the world's first 100 percent organic country (Fiedler 2013). In countries throughout Asia and Africa the "system of rice intensification" (SRI) is upstaging Monsanto's widely publicized GMO "golden rice", which we debunked in Chapter 2. Based on observation and adaption of villagers' upland rice cultivation techniques in Madagascar, the SRI as applied in drought-prone Bihar, India has produced 30–40 percent increase in yields using less seeds, less water, no herbicides, and no genetic modification (Vidal 2013).

Agro-ecological approaches like organic farming are being applied not only in rural areas but also in the important movement for urban agriculture that is gaining force in cities throughout the world, from the Bay area of Oakland, California (Food Think Tank 2013), to Rosario, Argentina (Polis 2010), to polluted Bangkok (Bangkok Post 2013). And climate change is also contributing to place agro-ecology in the limelight. As the *Image of Africa* report we cited in Chapter 3 documented, family farmers in Africa have been dealing with an unfriendly climate for as long as they can remember. The severe drought of the mid-1980s prompted farmers' associations to capitalize on traditional techniques and develop new ones that are proving their worth as climatic conditions become more severe. The zai system in Northern Burkina Faso, which involves digging holes in the dry season, placing a small amount of manure in them and then waiting for the rainy season to sow seeds in order to take full advantage of the moisture, is an example. A study conducted in Nicaragua following Hurricane Mitch in 1998 demonstrated that farming plots cropped with simple agro-ecological methods (including rock bunds or dikes, green manure, crop rotation and the incorporation of stubble, ditches, terraces, barriers, mulch, legumes, trees, plowing parallel to the slope, no-burn, live fences, and zero-tillage) had on average 40 percent more topsoil, higher field moisture, less erosion, and lower economic losses than control plots on conventional farms. On average, agro-ecological plots lost 18 percent less arable land to landslides than conventional plots and had 69 percent less gully erosion compared to conventional farms (De Schutter 2010d; Holt-Giminez 2002). Family farmers are not waiting for scientists and development experts to give them the answers. A seminar on food sovereignty policies in the context of climate change organized by the peasant network ROPPA in Niger in December 2012 provided an occasion for peasant platforms to exchange experience and to dialogue with researchers and decision makers on their own terms (ROPPA 2012b).

As noted in Chapter 2, over the past years a robust literature has accumulated demonstrating the beneficial effects of smallholder agro-ecological production modes and their ability to produce sufficient good food to feed the world (Pretty et al. 2006; De Schutter 2010d, IAASTD 2009; McKay 2012). It is progressively making inroads in institutional worlds. When the IPC tried to push agro-ecology in FAO following the 2002 World Food Summit as one of the pillars of the action plan for food sovereignty, the initiative encountered difficulties since the staff working to promote alternatives to the dominant industrial model were relatively few and were operating in a position of marginality (McKeon 2009, pp. 80–81). A decade later, a major FAO publication summoning up the strength of all the relevant technical units contrasted agro-ecological systems with technological agro-chemical interventionist approaches, with the former coming out on top (FAO 2011a). FAO has teamed up with the African Union and the International Foundation for Organic Agriculture (IFOAM) to promote mainstreaming of organic agriculture into the African development agenda (FAO 2013a). The 2013 UNCTAD Trade and Environment Report concludes that "a paradigm shift in agricultural development is needed: from conventional, monoculture-based and high external-input-dependent industrial production towards mosaics of sustainable, regenerative production systems that also considerably improve the productivity of small-scale farmers" (UNCTAD 2013, p. ii). Yet despite the by now undeniable evidence in favor of agro-ecological production approaches, the stakes are so high when agro-ecology confronts the economic interests of corporate industrialized agriculture that it is a fight to get the very term on the agenda at the CFS.

Appropriate markets

If the accumulated evidence of the benefits of agro-ecological peasant farming is massive, well documented, and backed up by analysis and theory, the same cannot be said for markets that are alternative to the globalized corporate-led value chains reviewed in Chapter 2. This is not to imply that there is nothing out there. Where denunciation is concerned, the food sovereignty movement and the rural peoples' organizations who are its backbone have opposed liberalization of agricultural trade through the WTO and bilateral trade agreements (BTAs) from the very outset. Their impact has been appreciable considering the stakes, particularly in terms of raising awareness on the part of their bases and of the public at large.

Social movement mobilization and advocacy contributed significantly to stalling the WTO Doha Round on agricultural issues. On some occasions they have helped to counter the even more pernicious impacts of bilateral trade agreements, particularly in the case of the EU's Economic Partnership Agreements (McKeon

2008). They have clearly and repeatedly highlighted the absurdity of a market system in which rules for agricultural commerce are fixed at global level despite the fact that only some 10 percent of agricultural products transit through the global market. They have censured the outcomes that result when global market prices are visited on the national and local scene to the detriment of local producers and food security. They have critiqued the way in which global policies and conditionalities have obliged states in the Global South to dismantle instruments with which they previously protected and managed their internal markets, like supply management and reserves. There is a solid bibliography of articulate, well-documented denunciation of the global "free" market. It ranges from thoughtful academic questioning like the works referred to in Chapter 2 (Weis 2007; Clapp 2012) to courageous position-taking by UN figures like the Special Rapporteur on the Right to Food's reports on how the WTO ignores food security (De Schutter 2008 and 2009c) to popular mobilization by global campaigns like those denouncing dumping of surplus European and US products on defenseless African markets.

In more propositional terms, there is, of course, vast experience of different kinds of markets throughout the world, but it has not been as thoroughly documented and theorized as have alternative production approaches. Chapter 2 cited multiple examples of emerging alternative marketing arrangements in the Global North that bridge the distance between producers and consumers in those regions of the world where supermarkets have established their hegemony and the process of distancing the first and final actors of the food system is most advanced. Here it is often a question of reconstructing local markets that had come close to disappearing, although they have resisted more successfully in many European countries than in the United States. Learning that not all lettuce was cellophane-wrapped iceberg was one of the delightful discoveries I made when I moved from Chicago to Rome in the 1970s. Food and agriculture workers in the Global North, another important constituency in the food system, are also actively building their "piece" of the movement. The US Food Sovereignty Alliance started life in October 2010 with a march in support of striking restaurant workers in the French Quarter district of New Orleans. The Coalition of Immokalee Workers, founded in 1993 by a small group of exploited tomato pickers in Florida, is an iconic example of how powerful political mobilization and intelligent alliance building can take on even the bigs of the food business.

BOX 5.3
A PENNY A POUND, PLUS POWER: THE COALITION
OF IMMOKALEE WORKERS CHANGES HISTORY

For most tomato pickers in the US, a bucket brings in 50 cents, a piece rate that has remained virtually unchanged for more than 30 years. Because the rate is set so low, a worker has to pick more than two and a quarter tons of tomatoes per day – the weight of a young elephant – to make the minimum wage.

Until 2005, no restaurant or grocery chain had ever taken responsibility for the fact that its profits played a role in creating such deplorable conditions and wages. When gross mistreatment of workers periodically made its way into the public eye, if anyone at all took the rap, it was the crew leader who managed the workers. Corporations who reaped the profits remained untouched. In this way, the system had been protected against any real change.

The Coalition of Immokalee Workers (CIW) is transforming all of this. In 2005, after a four-year boycott against Taco Bell, CIW won its first major victory when Taco Bell's parent corporation, Yum! Brands, agreed to pay a penny more per pound for their tomatoes. If paid by all major buyers, this seemingly small increase would nearly double farmworker wages.

"Labor is such a small percentage of the overall cost of getting food out from the field to the table," Greg Asbed, a CIW co-founder, told us. "Farm labor wages could be increased 100 percent and the consumer wouldn't even notice the difference." . . .

Beyond fast food chains, the CIW has convinced the natural grocery-store giants Whole Foods and Trader Joe's and food-service companies to sign similar agreements. In 2010, the Coalition won a commitment from the Florida Tomato Growers Exchange, which includes 90 percent of the state's tomato growers, to pass along the penny-per-pound bonus to farmworkers. Workers picking for farms that sell to participating retail companies receive the penny per pound bonus as a line item in their weekly paycheck. Since 2011, due to these agreements, more than $10 million have flowed from buyers, through farmers, into workers' paychecks.

Beyond increasing wages, the contracts require companies to sign onto the Fair Food Program, governed by a Code of Conduct. In each of these agreements, CIW actively participates in upholding the code, monitoring and reporting working conditions at farms, and conducting worker-to-worker education sessions on the farms on company time.

Bell (2013). Reproduced with permission.

In the regions of the Global South, harking back again to Chapter 2, markets that operate on logics different than that of the capitalist economy are still very much alive. In Africa, as the report by regional producers' networks cited earlier demonstrates, they account for most of the food consumed in the continent but are ignored by official statistics and penalized by development programs and corporate value chains. In cross-border markets in Cameroun traders are prepared to let people buy on credit because most of the producers, traders, and customers involved are well known to each other and trust, social conventions, and informal sanctions tie the system together (EAFF, PROPAC, ROPPA 2013 p. 7). In the Sikasso region of Mali, as in countries across Africa, local village markets where producers sell directly to consumers are by far the most important outlet for family food production and the most significant source of food for people in the region. An innovative initiative, in the same region of Mali, is a people-controlled grain stock exchange, which brings sellers and buyers together in a transparent market, recreating locally the functions of the original futures exchanges before they were distorted by financial speculation (*op.cit.*, pp. 16–17). Access to credit on appropriate terms is an important part of equitable and sustainable marketing and food systems in an era in which public support for agriculture has been practically eliminated by the liberalized market economy. In West Africa storage credit schemes operated by village associations allow family farmers to stock part of the cereal harvest as security for loans to meet immediate monetary needs. Peasant movements like the FONGS in Senegal are experimenting with a range of strategies, from buying into the capital of the national agricultural credit bank in order to influence its policies to setting up a decentralized network of credit houses tied to FONGS member associations (SOS Faim 2013).

In all regions of the world small-scale producers group together in cooperative arrangements of various kinds to seek to establish better market relations by storing and marketing collectively. In some cases these initiatives are sucked into the global value chain logic even when they start off as expressions of rural producers' movements. In others, however, autonomy is maintained and trust and solidarity play an important role. The Keenkenyoike Market and Slaughterhouse in Kenya is an example of a collective marketing initiative in the pastoralist world that combines affective and economic dimensions. Founded in 1981 without external support, the enterprise is self-organized and administered by elders of the Maasai pastoralist communities. Today the market trades more than 250 cattle per day and the slaughterhouse processes 160 per day. It offers its members 30 percent more for their livestock than in competing markets as well as social insurance mechanisms for the community (PROCASUR 2012). Halfway across the world, the island Republic of Palau affords another example of how economic activities need not be incompatible with other values. "The changes in Palauan agriculture reflect not a dichotomy between 'traditional' versus 'modern', but rather show a difference in orientation: is a farm 'profit-oriented' or 'family-oriented'? Is it focused on sales, or on services? Elements of commercialism can exist in harmony with traditional values; yet unbridled commercialization will render the 'family' in farming meaningless" (Bishop 2013). The Palau family farmers are working on establishing their version of a market, a multipurpose and multifunctional site called "the Meeting Place" that will act as a type of regional food hub as well as a center for training, strategizing, and building relationships.

An example from Colombia illustrates what can be done to promote people-friendly markets even under highly unfavorable conditions.

BOX 5.4
PEASANT FARMERS' MARKETS IN COLOMBIA

Since the late 1940s Colombia has had a long string of what may arguably be the most anti-peasant governments in the world. . . . How then did Colombian peasant organizations – some of whom are members of La Via Campesina, and others that are allies – together with nuns who promote ecological farming, and academic researchers in the city, win a very good public policy in the capital of Bogotá to promote peasant farmers' markets?

In the mid-2000s, the mayor's office wanted to restructure the distribution of fresh produce in the capital by creating a series of "inter-nodal" transfer point markets between rural agribusiness and giant super-markets chains. It looked like the peasants who had traditionally supplied Bogotá's wholesale markets with produce were about to be squeezed out of business. But the rural-urban coalition alluded to above put forth a counter-proposal, by which the city government should open and support ten new peasant farmers' markets. The mayor's office balked, saying that the peasants would turn the city's beautiful plazas into "shanty towns." But pressure tactics got them to accept one trial market. Much to their shock, the peasants were orderly and well organized, and urban consumers, starved for quality fresh produce, loved it. Between these good results and new mayoral elections, the city government reversed its position and agreed to open various markets. By 2010, some 2,500 peasant families were doing more than USD 2 million in annual business.

One goal of this peasant initiative was to have markets in neighborhoods of all social classes, and to always have agreed upon prices that are lower than supermarket prices, yet still very profitable for farmers because of the lack of middlemen. They have achieved that. Another goal was to change the stigmatization of peasants in the eyes of city dwellers as subversives to be eliminated to that of valued and trusted producers of healthy and affordable food. Surveys have shown that this change of image is indeed taking root. They wanted to use the markets to organize peasants and give them political training. So when they come to sell in Bogota they receive seminars on the public policy process, and have returned to their rural townships to demand farmers' markets there as well, and they have organized themselves in associations to share the cost of transport, which have in many cases successfully pressured rural municipalities to provide trucks to bring produce to market. Finally, the markets helped promote the transition to ecological farming. This has been done in a very clever way. All ecological farmers sell under a big green tent, with an agreement that their prices will be no higher than those of the conventional farmers in the other tents. Not surprisingly, the consumers flock first to the green tent, and only begin to buy in the other tents when everything "green" is sold. The other farmers get curious pretty fast. When they finally express interest in agroecology and ecological farming (which nobody pressures them to do), they are directed to the nuns who set them up with other peasants who become their agroecology mentors. . . .

In many of our own countries we feel a sense of hopelessness with regard to ever achieving policies to promote food sovereignty. Our governments just seem too hostile to peasants and too much in bed with agribusiness and supermarket chains like Walmart and Carrefour. When we feel that way, we should reflect on the experience of Bogotá. Surely if that's possible in Colombia, of all places, we should be able to do something anywhere.

Nyéléni (2013). 'Peasant Farmers' Markets in Colombia'. Nyéléni Newsletter No. 13. Reproduced with permission

Other market forms do without money altogether. Barter markets in the Peruvian Andes provide multiple benefits for their participants without pesos changing hands. In the middle area of the valley of Lares-Yanatile in Cusco a barter market is held every week, where nearly fifty tons of goods are traded each market day – ten times the volume of food distributed by the National Program of Food Assistance. The benefits of the Andean barter markets, governed by a decentralized web of local organizations, are multiple. They facilitate access to food security and nutrition by some of the poorest social groups in the Andes. They help conserve agricultural biodiversity through continued use and exchange of food crops. They contribute to maintenance of ecosystem services and landscape features. They ensure local, autonomous control over production and consumption and, in particular, control by women over key decisions that affect both local livelihoods and ecological processes (Pimbert 2009, p. 4). Lest the Peruvian example seem a folkloristic nod to past practices, we can note that in the United States the barter market amounts to $12 million annually and is growing steadily (Spitznagel 2012).

Examples like these from all parts of the world could be multiplied almost endlessly. Anyone who has set foot anywhere in the Global South – or elsewhere in the world where supermarkets and shopping centers have not squashed neighborhood commerce – knows that "traditional" markets are where the action is: the sites not only of exchange or purchase of basic goods but also of social transactions and identities. Some of the strongest memories I have retained from four decades of frequentation of the Global South involve markets: the weekly market in the deep south of Ethiopia where everyone was in their place – except for me, the first white person the children had ever seen and the object of benign but intense astonishment. Or waking in a guest house on the edge of a market in Mumbai and, well before consciousness informed me, knowing from the smells that I was Asia and not in Africa. This reappropriation not only of economic benefits but also of cultural diversities and social relations is a good part of what is going on in the farmers' markets and community-supported agriculture of the Global North. Yet not enough has been done on the terrain of markets to challenge the dominant paradigm, bringing practice and reflection together. This is understandable since, as we have seen in Chapter 2, the naturalized "free" market is the kingpin of the neoliberal world order.

Some surmise that the food sovereignty movement may have initially tended to denounce "the market" rather than to seek to recuperate it as a basic aspect of human life that has been co-opted by capitalism but need not be. To prove his point Canadian historian Jim Handy draws on Fernand Braudel's discussion of the economy of preindustrial Europe, characterized by three sectors or levels. The ground floor is one of extremely elementary "non-economy", the soil into which capitalism can never really penetrate. Then comes day-to-day economic life, or what we call the "market economy". And above that the zone of the "anti-market, where the great predators roam – the real home of capitalism", which, in Braudel's analysis, has been monopolistic and oligopolistic from the very outset. Handy notes perspicaciously that the peasant dispossession decried by food sovereignty "is not a product of the functioning of markets but rather of the perversion of markets through capitalism operating in the 'anti-market'. Food sovereignty, then, is radical not because of a rejection of the market but rather because of its dream of ending enclosure and dispossession at the hands of capital" (Handy 2013, p. 2). The natural enemies of the anti-market, he concludes, are peasant production and the intimacy of the market, and it is these that need to be strengthened.

As compared with the density of reflection about models of agriculture and modes of production, there is relatively little reflection – beyond affirmation of the need to prioritize and protect local markets – on how markets could and should be built in order to serve the needs and respect the rights of people. This is dangerous since the peasant family farm mode coupled with sustainable agro-ecological models of production requires markets that are appropriate to their characteristics in order to flourish. Specifying what it is that makes them appropriate is essential to avoid simply coupling small-scale producers like carriages to the engine of value chains, or co-opting the technicalities of organic farming and puffing them up into hypermarket green brands. It is also necessary in order to respond to what Harriet Friedmann, one of the pioneers of food regime analysis, calls the "price paradox" – the meeting point of producers who need good livelihoods and eaters who need affordable prices – which is naturalized by the role of markets as configured in capitalism (Friedmann 2013). The African farmers' organizations' Synthesis Report, which we have cited on several occasions, is a rare and rich source of such reflection coming from the world of social movements themselves.

The association Crocevia conducts an analysis of internal markets and peasant agriculture rooted in the reality of Italy, where it is still the dominant form. They note that, in the "modern" phase of agricultural development, the way in which the market is organized has a determining impact on the modes of production that can be adopted. As long ago as 1958, FAO recognized that "modern marketing is difficult without modern production. Attempts to transplant a marketing system developed to handle the specialized output of commercial farmers into a rural community quite different in character and outlook may only lead to difficulties" (FAO 1958, p. 3). Peasant, family-based production cannot be maintained unless it is coupled with a different, autonomous trade system, a different way of circulating food products and creating jobs along the way. This will not happen by chance. It is not a question simply of multiplying initiatives like farmers' markets. Building "appropriate trade" for small-scale food producers requires decentralizing the encounter between food supply and demand. Guarantees for consumers in terms of quality and convenience must be ensured. Collective rights covering natural resources are a necessary component. A trade system and local markets of proximity that are appropriate to family-based peasant agriculture have to be consciously constructed and supported by specific and differentiated public instruments, rules, and policies. Key issues to address are who controls the value chain, production costs, and producers' prices and market power (Onorati 2014). In the Global North, as in the Global South, these conditions cannot be ensured in the absence of measures to control importations and global supply (Paffetti and Amelio 2013).

In the academic world the work on "nested markets" seems to be the most pertinent to social movement concerns. Drawing on extensive field observation in Latin America, Europe, and Asia, Dutch rural sociologist Jan Douwe van der Ploeg characterizes the phenomenon of newly emerging markets as a reaction to developments in the main markets for agricultural commodities. The increasing gap between producer and consumer prices, with the intermediaries along the chain taking outsized profits, creates the *space* for alternatives to be developed. *Levers* for doing so are provided by the "possibilities to counter distance with proximity, artifice with freshness, anonymity with identity and genuineness, standardization with diversity and inequality with fairness". And the unsatisfactory nature of dominant market conditions creates a *need* for primary producers to construct new markets (van der Ploeg et al. 2012 p. 139). The normative frameworks in which these new markets are embedded (or "nested") are rooted in the social movements or the policy programs from which they emerge. They are grounded in local and regional resources and prioritize local and regional outlets. They are often supported by state agencies and involve the redistribution of resources to achieve specific agreed objectives. They are not centrally controlled but can link up whenever the need to do so arises. "Together the *specificities of place, product and network* (especially when knit together into a coherent whole) compose a nested market" (*op.cit.*, p. 141). Such markets need not be doomed to a niche existence. Under the pressure of trends like resource scarcity, climate change, and the food crisis, a scaling-up transition could be envisioned under the right conditions (Brunori 2011).

Seeking to move beyond a dichotomous distinction between "good" and "bad" food circuits and products, van der Ploeg proposes four leading questions that can be used to contrast different approaches to the politico-economic organization of markets, expressed in Table 5.1. This approach is just as appropriate to the defense and strengthening of existing local markets in the Global South as to the construction of new ones in the Global North. Bringing voices of theorization like these into dialectic rapport with the experiences of people is one of the key messages for the future, and we will come back to it in the concluding section.

TABLE 5.1 A schematic comparison of the general agricultural and food markets and the newly emerging markets

	General agricultural and food markets	Newly emerging markets
Who owns what?	Most linkages between production, processing, distribution and consumption of food are controlled by food empires	These short circuits are owned or co-owned by farmers
Who does what?	The role of farmers is limited to the delivery of raw materials for the food industry	The role of farmers is extended to embrace on-farm processing, direct selling and the redesign of production processes that better meet consumers' expectations
Who gets what?	The distribution of value added is highly skewed; most wealth is accumulated in food empires	Farmers get a higher share of the total value added
What is done with the surpluses?	Accumulated wealth is used to finance the ongoing imperial conquest (take-over of other enterprises, etc.)	Extra income is used to increase the resilience of food production, to strengthen multifunctional farming and to improve livelihood

Source: van der Ploeg et al. (2012). "Rural Development through the Construction of New, Nested Markets: Comparative Perspectives from China, Brazil and the European Union". *Journal of Peasant Studies*, p. 142. Reproduced with permission.

Research and knowledge

This reflection leads us quite naturally into a fourth important, transversal area in which concrete experiences of alternative ways of doing things are being conducted, that of research and knowledge. When I joined FAO in the late 1960s, my first assignment took me frequently to the photo archive hunting for images to illustrate reports on village level agricultural projects. The archive, I discovered, was full of photos like the one in Figure 5.2 with captions that read more or less like this: "Mr. So and So, FAO expert, and his counterpart demonstrate modern agricultural techniques to the peasants of such and such a country". It didn't take me long to decipher the message that was being conveyed. The people with the knowledge were the expert (white, male, identified by name) and his counterpart (male but dark-skinned, nameless but with a partial identity due to his relationship with the expert). The peasants (they too all male for the purposes of the photograph) were an amorphous mass of passive spectators or, at best, apprentices. The incongruity of this

FIGURE 5.2 Agriculture extension in the 1970s

message with the rural world I was beginning to discover was a trigger for a search to seek better ways of understanding and acting on reality.

It was a good time for this. The political excitement of 1968 was in the air, along with the enthusiasm of independence for many ex-colonies. Brazilian educator and philosopher Paulo Freire's work on "education as the practice of freedom" was turning traditional approaches to extension on their heads, highlighting the political dimensions of knowledge (or conscientization), and stressing the dialectic between practice and reflection (or praxis). Freire was associated with FAO through the Chilean Institute of Training and Evaluation (ICIRA) in 1968 before moving on in 1969 to a different Harvard University than today's, which gave him hospitality while he finished his masterwork, *The Pedagogy of the Oppressed.* So it was not unthinkable that the FAO program in which I worked could be in the vanguard of the creative flourishing of alternative ideas and action that characterized the period prior to the triumph of neoliberalism (McKeon 2009, p. 20). The Participatory Research Network formed in 1977 brought together engaged academics and practitioners seeking to help create popular knowledge rooted in communities and workplaces in order to empower the people directly concerned to act for structural transformations in their conditions of life (Hall 1981). More specific focus on agriculture and rural development emerged from development practitioners and researchers who were becoming increasingly frustrated with the top-down, technological package-oriented mainstream approaches to agricultural development epitomized by Green Revolution programs in Asia and the Training and Visit (T&V) approach to extension applied by the World Bank. Paul Richard's *Indigenous Agricultural Revolution* (1985) critiqued the notion of peasant ignorance and meticulously documented how research and development institutions fail to see the most effective innovations that take place, in farmers' fields outside the realm of formal science and laboratories. The "Farmer First workshop" held at the Institute of Development Studies in the United Kingdom in 1987 launched what became a highly popular current of work linked to the name of Robert Chambers. In the French-speaking world the "animation rurale" approach pioneered by IRAM promoted a bottom-up empowerment strategy similar to that of Freire's in newly independent French-speaking ex-colonies in Africa. Later on researchers associated with institutes like CIRAD, ORSTOM, CNRS, and GRET developed approaches that were open to confronting the logic of projects with that of peasants and to building more horizontal exchanges with the latter (Boiral et al. 1985).

The changing environment from the 1980s on, with the growing dominance of neoliberal policies and concentration of power in the global food system, curtailed the space for peasant knowledge. Participatory rural appraisal (PRA) methods born from a Farmer First approach have tended to become a-politicized or, worse, retooled into management tools for making it appear that investment projects fit more closely into the rural communities on which they impact (Mulvany and Moreira 2008). I witnessed this in FAO in the 1990s. What began as a diffuse, enthusiastic buy-in to participatory approaches by people throughout the organization who met over lunch to plot about changing the way things were done in our areas of work became the organizational "property" of a specific department, bringing it visibility, a budget line, and an injunction to apply the usual soulless institutional "toolkit approach" to mainstreaming. At the same time, the introduction of intellectual property rights has facilitated a takeover of agricultural research by the corporate sector, which now accounts for a good proportion of all agricultural research conducted and has bought its way also into the Consortium on International Agriculture Research (CGIAR) system, in theory public sector although administered by the World Bank (McKeon 2011a). The results are documented in a fascinating study on "how agricultural research systems shape a technological regime that develops genetic engineering but locks out agroecological innovations" (Vanloqueren and Baret 2009). The accreditation of genetic engineering and the relative indifference to agro-ecological innovation in the research community is the end result of interactions among the many factors that play a role in orienting agricultural research, from the values and worldviews of scientists to the focus on growth and competitiveness in todays' research policies, the tendency toward specialization rather than interdisciplinarity, the imbalance in the power of lobbies, and many more. "Genetic engineering, a technological paradigm that is well suited to scientific reductionism, is more successful in this technological regime than agroecological engineering, a paradigm that questions mainstream approaches within agricultural research" (*op.cit.*, p. 981).

Yet bottom-up alternatives to official research and knowledge approaches continue to emerge against all odds. The 2008 report of the International Assessment of Agricultural Knowledge, Science, and Technology for Development (IAASTD), launched by the World Bank and FAO in 2002 and involving more than eight hundred participants from relevant stakeholder groups, acknowledges:

> For many years, agricultural science focused on delivering component technologies to increase farm-level productivity.... But, given the new challenges we confront today, there is increasing recognition within formal Science & Technology organizations that the current agricultural knowledge, science and technology (AKST) model requires revision. Business as usual is no longer an option. . . . Once AKST is directed simultaneously toward production, profitability, ecosystem services and food systems that are site-specific and evolving, then formal, traditional and local knowledge need to be integrated.
> (IAASTD 2008, p. 3)

The IAASTD initiative was deserted by multinational corporations when they realized that the emerging evidence was in support of agro-ecological approaches rather than GMOs. The report was not endorsed by some governments like the United States and the United Kingdom that are closely linked to corporate interests and the dominant paradigm. Even its original promoters, the World Bank and FAO, refrain from referring to it. But it has provided authoritative support for approaches that were pioneered and are being followed by peasant-led or peasant-friendly action research and training activities in all regions of the world.

The best way to guard against institutional co-optation of people-centered research and training, my FAO experience taught me, is ownership by the concerned peoples' organizations themselves rather than by well-meaning researchers. The FONGS in Senegal has been engaged in participatory research from the mid-1980s on. The need to address the serious problem of soil infertility in the overexploited groundnut basin of Central Senegal led to a fruitful investigation and amelioration of peasant practices facilitated by an NGO team (ENDA 1987). Four years later a full-fledged approach to peasant-led investigation of an entire *terroir* (territory) had been developed, and farmer field schools were being pioneered in West Africa (Jacolin et al. 1991). By the mid-1990s the FONGS had integrated these approaches into its ongoing program, and the newly born national peasant platform was dialoguing with the national Institute of Agricultural Research. During a session on sustainable agriculture, which I helped to organize in 1995, the peasant animators facilitating the work thought nothing of dispatching someone to fetch a technician from the government research and extension service – previously regarded from the position of subordination illustrated in the FAO photo reproduced above – to respond on the spot to questions raised by participants. Four years later the peasant platform became a major actor in the national agencies for research and for rural training and advice, newly designed – thanks to their pressure –

to be more responsive and accountable to producers (McKeon et al. 2004, p. 17). It is this kind of appropriation over time that has enabled the authoritative peasant-led research on family farming in Senegal referred to in Chapter 2 and earlier in this chapter to build up its capacity to challenge industrial agriculture paradigms.

A similar patient trajectory has been followed in Brazil, where a national NGO founded in 1983, AS-PTA, has been working for three decades on campesino-led action-research, which has helped to build a powerful national movement promoting agro-ecology and opposing the use of GMOs. In Central America what came to be known as the "campesino-to-campesino movement" originated in the 1980s when Mayan campesinos in Guatemala pioneered methods of soil and water conservation and farmer-to-farmer pedagogy. Sharing them first with each other and then with small-scale farmers in Mexico, they developed effective practices of agro-ecosystem management, nonhierarchical communication, and local social change that eventually spread throughout the region (Holt-Giminez 2006).

The food sovereignty movement has provided a global framework for such experience. The action plan of the 2007 Nyéléni Food Sovereignty Conference included a strong plank on local knowledge:

> We … will identify local, collective, and diverse experiences and practices, as examples, recognising that they are ever changing and dynamic – not static – and gather strength through exchange and solidarity. … We will fight against all forms of intellectual property over life and knowledge, including the privatization and patenting of traditional wisdoms associated with food production. … We will support research that is done by the people themselves and their local organisations, that strengthens food sovereignty and helps preserve productive land, water, seeds and livestock.
>
> (Nyéléni 2007, p. 6)

Innovative ways in which aspirations like these can be put into practice are illustrated by independent farmer-led assessments of public research on plant breeding and the management of agro-biodiversity undertaken by "citizen juries" in West Africa, South and West Asia, and the Andean region in the context of an international initiative promoting "citizens rethinking food and agricultural research for the public good" (Pimbert et al. 2010). A range of other initiatives are evoked in a recent issue of the newsletter of the food sovereignty movement, Nyéléni, dedicated to "creating knowledge for food sovereignty". These include the encounters between activists and engaged academics in Yale and The Hague referred to in Chapter 3 and the experiment of the CFS's High-Level Panel of Experts, which welcomes the knowledge of social actors and practitioners. Some of the most interesting come from the world of indigenous peoples, who have been playing a more assertive role in the food sovereignty movement over the past few years and "whose epistemologies question the mechanistic worldview of positivist science". The editorial notes the need to challenge academic knowledge but also to be open to being challenged by it. Willingness to listen, the value attached to diversity, the constant attention to rooting knowledge creation in experience and to the human qualities and values of the people who give breath to it: these are among the characterizing elements of this movement to "radically transform dominant knowledge and ways of knowing":

> To develop knowledge for food sovereignty we need to be humble and respectful of other voices and perspectives. We need to be bold in order to experiment with methods and ideas that may seem "unscientific", while also working to demonstrate the quality in our inquiry processes. We need to be playful in order to move lightly through the many obstacles on this path while keeping our curiosity alive. With these challenges in mind, one research question emerges which we invite you to join us in reflecting on: How do we nurture the human qualities that we need in order to develop knowledge, together, for food sovereignty?
>
> (Rahmanian and Pimbert 2014, p. 1)

Taking on Goliath

What could help build the political clout of the myriad local peoples' practices summarily referred to above to the point where they could effectively call governments to account and take on the Goliath of corporate power? This is the million-dollar question, but some parts of the answer are fairly self-evident. The cornerstone of a winning strategy, as we have seen it emerging from the examples we have reviewed, is that of maintaining the autonomy and the identity of the "alternative" experiences and models and resisting the strong pull toward co-optation into the economics and the discourse of the dominant food system. Building on this bottom line, important contributions to a winning strategy can come from capacity building, linking small-scale producers with other sectors of their societies, transnational networking – both horizontal and vertical – alliance building, and interacting with governance spaces at different levels.

Building capacity and alliances – who and how?

The primary agents of alternatives are peoples' organizations and social movements, and one imperative is that of helping them strengthen their capacities to resist, propose, and mobilize. But how, with the help of whom, and on what terms? "Capacity building" has become a buzzword in the development establishment. Strengthening rural peoples' organizations (POs) has become a relatively frequent component of development cooperation programs. The problem, as thoughtful World Bank, IFAD, and FAO staff themselves admit, is that "when we succeed in developing projects that support peoples' organizations we tend to reinforce those functions of the POs that are most in line with the mandate of our agencies and our vision of development, and thus risk downgrading the essential more political functions they perform" (McKeon and Kalafatic 2009, p. 10). When movement building is dependent on project funding, donor conditionalities are the order of the day, although they are often disguised as technical or administrative "necessities" (McKeon et al 2004, pp. 51–52; McKeon 2009, pp. 177–178). Oodles of money may be available for establishing cooperatives that reliably feed value chains, and little or none for strengthening local markets or supporting peasant-operated training programs. Governments have been known to create their own docile national farmer networks, in competition with autonomous ones, with support from aid programs. Under cover of "coordination" donor partners club up and occupy the space of interaction with national or regional authorities, crowding out national actors and their legitimate negotiation with their governments.

Fortunately there are some partners, mostly NGOs, who have built long-term relations of complicity with emerging peasant movements and are willing to take on the challenge of profoundly transforming traditional donor-recipient relations into ones of solidarity. There is also a growing interest in the food sovereignty agenda on the part of engaged academics that opens perspectives of support for strengthening the analytic capacity of the movement's components to strategize and to turn their experience into evidence. Social movements need to be able to autonomously design their training efforts in order to meet priorities like that of building networks of leadership capable of playing their political and organizational roles in a fashion that promotes control from the base up. In the long term, solutions to resource mobilization for capacity building are to be found, on the one hand, in successful action by small-scale producers' organizations to help their members enhance their livelihoods and defend their autonomy from debt-inducing value chains, so that they are in a position to contribute to the costs of their organizations. On the other hand, they lie in pressuring national and regional governments to make available to smallholder food production and local food systems the share of public funding that they merit. We will return to this in the next chapter when we discuss how the issue of investment in agriculture is being treated in the Committee on World Food Security.

A second challenge in terms of heightening the political weight of alternative food initiatives is that of going beyond the initial peasant producer focus of food sovereignty and building links among different pieces of movements within a same society. This is a central message of *Food Movement Unite!*, a composite presentation of food movement experiences published by the California-based organization Food First (Holt-Giminez, 2011). Efforts in this direction are underway in all regions. The "Africa Can Feed Itself" campaign, launched by the West African peasant network ROPPA, binds small-scale producers together with urban consumers in defense of foods that form part of the cultural heritage and identity of the region and the basis of its domestic food economy. These products are under siege from low-cost and frequently low-quality imports from abroad, often introduced under cover of food aid. The campaign translates from communication into concrete actions like local cereals processed by rural women into forms that their urban sisters can cook more easily or the introduction of products like bread made from 30–50 percent locally produced millet flour. Fiercely horizontal organizations like Urgenci, discussed in Chapter 2, promote links between specific groups of producers and consumers around common objectives grounded in their shared territories. Food sovereignty alliances and committees have sprung up at the national level in countries around the world, bringing together a wide range of associations and initiatives coming at food issues from different directions.

The challenge of building "unity in diversity" is often not an easy one to tackle, as illustrated by the long-term process of bringing "farmers, foodies and first nations" together under the banner of food sovereignty in Canada (Desmarais and Wittman 2013) or the need to take deep-rooted racial issues into account in building a food sovereignty movement in the United States (Detroit Black Community Food Security Network n.d.). Similarly, in the Global South rural social movements are addressing issues of conflicts that arise between different communities and groups of people who share territories, like farmers and pastoralists or indigenous peoples and peasants. These conflicts are often exacerbated, if not caused, by pressures on territories coming from outside, like privatization of common land and other resources. Nonetheless, it is in the interest of the people themselves to find ways "to ensure the peaceful coexistence of diverse communities in territories by strengthening our organizations and multi-sectoral alliances so as to democratically negotiate and share territories" (Nyéléni 2007, p. 3). An illustration of this kind of effort are the dialogues underway in India among the different categories of rural peoples who depend on common resources – peasants, landless, artisanal fisherfolk, pastoralists, dalits, forest indigenous peoples – aimed at overcoming their internal conflicts so that they can fight together against government intentions to give land to corporate farming.[2]

A third dimension of intra-movement relations is that of building transnational links among movements: horizontally among groups in different parts of the world and vertically from local action to global advocacy. Organizational modes that are able to operate effectively globally while respecting egalitarian horizontal exchanges and the autonomy of locally rooted action are the much quested-after holy grail of social movements generally, including the food sovereignty movement. Even the World Social Forum, established as an open, decentralized space for horizontal discussion, has not escaped accusations of falling into the traps of centralized decision making, capture by resource-rich NGOs, and dubious partnerships with the private sector (Holmes 2013). One of the central features that characterizes Via Campesina is the in-principle absence of a policymaking secretariat. "Integral to the functioning of Via Campesina is the absence of a sovereign authority dictating what any member organization or country can do. This suspicion of policies imposed from above is unsurprising within Via Campesina, an organization forged in resistance to autocratic and unaccountable policy making, largely carried out by the World Bank together with local elites" (Patel 2009, p. 669). "One of our internal debates is how to maintain political power at local, national and regional level so as to keep the movement's horizontal structure, albeit at the expense of a certain international efficiency", reports VC leader Paul Nicholson (2012, p. 2). Even so, some critics feel that locally embedded micro-resistance risks being overshadowed by protest summitry and large-scale mobilizations rather than serving as building blocks for global contestation (Ayres and Bosia 2011).

Networking is complicated by issues of who represents whom in the agricultural world, particularly at the global level. The networks we have cited most often in this book – like La Via Campesina and ROPPA – are ones that have a genuine peasant base and share certain important characteristics: they have followed trajectories building from the local level; they focus on attaining benefits for their national and local memberships, to whom they are accountable, and not on achieving global visibility per se; their platforms are based on a broad social, economic, and political vision that goes beyond economic and material claims. In contrast, the global scene is populated with other, less transparent networks whose legitimacy as representatives of small-scale producer movements is questionable. These include organizations like the World Farmers' Organization, where big commercial farmers' organizations of the Global North are dominant but that claims to speak for farmers generally in global policy forums. Another variety of problematic mechanisms are those with hybrid membership including both peoples' organizations and NGOs, or rural producers' organizations and private sector enterprises, or civil society organizations and international institutions. The International Land Coalition (ILC) illustrates this last variety. Housed in IFAD, its membership comprises civil society organizations and intergovernmental institutions including the World Bank, IFAD, and FAO. Abundantly funded, by IFAD and the European Commission in particular, it is able to move quickly to occupy spaces while social movements are painfully organizing and mobilizing resources. As we will see in the next chapter, the ILC is positioning itself as a channel for civil society input to stakeholder negotiation processes regarding land tenure issues, a role that it has no legitimacy to perform (McKeon 2012).

Yet building broader alliances among civil society actors working for change in food systems is essential. With whom, and how? A thoughtful analysis of how the neoliberal and reformist components of support for the corporate food regime stack up against the progressive and radical components of alternative food movements has led some analysts to identify the progressives as "swing actors" who could go either way. They urge more radical food sovereignty movements to forge alliances with the progressive food justice world in order to avoid isolation and to work effectively for regime change (Holt-Giminez and Shattuck 2011). This reading seems to resonate with Via Campesina's own self-assessment on its twentieth anniversary: "Very early on La Via Campesina began forming alliances with other progressive forces in efforts to mobilize a global civil society movement to challenge neoliberal capitalism. Over the years it consolidated strategic alliances with key grass-roots urban-based social movements, other rural movements, progressive non-governmental organizations and other allies" (Desmarais and Nicholson 2013, p. 6). This is not to imply that all is peaches and cream in food movements. Relations between peasant movements and NGOs have tended to be fraught given the longstanding habit of many NGOs of "speaking for" the rural poor and raising funds ostensibly on their behalf. Peoples' organizations are increasingly insisting on speaking for themselves, but big international NGOs continue to conduct high visibility advocacy campaigns on issues that are the life and blood of peasant movements without consulting them or giving visibility to their collective efforts (McKeon 2009, p. 177). We will come back to this issue in the next chapter since the food crisis and the reform of the CFS, by up-scaling food issues into a fertile and remunerative terrain for NGO advocacy, has put a new twist on this behavior.

In order to ground discourse about building alliances in reality, it is worthwhile to cite just a few of the multitude of concrete terrains on which they have been and are being constructed. The international Nyéléni forum on food sovereignty in 1997 provides a truly literal example since it involved the collective physical construction of a meeting place in rural Mali that has since been operated as a training center by the national peasant platform. The organization of the forum represented a deliberate and carefully thought-out effort by La Via Campesina (not without some understandable internal turmoil) to share "ownership" of the concept of food sovereignty and to ensure that it was rooted in and built up from peoples' initiatives throughout the world. The methodology for the selection of the invitees and the organization of the discussions was meticulously planned to give voice to peoples' initiatives. Particularly close NGO allies were co-opted as workers, helping out with tasks like reporting. The forum undoubtedly succeeded in broadening and deepening the concept and practice of food sovereignty and the sense of belonging to a worldwide movement. It is a movement without an institutional governance, since the organizing committee did not perpetuate its existence. It dissolved after the forum into a broader informal group of "involved organizations" responsible for bringing out the Nyéléni Newsletter, which aims to be the voice of the international movement of "hundreds of organisations and movements engaged in struggles, activities and various kinds of work to defend and promote the right of people to Food Sovereignty around the world" (www.nyeleni.org/?lang=en).

The organizational methodology of the IPC network was the inspiration for that of the Nyéléni forum. The IPC has been the main vehicle for global alliance building of social movements and civil society in the area of food and agriculture. We encountered it in Chapters 1 and 4 as the foundation for the involvement of rural peoples' organizations in the reform of the CFS. A self-evaluation conducted in June 2008, soon after the eruption of the food price crisis, identified some of the characteristics that have facilitated the functioning of the IPC as an effective space for social movements. The fact that it operates not as a hierarchical, representative organization but as an autonomous facilitating mechanism was felt to be a fundamental success factor. "Each sector can speak for itself, with no forced consensus as in other UN processes". At the same time, the IPC is not a neutral space. "The political statement of food sovereignty is what we have in common. This allows us to develop common strategies while respecting the voice of each component". Diversity is a recurring term. "Bringing together the different regions and rural producer constituencies makes it possible to get interesting analysis that's not taking place anywhere else". This diversity has also stimulated virtuous behavior changes. The NGOs involved have learned to put their expertise at the service of peoples' organizations. Indigenous peoples, who tend to think of themselves as a separate category, have understood the importance of learning from the struggles of other groups like pastoralists. Strong organizations, like La Via Campesina, cite the IPC as a space that has helped them learn to listen (McKeon 2009, pp. 113–114). The IPC is now restructuring itself to meet the new challenges it faces in the post–food crisis era and to further clarify the different identities and roles of peoples' movements and NGOs (Colombo and Onorati 2013, p. 69).

The EuropAfrica platform (www.europafrica.info) is a more circumscribed illustration of respectful and effective alliance building between regional African small-scale producers' networks and European civil society organizations, not only NGOs but also family farmer organizations and other pieces of food movements. Based on longstanding relations of trust between some European NGOs and the African peasant movement, the EuropAfrica project started off a decade ago with a dialogue that led to a common vision of the model of agriculture and the kind of food systems that the group intended to defend. The dialogue was not among leaders alone. It involved peasant-to-peasant exchanges that, in the words of the first President of ROPPA, did more than a hundred speeches to bring home to African peasants the fact that the conflict is not between North and South but between two different models of agriculture that confront each other around the world. Over the years EuropAfrica has made a significant contribution to fighting the Economic Partnership Agreements (EPAs) through advocacy targeting both the European authorities and the African Regional Economic Commissions responsible for negotiating them. It has facilitated African networks to learn from each other and from the European experience of regional agricultural policies. It has provided a space for building up an intra-African understanding of what models of agriculture and what kinds of food systems feed Africa today and require investment for the future, generating documents that are weighing in on policy decision making in Africa, Europe, and globally (EAFF, PROPAC and ROPPA 2011 and 2013). As in the case of the Nyéléni forum and the IPC, common political objectives, respect for the different roles of peoples' organizations and NGOs, a methodology privileging dialogue, and a nonhierarchical approach to organization have contributed to alliance building. Examples could be multiplied. The Global Campaign on Agrarian Reform launched by La Via Campesina and FIAN in 1999–2000 with a particular view to bringing local land struggles to global attention (Borras 2008) and the more recent Dismantle Corporate Power campaign (www.stopcorporateimpunity. org/) highlight another important characteristic of social movement networking. Mobilization and campaigning is built not on single-minded, centrally determined targets and slogans – "NGO style" – but on the concrete objectives and situations of hundreds and hundreds of local struggles. We will return to these issues of addressing differences in both objectives and methodologies among different segments of the radical and progressive movements when we assess the operations of the CFS Civil Society Mechanism in the next chapter.

Subglobal governance: building upward

For now we will close this chapter by looking at another significant factor in building food governance from the bottom up: that of interaction at different levels between citizen movements and governance spaces. Subnational governance has become an important interface locus. On the one hand, authority to regulate regarding a range of food-related issues has been divested to decentralized authorities in many countries. On the other, local movements are increasingly allying with local governance to challenge hierarchically superior rule makers. This was what was happening in March 2011 when the town of Sedgewick, Maine became the first in the United States to pass a food sovereignty ordinance. In doing so, it declared its citizens' right to produce and sell local foods of their choosing, without the oversight of inhibiting state or federal regulation. The rights asserted here concern not only the interface of personal choice and government oversight, but also broader issues of the organization of food systems. These include "the right to community self-government in matters relating to food, the local spatial scale as a basis on which to organize a food system and, by extension, the need for scale-appropriate regulations for small-scale production for direct sale" (Kurtz et al. 2013, p. 8). There is a vision of territorial self-determination at work here, whereby "societies can be self-governing via their rural producers, agricultural capacities and domestic food needs" (McMichael 2014, p. 2).

Municipal food policy councils are a fast-spreading tool for occupying this strategic space, particularly in countries where urbanization is advanced and there is a strong tradition of citizen involvement in local affairs. The granddaddy of them all is said to be the Knoxville, Tennessee, Food Policy Council founded in 1982 to address the city's failure to provide affordable, nutritious food to all of its residents. Over the past three decades the approach has spread quickly. Whether the initial initiative comes from local government or local citizens, the idea is to bring together all stakeholders in a community food system and give them a say in constructing a system that reflects their values. In the words of the Chair of the Boulder County, Colorado, Food and Agriculture Policy Council, "At first we only had a collection of special interests. But now we have a vision that everyone can share and work for" (Burgan and Winne 2012, p. 5). The United States and Canada have been the most fertile terrain for this kind of initiative thus far. The United Kingdom started to follow suit with the establishment of a Food Policy Council in Brighton in 2011.

Diffusion of community-level food action has been facilitated by the growth of horizontal networking of local authorities and experiences over the past two decades. A Resilient Urban Food Systems Forum in Bonn in June 2013 featured good practices from as far-flung a range of cities in the Global South as Bobo-Dioulasso in Burkina Faso, Kathmandu, Nepal, Kesbewa, Sri Lanka, Dumangas, the Philippines, as well as Belo Orizonte, birthplace of Brazil's Zero Hunger program (Resilient Urban Food Systems 2013). The first "City-Countryside-Organic" Congress, held in Berlin in January 2014, highlighted the important influence

that municipal administrations can have on food, agriculture, and diet by deciding what kind of food is prepared and offered in public canteens, by choosing to
whom to lend public land, and by offering education and information in order
to contribute to well-informed decisions of their citizens on what kind of food
to buy. Municipality of Bogota support for peasant farmer markets cited earlier in
this chapter is an example of what can be achieved by peoples' pressure even in
unpromising circumstances. Subnational regional governance is another level that
lends itself to dynamic interaction between citizens and authorities. In Italy regions
are responsible for many of the important choices made in the implementation
of the European Common Agricultural Policy. In France a complex of region-
ally rooted cultural and regulatory conditions succeeded in limiting the capacity
of supermarkets to restructure fresh fruit and vegetables value chains to their own
advantage and to small-scale producers' disadvantage (Gibbon 2004). Rural peoples'
organizations privilege the regional level as a strategic locus in which to push for
people-centered alternatives based on cooperation and complementarity – including in the field of food provision – rather than competition (Berrón et. al. 2013).

Citizen action at local levels can be more or less politicized, more or less conscious of links between local and global dynamics according to the circumstances.
The Toronto Food Council, one of the most radical and comprehensive in its views,
recently protested against the impacts that the Canada-EU trade agreement (CETA)
will have on sustainable local food systems in Canada and requested the City of
Toronto to seek exemption from its provisions (Baker 2012). Dynamizing the dialectic between the local – where peoples' organizations have direct possibilities of
intervening in policy choice – and other levels can make an important contribution
to building both citizen awareness and more equitable and sustainable global food
governance. A discernable shift is underway, in some cases, from conceiving of scale
in terms of boundaries (local-national-international) to conceiving of it in terms of
relationships. Here "the local is seen as a starting point in the construction of food
sovereignty which must then extend to the regional and national scales" (Schiavoni
2014, p. 11).

The destiny of the nation-state in a context of globalization is the object of
much controversy. We have discussed in Chapter 4 a range of ways in which its
authority in the field of food and agriculture is challenged by international trade
policies, global economic actors, and a wide variety of transnational mechanisms
in which the nation-state is not the basic building block. One analyst of globalization notes that the expansion of global regulatory powers has increased the power
of some of the pieces of the nation-state – notably the executive branch and central banks – over more democratic organs like parliaments.[3] Some go so far as to
maintain that the nation-state is an outworn reality that has lost its functions and
power. Others feel that, on the contrary, "the capacity of the nation-state to mediate between the local and the global is critical to how global pressures enhance or
weaken the rights of local citizens" (Gaventa and Tandon 2010, p. 8). Social movement activists themselves have no doubts about the importance of their interface
with national authorities, for better or for worse, in the present context. Too often

national governments can be accomplices in corporate deals that rob rural people of their land and livelihoods or, worse still, actors of repression of peasant struggles and in these cases they must be strongly contested. In a more positive perspective, they may be pushed to fulfill their responsibility as defenders of their citizens' interests or, at the very least, to exercise accountability. As we will see in the next chapter, a stronger role for the public sphere as against corporate private sector interests is a key component of social movement advocacy around investment in agriculture in the Committee on World Food Security.

Building interface with authorities is a process over time, not a once-off confrontation. The West African peasant movement ROPPA and its national platforms have emphasized from the outset that their own national governments and regional authorities are their primary interlocutors. At the time of the forum in January 1993 that led to the establishment of the national peasant platform in Senegal, the authorities were deaf to any suggestion that rural people might have something to say about the agricultural structural adjustment policies they were negotiating with the World Bank and the IMF. It took all the acumen of the peasant leadership to bring the government to a table that – for once – the peasants themselves had laid.

BOX 5.5
OBLIGING THE GOVERNMENT TO ENGAGE

From dusk to dawn of a night in January 1993 just a few weeks before vociferously contested national elections were to take place, towns and villages throughout Senegal were papered with posters announcing a national forum on "What Future for Senegal's Peasants?", a politically delicate topic since 70 percent of the electorate were rural dwellers drawing their livelihoods from agriculture. Much to the surprise of the President's office, which had ignored the organizers' invitations for weeks, the poster asserted that the President himself would open the Forum. When the farmers' federation responsible for the event was queried on the phone, they replied by taking rhetoric at face value and turning it to their advantage, a twist that has come to characterize them: "We represent the majority of the Senegalese people. It would be inappropriate for us to meet in the absence of the Father of the Republic".

McKeon et al. (2004). p. 8

The Senegalese government was not the only authority denying the right to voice of the principal agricultural actors in the country at the time. FAO, although it had supported the preparations for the Forum through the civil society program that I coordinated, got such cold feet that the peasant movement had to cover my travel expenses to attend it. As a sincerely and severely worried colleague put it, "You know, Nora, farmers don't have the right to have ideas about agricultural policies. That's the purview of governments".

The progress that the West African movement has made since then in bringing its claims to the negotiating table is remarkable. It has required strong mobilization just as much as dialogue. ROPPA has engaged in negotiations on agricultural and trade policies in the context of the regional UEMOA and ECOWAS groupings and the continental NEPAD/CAADP, and on a myriad of more specific issues ranging from cotton to land tenure and financing of agriculture. Recognition of family farming as the basis of agricultural development and food sovereignty as the overarching principle has been enshrined in the West African regional agricultural policy, ECOWAP, adopted by heads of state in 2005 (ROPPA 2012a; McKeon 2012). Food sovereignty has also been incorporated in national law in Senegal and Mali. National peasant platforms have been recognized by the governments of all of the ECOWAS countries and involved to a greater or lesser degree in negotiations on national agricultural investment programs and other key dossiers (ROPPA 2012b). Adopting the difficult-to-translate French term, peasant organizations have become "incontournable" (impossible to ignore). This does not mean – much to the contrary – that the struggle is over. Listening to social actors has not entered firmly into the practices of governments, and, when it does take place, it often adopts window-dressing modalities. Implementation of policies lags behind adoption. There are notable contradictions between the regional agricultural policy and sectoral policies. Decisions like the Common External Tariff adopted by ECOWAS heads of state on 26 October 2013, which fails to adequately protect the West African market space, weakens the ECOWAS position in the trade negotiations with the EU and risks permitting invasion by European products and investments (ECOWAS Peoples' Summit 2013). But the West African peasants are firmly seated at the negotiation table and are widely recognized to voice truths even when the authorities try to sweep them under the carpet.

Cases in which social movement engagement is helping to foster changes in national policies in the direction of "alternative" food systems can be found in all regions of Africa. In Namibia the practice of holistic range management by farmers and pastoralists themselves, as opposed to simplistic top-down dictates to reduce stock numbers, has been so successful that the government listened to stakeholders and incorporated their flexible management approaches into national policy (FAO 2013a, pp. 49–50). In Cameroun broad mobilization by producers and consumers against European dumping of frozen chicken sensitized public opinion and pushed the government to introduce higher import tariffs (GRET n.d.). The flourishing Kenyan milk sector was liberalized in the framework of structural adjustment and WTO rules promoting a rise in imports of milk powder from the European Union, with the result that by 2001 Kenya had gone from near self-sufficiency to net imports. Local producers mobilized to fight successfully for protection of the milk market, and today Kenya's dairy industry is one of the most developed in sub-Saharan Africa (GRET n.d.; EuropAfrica 2010). The mobilizations around seeds in Korea and Indonesia cited earlier are examples of social movement action in Asia that has won important results at national level. In the mountainous area of Northern Pakistan the Shimshali community has succeeded in opposing the appropriation of their land for national parks and "community-based" conservation projects such as trophy hunting and are implementing instead a model of eco-logical sovereignty that challenges the very logic of protected areas in international conservation (Ali 2010). Social movement pressure led to the inscription of food sovereignty in the interim constitution of the post-monarchy Nepalese republic in 2007. Three years later, the Supreme Court made a landmark decision in favor of the justiciability of the right to food in response to a public interest petition (Right to Food and Nutrition Watch 2013 p. 94).

Latin American social movement relations with national governments were almost unrelievedly confrontational during the epoch of military and elite regimes. They have evolved over the past years with the advent of governments that cham-pion some of their same objectives – however problematically – and of transna-tional groupings that resist the free trade policies forced on Latin American states by their Northern American big brothers (Araujo 2010). In Nicaragua, Bolivia, Ecua-dor, and Venezuela food sovereignty has been introduced into national law. Brazil's Zero Hunger program, introduced in in 2003, has achieved undeniable progress although there is room for improvement. In the first six years of its implementation 20 million Brazilians climbed out of poverty, early childhood malnutrition fell by 61 percent, and small farmers' incomes rose by 58 percent (Inter-réseaux 2012).

BOX 5.6
THE ZERO HUNGER STRATEGY'S PRINCIPLES

Strong political will: Lula's arrival

President Lula made food and nutrition security (FNS) a political priority during his election as president of Brazil in 2003. Yet, the context was not in his favor. The country's debt was 57 percent of GDP, inflation was close to 12 percent, and unemployment had reached 11.5 percent. The country was forced to call on the IMF. Surprising everyone, when he took office, Lula promised to lower the debt (he announced a 10 percent public budget cut). At the same time, he found the means to set up the Zero Hunger strategy, grouping together sev-eral existing programs (that were previously not coordinated) around several major goals: strengthening family farming, improving access to food, income-generating activities, and social participation. The reasoning was as follows: to remedy the problem of access to food, it was necessary to cut food prices and better protect populations that were excluded from the food market (the unemployed, children, etc.), which should simultaneously increase demand and therefore offer better outlets for local farming.

Combining social (relief) actions and development

The Zero Hunger strategy's main ambition was to combine emergency and long-term measures to attain its objectives. In this sense, we can say that the Zero Hunger strategy was not merely a set of social policies. Indeed, while the government did, for example, set up free distribution of food baskets, structural measures were also set up at the same time (vocational training programs, microcredit, family farming support, etc.) to enable a true exit from the cycle of hunger and poverty.

Connecting the rural and urban worlds and tailoring support to these zones

In rural areas, the government aligned its action on developing family farming and land tenure. Little by little, rural development policies evolved and acted from all angles on the problem of poverty, hunger and inequalities in rural areas: from producer to consumer, and from supply to demand. In urban areas, the challenge was to set up measures to fight hunger and poverty without triggering dependency. What is more, Zero Hunger sought to strengthen the ties between rural and urban areas, and between family farmers and urban consumers.

The strategy's intersectoral approach

Integrating the fact that food security and poverty are multidimensional problems, the Brazilian government bet on a comprehensive and intersectoral strategy: links between programs, coordination between the various ministries in charge. The most telling example is the National School Meal Program (PNAE). This program aims to provide free meals to students in public schools. And 30 percent of the food purchased for these establishments must come from local family farms. The foodstuffs are purchased through the Food Acquisition Program (PAA). In this way, accomplishing the goal of facilitating access to food makes it possible to support local family farming by ensuring outlets at remunerative prices. In 2008, more than 100,000 farmers sold their crops to the PAA, for nearly 17 million people.

Steering under the sign of civil society participation

Finally, it is impossible to speak of Zero Hunger without mentioning the determination to give an important role to civil society in the strategy. This principle, written into the 1988 Constitution, takes the form of representatives' seats in bodies (such as the local councils, or even the National Council of Food and Nutritional Security (CONSEA), the importance of arenas for discuss-ion and debate, the promotion of civil society initiatives, and municipal, fede-ral and national governance). More specifically, the National System for Food and Nutrition Security (SISAN) is coordinated by two institutions: CONSEA and CAISAN (the Interministerial Chamber for Food and Nutritional Security), which are based on the deliberations of the National Conferences on Food Security. These conferences are held every four years, involving thousands of people (civil society, private sector) and guiding policy.

Inter-réseaux (2012). *Brazil's Zero Hunger Strategy.* Rural Development Briefing, September 2012. Reproduced with permission

Implementation of the right to food is one way of tracking progress in set-ting in place national frameworks and legislation that are supportive of equitable food governance and sustainable food systems. As we noted in Chapter 2, civil society was behind the introduction of the right to food into the World Food Summit agenda in 1996 and in the negotiation of the Voluntary Guidelines to Support the Progressive Realization of the Right to Adequate Food in the Context of National Food Security in adopted in 2004. The tenth anniversary of adoption of the Guidelines has stimulated stocktaking regarding the degree to which they have translated into action at national level. In his final report to the UN General Assembly before stepping down after six years of service as the UN Special Rapporteur on the Right to Food, Olivier De Schutter wel-comed what he called a "rights resurgence". Countries in Latin America and Africa have blazed the trail. South Africa, Kenya, Mexico, the Ivory Coast, and Niger have already given direct constitutional protection to the right to food, while reform processes are underway in El Salvador, Nigeria, and Zambia. Right to food framework laws have been adopted in Argentina, Guatemala, Ecuador, Brazil, Venezuela, Colombia, Nicaragua, and Honduras, with several other Latin American countries in the process of developing similar measures. Countries including Uganda, Malawi, Mozambique, Senegal, and Mali have adopted, or are in the process of adopting, framework legislation for agriculture, food, and nutri-tion that enshrines rights-based principles of entitlements and access to food. In other countries, like India, the judicial system is in the forefront of defending citizens' right to food. In all of these cases, "the mobilization of civil society and social movements has played a key role in support of the legal developments" (De Schutter 2013, para. 53).

Institutionalization of food sovereignty and the right to food, at whatever level, is not a simple affair. It can be a time consuming and complex process, and one that is difficult for social movements to follow and control. Once legal frameworks and policies are in place, their implementation often lags behind. Dangers of co-optation are always present, and movements are well aware of the need to keep mobilization and protest alive even while engagement is underway (Claeys and Lambert 2014, p. 16).

We began this rapid review by emphasizing that it was not intended as a simplistic celebration of peoples' local strategies of resistance and alternative building. Rather, it is a reminder that, whatever the challenges, concrete action is underway around the world to build more equitable and sustainable food systems at subnational, national, and regional levels. This action is often grounded in "everyday politics" of the kind that occurs when people facing a tightened squeeze on their livelihoods seek solutions to the challenges they face. Such activities, van der Ploeg notes, can go beyond contesting vested interests to create new pathways by reconstituting existing patterns for the production, allocation, and use of resources in ways that dominant regimes find difficult to capture, particularly when "(more or less) consistent rural development policies are in place" (van der Ploeg 2012 p. 155). The material and economic component of alternative building – beyond policy advocacy and "righteous resistance" alone – is fundamental in empowering the actors of change.

The impact of policies and programs from outside and above the locus of alternative building is far too often negative. The African reports in the Image of Africa project we discussed in Chapter 2 describe how people affected by the drought of the mid-1980s reacted by adopting internal solidarity mechanisms, a host of self-help measures, and even elaborating alternative development strategies based on "an effort to make better use of local resources and knowledge, to exploit seasons and potentialities which had previously been under-used, greater attention to re-establishing the disrupted equilibrium between people and their environment, the development of new capacities, and a growing awareness of the need to work and plan together in order to defend common interests" (McKeon, 1988 pp. 5–7). They regretfully reported that government programs and donor aid had ignored the efforts of the people directly affected, in the best of cases, and often actually undermined them (*ibid.*, p. 19).

Recent research conducted on the basis of 118 cases in the UN Framework Convention on Climate Change (UNFCC) database confirmed the wealth of local strategies to address climatic stress and concluded that some form of institutional support is fundamental to ensuring the success of these strategies. The records show that in 61 percent of the cases such support comes from most often informal civic institutions as compared to 6 percent for public institutions and 5 percent for private sector initiatives (Agrawal 2010 p. 182). The same kind of perverse logic of official nonsupport for local peoples' strategies applies in the "developed" West. Government subsidies and Michelle Obama's campaign "to eradicate food deserts" are facilitating retail giants to move into inner cities of the United States, trouncing on inhabitants' self-help community efforts and vying for the food dollar of the urban poor (Holt-Giminez 2011, p. 316). This need not be the case, however. National law can sanction and support local efforts, as in the case of the German Renewable Energy Act of 2000, which has stimulated community-managed clean energy facilities throughout Germany. UN Special Rapporteur on the Right to Food, Olivier De Schutter, dedicated his last briefing note to the potential of public procurement to have profound transformative results if governments commit to linking right to food goals to their procurement contracts, purchasing from local, sustainable small-scale producers rather than sourcing indiscriminately from global markets in the search for the cheapest opportunities. "By creating a demand for sustainable diets, governments have the power to set a positive trend and accelerate a transition towards sustainable food systems that respect the rights of vulnerable groups, including small-scale food producers. Public procurement policies also represent a rare opportunity to link the right to food of consumers and of producers in a meaningful way" (De Schutter 2014c, p. 19), as is illustrated in the case of the Brazilian Zero Hunger featured earlier in this chapter.

Recalling these realities is propaedeutic to returning to the global level to assess the difference that a forum like the reformed Committee on World Food Security could make. Clearly, it would make none if people were not in action around the world. As a representative of La Via Campesina stated at a recent CFS plenary, "Each government represented here refers 'back to capital' when the negotiations get tough. We have 172 capitals. When we are strong there we are unbeatable here". Geoff Tansey concludes his thoughtful reflection in *The Future Control of Food* by remarking, "We need to rethink the way we make global rules and the nature of international negotiating processes. Ensuring food security requires action from local to global levels. But much of the current approach undermines and devalues the enormous capacity that exists for innovation and action at a local level" (Tansey and Rajotte 2008, p. 214). Our brief exploration of peoples' action has highlighted areas in which they are building up traction power and where changes in paradigms, regulations, and resource allocation at the global level could make a difference. In the next chapter we will return to the reformed Committee on World Food Security to assess the degree to which it is proving to constitute a forum in which changes of this nature can take place.

Notes

1. Interview with Antonio Onorati, April 2014.
2. Communication by Ladji Desai of WAMIP to a social movement strategy meeting on implementing the CFS tenure guidelines, held in Heidelberg from 4–7 February 2013.
3. Communication by Saskia Sassens at the International Studies Association convention in 2013.

6

BUILDING A BETTER FOOD SYSTEM, FROM THE TOP REACHING DOWNWARD

Chapter 4 discussed the reform of the Committee on World Food Security and briefly presented its most innovative aspects. We suggested that this new forum could do a better job of promoting inclusive and equitable global governance of food aimed at defending the right to food of the world's population than any existing one. We underscored the decisive role that social movements and organizations directly representing those most affected by food insecurity had played in mobilizing political will for the reform and in helping to shape the new CFS. Five years down the road, how is this promise playing out? Is the reformed CFS, in fact, offering a political space in which the deficiencies of global food governance discussed in Chapter 4 can be addressed? In which all interested actors are present and power relations among them are recognized and corrected to the benefit of the most marginalized? In which understanding of where food insecurity comes from and how to overcome it is better grounded in structural realities and lived experience? Has the presence of those most affected influenced the outcomes of the debates and negotiations that take place in the CFS, and are they proving to be supportive of the kind of territorially based initiatives to build better food provision that we reviewed in the last chapter?

This very initial assessment of the CFS's performance will concentrate on two interconnected issues that are at the center of the clash between opposing approaches to food systems we have illustrated earlier: access to land and investment in agriculture. It will review concrete initiatives to negotiate and implement global guidelines on tenure of land and other natural resources, and to develop principles to guide investment in agriculture so that it enhances national food security. Beyond these two core initiatives it will also examine more briefly progress made and obstacles encountered in developing the CFS's Global Strategic Framework for Food Security and Nutrition (GSF). It will touch on the hardcore taboo issues that the Committee is having most difficulty in taking up – like trade, price volatility,

TABLE 6.1 An ideal checklist for the Committee on World Food Security in an ideal world

Is it helping to:

Address the following deficiencies of global food governance?	Support the following kinds of alternative building?
- Fragmentation - Lack of inclusiveness of those most affected - Insufficiently human rights based - Dominance of productivist and "free" market paradigm as route to "food security" - Inadequate, top-down articulation among different levels - Inadequate implementation, monitoring, and promotion of accountability - Power relations affecting decision making, particularly corporate influence and donor conditionalities - Spread of informal, private sector, or hybrid mechanisms lacking political oversight and accountability - Lack of effective, enforceable regulation.	- Multifaceted family-based small-scale production and reproduction units - People's access to and control over resources: land, water, biodiversity, and seeds - Sustainable agro-ecological models of production - Locally embedded markets/food systems that are supportive of family farming and rural economies - Research and knowledge that incorporates and supports local peasant knowledge and practices - Food sovereignty paradigm and the right to food - Subsidiarity and inclusive decision-making mechanisms at all levels.

and biofuels – and on prospects for bringing them to the table. It will assess how the autonomously established Civil Society Mechanism is carrying out the difficult mission it assigned itself. It will look at how the reformed CFS is addressing the function of monitoring the degree to which its decisions are being implemented and the difference they make, leading us to a discussion of the key issue of account-ability in the concluding chapter of the book.

Land grabbing and governance[1]

It is hardly a novelty for people with power to take possession of land and expro-priate those who formerly inhabited it. Think of the enclosures of the commons that got underway in England in the 16th century, or the aftermath of Columbus's "discovery" of America, to name only two well-known examples. But the form that what has been baptized "the global land grab" is taking today has some distin-guishing features, as was suggested in Chapter 2. It has arisen in the context of the multiple, interlinked crises of food, energy, climate, and finances to which we have referred in earlier chapters. It is inserted in an emergent food regime characterized

by the consolidation of corporate control; the emergence of new exporting powers; and the reinvention of land and food as objects of investment, speculation,
and financialization (McMichael 2012a). The economic and geopolitical interests
behind this global food system, as we have seen, have been buttressed by rhetoric
touting the "modernization" of agriculture, "free" markets, and technological innovation, and stigmatizing as archaic relics the peasant and family farming systems that
now lay claim to most of the world's agricultural land. The global land grab is supported by the myth that there is substantial availability of "idle", unoccupied excess
land in the targeted countries that "might as well be put to good use". A further
faulty argument – which we have debunked in Chapter 2 – is the suggestion that it
is useful to convert large expanses of land from food production to agrifuels or to
play other remunerative (for corporations) roles in the "green economy" like serving as carbon sinks (TNI 2013, pp. 5–6). Although the impetus for large-scale land
acquisitions often comes from foreign states and capital, national elites in countries
in the Global South where land is being grabbed also play an important role. The
resulting maze of actors, motives, complicities, trajectories, and narratives has made
today's land grabbing a particularly difficult process to decipher and to govern.

The dimensions of this phenomenon are distressing, although it is difficult to
obtain complete data due to the secrecy that surrounds many of the transactions.
It was reported in 2012 that deals amounting to a total of 203 million hectares had
been approved or were under negotiation worldwide between 2000 and 2010, with
a strong acceleration in 2007–2008. This amounts to over eight times the size of
the United Kingdom (Anseeuw et al. 2012, p. 4). Although Africa is the major target, the phenomenon is worldwide. It includes Europe and North America, where
smallholders' farmland is threatened by the consolidation of industrial agriculture
enterprises, urban encroachment, or institutional investment (Oakland Institute
2014). The impacts of land grabbing in terms of dispossession of small-scale producers and the disruption of their food production role are significant, particularly
since the amounts of land being leased or sold in food insecure countries are high.

It was civil society that blew the whistle on this evolution. On the eve of an
FAO-sponsored Food Crisis Summit in June 2008, the civil society statement "No
More 'Failures-as-Usual'" demanded an immediate halt to the "new enclosure
movement" that was converting arable, pastoral, and forest lands to fuel production
(IPC 2008). A few months later GRAIN issued an influential report, *Seized!*, and
land grabbing hit the headlines (GRAIN 2008). It sparked mobilizations by social
movements around the world and obliged governments and international institutions to admit that something was amiss.

Prevailing governance mechanisms were hardly in a state to deal with this phenomenon when it gained public attention. Consideration of the politically fraught
issues of land tenure and agrarian reform had winged its way through successive
global conferences over the preceding half century – starting with the UN Conference on Agrarian Reform in 1966 – without succeeding in putting internationally
agreed guidelines in place. The International Conference on Agrarian Reform and
Rural Development (ICARRD), co-organized by the Brazilian government and

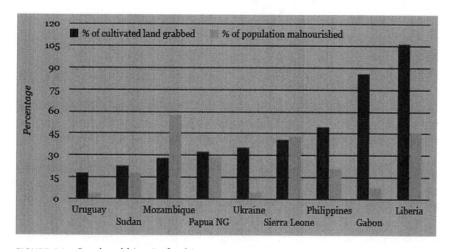

FIGURE 6.1   Land grabbing in food insecure countries

Source: Jacobs, Ryan (2013). "Charts: The Top 5 Land-Grabbing Countries", *Mother Jones*, 6 February 2013. Reproduced with permission.

FAO in 2006, came closer thanks to strong pressure by rural social movements networked in the IPC (McKeon 2013a). Access to land along with agrarian reform had been one of the four substantive pillars of the food sovereignty action plan adopted by the civil society forum in Rome in 2002. The IPC network of rural social movements had lobbied strongly in favor of holding the ICARRD. They organized an autonomous parallel civil society forum with well-defined opportunities to interact with the official deliberations and had a meaningful impact on the outcome of the conference. Their drafting victories included the recognition of collective – not just individual – rights to land; acknowledgment that land is a cultural, social, and historical – as well as economic – asset; reference to "control of" and not simply "access to" land; and explicit mention of the right to food and food sovereignty (Borras, 2008; ICARRD 2006; McKeon 2009, pp. 98–100). ICARRD brought agrarian reform back onto the agenda of FAO's normative work, although powerful FAO members like the United States and the European Union did their best to slow pedal follow-up. They preferred to leave the initiative in this area to the World Bank and its market-led approaches to land reform whereby "willing buyers" encounter "willing sellers" in an illusorily power-free playing field.

The voluntary guidelines on responsible governance of tenure of land, fisheries, and forests in the context of national food security

FAO began work in 2008 to formulate "Voluntary Guidelines on Responsible Governance of Tenure of Land and Other Natural Resources" as recommended by ICARRD. The IPC was invited to take part in the process. Over the following months regional civil society consultations were organized that enabled rural social movements to autonomously develop their own ideas about the framing, the scope, the principles, and the content of the guidelines. The IPC wanted them to be the object of an intergovernmental negotiation in which social movement views could be heard, and not simply the result of a technical consultation among stakeholders. The reform of the CFS provided the forum in which this became possible. The agenda of the first session of the "new" CFS in October 2010 featured "land tenure and international investment in agriculture". The background paper indicated that the output of the FAO Guidelines initiative would be adopted by the purely intergovernmental FAO governing bodies, which had not been "infected" by the participatory spirit of the reformed CFS. The final CFS session report, instead, went out of its way to laud the inclusive and decentralized approach that was being adopted for the development of the Guidelines and determined that they would be negotiated within the Committee itself (CFS 2010b, para. 26 i). This outcome can be largely attributed to the innovative format of the reformed Committee whereby political decisions are made in plenary sessions in which civil society and social movements are full participants (this particular one went on until 3:00 a.m.) rather than in closed-door drafting committees as is normally the case in intergovernmental forums.

The negotiation of the Guidelines took place from July 2011 to March 2012, with growing engagement by key actors as the political importance of the process became progressively evident. The initially reluctant United States agreed to chair the process. The Africa Group, largely absent at the outset although its region is a prime target for land grabbing, made a remarkably successful effort to strategize and defend its positions. It was supported in its positioning by the fact that the African Union had itself adopted a framework and guidelines on land issues in 2009, a good example of the importance of subsidiarity and multilevel synergies. Latin American countries where tenure laws are in revision and the giant China, where land grabbing is an explosive internal issue, came on board as they realized that they would be obliged to apply the Guidelines to their own situations once the ink was dry on the paper. The Middle East galvanized over the issue of tenure rights in occupied territories. The private sector network fought to legitimize and protect foreign investment, in alliance with Canada, Australia, and the United States. For its part, the EU tended to defend a rights-based approach and a focus on small-scale producers and indigenous peoples. The Civil Society Mechanism's negotiation team, led by the IPC land group, based its engagement on its autonomous vision of the guidelines. It agreed on a politically acceptable baseline outcome and laboriously drafted and defended alternative wording. Debate in the room was supported by mobilization outside. Indigenous peoples' (IPs) representatives were able to bend the iron resistance of the Canadian delegation to tolerable wording on respect for recognized IP rights by activating First Nation leaders in Canada who put pressure on the government back home. A delegation led by a peasant leader from Senegal brought to the podium and delivered to the Chair the declaration denouncing land grabbing that had been adopted by the Dakar World Social Forum in February 2011 along with the list of the hundreds of organizations in all regions of the world that had signed on to it. Throughout the negotiations the testimony and proposals brought to the debate by organizations of those most directly menaced by violations of their rights to land and other natural resources were particularly effective.

The final adopted text received a cautiously positive assessment from the rural social movements that had engaged in the process (Seufert 2013). The very fact that, for the first time in history, global guidelines on tenure of land and other resources had been negotiated and adopted in an inclusive intergovernmental forum was grounds for satisfaction. The Guidelines are based on the principles and interpretations of universal human rights, making them legally relevant at national and international levels even though it did not prove politically possible to eliminate the term "voluntary" from the title. Battles had been won on critical issues like protection of customary tenure, a strong gender approach, priority to restitution, and redistributive reforms favoring the most vulnerable, affirmation of states' obligations to regulate their corporations' operations beyond their own territorial boundaries. There is an important section on "general principles of implementation" to which civil society made significant contributions (CFS/FAO 2012 Part 2, 3B), which defines in detail what is implied by the often invoked and seldom applied term "consultation and participation". It recognizes that equity and justice require empowerment of the vulnerable, and it insists on accountability of individuals, public agencies, and nonstate actors. At the same time, the Guidelines do not address some of the issues that social movements felt were important, like the water grabbing. which – as we saw in Chapter 5 – so often accompanies land grabbing, or the qualitative question of how land should be used and managed sustainably. They do not extend to non-indigenous social groups the principle of free, prior, and informed consent (FPIC) affirmed in the 2007 UN Declaration on the Rights of Indigenous Peoples. They are too weak in prioritizing essential support to small-scale producers. Above all, they "do not explicitly challenge the untruth that large-scale investments in industrial agriculture, fisheries and forests are essential for development" (CSOPVGN 2012) although they do include safeguards to control the impacts of large-scale transfer of tenure rights (Monsalve Suárez, 2012b).

From adoption to implementation

The negotiated text (CSF/FAO 2012), like any compromise, leaves ample room for multiple interpretation on many points. The Guidelines need to be applied to specific situations in order to be transformed from "soft" into "hard", binding law. Who takes the initiative, in what way and with what interests is of key importance. The adopted text clearly underlines the responsibility of states for implementation, monitoring, and evaluation and calls on them to set up multi-actor platforms and frameworks to do so. The realization of the right to food is cited as a benchmark for measuring impact. The CFS is designated as the global forum for assessing progress in implementation, and it is specified that participants other than governments have the right to contribute to reporting.

Although the CFS has a mandate to monitor how its decisions are applied, it is not itself charged with their implementation. With the adoption of the Guidelines, technical oversight responsibility for promoting their implementation passed to FAO as the UN agency with main normative responsibility for natural resource tenure issues. This primacy has consistently been contested by the World Bank and other proponents of market-led approaches whenever FAO has had the courage to flex its normative muscles, as on the occasion of the ICARRD conference. Powerful and contrary member states are able to condition FAO's action both by the positions they take in its governing bodies and by failing to make available resources to enable FAO to provide technical assistance to countries requesting it. In the case of the Guidelines, FAO proposed the establishment of a multilateral facility to receive contributions from donors interested in supporting national-level implementation. Social movements strongly defended this proposal as a way of providing support for implementation under collective and inclusive oversight rather than allowing each donor to bilaterally push implementation in the direction of its interests. However, although a few donors have separately deposited funds with FAO to support Guideline implementation,[2] the idea of a multilateral facility has not gotten off the ground. Other actors like the G8, the World Bank, and the International Land Coalition (ILC) are advancing on their own, backed by significant resources, in accordance with their visions of what is needed. In the meantime, FAO moved ahead as soon as the Guidelines were adopted with awareness raising and capacity development, and is responding to country requests for support within the limits of available resources (Arial et al. 2012). A series of technical guides is being developed to help apply the Guidelines to specific sectors – like fisheries, forestry, or the commons – or constituencies – like indigenous peoples or women.

The social movements have developed their own implementation strategy separate from, although interacting with, the official process.[3] It takes local peoples' struggles to defend their access to resources as its point of departure. The Guidelines are considered to be useful only to the degree to which they support these struggles through their content, their strong grounding in human rights, the inclusive decision-making processes they stipulate, and the opportunity they provide for "naming and shaming" recalcitrant actors in a global forum. Social movements are normally strong in legitimacy but weak in access to resources to support their action, and Guidelines implementation is no exception. Nonetheless, more has been happening around the world in the short period since their adoption than might have been expected. In all regions, countries have been identified in which peoples' movements are engaged in land-related mobilization processes that could benefit from being linked to the Guidelines. In India the standards of the Guidelines were applied to the Land Acquisition and Rehabilitation and Resettlement Bill (LARR) when it was under review in parliament in 2013. On 14 August 2013, following one hundred days of farmer and pastoralist protest, the Government of the State of Gujarat gave in and rescinded its authorization to sell land that constituted the common grazing area of forty-four villages. The demonstrations were substantiated by a point-by-point analysis of ways in which the government decision had violated principles of the Guidelines (IPC forthcoming).[4] In Mali the National Coordination of Peasant Organisations (CNOP) has joined with other civil society organizations to found a "Malian Convergence against Land Grabbing", which provides legal assistance to communities that risk losing their land, trains local land facilitators, undertakes advocacy and communications campaigns, and channels peasant input to the land law proposal currently under negotiation with the support of the IPC land group. A mission by FIAN in late 2013 backed their protests against land grabbing in Southern Mali by communicating to the President of the Republic a detailed account of what has occurred and of the provisions of international and continental frameworks that have been violated. In Uganda local fishing communities around Lake Victoria are being engaged in communal dialogue to discuss current land and water grabbing practices and possible solutions, drawing on the Guidelines and existing national land laws. In Argentina peasant organizations are applying Guideline standards to influence discussions underway concerning land allocation and use. In Italy, where decisive decisions on land are made at a decentralized level, "movimenti contadini" (peasant movements) are using the Guidelines in their advocacy approaches to regional governments. A report documenting the extent of land grabbing in Europe was presented in the European Parliament on 25 June 2013, and a campaign was launched for adoption of a Directive that would apply the Guidelines in the European context (TNI 2013). Ways are being explored of using the Guidelines as a baseline for impact studies on large investment projects and for assessments of what the international financial institutions and bilateral aid agencies are doing in the name of implementing the CFS outcome. Support to the IPC land group to develop a training manual for use at grassroots level has been forthcoming from FAO, and IFAD has funded a project to help La Via Campesina member organizations in different regions use the Guidelines locally.

It is hardly surprising that the proponents of large-scale land acquisitions, as land grabbing is termed in official parlance, are attempting to use the Guidelines as an instrument to do just the opposite of what they are intended to do: open up the way to effective and legal dispossession of rural people. Perhaps the most blatant example of this strategy is the New Alliance for Food Security and Nutrition adopted by the G8 under the US Presidency in May 2012. The New Alliance, an effort to open up African markets to TNC agribusinesses under cover of fighting hunger, claims that it will assist the governments of the African countries selected to pilot this program to apply the Guidelines in their national contexts. A check of the agreements that have been signed with these governments reveals that the G8 interpretation of Guideline implementation translates into kick-starting a market-based approach to land transactions by demarcating village lands and issuing land tenure certificates to individual farmers (Oxfam 2013; McKeon 2014). To a Western reader accustomed to the apparent advantages of possessing private property in a capitalist economy, this might seem like an empowering step, but it isn't. African small-scale producers are resisting this procedure because it fragments the commons, which are an indispensable ingredient in rural livelihoods – particularly for pastoralists – and violates traditional community practices. It also constitutes a first step to expropriation since poor producers with little or no access to credit and other services are very likely to end up selling their land if they have title to it. Small-scale producers' organizations have not been involved in the negotiation of the agreements in any of the countries, despite the usual participatory rhetoric (Oxfam *op.cit.*, McKeon *op.cit.*).

The value added of the Guidelines is their potential contribution to developing or strengthening national legislation that defends peoples' rights to land and helping to ensure it is applied. This, of course, will not happen without strong mobilization and social pressure from the base. A recent collection of case studies in Asia highlights the primary responsibility of governments in land grabs and the need to raise community resistance to national level and to make governments answerable (PANAP 2013, p. 6). Civil society is advocating respect for the Guidelines' invitation to governments to establish national multi-actor platforms to assess the existing situation of land governance, identify gaps, and propose action to fill them. The objective is to ensure that delicate decisions on land issues are made in political negotiation by governments and national actors – particularly the most vulnerable and threatened by expropriation – guarding against donor conditionalities and corporation enticements. "Experience shows that good results require enough social pressure from below to shift the balance in favour of those who should be prioritised from a social justice perspective – and just how much social pressure from below will be enough depends on many situational factors" (TNI 2013, p. 24).

The insistence on multi-actor platforms could provide producers' organizations with an arm to use in challenging programs such as the New Alliance at the national level, particularly if the CFS as the global political reference and FAO as lead implementing organization are able to enforce the Guidelines' implementation principles and monitor their application. However, the G8 and the World Bank continue to attempt to wrest leadership for these functions. The G8 Summit in Lough Erne, Northern Ireland, in June 2013 had before it a proposal to launch a "global land transparency initiative", billed as a big piece of the cure for land grabbing. The focus on transparency on the contrary "is unlikely to produce anything more than just more transparent land grabs" (TNI 2013, p. 24) unless unequal power relations are addressed.

What needs to be monitored, how, and by whom, to go beyond transparency and address structural issues? Social movements had proposed the establishment of a global land observatory situated within FAO, the UN agency mandated to exercise normative authority in this field. It has not proved possible to mobilize the necessary political will and funding to carry this proposal forward. On the contrary, a Land Observatory has been established under the auspices of the well-resourced International Land Coalition (ILC), whose composition and governance, as we have seen in Chapter 5, are hardly a showcase of coherence and legitimacy (Borras 2010; McKeon 2013a). A "Global Land Indicator Initiative" (GLII) was launched in 2012, outside of the purview of the CFS, by UN-Habitat, the World Bank, the ILC, and others with the declared aim of harmonizing monitoring efforts around land tenure and governance. It risks preempting the initiative on monitoring and developing an approach based on expert assessments and quantitative surveys that does not jibe with the objectives, the content, and the human rights–based framework of the negotiated Guidelines. In the assessment of the IPC land group, one reason why the CFS Guidelines are distinctive is that they acknowledge that land governance is not neutral and make clear suggestions as to who ought to be emphasized in allocating tenure rights from a social justice and human rights perspective. The GLII proposed indicators gloss over the issue of whose rights count and "push the discussion backward toward an imagined neutrality" (IPC 2014). FAO's situation in all of this game playing is not an easy one since, as an intergovernmental agency, it finds it difficult to dissociate itself from initiatives taken by some of its most powerful members. The fact that the secretariat is organized on the basis of specialized technical units also makes it more difficult for FAO to pursue strategic normative objectives. The establishment by the Director-General of an organization-wide task force for implementation of the Guidelines headed up by a politically astute director seeks to address this perennial problem of a technical agency whose work inevitably has political implications. Efforts are being made to build synergies with the IPC land group in applying the Guidelines at country level in order to ensure that rural peoples' organizations and their perspectives are well represented.

What do social movements have going for them to oppose to these displays of power? The bottom line is their rootedness in local struggles around the world and their capacity to put the Guidelines at the service of peoples' action, perhaps the most effective potential counter-power to that of corporations. Work led by the IPC land group over the coming months to train "land facilitators", develop communications materials, and provide horizontal "movement-to-movement technical assistance" to groups of activists operating in specific national contexts will be key in this regard. Alliance building, discussed in more general terms in the previous chapter, is also essential. In the case of land grabbing, more than that of some other issues on the global agenda, rural social movements have been facilitated in building alliances with engaged academics by the fact that the academics themselves have clustered in networks.[5] While promoting a veritable flurry of academic conferences and publications on land grabbing, they are providing "evidence-based" support for activist platforms, helping to identify possible blind spots in activist strategies and analyzing emerging issues.

In terms of broader alliances, the existence of three competing political tendencies among state and nonstate actors with regard to global governance of land grabbing has been hypothesized. The different objectives they espouse shake down roughly into the categories of conservative, reformist, and radical. "The first is *regulate in order to facilitate land deals*, the second is *regulate in order to mitigate adverse impacts and maximize opportunities of land deals*, and the third is *regulate to stop and rollback land deals*" (Borras et al. 2013. p. 168). This, the authors surmise, should lead us to expect at least three visions of the Guidelines. The first two positions might find themselves allied by their tendency to emphasize procedural issues like transparency over structural ones, leaving the politically and strategically oriented third position – that of the social movements – out in the cold. It is essential, in their view, to work instead toward an alliance between the second position, with its tactically popular concern for urgently targeting the unacceptable impacts of land deals, and the third position with its more radical but tactically weaker insistence on addressing the structural causes of land grabbing and proposing strategic alternatives. Broadening alliances is of necessity accompanied by a broadening of the way issues, claims, and targets are framed. "Land sovereignty" is one proposal that has been put forward as a broader master frame that resonates with the concept of food sovereignty (Borras and Franco 2012). Whatever the terminology adopted, the framing needs to bridge North-South and rural-urban gaps. Not enough has been said about land concentration issues in the Global North, and governments in these areas tend to consider the Guidelines an instrument of relevance to the South but not to their own backyards. And not enough has been said to link land occupation and urban agriculture in urban "food deserts" to agrarian struggles in rural areas as reactions in different settings to the same oppressive global food regime.

Over the past months it has become increasingly evident that the Tenure Guidelines are situated at the heart of an exceedingly contentious combat for control of land and the wealth it produces. In almost Manichean fashion, national and transnational capital and its unending need to obtain profits appears to be pitted against the small-scale producers and communities for whom their territories are not only the basis of livelihoods but also of deep intergenerational social and cultural values. Governments, in this scenario, are often playing the extremely ambiguous role of facilitating the former while proclaiming productivist and hunger-fighting rhetoric to demonstrate that they are really serving the interests of the latter. The confrontation around the implementation of the Guidelines is proving to be just as intense as that around their negotiation, if not more so. But the fact that the Guidelines exist and are being used to support local struggles and to help call governments and corporations to account is an undoubted "plus" of the CFS, and one that could not have been achieved in a less inclusive and explicitly political global forum.

Investment in agriculture and governance

Land grabbing is only the most visible and easiest to denounce piece of a broader and more complex trend. The bigger story is the concern to consolidate the global corporate-led food system, shaken by the multiple crises of these past years, and open up to it those growing markets – principally in Africa – that have escaped its penetration thus far. As we have seen in Chapter 2, integrating those smallholders who can make the grade into global value chains can be a more profitable strategy than land grabbing since it asserts corporate control over small-scale producers' resource basis and production choices while leaving them on their land to shoulder all the multiple risks that agriculture entails. This is why the debate and negotiations in the CFS surrounding the broader topic of investment in agriculture is so important. As an IPC member put it during a recent strategizing meeting, "It's not just about grabbing land, but about grabbing the right to produce. It's easier to devise measures to protect communities from being expelled from their land than to counter the fact that roads lead to seaports instead of connecting small-scale producers to internal markets".

We will trace the development of the debate on agricultural investment in the CFS in some detail since it provides us with an opportunity to revisit – in hands-on operational terms – issues like the power of paradigms, the interests behind global food chains, and the nature of evidence-based decision making that we have discussed more abstractly in earlier chapters. This review will also offer a glimpse of what actual negotiation looks like for readers who have never witnessed it. Finally it will enable us to follow the engrossing process of what is involved in putting an innovative institutional proposal like the CFS into practice.

Investing in agriculture has been at the top of the agenda of the reformed CFS since its first session in October 2010. In the same late night session in which it was agreed to negotiate the Guidelines on responsible tenure, the CFS declined to rubber stamp a set of Principles for Responsible Agricultural Investment (PRAI) that had been launched by the World Bank, FAO, IFAD, and UNCTAD in January 2010. The PRAI were promoted by G8 members who took the line that the surge in large-scale foreign investment in developing country agriculture – including land acquisitions – was to be welcomed as a contribution to solving the food crisis since it would stimulate food production and the economy in general. All that was needed was to "discipline" it with a code of conduct, formulated in closed-door discussions by the four multilateral institutions, that investors would be asked to voluntarily apply to their operations. Conscious of the lack of any kind of a consultative process behind the PRAI, their supporters sought to obtain an "en bloc", no-questions-asked investiture of legitimacy from the CFS. On the other side of the fence, the IPC network, other civil society organizations, academics, and public figures like the Special Rapporteur on the Right to Food denounced the PRAI as a "move to legitimize the long-term corporate (foreign and domestic) takeover of rural people's farmlands" (GCAR, 2010) by positing large-scale investments as the solution to rural poverty and hunger (Borras and Franco 2010; De Schutter 2009b and 2010a). In the CFS the refusal to endorse the PRAI was supported by G77 and European member countries which recognized that the PRAI did not have an easy fit with the Committee's food security mandate or an appropriate consultative process behind them. This bloc won the day. The PRAI were simply "noted" rather than endorsed. It was decided instead that, once the Tenure Guidelines had been approved, the CFS would open up its own inclusive consultation to formulate principles which could help ensure that agricultural investment promotes food security (CFS 2010b, para. 26).

To coordinate its input to the debate, the Civil Society Mechanism set up an agricultural working group in May 2011, chaired by two small-scale producer organization leaders and open to participation by CSOs and social movements around the world. A technical team of NGO experts and engaged academics provided support for its reflections. Two cross-cutting objectives were defined, one proactive and the other defensive. These were to:

1. achieve more support and opportunities for small-scale food producers and their models of production through enabling public policies, support programmes and research; remunerative prices; access to domestic markets through appropriate infrastructure and credit; value addition through such means as small-scale processing, cooperative enterprises.
2. protect small-scale food producers from corporate take-over by resisting land grabbing, value chain/contract farming approaches for linking producers to markets, initiatives to stimulate adoption of GMOs, etc. and public–private partnerships promoting these corporate strategies.

(CSM 2011a, p. 1)

Investing in smallholder agriculture

The civil society voice had a first opportunity to begin to shift the terms of the debate during a policy discussion on "How to Increase Food Security and Smallholder-Sensitive Investment in Agriculture" held during the annual CFS plenary session in October 2011. This debate also constituted an initial experiment with piecing together technical preparation and political decision making in innovative ways in an inclusive setting. The normal intergovernmental procedure would have called for preparation of a secretariat background paper discretely suggesting policy issues that the governments might wish to address, with NGO observers intervening only at the end of the debate. In the reformed scenario the CFS called on its newly established High-Level Panel of Experts (HLPE) to prepare a report on the topic that was expected to provide a foundation for evidence-based decision making. Drawing on this paper and assisted by members of the Advisory Group representing nonstate CFS participants, the CFS secretariat was expected to prepare a list of draft decisions to go to the CFS plenary (the "decision box" in CFS parlance) for political attention. The process was understandably full of glitches the first time around. The HLPE report was not available in time to be taken into consideration in the preparation of the background documentation, organizational problems among the Rome-based agencies intervened, and in the end the habitual secretariat-dominated modality of drafting kicked in. The CSM protested strongly against the way in which the document (mis)treated what it considered to be the key questions.

BOX 6.1
CHANGING THE TERMS OF THE DEBATE: CIVIL
SOCIETY COMMENTS ON THE DRAFT CFS DISCUSSION
PAPER ON "HOW TO INCREASE FOOD SECURITY
AND SMALLHOLDER-SENSITIVE INVESTMENT IN
AGRICULTURE"

Although the paper purports to be "smallholder focused and sensitive", we find very little in it that addresses smallholders' stated needs and proposals and quite a bit that seeks to ensure an environment for safe and profitable investments from outside the smallholder sector.

Food production by whom?

Promoting an autonomous smallholder food production sector entails multiple benefits as compared with large-scale industrial agriculture: not only food production but also food security starting with smallholder families themselves, employment creation, environmental protection, social security, poverty reduction, etc. This means that the top priority in reorienting investments and policies should be to tackle the constraints that smallholders face. The draft paper seems to ignore the fact that smallholders now produce up to 80 percent of the food consumed in developing countries even though they are receiving insufficient policy and program support and, as a result, are performing below their potential for productivity. It also glosses over key constraints without suggesting remedies. The whole issue of the importance of stable markets and prices and sufficient incomes for smallholders, which are the key issue for investment in food production, is hardly dealt with.

Adopting what model of agriculture?

Promoting sustainable agriculture adopting agro-ecological approaches is
    essential in order to increase resilience and contribute to meeting chal-
    lenges of climate change while also working toward food security goals.
    The draft paper largely ignores the issue of sustainability.
It also fails to acknowledge the traditional knowledge and existing capacities
    of smallholders and seems to assume that they have only needs that will
    have to be attended to by research and education establishments external
    to the rural milieu.

Whose investments to promote?

The definition of investment adopted in the draft paper is seen essen-
    tially through an economic lens. We cannot accept that the nature of

corporate investment is at all comparable to smallholder investment since this would reduce the role of smallholders to solely seeking financial returns as does corporate investment.

The draft paper recognizes that smallholders themselves account for the bulk of investment in agriculture. However, it does not go on to acknowledge that foreign investment – both ODA and FDI – are of marginal importance. Instead it dedicates disproportionate space to corporate investment in agriculture. It posits "win-win" outcomes without documenting them. It acknowledges that there are "risks and conflicts of interests from corporate investments" but does not discuss them or suggest what needs to be done about them. It does not question the fact that a lot of concern is expressed about the need to "guarantee" corporate investments, yet no one seems to be bothered about "guaranteeing" the investments made by smallholders themselves.

Connecting smallholders to markets – under whose control? Which markets?

The draft paper does not discuss clearly the key issue of what approaches to connecting smallholders to markets can best reinforce their power within value chains and strengthen sustainable domestic food systems.

It does not address the negative impacts of vertical integration in markets that have resulted in monopolistic and oligopolistic control by transnationals.

What role for the state?

The role of the state, beyond providing infrastructure, information, and "a good business environment", needs to be expanded to include such obligations as ensuring access to resources and building and regulating local/national/regional markets.

During the plenary session small-scale food producers' organizations defended the CSM's positions with force and undoubtedly swayed the outcome. The background paper had been strongly oriented in favor of corporate investment, public–private partnerships, and global value chains. The decisions approved by the CFS, instead, recognize the primacy of small-scale sustainable food production and the fact that small-scale producers are the major investors in agriculture. They recommend that member governments and other CFS stakeholders "ensure that agricultural policies and public investment give priority to food production and nutrition and increase the resilience of local and traditional food systems and biodiversity".

These positions, immortalized in the report of the thirty-seventh session of the CFS (CFS 2011, paras. 24–29), have become what is called "accepted language" in intergovernmental negotiation parlance and cannot be watered down or ignored. As is represented in Figure 2.4 on p. 54 of Chapter 2, they were subsequently corroborated by the 2012 edition of FAO's flagship publication, *The State of Food and Agriculture*, dedicated to the theme of investments in agriculture.

Acknowledging the need to look at the issue more deeply, the CFS requested its HLPE to prepare a study of constraints to smallholder investment in agriculture and policy options for addressing them. This paper would provide a basis for further discussion on "investing in smallholder agriculture" at the annual CFS session in October 2013. The procedures for the preparation and organization of the policy discussion were somewhat different than in 2011, reflecting lessons learned from the first experiences. The HLPE had adjusted its production schedule in order to make its report available earlier. Internal discussion among the five members of the HLPE team itself was highly intense, reflecting the different paradigms under which they were operating. Contested points included how to define the very terms under discussion ("smallholder" and "investment"), how to assess different models of production and markets, what should be the role of the public sector as compared with that of private investment or "public–private partnerships" (PPPs), the impact on smallholders of contract farming, and other corporate-led approaches to value chains. Even the issue of what constitutes evidence was subject to debate. Documents prepared by small-scale producers' organizations themselves, like the African report we have cited on several occasions in earlier chapters, were not included in the bibliography since some team members considered that they were not "scientific". The arbitrary nature of this judgment is evident considering that the lead author of the African farmers' document was also a member of the HLPE team.[6] Nonetheless, the output was excellent on the whole (HLPE 2013). As in the case of the IAASTD report referred to in Chapters 1 and 5, the fact that an "objective" academic publication corroborated much of the evidence and many of the positions advanced by small-scale producers' organizations themselves provided significant discursive support for the latter.

According to the new procedures, the HLPE report would be the main background document for the discussion. All that needed to be prepared was a "decision box" for which the recommendations contained in the HLPE report would be the starting point. As in 2011 the CFS secretariat retained final responsibility for this task, but participation in the drafting had been broadened beyond the Advisory Group to include the governmental Bureau members as well. Accustomed to being the uncontested masters of the game, they had found themselves in the uncomfortable situation in 2011 of having had less of a hand in crafting the draft decisions than the nonstate members of the CFS and were determined to reassert their authority. Another difference was a more active engagement by the private sector. Over the two intervening years the major agrifood corporations had assessed the growing significance of the CFS as a policy forum and, taking their cue from the CSM, had organized their own autonomous Private Sector Mechanism in order to heighten their impact. A final innovation was the introduction of a strong facilitation role for the Rapporteur of the CFS plenary session policy discussion, whose responsibility it was to shepherd the decision box relatively painlessly toward consensus and adoption.

Discussions during the drafting process were highly contentious. The CSM, backed by Africa and to some degree China, insisted on the centrality of small-scale food producers as the main actors of food security worldwide. Appealing to classic growth theory, on the contrary, the US-Canada-Australia axe backed by the PSM attempted to transform the framing into one of "increasing productivity across the agricultural value chain and the full market system, not just smallholders". Interesting discursive skirmishes took place. Is "the market" a homogenous given, or are there different kinds of markets that offer different conditions for smallholders? Are "traditional practices" and "agro-ecology" in a separate and inferior universe as compared with "technology and knowledge", or are they, instead, forms of technology and knowledge that could be considered particularly valuable given the challenges of climate change? Is the rosiest future one can imagine for smallholders one of graduating "out of subsistence" and into global value chains, or is there a totally different vision out there? Battle lines were drawn around the right of the CFS to even remotely approach discussing anything that concerned global trade issues and transgressed on WTO terrain, the relative roles of the public sector and private investment, the positive or negative implications of land titling for smallholders, and whether or not to foresee any kind of meaningful role for the CFS in follow-up to the debate on smallholders.

In the end the draft that went to the CFS plenary was felt by civil society to be an acceptable basis for discussion.[7] Little debate on the decision box as such took place in the plenary, however. The line-by-line discussion was consigned to a mechanism baptized "Friends of the Rapporteur" that would meet separately to try to achieve consensus on a text to be brought back to the plenary two days later. Plenary interventions focused on making statements of principle on the topic, reflecting the fault lines that had already emerged clearly in earlier debate. Most of the governments who took the floor praised the quality of the HLPE report and expressed awareness of the importance of the smallholder sector. "Smallholder farmers make an important contribution," the Chinese delegate stated with no little authority given that "more than 90 percent of all farmers in China are smallholders" and close to 20 percent of the world's population are Chinese. The Private Sector Mechanism reiterated the need to help smallholders "break the subsistence cycle" and become small entrepreneurs, and the United States suggested that they were helping to do just that through the G8 New Alliance for Food Security and Nutrition by increasing their access to new technologies and seed varieties. The CSM politely but firmly replied that "we don't want to become small entrepreneurs – we have our own technologies and market systems that we have developed ourselves, for which we want to have public sector support." The Africa Group made the most explicit and sweeping statement: "What we need is a paradigm shift. Smallholders are the basis of our food security. The emphasis should be not on encouraging outside investment but on facilitating those who are already producing".

The negotiations in the "Friends of the Rapporteur" group did manage to arrive at consensus. Its legitimacy was undermined, however, by the fact that the presence of the Global South was weak given the difficulties of small delegations to adequately cover all that was taking place at the same time in various "rooms" of the CFS. The debate was respectful and characterized by fair play and listening, thanks in good part to the skills of the Rapporteur. Communicative high points of the kind that never get into reports included the Swiss delegate handing out chocolate to keep spirits high as the debate continued late into the night, and the La Via Campesina representative explaining to an astonished Australian delegate (noted for his earlier statement that "the market is the market") why global phyto-sanitary regulations developed with agri-industry in mind penalize small-scale family farmers. Although resistance to dethroning the domination of WTO free trade regulations over food security concerns continued to prevail, some progress was made in winning recognition that there is not just one market and that different markets serve different masters. The resulting text whisked through plenary without difficulties. In the end, the CSM's assessment of the outcome was essentially positive. Some important points had been won, and the "agreed language" could be brought to bear on the negotiation of responsible agricultural investment principles (rai) that the CFS had decided at its first session to undertake in alternative to endorsing the World Bank/ IFAD/UNCTAD/FAO PRAI.

BOX 6.2
THE ADOPTED TEXT

- Recognizes – once again – that smallholders play a central role for food security, are the main investors in their own agriculture, and contribute to a range of other benefits.
- Invites governments and national stakeholders, especially smallholders' organizations, to develop a country-owned vision for smallholder agriculture and bring it to bear on a range of relevant policies and budgets.
- Emphasizes the importance of legal recognition of and respect for the rights of smallholder farmers and strengthening their organizations.
- Acknowledges the need to document the state and evolution of smallholder agriculture.
- Advocates promoting smallholders' ability to access, breed, produce, conserve, exchange, sell, and use the seeds they need and supporting conservation and development of agricultural biodiversity including through agro-ecological approaches (a hard-fought successful battle to win a mention of agro-ecology).
- Calls for strong promotion of responsible governance of land and natural resources with emphasis on securing access and tenure for smallholders in accordance with the Tenure Guidelines adopted by the CFS.

- Prioritizes public investment in support of smallholders own investments, which are recognized to be multiform and not just monetary.
- Calls for strengthening participatory research combining traditional knowledge with the findings of scientific research.
- Recognizes that the constraints of smallholders in relation to sanitary and phyto-sanitary regulations need to be taken into account.
- Supports the development of and access to markets that are remunerative for smallholders and rural economies; recognizes the importance of nonmonetary exchanges and of local food systems.
- Foresees that experiences in applying these recommendations be presented at the CFS in 2015 and that the HLPE report and the CFS recommendations be taken into account in the consultation on rai principles.

CFS (2013). paras. 29–50

Responsible agricultural investment principles (rai)

It would be tempting to adopt a metaphor like that of a tug-of-war to describe the saga of the CFS consultation on principles for responsible agricultural investment. Indeed, the major "pullers" are the two opposing teams we have encountered many times in our exploration of food systems and global governance. But this image is too unilateral and static to render the complexity of the actors, interests, and positions at play. Although the hardcore members of the two factions can be identified and are not likely to change their affiliations, others are harder to pin down. Where to put a Latin American regional group, GRULAC, which includes both major agricultural exporters and countries where the vast majority of the population are indigenous peoples and peasants? Or even a single government like that of Brazil, an emerging power, which is attempting with considerable difficulty to maintain a dual agricultural economy requiring defense of the interests of large-scale export-oriented, often GMO monoculture, on the one hand, and support for the small-scale family farming that occupies the bulk of the population, on the other? During the negotiation of the Tenure Guidelines, the Africa Group had been facilitated in adopting unitary positions, most often defending the interests of smallholders, by the fact that they could use the African Union's continental land policy as a reference point. Nothing similar exists, however, where agricultural investments are concerned. On the contrary, donor and corporation-driven initiatives like Grow Africa and the G8 New Alliance for Food Security and Nutrition have been able to woo the AU and NEPAD into an uncomfortably promiscuous bed with them, and individual governments or statesmen are bought off by outside investors on a daily basis. The EU had been a major ally of civil society during the Tenure Guidelines negotiations, particularly in defense of human rights, although it is hardly a babe in arms where land issues and land grabbing is concerned. In the case of agricultural investment writ large, however, the level of incoherence between EU development policies and its trade, investment, and competition policies reached dramatic proportions. And how about a big player like China, a major investor in agriculture both at home and abroad, contesting the dominance of Western donors and trade partners in key regions like Africa?

The lead-up to the official launch of the rai process in June 2012 was dedicated to determining just what the consultation would look like, a contentious matter in itself. Those supporting the World Bank–promoted PRAI that the CFS had refused to endorse tried repeatedly to place them once again at the center of the consultation. When this effort failed, they sought to postpone, limit the inclusiveness, and downgrade the importance of the consultation. Civil society organizations were concerned to get the debate out of Rome and into the field. They took advantage of the biannual FAO Regional Conferences held during the spring of 2012, preceded by civil society consultations, to hold a first round of reflection on what those most directly concerned considered to be the main issues. Coming from a totally different planet, in April 2012 the Administrator of USAID, Rajiv Shah, made a lightening visit to FAO to convince all concerned that the corporate private sector–led New Alliance for Food Security and Nutrition that President Obama was intending to propose to the G8 at Camp David the following month represented the definitive answer to "lifting 50 million people out of poverty in 10 years". The long silence that followed his eminently self-satisfied and PR-perfect presentation was broken at last by one of the most authoritative African government representatives to FAO and the CFS, who wearily remarked, "When will you people stop marching into our continent to impose your solutions to our problems rather than supporting the ones we have put in place?"

The Tenure Guidelines were adopted at a special session of the CFS on 11 May 2012, opening the way to the official launch of the rai consultation. In the view of the social movements, the Guidelines' language on agricultural investments was a great improvement over the PRAI and a basis on which to build. Comparing the two helps us to understand what it is that can make a difference in international regulations from the viewpoint of those whose rights – in theory – are intended to be protected.

BOX 6.3
THE FAO TENURE GUIDELINES AND THE PRINCIPLES FOR RESPONSIBLE INVESTMENT IN AGRICULTURE (PRAI): WHAT IS IT THAT MAKES A DIFFERENCE IN INTERNATIONAL REGULATION?

1. The Guidelines are anchored in existing obligations under international human rights law. They do not bank on corporate social responsibility schemes as the PRAI do. Instead, they highlight the role of States in respecting, protecting and fulfilling legitimate tenure rights and the regulatory powers they need to wield to comply with these obligations.

2. The Guidelines recognize that States should support smallholders' investments, since they contribute significantly to food security, nutrition, poverty eradication and environmental resilience. The PRAI do not recognize this crucial role and do not prioritize support for smallholders' investment.

3. Unlike the PRAI, the Guidelines include the principle of "no harm to and respect for" human rights, as well as compliance with ILO standards. They relate responsible investment to promoting local food production systems.

4. The Guidelines call on States to introduce special safeguards against the risks posed by large-scale transactions in tenure rights and urge them to consider promoting production and investment models that do not result in the large-scale transfer of tenure rights to investors. This is in stark contrast to the PRAI, which do not question the desirability of large-scale appropriation of resources and simply recommend micro-management of the risks it entails.

5. Unlike the PRAI, the Guidelines require States to ensure the right to Free Prior and Informed Consent of Indigenous Peoples (FPIC). They establish a new standard about how consultations with non-indigenous groups, not covered by FPIC, should be conducted. They make it clear that it is the duty of States to ensure that affected people are properly consulted and that independent and prior impact assessments are carried out.

6. The Guidelines highlight the responsibility of States that invest or promote investments abroad to ensure that their conduct is consistent with the promotion of food security and their existing obligations under international human rights law. They also call on home States of transnational corporations to ensure that these businesses are not involved in abuse of human rights and legitimate tenure rights. States are enjoined to provide access to effective judicial remedies for negative impacts on human rights and legitimate tenure rights by business enterprises. Such provisions are lacking in the PRAI.

7. The Guidelines call on non-state actors, including business enterprises, to respect human rights and legitimate tenure rights and provide for remedy where they have caused or contributed to adverse impacts on human rights and legitimate tenure rights. The PRAI do not include any similar provisions since they conflate the roles of different actors and do not spell out the specific obligations and responsibilities of businesses and of investor States.

From Monsalve Suárez (2012b). *The Right to Food and Nutrition Watch*, 2012. Reproduced with permission

Substantive work on the rai consultation finally got underway with the establishment of an inclusive Open-Ended Working Group (OEWG), which held its first meeting on 2 July 2012. The group was expected to provide input and feedback for the preparation of a draft text by the CFS Secretariat and the OEWG Chair. This draft, following several iterations in Rome and in regional consultations, would be the object of negotiation in the OEWG and, finally, adoption in the CFS plenary session in October 2014. As the tortuous process moved forward, the CSM decided, as they had done for the Tenure Guidelines, to formulate their own version of what social movements felt strong and positive principles regulating agricultural investment should look like. This autonomous process would be separate from, but would communicate with, the official one. There were several reasons behind this strategic decision. It would help to clarify the social movement vision that needed to be defended in the official negotiations. The movements' struggles and demands should be taken as the starting point, not a negotiated compromise on a watered-down text. Independently of what the official outcome of the rai consultation might be, the civil society process could contribute to building a broad front against destructive agri investments and for public investment that supports and defends smallholder food production and local food systems. Finally, if the negotiations in the CFS went badly and social movements were dissatisfied with what the governments adopted, it would be easier to dissociate themselves if they could contrast their version of the principles to the official outcome.

The autonomous civil society consultation was kicked off at a session organized at the World Social Forum in Tunis in March 2013 and proceeded through discussions organized in all regions. Participants in the consultations insisted that the rai outcome should go beyond simply stating general principles and should provide guidance to governments as to how to apply them. It should entrench the principle of monitoring in order to hold governments and investors accountable. Some key concepts came up for discussion in all regions. The need to question the agricultural "modernization" paradigm was underlined. The concept of investment had to be reclaimed. It is not just about the mobilization of financial resources but about the commitment of multiple resources (financial, natural, human, social, cultural) to realize a range of goals, not just an economic return. Food sovereignty should be the overarching framework. Stronger condemnation of land and resource grabbing needed to be included. Legally binding regulatory systems had to be devised to discipline large-scale investors and provide safeguards in a range of areas including seeds, biodiversity, and indigenous knowledge. Specific attention needed to be paid to the impact of bilateral and multilateral trade and investment agreements, breaking the taboo imposed in the CFS by the "free" trade claque.

In parallel, the CSM was playing the difficult acrobatic act of interacting with the official rai consultation. In the case of the Tenure Guidelines the draft text had been formulated by an FAO technical unit dedicated to tenure issues through a three-year-long participatory process and brought to negotiation under the direction of a politically strong, technically competent and well-supported US Chair. The rai draft, on the contrary, had to be pulled out of thin air by an understaffed and overworked CFS secretariat with only ad hoc technical support from FAO and IFAD staff who were not necessarily familiar with the CFS. The Swiss Chair of the OEWG, although well meaning and committed, had nothing like the political stature of her Tenure Guidelines equivalent. The result was a muddied process that finally resulted in a Zero Draft released on 1 August 2013. This draft was taken to a series of multi-stakeholder regional consultations, starting in November 2013 and continuing through the first months of 2014. A revised Draft One was unveiled on 1 April 2014, and the actual negotiations got underway in Rome from 17–24 May 2014. As they opened the CSM was prepared to defend detailed alternative language proposals backed up by a clear definition of social movements' "red lines" – the points that they considered to be nonnegotiable. These were based on a distillation of the results of two years of autonomous consultations, articulated into thirteen points that were developed in a four-page position paper.

BOX 6.4
CIVIL SOCIETY ACTIONS AND POLICIES ON INVESTMENT IN AGRICULTURE

1. Investments must contribute to and be consistent with the progressive realization of the right to adequate and nutritious food for all.
2. Investments in food and agriculture must ensure protection of ecosystems and environments.
3. All investments in food and agriculture must ensure decent jobs, respect workers' rights, and adhere to core labor standards and obligations as defined by the International Labour Organization (ILO).
4. All investments in agriculture and food systems must ensure decent incomes, livelihoods, and equitable development opportunities for local communities, especially for rural youth, women, and indigenous peoples.
5. Investments must respect and uphold the rights of small-scale food producers, indigenous peoples, and local communities to access, use, and have control over land, water, and other natural resources.
6. All investments must respect the rights of indigenous peoples to their territories and ancestral domains, cultural heritage and landscapes, and traditional knowledge and practices.
7. All investments must respect women's rights and prioritize women in benefit sharing.
8. States must mobilize public investments and public policies in support of small-scale food producers and workers. Small-scale food producers, workers, and their organizations must be meaningfully involved in the formulation, implementation, monitoring, and review of these investments and policies.

9. States must protect small-scale producers and workers from market fluctuations and price volatility by regulating local, national, regional, and international food markets and curbing food price speculation.
10. States must respect and support timely and nondiscriminatory access by small-scale producers, workers, indigenous communities, local communities, and the public to justice; grievance mechanisms; fair, effective, and timely mediation; administrative and judicial remedies; and a right to appeal.
11. Trade and investment agreements and treaties must not undermine or compromise the rights of small-scale food producers, workers, indigenous peoples, or food sovereignty. States must monitor and assess the impacts of such agreements on the realization of the right to food and take appropriate action where necessary including through renegotiation or cancellation of the agreements/treaties.
12. States should enact appropriate national laws to regulate and monitor extra-territorial investments and investors. In so doing, they should apply the *Maastricht Principles on Extraterritorial Obligations of States in the Area of Economic, Social, and Cultural Rights*, as the guiding document.
13. The effective, meaningful, and democratic participation of small-scale food producers, workers, and indigenous peoples, particularly women, must be guaranteed in the planning and decision making around agricultural investments, area development, and land and resource use and management.

Civil Society Mechanism (2014)

The negotiations were just as complex and contentious as civil society had expected. A week did not suffice, and another negotiation session had to be planned. There was strong pressure to speed the process up in order to ensure endorsement of the principles at the CFS plenary in October 2014 at the expense of the quality, legitimacy, and ownership of the final product. There was also a push from those parties who preferred light principles and minimum accountability to compress the essential final section that spells out the roles and responsibilities of each category of actors and arrangements for implementation and monitoring. As this book went to press, the final outcome was not yet known, but the CSM was prepared to negotiate strongly and to react forcefully if it judged that the document adopted by governments was not acceptable.[8]

What has and hasn't been achieved

By the end of its fifth year of life, the CFS had undertaken a strenuous program of work on agricultural investment. The preceding account does not include the myriad Open-Ended Working Group meetings or the monthly encounters of the

CFS Bureau and Advisory Group at which investment was reviewed along with other issues. Nor does it do justice to the quantities of emails and documents that circulated between meetings, of which the civil society communications were dutifully subjected to Google translations from the ubiquitous English into French and Spanish and commented on in multilingual Skype calls scheduled to reconcile the time difference between Quito and Bangkok. Across the different processes involving agricultural investment, the CSM, as we have seen, had made considerable progress in reframing the terms of the debate and achieving global normative instruments that are more supportive of small-scale food producers and local food systems than those emerging from other global forums.

The five years of reflection, consultation, and negotiations had also helped the proponents of change in the system to identify the hardcore issues on which their opponents dig in their heels and on which constant vigilance and further reframing efforts are required. One is the need to fight against the universalizing and homogenizing tendencies of the global food regime. This requires making a clear and incontrovertible distinction between the different logics and interests of small-scale producers and local food systems, on the one hand, and, on the other, agribusiness-promoted vertical value chains that can allow (how many? which?) small-scale producers to be "promoted" as small-scale entrepreneurs. There is a persistent tendency to pay sanctimonious homage to smallholders – women above all – in the premises of guidelines, principles, and declarations but then to move on to propose policies that head in a different direction. As we saw in Chapter 5, civil society and social movements, backed up by academics and technically qualified NGO allies, have done a good deal of work on modes of production, opposing agro-ecological approaches to industrial monoculture agriculture. Given the persistence of the productivity mantra and the G8/corporate sector allergy to any mention of agro-ecology in CFS literature, however, they still need to further problematize the term "modernization" and to reinforce the demonstration of their argument that agro-ecological peasant agriculture can be more productive than industrial agriculture while also providing a series of other benefits. The overwhelming superiority of small-scale producers' locally based, horizontal, diversified practices of seed breeding as compared to that of corporations – globalized out of nature, vertical, and super-selective – is a particularly strong talking point.

More effort is needed also, as we saw in Chapter 5, in the area of analyzing the nature of markets that are congenial to smallholders, rural economies, and sustainable production models. It is necessary not only to demonstrate the falsity of the assertion that the agribusiness value chain vision could provide an avenue to food security and attainment of the right to food for all but also to convince as many governments as possible that it is not in their political interests to embrace this vision. An alternative to the "value chains" discourse dominant in the official literature is a work in progress. Pieces of such a different approach exist in social movement practice, as we have seen in previous chapters. However, they have not yet been brought together into a convincing overall scenario of how diversified local food systems based on a collaborative, and not solely economic, idea of values and exchange could operate, how they might relate to – but be protected from – international markets, and how they could effectively meet the world food demand. The issue of whether coexistence of local food systems with export-oriented large-scale industrial agriculture is possible, and if so, under different what conditions, has not been decisively addressed by social movements. It was glossed over in the HLPE report on smallholder agriculture, although it has been treated by the Special Rapporteur on the Right to Food (De Schutter 2011a, pp. 543–547). Rural social movements, particularly in Africa, are under pressure from their bases, who are becoming impatient with their organizations' early concentration on policy advocacy and capacity building and are pushing for more attention to economic activities and improved revenues. They are prone to fall into the logic of vertical agribusiness value chains unless approaches to value addition whose benefits reward producers and dynamize rural economies are available to them.

BOX 6.5
WHY CFS POLICY DECISIONS ON AGRICULTURAL INVESTMENT MATTER: THE CASE OF AFRICA

Africa is a particularly attractive target for corporate investments and financial speculation. "Africa represents the 'last frontier' in global food and agricultural markets. It has more than half of the world's uncultivated but agriculturally suitable land and has scarcely utilized its extensive water resources. As Africa's population, incomes, and cities grow and spur the development of domestic markets, the prospects for agriculture and agribusiness will be better than ever" (World Bank 2013, p. 2). Corporations and financial actors lead the assault on Africa's territories and economy, but they act in strong complicity with governments in both the North and the South who are defending particular political and financial interests over those of the present and future citizens to whom they ought to be accountable. Initiatives like the G8's "New Alliance for Food Security and Nutrition" and the "Grow Africa" program promoted by the World Economic Forum, clothed in language of fighting hunger, aim at privatizing Africa's natural resources, opening up its agrifood markets to corporations, and institutionalizing an industrial model of agriculture along with value chains that whisk benefits away from rural economies (McKeon 2014). The challenge over the coming years will be to see whether, with appropriate support from public policies and investment programs, the rising demand for food in Africa can be met instead by Africa's family farmers and food webs adopting environment and climate-friendly agro-ecological approaches. Africa's small-scale producer organizations are investing energy in CFS policy debates because it provides them with international normative guidance, adopted by their governments, on which they can draw in calling them to account.

Other issues on the CFS agenda

We have concentrated on the CFS's treatment of land tenure and agricultural investment since they are the thematic areas in which social movements and the food sovereignty group have invested most energy. The CFS menu, however, is more extensive, and on some issues civil society has not fared as well. Two examples are price volatility and biofuels, which have been the object of HLPE reports and policy discussions in CFS plenary respectively in 2011 and in 2013. In both cases the HLPE report was considered by civil society to be a useful basis for discussion. In both cases, however, the process of moving from HLPE evidence to CFS policy decisions was flawed, giving primacy to narrow, short-term interests of corporations and the governments who support them over the concerns expressed by civil society and negatively affected countries. In 2011 the civil society delegation walked out of the room when the Chair persistently ignored their positions and promoted a price volatility work plan developed by the G20, outside of the CFS space (CSM 2011b). In 2013 they denounced the decision box on biofuels that reached the plenary on the grounds that it did not reflect the evidence and recommendations of the HLPE report and complained that the "Friends of the Rapporteur" mechanism had given undue weight to the views of countries defending the interests of their own biofuels industry, across the North/South divide from the United States to Brazil.

A definitive civil society analysis of the "why" of these different outcomes has not yet been delivered. One might consider that the issues addressed on these two occasions were particularly ungovernable. The price volatility discussion went to the heart of the debate, unsuccessfully conducted in the G8/G20, on how to regulate the speculation that had proved to be so damaging to advanced capitalism itself with the financial crisis of 2008. The biofuels debate targeted specific interests and policies of a range of powerful producer states and was directly related to defense of the neoliberal trade paradigm and the industrial agriculture mode of production. But then, the same can be said of the treatment of land and investment issues in the CFS. At a more operational level, the quality of the facilitation and backstopping conducted by the secretariat and the Rapporteur in the case of the investing in smallholder agriculture decision box was undoubtedly superior to that of the biofuels box. In political framing terms, there has been a clear advantage to taking land as an entry point (given the outrage effect of land grabbing practices) or smallholders (considering their potential political weight in areas of the world where they constitute the majority of the population) as compared with the more technically complex issue of price volatility to which social movements have found it more difficult to relate.

This last remark leads us to underline a final significant factor. The outcomes of policy decision making in the reformed CFS have been more in line with its mandate and with civil society objectives in cases in which social movements in all regions have been strongly engaged than in those where – for lack of time, resources, or interest – they have failed to engage and have left it to the NGO component of the CSM to conduct the battle. We can corroborate this statement by looking at the fate of another CFS outcome that, on the face of it, would appear to be just as arcane and difficult for a social movement to fathom as the price volatility dossier. The Global Strategic Framework for Food Security and Nutrition (GSF) was adopted by the CFS in October 2012 following a contentious two-year nego-tiation process. The very idea that the CFS develop such an instrument had been strongly opposed, during the reform process, by those governments who wanted to limit the Committee's mandate to anodyne policy convergence and coordination building on "best practices" (intergovernmental parlance for avoiding anything that smacks of political decision making). The Global Strategic Framework was under-stood by both its promoters and its opponents to constitute a mechanism for pro-gressive paradigm change taking the right to food and food security – rather than economic growth or "free" trade – as the organizing principle. Despite the GSF's apparent abstraction, the CSM working group that was established to intervene in its negotiation was led by social movements. Alliances were built with governments who, although they might have diverging positions on any particular issue, agreed that it was appropriate for the CFS to progressively develop an overarching strategic framework.

The concluding round of contentious debate on the GSF focused on whether or not to include a final section listing issues with important implications for food security on which consensus had not yet been reached. This was intended as a reminder that there was more work to be done on questions that some govern-ments would be glad to continue ignoring. The list included such hot topics as the need for the international trade system and trade policies to address food security concerns, the impacts of intellectual property systems and biotechnology on food security and nutrition, and the need to seek a common understanding of the term "food sovereignty". The United States strongly opposed inclusion of this last sec-tion in the document. It went so far as to address a diplomatic "demarche" com-municating its position to a number of governments including those of African countries who were to be rewarded with US funding in the context of the G8 New Alliance. These strong-arm techniques were denounced by civil society but also by the majority of the member governments who were concerned to respect the procedures and defend the legitimacy of the CFS. As the Africa Group put it, "There was consensus on this document. We negotiated in good faith. We all have to follow the same spirit and move ahead. This is the spirit of the CFS and we stand by it." The confrontation finished in plenary with a red-faced US delegation and a compromise whereby the final section was included, but the reference to food sovereignty was deleted. "Only for now . . . ", civil society prophesized. Even without it, the GSF was considered by the CSM to be an important success. It is the first global framework on food adopted by intergovernmental consensus that systematically mainstreams the right to adequate food and other related aspects of human rights international legislation. It stresses the central role of small-scale food producers as key actors for achieving food security and nutrition. It calls on all stakeholders to ensure coherence of policies that have a direct or indirect impact on food security and the right to food. It can be used by social movements as a tool for awareness building, advocacy, and monitoring policy coherence at national level (CIDSE et al. 2013). It can be chalked up as another CFS product that could not have been obtained elsewhere.

The Civil Society Mechanism as an innovative interface

Before bringing this provisory assessment of the reformed CFS to a close, we need to take a look at the performance of the autonomous Civil Society Mechanism (CSM), one of its major innovations. We have reviewed the characteristics of the CSM in Chapter 4, focusing on those that have taken it far beyond prevailing practice in other intergovernmental forums (McKeon 2009; McKeon and Kala-fatic 2009). Some aspects of the overall reform for which civil society had fought have been fundamental in terms of providing a favorable environment in which the CSM could operate. The agreement that the CFS constituencies other than governments would be full participants in the debate and would interact with the Bureau in intersessional activities all year round is one of these. The fact that the autonomously designed CSM is accepted to be an inherent and important part of the overall design has enhanced its weight and facilitated mobilization of resources for its operations from supportive governments. The decision that the private sector would be assigned a separate space of its own rather than mixing it up with civil society is another important point. An underlying principle in the civil society vision of the CFS design is to clearly delineate the separate spaces of different actors with their different identities, roles, and interests, and to protect the Committee itself as an arena for political engagement and negotiation among them.

Overall, there is no doubt that the CSM's performance over the first five years of its existence has been laudable. CFS member governments were pleasantly surprised at the first plenary session of the reformed Committee when the civil society contingent succeeded in presenting a document describing its autonomous structure, designed in consultation with networks and organizations in all regions and validated at a global civil society forum. Civil society has successfully occupied the global policy space it helped to create and has accredited social actors whose presence in other international arenas has been largely episodic or regimented. The CSM's invariably substantive and disciplined input is appreciated by all parties. The fact that its positions are voiced by representatives of sectors who are most affected by the decisions under discussion has enhanced their legitimacy. The Mechanism is attracting attention throughout the UN world as a practice to be emulated. An expert panel established to review the UN Environment Programme's NGO-dominated relations with civil society in which I was recently asked to participate unanimously recommended adapting the CSM approach to UNEP conditions, while recognizing that this mechanism was the outcome of a process of social movement engagement and could not be "cut and pasted in" elsewhere (UNEP 2013). In terms of results obtained the CSM has been successful in influencing the terms of the debate and the outcomes of negotiations, particularly when social movements have engaged strongly. It has also used the opportunity of close and continuous interaction with government representatives to build alliances and a practice of dialogue.

The internal functioning of the CSM has been subject to hiccups, as could be expected of a brave new experiment in civil society self-governance. As described in Chapter 4, the CSM was designed to ensure pride of place and visibility to organizations directly representing small-scale food producers and other categories of those most affected by food insecurity. The intention was to assign political leadership to legitimate peoples' organizations and social movements and back them up with the technical and analytic support necessary to develop proposals on complex issues, drawing on capacities of NGOs and academic allies. It was recognized that the CSM would be both an opportunity and a challenge from this viewpoint. Five years down the line, there have certainly been positive outcomes of reflecting and negotiating together in the thematic working groups the CSM has established. More organic links have been built between peasant farmers' organizations, which have tended to be the most solidly organized and visible rural peoples' constituencies, and others like agricultural workers, fisherfolk, and the urban poor, as well as indigenous peoples. Building solidarity and a common frame of understanding among different sectors of the marginalized is an important part of constructing a strong food movement.

But there are problems as well. If the CSM is an arena for alliance building, it is also one of internal conflictuality as organizations and individuals vie for visibility and decision-making power. The worst offenders, as always, are those that are not accountable to a broad membership that is directly affected by the policies under discussion in the CFS. The various constituencies of the food insecure are numerically dominant in the CSM's governance, but there was a perceived danger from the outset that they could find it difficult to consistently play the leading role. On the one hand, it was far from certain that people's organizations would be able or willing to invest sufficient energy in the CSM to ensure that their positions create the basis for the overall civil society platforms. Potentially problematic issues were seen to include the dominance of the English language, the documentation overload generated by intergovernmental processes, insufficient human resources to dedicate to international negotiations, the time required for consultation within social movements, and the need to make global issues relevant to local struggles. Additionally, there is a tendency for NGOs, even with the best of intentions, to allow their superior resource basis, their constant presence on the Roman scene, and their appetite for following the arcane convolutions of CFS process to post them in leadership positions in what has become an increasingly attractive policy forum. The food crisis, land grabbing, and biofuels have become high visibility issues. They are attracting the interest of big NGOs for whom advocacy is a public service activity but also a key element in their resource mobilization.

Even NGOs that are strong players in the CSM/CFS suffer from internal policy incoherence. Their representatives in Rome participate with conviction in developing collective positions against the G8 New Alliance and denouncing efforts by the World Bank and other powerful players to hijack implementation of the Tenure

Guidelines. Yet they take part in initiatives like that of the Global Land Indictors, referred to earlier in the chapter, that are contested by the social movement component of the CSM. OXFAM America agreed to serve in the Leadership Council of the New Alliance over the protests of CSOs in the CSM. Action Aid has used EU project funding to establish an International Food Security Network (IFSN), which enrolls a mixed bag of local NGOs and peasant associations under Action Aid leadership. This is only one of several networks that are headed up by NGOs but claim to include and represent peoples' organizations, muddying the waters of relations among different components of civil society. Large NGOs have launched major campaigns against hunger and land grabbing in which their superior capacity to capture media attention can operate to the detriment of less well-endowed civil society efforts that privilege the visibility of small-scale producers' organizations. The reports and information materials they publish generally do not highlight the collective resistance struggles that Southern peoples' organizations are conducting, reserving visibility for the NGO. The positions that they advocate "on behalf of" the poor are often developed without systematic political engagement with concerned peoples' organizations and may not even reflect the positions for which these organizations themselves are lobbying. These NGOs tend to fall into the middle-of-the-road category of actors to which we have referred earlier in discussing alliances around land grabbing. A continued challenge is that of finding ways of building collaboration without having the agenda be overtaken by them. Or more broadly, as suggested in Chapter 5, managing to tilt the "progressive" forces concerned with food issues toward a "radical" agenda that contemplates significant structural change and away from the siren call of the "reformist" trend (Holt-Giminez and Shattuck 2011).

The CSM is conducting a self-evaluation that will assess to what degree the objective of prioritizing organizations representing those most affected by food insecurity has been attained and what changes need to be made to improve performance. Another key issue under examination is that of the degree to which the CSM has succeeded in bringing its priority concerns into the CFS. In the first session of the reformed CFS, taking the other actors somewhat by surprise, social movements and other CSOs succeeded in strongly conditioning the initial CFS policy agenda. More recently, with the institutionalization of a rather cumbersome agenda-setting mechanism and the stronger engagement of big players, civil society has had difficulties in winning a spot on the agenda for the topics that social movements have prioritized: agro-ecology, governance of biodiversity and genetic resources, food sovereignty. Underlying this tactical difficulty is the challenge of maintaining a vision of overall paradigm and system change while fighting for piece-by-piece, issue-specific victories that can relatively easily be waylaid by defenders of the current global food system. This is both a political and an epistemic fight against morselization, technicalization, and co-option.

Another related problematic area regards the terrain on which dialogue and decision making take place in the CFS, the atmosphere that reigns, and the rules that prevail. A good deal has been said and written about the difficulties that social movements run up against when they engage with international institutions and about how intergovernmental forums privilege window-dressing modes of participation by nonstate actors in order to avoid their inclusion in political process (McKeon 2009, pp. 173–179; McKeon and Kalafatic 2009; Higgot 2001). Some of the issues involved here have been addressed in the reformed CFS and with the creation of the CSM as an autonomous interface mechanism. However, the basic scenario of the CFS continues to conform to intergovernmental practice, and it is one that is profoundly foreign to social movements (Brem-Wilson 2013). How to remodel global policy decision making spaces like the CFS so that they become more suited to performing their expanded multi-actor, multisectoral, and multilevel mandates? Insights in this regard are more likely to come from the CSM than from the governments or secretariat. And they are more likely to come from social movements than from the NGO components of the CSM, which tend to be more easily sucked into the fascination of the global game because they are less intimately rooted in local realities. "Have we succeeded in bringing the voice and the urgency of peoples' struggles into the room?" is a constant query coming from peoples' organizations in civil society self-evaluation at the close of important CFS sessions. It can be done. A page-turning moment in the International Conference on Agrarian Reform and Rural Development (ICARRD) came when hundreds of rural women marched directly into the plenary session to present their petitions to the assembled delegates. But ICARRD took place in Brazil in a relatively permeable conference center where a permissive session chair could pretty much determine what was allowed. The FAO Headquarters in Rome is an impenetrable fortress by comparison, and bringing the masses into the Plenary Hall is about as unimaginable as entering the Sistine Chapel to lobby the conclave about the choice of the next Pope.

A promising transformational practice that is already being adopted in the CFS is the regional consultations that have been organized in the context of the Global Strategic Framework, the Tenure Guidelines, and the rai principles. Decentralization and contextualization of the debate brings it closer to local realities and allows civil society to knock more loudly on the door of national government accountability. As indicated above, in the two latter cases regionalization of the debate has been accompanied by the development of autonomous civil society texts. These documents contribute to building broad-based popular movements for whom influencing CFS outcomes is, as it should be, just one piece of the overall strategy. For social movements it is essential to orchestrate mobilization so as to enhance the kinds of power that they can wield against those that corporations and powerful states exercise when they deliberate in closed-door forums, apply political conditionalities, and proffer financially enhanced handshakes. Making things visible so that they cannot be denied; building local peoples' awareness of their rights, how they are being violated, and what they can do about it; politicizing the agenda by such means as public mobilization strategies around World Bank meetings, the G8 New Alliance, and corporate agricultural investment conventions; linking up land and investment issues under debate in the CFS with other social movement mobilizations targeting corporations, the WTO, bilateral trade, and investment agreements – these are some of the ways in which social movements can play David to the Goliath of the global corporate food system. They are the indispensable complement to engagement in a global forum like the CFS, and not enough attention has been given thus far to strengthening these synergies.

Bringing CFS outcomes home

In the end, what will make the difference for social movements – and for the CFS as a whole – is building links between the global policy space and local realities by "bringing home" the outcomes of CFS negotiations. Rural peoples' organizations and social movements can justify their investment in global engagement only if it generates support for local struggles and alternative building and opens up political space at national level. It is not a question of choosing between a top-down or a bottom-up approach to campaigning, policy work, and accountability claiming. The two must be mutually reinforcing, with local and national mobilization providing the popular energy for global policy work that otherwise would be reduced in its legitimacy and its urgency, and the latter accessing outside support of various kinds for local struggles. Urging governments to implement their global commitments and calling them to account if they fail to do so is a powerful global–local bridge builder. It is a hallmark of international human rights "soft law" and of the monitoring and appeals machinery of the Human Rights Council, which civil society and allies like the Special Rapporteur on the Right to Food are seeking to bring to the CFS. Monitoring is also an important tool for collective learning. Monitoring the national implementation of CFS decisions, with appropriate indicators and benchmarks, can feed back into the formulation of guidelines at global level and, over time, can lead to adjusting objectives and paradigms (De Schutter 2014a, p. 238).

The crafting of the section of the Global Strategic Framework that discussed the principles governing monitoring was a major achievement in this direction. They should be human rights based. They should make it possible to hold decision makers accountable. They should be participatory and include all actors involved, particularly the most vulnerable. They should be simple, comprehensive, easy to understand, and appropriately disaggregated (CFS 2013b, paras. 92–93). The CSM is seeking to use this victory to facilitate meaningful implementation of a highly contested paragraph of the CFS reform document that identified promoting accountability as one of the functions of the new Committee and enjoined the CFS to develop an "innovative mechanism" to monitor progress towards agreed upon objectives (CFS2009 Rev. 2, para. 6ii). Work on this task has been hampered, on the one hand, by the allergy of governments toward being held accountable and, on the other, by the propensity of FAO technicians for complicated monitoring approaches relying dominantly on quantitative data. The monitoring principles included in the GSF should open the way to building on the considerable experience in participatory monitoring and building accountability that has been accumulated in the context of the human rights framework and structures. They underscore the fact that the monitoring function needs to be carried out at the national level by a multi-actor platform and to include qualitative information, based on concrete cases, of the kind that social movements are best placed to provide. It needs to go beyond simply looking at whether CFS decisions have been implemented and assess also the outcomes. National-level monitoring, where governments feel more in control, needs to be linked to the global monitoring function of the CFS. The onus is on civil society to come up with doable proposals that can successfully take the CFS beyond the comfort zone of most governments.

A CFS balance sheet

The questions we have raised regarding the CSM are central in assessing the performance of the CFS as a whole, given civil society's dominant innovating role in the reformed Committee. For the CFS, as well, the balance sheet can only be positive. In terms of terrain covered and outputs, the work on land and agricultural investment at which we have looked in some detail would be sufficient in itself to justify five years of activity without considering important accomplishments in other critical areas like social protection measures or food insecurity in areas subject to protracted crises. As we have seen, the CFS's inclusive nature and its food security and right to food mandate confers qualities on its outputs that cannot be achieved elsewhere. The reformed CFS has undoubtedly made important strides in gaining policy significance over the past five years. Big food security actors who had snubbed the "old" CFS are back in force – agrifood corporations, the World Bank, powerful countries like the United States. Regions like Africa, which had tended to be passive participants in the global debate, are making efforts to build up their presence. Conflictuality on key issues is coming out into the open and is tending to gravitate toward the CFS as the foremost food security policy space. This is a positive indicator of success. The fact that the new CFS cannot be ignored is impacting on actors who were used to deciding in splendid isolation, like the G20 (on price volatility) and the World Bank (on the PRAI). This is already a significant result in itself, and it was not a foregone conclusion. As a member of the EU delegation remarked to me at the close of the reformed CFS's first plenary session in 2010, "When this whole reform business came up on the screen we thought the CFS was a dead duck. Now it may not be a swan but it certainly is up in the air and flying".

From a once-a-year Rome-based plenary meeting, the CFS has developed into a year-round process that is making forays into the regions. The governmental Bureau, the Advisory Group bringing in the voices of the nonstate CFS participants, and the secretariat – expanded beyond the FAO to include IFAD and the WFP – are engaged together in an on-the-job and often messy experiment in developing new approaches to global political process. One important element in this experimentation is that of progressively constructing clearer and more effective relations between political debate and technical support. The technical basis for debate and decision making in the CFS has evolved beyond the secretariat to embrace the High-Level Panel of Experts, itself an experiment in extending the concept of research to accept nonacademic sources of knowledge. The quality of the HLPE's work is generally recognized to be high. Some reports, like that on smallholder investment, are having significant impact not only within the CFS but on strategic reflection more broadly. But there is room for improvement. Rather than going for weak consensus among HLPE team members, the reports could use intra-team controversy to help frame and stimulate informed political debate in the CFS. More could be done to strengthen systemic analysis with a political economy dimension, and to bring qualitative data from social movements to bear on the issues under discussion.

Putting the expanded political component of the CFS into operation has proved to be even more problematic. Political debate has broadened from governments alone to include other concerned actors, but just what that means in practice is still being determined. The CFS reform document indicates that the nonstate actors participate on the same footing as member governments except that "voting and decision taking is the exclusive prerogative of Members" (CFS 2009, para. 10). This procedure met with civil society approval when the reform was under discussion, since they prefer that governments make decisions and be held accountable for them. But determining exactly when the shift from discussion to decision making takes place is a difficult call to make, particularly when the objective is to build consensus rather than to decide by voting. The moment of decision making in the CFS seems to hop around like a hyperactive frog in an electrified pond. Already the HLPE reports tend to favor consensus over clarifying the terms of contention. The process of drafting the decision box that goes to the CFS plenary also risks turning into an exercise in conflict-calming pre-negotiation. Once the annual CFS session arrives, negotiation tends to evade plenary debate and take up residence in the "Friends of the Rapporteur" mechanism where big players dominate and too much depends on the capacities of the Rapporteur. A proper equilibrium has not yet been attained between arriving at decisions and allowing full debate on what will invariably be contentious issues if they merit making decisions about them. Ensuring that adequate weight is given to the various voices that are raised in the debate, taking differences of power and interests into account, is also a work in progress. The consensus-seeking mode of intergovernmental process risks being extended to this more inclusive forum where powerful actors who champion one paradigm of organizing the food system sit side by side with small-scale food producers' organizations whose vision is totally different. Seeking "balance" by negating these differences and giving a bit to one side and a bit to the other is unacceptable from the viewpoint of social movements.

It is fair to say that the reformed CFS is addressing with some success the first four deficiencies of global food governance listed in the ideal checklist with which this chapter opened: fragmentation (with all concerned actors in the room), lack of inclusiveness of those most affected (with priority voice for organizations representing the food insecure within an autonomous CSM), insufficiently human rights based (with the right to food specified in its mandate), and dominance of productivist and free market paradigm (with the HLPE reports and the successful work conducted by the CSM to change the terms of the debate). It has begun to make efforts to address the fifth – inadequate subsidiarity – by seeking to regional-ize its deliberations and to collaborate more systematically with existing regional authorities, and the sixth by putting in place a system for monitoring implementa-tion of its decisions. The three last deficiencies listed are the most difficult to correct since they get to the heart of the power relations that keep the corporate-led global food system in place: multiplication of private sector or hybrid governance mecha-nisms, weight of corporate influence, and lack of effective and enforceable regula-tory power. The unwillingness of the "free" market proponents to allow the CFS to tread on the terrain of international trade agreements is an obstacle. Defenders of the corporate food regime have not been able to get their way in the CFS thus far, but they will certainly not stop seeking to do so, and they will continue to exercise the option of ignoring or subverting CFS normative guidance that does not serve their interests.

The reformed CFS has taken a giant's step by adopting the right to food as its lens for reading contentious issues impacting on food security and the inescapable reference point for policy coherence, although determined umpiring is required to keep some members on track. It has taken another by bringing most of the con-cerned actors into the room, particularly those most affected, whose voices are less often heard. It is, however, laboring under the very basic dilemma that the national governments who remain its end-of-the-line decision makers are prone to engaging in global food issues with a view to defending narrow, short-term national interests defined in terms of a paradigm that pumps for globalized trade and productivism. Yet they are the only actors who could potentially defend their citizens against the impacts of multilateral and bilateral trade and investment agreements that violate their right to food and that – unlike the human rights framework – are enforced by "hard" international law. The UN Special Rapporteur on the Right to Food has provided detailed and lucid guidance regarding incoherencies between trade regimes and the right to food, which current global governance mechanisms are failing to address (De Schutter 2008 and 2009c). It is the same governments who sit in the CFS and the WTO, and hence, in theory, they could be called upon to address their policy incoherencies. India, speaking on behalf of the G33 at the WTO Ninth Min-isterial Conference in Bali in December 2013, did just that by successfully defending its rights-based Food Security Act. In the words of Indian Minster of Commerce, Anand Sharma, "For India food security is non-negotiable. Governments of all developing nations have a legitimate obligation and moral commitment towards food and livelihood security of hundreds of millions of their hungry and poor. Public procurement at administered prices is often the only method of supporting farmers and building stocks for food security in developing countries" (Wise 2013b). In the concluding section of this book we will try to explore what would be required to bring this kind of logic to bear more forcefully on the global governance of food.

Notes

1. See McKeon 2013a for a more detailed discussion of the negotiation of the CFS Tenure Guidelines from a social movement perspective.
2. Including Switzerland, Belgium, Germany, the European Commission, Italy, and the United Kingdom, with interest expressed by Denmark, Belgium, France, Sweden, and Canada.
3. It draws its inspiration from the International Peasant Conference: Stop the Land Grab! held in Mali in November 2011 (http://viacampesina.org/en/index.php/main-issues-mainmenu-27/agrarian-reform-mainmenu-36/1127-stop-land-grabbing-now).
4. This manual will be accessible, when published, on the FAO website for the Guidelines: www.fao.org/nr/tenure/governance-of-tenure/it/.
5. The most noteworthy of these are the Land Research Action Network (LRAN), the Transnational Institute (TNI), the Initiatives in Critical Agrarian Studies (ICAS) housed at the International Institute of Social Studies (ISS), and the Land Deal Politics Initiatives (LDPI).
6. Communication by Mamadou Goita to the CONCORD European Food Security Working Group, 3 June 2013.
7. This was not the case for the other policy discussion, on biofuels, that took place at the fortieth session of the CFS, as we shall see shortly.
8. The rai principles were endorsed by governments at the 41st session of the CTS in October 2014. The statements expressing the concerns of the CSM regarding the content of the rai can be found at www.csm4cfs.org/news/principles_for_responsible_agricultural_investements.13/

7

WHERE TO NOW?

We have yet to see an economy whose driving mechanism is neither direct coercion by the state nor the compulsions of profit but democratic self-determination, which need no long subordinate all human values to the wasteful and destructive imperatives of accumulation. That kind of advance in democracy would require a system of social relations as different from capitalism as capitalism was from feudalism.

Ellen Meikins Wood, *The Pristine Culture of Capitalism*, p. 176

Where have we gotten to?

This book took off from the food price riots of 2007–2008 to conduct an exploration in time and in space of how our food provision is ensured today. It has reviewed the dominant corporate-led global food system and the multiple ways in which it visits negative impacts on society and the environment. Even those readers who are not totally convinced may, I hope, have opened their minds to the evidence and the reasoning presented here. They may have begun to ask themselves whether it might not be imperative to find ways of deviating from the collision course with the limits of tolerance of our world in which we seem to be engaged.

The urgency of taking action is evident since corporations and states, left to their own devices, will not virtuously self-reform. A balance sheet published by two thoughtful academics in early 2012 found that:

A paradigm shift is underway, caused by the deepening integration of agricultural, energy, and financial markets in a resource-constrained world made more vulnerable by climate change. Powerful multinational firms dominate these markets. Many benefit from current policies and practices, and some are directly involved in new agricultural development programs, either through public–private partnerships or in programs such as AGRA. Their interests

heavily influence national and global policies, slowing, diverting, or halting needed action. This leaves international institutions promoting market-
friendly reforms but resistant to imposing needed regulations on those food
and agricultural markets.

(Wise and Murphy 2012, p. 34)

Revisiting their assessment a year later they concluded that, despite the urgency,
"world leaders largely squandered their opportunities in 2012" (Murphy and Wise
2013, p. 1).

A recent FAO review of food and agricultural policy decisions taken by ten
African countries since 2008 (Demeke et al. 2014) evoked the following comment
from a former FAO policy analyst:

> The policy decisions taken by governments in the wake of the crisis show
> that they have mainly considered the food crisis as a supply crisis and have
> responded by subsidising and promoting well-known technologies that in-
> crease production, the so-called green revolution technologies. As a result,
> it is most likely that the majority of poor smallholder farmers, who do not
> have the financial means to buy inputs, will not have benefited from these
> subsidies, despite targeting efforts made in some countries and despite the
> establishment of special credit programmes. Moreover, this reaction to the
> crisis will not have been in favour of the very much required transition to
> more sustainable agricultural practices.
>
> (Maetz 2014)

In his final report at the end of his tenure as UN Special Rapporteur on the Right
to Food, Oliver De Schutter reiterated that "a narrow focus on improved productivity risks ignoring the wide range of other variables that foresight exercises should
take into account. . . . Any prescription to increase yields that ignores the need to
transition to sustainable production and consumption, and to reduce rural poverty,
will not only be incomplete; it may also have damaging impacts, worsening the
ecological crisis and widening the gap between different categories of food producers" (De Schutter 2014b, p. 8).

For its part, the food sovereignty movement gives the floor to the young people
who will be the beneficiaries or the victims of tomorrow's food system:

> Young people in the rural areas of the world are facing one of the greatest
> challenges in all history: gathering the testimonies of the farmers' struggle
> and at the same time facing the new challenges for the construction of a
> radically different world. All over the world, the neoliberal capitalist system
> has imposed a political and economic model of industrial agriculture, inten-
> sive monoculture and of land grabbing driven by transnational corporations
> with the approval of national and local governments. This model – which
> promotes the privatization of all natural resources including land, forests,

water and planted seeds – destroys livelihoods and rural cultural heritage, and exhausts Mother Earth.

(Nyéléni Newsletter 2014, p. 2)

Adopting different language, these diversely authoritative sources transmit the same message – the old is digging in its heels and is slowing, diverting, or halting needed action. E.P. Thompson, the author of the epigraph placed at the beginning of this book, describes the profound recasting of power and culture that took place in 18th-century England leading up to the moment when "the gentry lost their self-assured cultural hegemony [and] it suddenly appeared that the world was not, after all, bounded at every point by their rules and overwatched by their power" (Thompson 1991, p. 96). The new that was being rung in at that time was energetic "young capitalism" sparking class consciousness among those who had previously been "plebs" (*ibid.*, p. 23). Capitalism has aged since then, and in its mature form it seems today to have become a force blocking the new. The plebs who were becoming members of a class and citizens in a society in 18th-century England seem to have largely been transformed today into solitary consumers. What hopes are there to open up space for dialectic to operate once again, and how are we to go about it?

Why is this time different?

On several occasions in the course of this book we have noted capitalism's recurrent capacity to generate crises and then turn them to its advantage. David Harvey, a long-time analyst of capitalism from a Marxist viewpoint, reminds us that crises are essential to its reproduction. "It is in the course of crises that the instabilities of capitalism are confronted, reshaped and re-engineered to create a new version of what capitalism is about" (Harvey 2014 p. ix). We have seen this capacity at work in the current flourishing of market- and technology-based solutions to hunger, malnutrition, climate change, and the glorification of the private sector and corporate capital as paladins of development. Is there any reason to believe that the reshaping effort might not work this time around? Might there something different operating today?

Voices in the academic world are being raised with increasing strength to argue against neoliberal doctrine and in favor of government intervention to regulate and correct market dynamics within a capitalist system. Such Keynesian ideas, which have gained ground since the financial crisis of 2007–2008, find lucid and articulate exponents in thinkers like Noble Prize winners Paul Krugman and Joseph Stiglitz. The latter's latest book questions whether US society can continue to pay the high price of inequality that, in his view, stifles what he considers to be the dynamic potentials of capitalism (Stiglitz 2014). French economist Thomas Piketty's *Capital in the Twenty-First Century* (2013) argues that capital's propensity to accumulate and become ever more concentrated is not the result of market failure but a natural, inherent tendency. He holds that the resulting growing inequality, which he too sees as a threat to democracy and social order, can only be reversed through state intervention.

The question "Does capitalism have a future?" is in the air (Wallerstein et al. 2013). A convinced "no" comes from Harvey, who identifies what he feels are fatal internal contradictions. One of these is the drive to accumulate capital beyond the means of investing it. More and more capital, he notes, is being invested in search of rents, interest, and royalties rather than in productive activity, and this trend is reinforced by "the immense extractive power" of the provisions for intellectual property rights referred to repeatedly throughout this book (Harvey *op. cit.*, p. 241). The second is capitalism's imperative to use the cheapest methods of production, leaving consumers bereft of adequate means of consumption and expanding mass unemployment. We have discussed the trends of financialization and de-peasantization in Chapter 2. Like a sorcerer's apprentice, productive capitalism seems to have lost control of the economic globalization it yearned for, and it is overwhelmed by the ascendency of financial capital that has ensued.

The third fatal contradiction listed by Harvey is also central to the food nexus. This is the necessity to exploit nature and the environment to – and beyond – its limits. Capitalism has managed to overcome this difficulty and maintain profitability in the past. The negative ecological aspects of these past adaptations are cumulative, however, and the inflexion point in capitalism's exponential growth today is pushing toward exasperated commodification and privatization of nature and intensification of pressure in areas like climate change, biodiversity, and food security (*ibid.*, p. 253). Concerns of this kind have been voiced in Chapter 2 and elsewhere in this book, coming from a wide range of sources of various kinds including intergovernmental institutions like UNCTAD and UNEP and multi-authored scientific assessments like the IAASTD. Adding to the stock of evidence, the Fifth Assessment Report of the Intergovernmental Panel of Climate Change (IPCC) states unequivocally that global warming is cutting into food supply and fueling wars and natural disasters (Goldenberg 2014). The urgency of transiting to a food system that can help to "cool the planet" rather than heating it, as La Via Campesina puts it, is evident. Speaking during the release of the IPCC report on 30 March 2014, climate scientists indicated that the Green Revolution model of agriculture is likely to fail in the face of temperature extremes and changing rainfall patterns (Gaia Foundation 2014). This is no surprise since, coming at capitalism from a food perspective, we have already taken note of the profitability crisis from which industrial agriculture is suffering today due to a fall in nitrogen efficiency and loss of biodiversity (McMichael 2012b, p. 65) and dysfunctions of genetic modification that have triggered decreases in productivity and increases in the need for pesticide applications.

The limits that risk being exceeded are social and political as well as natural and ecological. Like the capitalist economic system of which they are a part, global food regimes historically alternate between periods of economic liberalization and reformist periods that governments enact in response to the social unrest caused by the impacts of liberalization. Calls for reform have been mounting since the 2007–2008 food price crisis, yet governments and multilateral organizations are offering only more of the same neoliberal policies (Holt-Giminez, 2011, p. 318).

The foreseeable future trajectory for the present corporate-led food regime could lead in the direction of a two-track food system offering high-quality food for the rich and low-quality mass-produced food for the poor, along with dispossession of the majority of the population in the Global South, hardly a recipe for social peace.

BOX 7.1
THE MULTIFACETED CRISIS OF MARKET RULE

- a crisis of neoliberal capitalism and its focus on redistribution, rather than production, of material wealth, with large/institutional investors shifting funds to agricultural commodity speculation;
- ecological crisis, stimulating green investments as governments and public authorities devise incentives and protocols enabling "ecosystem service" financing;
- food crisis, with price inflation, rising hunger, depletion of reserves, food export bans, and food riots, stimulating new enclosures as investors capitalize land for food and fuel;
- trade regime crisis as states and sovereign wealth funds override WTO rules by commodifying agricultural land offshore for non-trade-based access to food and fuel for the investing country;
- a crisis of governmentality, mortgaging public capacities to austerity programs associated with structural adjustment policies – conditioning policies favorable to land/green grabbing for host states in the global South; and
- a general legitimacy crisis reflected in contestation over the content and consequences of governance of humanity's relation to land and ecosystems.

Adapted from McMichael (2014)

So, it is not unreasonable to entertain the hypothesis that this time may be different. It may prove possible to leave capitalism behind us as an organizing principle of human society that has held sway, after all, for not more than five centuries out of a total of our six millennia of recorded history. If not that, it may be time – at the very least – to introduce so significant a series of measures regulating markets and empowering communities that the result is "something truly new" (Friedmann 2009). The overwhelming and homogenizing power of the naturalized market and predatory capital has paralyzed the dialectic between different ways of conceiving food and organizing food provision. Yet there are cracks in the system, both internal to capitalism and the corporate-led global food regime as we have rehearsed above, and external.

This book has adopted food regime analysis as a privileged lens for reading the evolution of global food provisioning from a political economy viewpoint. This big picture provides a context within which to situate an examination of specific components of food provisioning – like choice of technology, market organization, models of production, and others – and of how actors and functions are linked together operationally in different food systems. Food regime analysts judge that it is too early to determine whether the corporate food regime – as the latest of the successive forms of how capitalism has reorganized world agriculture to permit continued accumulation – has run its course or whether it is simply restructuring (McMichael 2013a, p. 109). The current crisis of accumulation is a compound one. It combines the structural tendency of capitalism to erode its conditions of production (labor, nature) with the more conjunctural tendency of neoliberal capital to turn away from investment in production and toward various forms of financial speculation. Agrifuels production, enclosure of land and other natural resources, promotion of a bioeconomy that transforms the very bases of life into exploitable market values – these are components of capital's response to the current accumulation crisis (*ibid.*, pp. 114ff). Their ecological, economic, and social sustainability is subject to doubt, as we have seen. In food regime terms, such restructuring efforts are accompanied by changes in state/capital relations. The impasse in which the WTO multilateral trading system has found itself is indicative of this kind of change (*ibid.*, p. 125). It has opened the way to a series of bilateral and multi-bilateral arrangements in which states and investors combine in a dizzying multitude of ways.

Food regime analysis also posits a strong role for social contestation in the transition from one configuration to another. It is a hypothesis of this book that the food sovereignty movement constitutes a counter-force that has the potential of substantially altering the basis of food regime organization by helping to fragment global hegemony and reconstitute a territorially rooted and governed approach to food provision. Previous chapters have reviewed the increasingly grounded and articulated alternatives to various aspects of the corporate food regime that are building up from the local level around the world and how they are interacting with subglobal governance sites. We have examined food sovereignty as a paradigm that substitutes for the "free" market-productivist-modernization package in all its dimensions. It is rights based, including the rights of Mother Earth. It is attentive to ecology, the environment, and biodiversity. It fights climate change and builds resilience. It is territorially rooted, bridges the distance between producer and consumer, and furnishes healthy food for all. It binds agro-ecological modes of small-scale production with modes of processing and distribution that are appropriate to them and that create employment and stimulate local economies. It operates against inequalities. It is "the real choice" (Cranbrook 2006). Finally, this book has documented the advent, thanks in good part to pressure from the food sovereignty movement, of a global governance site that is not like the others. The reformed CFS is a source of inclusively debated, paradigm-changing normative guidance. It is committed to building links with multi-actor policy platforms at regional and national levels in a logic of subsidiarity. This is only a timid beginning in terms of establishing a system of global food governance that can be supportive rather than repressive of action for change coming from the base. How to move further in this direction?

In the introduction we promised that we would explore possibilities of defending common goods and public interests in a globalized world that the market has come to rule. Past chapters have come some distance in this direction, particularly in terms of identifying what ought to be promoted in the common interest. We now need to give more attention to the "how" part of the equation, not providing solutions but pointing to fruitful terrains in which they can be and are being sought. We will start by looking at what it might take for global governance sites to do a better job in defense of a better world.

Revisiting global governance and public/private spheres

Chapter 4 referred to the transition from purely intergovernmental process to multi-actor global governance as an introduction to talking about the 2009 reform of the Committee on World Food Security. Now we return to this evolution in a forward-looking perspective. The Commission on Global Governance whose conclusions we cited took a normative and aspirational view of global governance. They viewed it as a long-term process of inclusive global integration based on common values and targeted to defending global public goods. Some critics, however, judge the global governance project to have suffered the fate of other initially progressive normative concepts, evolving, instead, into an attempt to conceal the negative tendencies of neoliberal late capitalism. In this vision, global governance is seen not as a counterforce to, or a regulative mechanism for, economic globalization but as its ideological companion (Pattberg 2006, pp. 13–14). Global governance is, in their view, neoliberal global governance, and the political actors and interest groups engaging in its spaces are often unable to move beyond neoliberal terms of debate (Duncan and Barling 2012, p. 145). Other students of global governance speak of it as "a functional necessity of a more global world". In this vision it is intrinsically neither good nor bad. Whether it has beneficial or harmful effects depends on how it is practiced and the degree to which it is accountable (Scholte 2011, pp. 14–15).

The food sovereignty movement that played such an important role in crafting the reformed CFS has some very clear ideas about how governance at all levels should be practiced in order to generate beneficial effects and offer a fighting chance of changing the terms of the debate. One has to do with maintaining clarity about what players, in addition to states, are recognized as having what kinds of legitimate roles in different aspects of governance activities. Clearly spelling out the identities, interests, roles, and responsibilities of different actors is fundamental in their vision. A related requirement is the need to ensure that normative decision making is unequivocally maintained as a political act, engendering the political accountability of those who make the decisions. It is not to be confused with technical evidence gathering, managerial prescriptions in the name of efficiency, or multi-stakeholder pyjama parties. Chapter 4 has mapped the maze of different forms and levels of rule making and application that exist in today's globalized world. Some of them are reasonably accountable to the people they are ultimately expected to serve through some form of political oversight – others not at all. We have noted the vigor with which pieces of the international community proposed an administrative, managerial solution to the 2007–2008 food crisis allied with an apolitical smokescreen of partnership that would leave decision making with corporations and powerful donor country governments. The reform of the CFS was a victory for political decision making, informed by effective evidence giving by those most affected and allied to accountability. Making this happen in practice, as the last chapter has recounted, is a constant battle and a work in progress.

Facile representations of the state, the private sector, and civil society as three components of global food governance with equal status and weight are deleterious in this regard. So are protestations that these categories are no longer terribly relevant and that what counts are the governance functions that need to be fulfilled and who actually weighs in to address them. Such assessments are off the track politically, although they may shed light on the increasing complexity of governance arrangements and why private authority emerges when it does (Green 2014, p. 166). Neither one nor the other, however, helps us to understand the political reality of a world in which the corporate private sector wields enormous power, to the point of often rendering states subservient. They do not help equip us to resist attempts to privatize governance in the form of public–private partnerships, which fail to define the obligations and regulate the behavior of the private partners. PPPs are billed as win-win affairs since, in theory, they make it possible to profit from the capacities and resources of private entities and shift some of the risk of service provision to them while anchoring accountability solidly in the public sector. In reality, accountability tends to drop out of the picture altogether while corporations manage to maximize their profits and evade the bulk of the risks involved in investment by pushing governments to twist rules and regulations to their advantage. In the field of agriculture and food security PPPs like those envisaged in the G8's New Alliance for Food Security and Nutrition pit the interests of powerful corporations against those of peasant farmers, with governments too often rooting for the former. But who needs governments in the PPP cosmology? The companies claim that they themselves have the interests of small farmers at heart in the value chain logic. As the head of strategy at fertilizer giant Yara puts it, "We take a certain share of the profits but it makes no sense for us to screw the farmer. It is short-sighted if you are an input supplier" (Tran et al. 2014). The Global Redesign Initiative (GRI) launched by the World Economic Forum in 2009 carries this vision of who-needs-governments, or regulations for that matter, to the level of global governance of just about everything, from developing a common values framework to eradicating poverty or addressing global risks and security (WEF 2010; Sogge 2014). Civil society in the CFS, instead, is advocating strongly for "bringing back the State" (Kay 2014).

What to do with the private sector in our forward-looking exploration? The term itself is just as fuzzy as that of "civil society", which we discussed in Chapter 4. Applied to the field of food and agriculture, FAO defines it as "including enterprises, companies or businesses, regardless of size, ownership and structure". The range, in size, is from smallholder farmer organizations to the largest international corporations. The category includes industry and trade associations "that represent private sector interests" but not philanthropic foundations, although many would maintain that some of the most powerful of these are also staunch defenders of private sector interests (FAO n.d.). Definitions such as these paste over the enormous differences in nature and interests that exist between actors like small-scale food producers and large-scale export-oriented industrial agriculture enterprises, a point that the Civil Society Mechanism has forcefully reiterated in negotiations in the CFS. It is universally recognized that small-scale producers are responsible for the bulk of investments in agriculture and of food production today, a reality that has led the African movements to propose that the acronym "PPP" be reframed as public-peasant partnerships (McKeon 2013c, p. 16).

The separating out of the categories of public and private is, of course, not a natural given but an historical, culturally specific process. It took on particular significance in Western Europe in the period of the 16th–18th centuries as it accompanied the replacement of the paternalist moral economy of feudalism by the market economy, the evolution to which the opening epigraph of this book refers. The detachment of the title to property from allegiance to a sovereign had the effect of turning it into an economic rather than a political category and laying the ground for the modern association of the public sector with "politics" and of the private sector with "economics" – with the market behavior of private individuals (M. McKeon 2005, pp. 17–18). At the same time, with the defeat of the old regime – fueled by the capitalist revolution – the political theory that authority came from the top down was challenged and replaced by the theory that authority came from the bottom up, creating space for private citizens to reflect on and criticize state policy. Liberalism celebrates all of these changes as an unmitigated "good thing". In crediting the "moral economy", however, Thompson points out that the old regime assumed that the rulers had responsibility for the welfare of the ruled. Under capitalism, instead, this sense of moral responsibility has evaporated, in part because of the primacy of the moral principle of equality (suggesting individual responsibility for failure) whereas the old regime took inequality to be "moral". In his influential work *The Great Transformation* (1957), Karl Polanyi spoke about the "discovery of society" as involving the progressive replacement of preindustrial conceptions of moral economy, through social pressures, by rationalized notions of civil rights and social protections (Patel and McMichael 2010, p. 13). Polanyi himself judged that, in the long term, the self-protection of society that was put in place to tame the excesses of the market would prove incompatible with the functioning of the capitalist economic system (Polanyi *op.cit.*, p. 129). He posited two alternative solutions. Either the democratic principle must be extended from politics to economics, or the democratic "public sphere" will be abolished altogether (Polanyi 1936 quoted in Patel 2005, p. 80).

It is in this democratic "public sphere" that the tendencies represented by the reformed CFS can be situated and – hopefully – reinforced by extending their authority over the economic world.[1] To what exactly does the term refer? In the words of one of its most authoritative theorists, Jürgen Habermas,

> A portion of the public sphere is constituted in every conversation in which private persons come together to form a public. They are then acting neither as business or professional persons conducting their private affairs, nor as legal consociates subject to the legal regulations of a state bureaucracy and obligated to obedience. Citizens act as a public when they deal with matters of general interest without being subject to coercion. . . . We speak of a political public sphere when the public discussions concern objects connected with the practice of the state. The coercive power of the state is the counterpart, as it were, of the political public sphere but is not a part of it. State power is, to be sure, considered "public" power, but it owes the attribute of publicness to its task of caring for the public, that is, providing for the common good of all legal consociates. Only when the exercise of public authority has actually been subordinated to the requirement of democratic publicness does the political public sphere acquire an institutionalized influence on the government.
>
> (Habermas 1989, p. 231)

Sympathetic critics note that the institutional presuppositions for a legitimate and effective public sphere that Habermas tacitly postulated situates it in relation to a sovereign, territorial nation-state. These include a state apparatus exercising power over a bounded territory and its inhabitants, a national economy subject in principle to state regulation, a national citizenry possessing a set of general interests, a national language constituting the medium of public sphere communication, a national literature fostering an imagined community and shared identity, and a national infrastructure of communication. Such conditions do not obtain in a globalized world. "If economic governance is in the hands of agencies that are not locatable in the Westphalian space how can it be made accountable to public opinion? Moreover, if these agencies . . . are systematically reversing the democratic project, using markets to tame politics instead of politics to tame markets then how can citizen public opinion have any impact" (Fraser 2007, p. 17)? The invitation is not to jettison the concept and the aspiration of public sphere but to rethink what the conditions of legitimacy and efficacy posited by Habermas mean in a post-Westphalian world.

In a global governance context the condition of legitimacy could translate into a requirement that "all who are affected" – based not on shared citizenship as in the nation state but on "co-imbrication in a common set of global structures and institutions that affect their lives" – be able to participate as peers (Fraser *op. cit.*, p. 23). This is a requirement that the reformed CFS has fulfilled far better than other global governance spaces, but it is not enough. For one thing, the articulation between the people in the room and the vast constituencies whose voices they are expected to represent is insufficient. The representativity of governments tends to be assumed but shouldn't be, as has often been acknowledged. There are problems of inclusiveness of the range of concerned actors consulted at the national level, particularly the most vulnerable. There are also issues of intrusion in national decision making and position defining by outside actors, from donor governments and international agencies to corporations. Of the constituencies other than governments present in the CFS, the CSM has done the most to ensure that the positions it brings to CFS plenaries are the outcome of broad consultation in the regions. The Private Sector Mechanism, instead, represents essentially the views and interests of agribusiness corporations. Their delegations may include a few leaders of commercial farmers' organizations, but the small and medium enterprise sector is absent despite the key role it plays in food systems. An even greater limitation, however, is the string of illogical thinking that starts off from the reality that the corporate private sector has enormous influence on food security and hence has to be taken into account in seeking solutions to hunger, food insecurity, and malnutrition. Thus far no one would disagree. But *how* to take it into account? Should the corporate private sector be "in the room" on the same footing as governments and civil society, helping to define normative guidance that is expected to defend common goods like the right to food of the world's population and the ecological and climatic health of the planet we are leaving to our children? Or should norms be designed on the basis of sound evidence, privileging that provided by the most affected, and adopted by governments who are constitutionally obliged to be accountable to their citizens and should be held to the fulfillment of this obligation?

The in-the-room champions advance two basic arguments. On the one hand, they hold, agribusiness corporations have great positive contributions to make to attaining the right to food and a healthy environment through their technology, managerial know-how, and capital – a position that I hope this book has demolished or at least put severely into question. Secondly, if they don't participate in framing the normative guidance, they are not likely to respect it. This is more than highly doubtful. On the one hand, if they do participate, the normative effectiveness of the output risks being watered down, even to a point close to irrelevance. On the other, corporations are far more likely to respect norms when they are legally obliged to do so than when they are invited to comply voluntarily. As West African peasant leader Mamadou Cissokho has put it, "We don't want 'responsible investors'. We want a legislative framework that protects us effectively and investors who are obliged to respect the law" (Cissokho 2012).

Regulation – hard or soft? Public, private, or hybrid?

The search for regulation evokes the second condition posited by Habermas for a meaningful public sphere. Attaining efficacy necessitates public powers able to translate citizens' deliberations into binding law and ensure that it is respected. This provision makes sense in the context of the nation-state, although it is far from being universally fulfilled. It is less easy to imagine at the global level. Global governance does internationally what states do at home with the notable exception of the lack of enforcement authority (Monsalve Suárez and Aubry 2014). The challenge is to construct new transnational public powers that possess the political and administrative power to solve transnational problems and make them somehow accountable to new transnational spheres (Fraser *op.cit.*, p. 23). We have examined in Chapter 2 the complex maze of multiscalar sites of formal and informal rule making that impact on food systems. The idea of a single global organ dictating binding rules on all aspects of food provision is unlikely and probably not even desirable.[2] What we are interested in is a system that can produce and enforce authoritative global normative guidance, and at the same time reinforce public policy space and accountability at levels where inclusion of the most affected is most feasible and where diversity can flourish. On the contrary, a good deal of the transnational governance that has been implemented over the past couple of neoliberal decades, from structural adjustment regimes to the WTO and beyond, has had the effect of overriding social compacts at national and regional levels and substituting private for public goals.

The enormous influence that corporations exercise in the area of food has been underscored in Chapter 2 and elsewhere in this book. The UN Special Rapporteur on the Right to Food sets the scene for a discussion of how to address it in his report on agribusiness and the right to food. "Food systems have been undergoing deep transformations in recent years due to the food processing sector becoming increasingly globalized and dominated by large transnational corporations. . . . These imbalances of power in the food systems can and must be corrected" (De Schutter 2009g, p. 1). To do so requires putting in place clear legal frameworks with robust monitoring and enforcement mechanisms. But existing regulation mechanisms that meet this description tend to privilege corporations, in no small part because of the influence they exercise on how these mechanisms are framed. The most stringent regulator, the WTO, has been corporation-friendly from the time of the 1994 TRIPS agreement discussed in Chapter 2 to the decisions on Trade Facilitation that are at the heart of the WTO Bali Package adopted in December 2013. These measures remove public interest customs and border procedures to put in place easier trade flows, clearly benefitting the TNCs that dominate the export-import market at high cost to developing countries. WTO regulations are legally binding and egregiously enforced though the Dispute Settlement Mechanism (TNI and SPI 2013). The same kind of logic applies to the mushrooming free trade agreements (FTAs) and bilateral investment treaties (BITs) to which we referred in Chapter 2. These most often include an investor-to-state dispute settlement mechanism, which allows corporations to jump beyond the reach of domestic legislation and judiciary and protect their interests by suing governments in global spaces like the International Centre for Settlement of Investment Disputes (ICSID) associated with the World Bank. Judicial norms designed to protect human rights and environmental standards, instead, go unprotected. In the judgment of Professor Jeffrey Sachs, Special Advisor to the UN Secretary-General on the Millennium

Development Goals, what we have amounts to "a culture of impunity based on the well-proven expectation that corporate crime pays" (Brennan 2014). The screen of opacity surrounding these agreements is so well defended that European civil society organizations concerned about the likely social, economic, environmental, and health impacts of the Transatlantic Trade and Investment Partnership have given the name "eu-secretdeals.info" to the website they have set up to publish and critique leaked negotiating texts.

As indicated in Chapter 2, corporations weigh in strongly not only in framing binding multilateral trade agreements but also in defining and maintaining the standards that feed into them, through the Codex Alimentarius and other channels. I have recounted elsewhere the outrageous lobbying behavior of the sugar industry in an FAO technical committee in the early 2000s where measures to limit sugar use for health reasons were on the agenda (McKeon 2009a, p. 171). Current efforts by the WHO to halve the amount of free (i.e. corporate-added) sugar recommended for peoples' diets based on evidence that links it to obesity and heart disease is sparking industry reactions once again. WHO's Director-General, Margaret Chan, has compared their tactics to those employed by the big tobacco companies, which for years tried to suppress scientific evidence that smoking was bad for peoples' health (Ungoed-Thomas and Mansey 2013).

Outside of the multilateral and intergovernmental frameworks, recent years have seen a rapid rise in private food regulation and participation by corporations in various forms of voluntary multi-stakeholder regulatory initiatives. Indeed, corporations and retailers use their discursive power to try to establish the superiority of corporate self-regulation and corporate social responsibility schemes over governmental and intergovernmental regulation (Clapp and Fuchs 2009, p. 10). They are concerned to legitimize their authority, a necessary step given the fact that these nonelected actors – retailers in particular – are designing and enforcing rules and norms that their structural power renders quasi compulsory. To do so they point to their presumed effectiveness and expertise, as well as their declared concern for consumer health and social and environmental issues. A recent study finds little evidence of a significantly positive impact of private food governance on the well-being of the food system. What benefits are generated tend to accrue to a small group of the global population (accrediting the hypothesis of a two-track food system), while retail standards tend to have negative effects on small-scale producers and small retail shops (Fuchs and Kalfagianni 2010, p. 26). Other students of private food governance have reached similar conclusions (Nestle 2007; Lang and Heasman 2004; Lang et al. 2009; Clapp and Fuchs 2009).

Those who feel that it is possible to reform the dominant food system without making deep structural changes champion corporate social responsibility (CSR) initiatives as a way of promoting virtuous business behavior and habilitating corporations to play responsible roles in public–private partnerships. Such initiatives are regarded with distrust, instead, by many civil society organizations and social movements which are seeking to bring about more radical transformation. Corporate *accountability* is a preferred approach for many of these actors. The corporate accountability agenda advocates proposals to establish institutional mechanisms that hold companies to account, rather than simply urging them to improve standards or to report voluntarily. These can include complaint procedures, independent monitoring, compliance with national and international law and other agreed standards, mandatory reporting, and redress for malpractice (Utting and Clapp 2008).

Voluntary CSR initiatives aim to convince businesses and corporations that it is in their best interest to act responsibly with regard to environmental and social issues, while recognizing that shareholder profits is their bottom line. These approaches encounter several mutually reinforcing pitfalls (Clapp 2014). Those initiatives that take the form of broad sets of principles, like the UN Global Compact, are vague and weak in terms of what they ask for and the implementation and enforcement measures they foresee. Despite this minimal scale of commitment, they attract low rates of participation. This is true for the more rigorous certification mechanisms as well, even though the costs for complying with these voluntary standards tend to fall on the producers rather than the corporations. Low rates of participation can be explained in good part by the fact that the "business case" for adhering to these schemes is often weak. It may hold for firms who make social and environmental responsibility a key feature of their business models, but these are a small minority of concerned companies. Even in these cases, firms often go for CSR measures that are also cost cutting, like energy efficiency, and ignore more difficult measures such as biodiversity conservation (Clapp and Thistlethwaite 2012). Voluntary initiatives like CSR can be counterproductive in terms of improving corporate performance since they can offer businesses and investors an easy and low-cost way of dissociating themselves from the negative externalities of their action. In fact, coupling business with social standards in this super-soft fashion may be more likely to impact negatively on social standards than positively on businesses. Human rights services performed to legitimize corporate behavior is becoming a business in itself with the result of depoliticizing human rights concerns by translating them into technical standardized language and deflecting attention from the issues of inequality and oppression which they are intended to address (Tuta 2014).

If adopting voluntary approaches to change the behavior of corporations that are actually involved in the production, processing, and marketing of food is of doubtful effectiveness, the outcomes are even more unlikely when applied to financial institutions and speculative investment. Tracing financial investment in abstract products like derivatives to identifiable actors and to real-world outcomes is extremely difficult (Clapp 2014). And yet financial markets are at the very heart of contemporary capitalism. The several thousand trillion dollars that flow each year into commercial financial transactions dwarf transactions in "real" goods and services, which amounted to only some US $77 trillion in 2011. What governance of these markets exists is in the hands of select groups like the G8, G20, and the OECD. The entrenched structure of finance capital generates strong resistance to regulation on the part of a range of economic and political elites whose interests are backed, as always, by the ideational power of neoliberal discourse (Scholte 2013). The division of labor that existed between industry chiefs and political class during the heart of the reign of productive capitalism seems to have melted down into a sliding-door world of elites based on participation in boards of direction, who move effortlessly from industry and banks to government and back again.

What can we conclude from this rather gloomy panorama of the present state of affairs regarding the extension of public sphere from the political realm to the economic? One obvious acknowledgment is that there is much more work to be done in this essential field, in conceptual and normative terms as well as in advocacy and mobilization. Yet this does not mean that nothing is moving. Even in the difficult area of financial trading, a number of countries – including ones with deep and fast-growing markets like Hong Kong, Singapore, South Africa, India, and Switzerland – have applied financial transaction taxes (FTTs) that raise their governments billions in revenue every year. Eleven European countries are poised to join them by implementing a proposed FTT of between 0.01 percent and 0.1 percent on trades in stocks, bonds, and derivatives. In the judgment of former banker John Fullerton, a tax of this nature, falling disproportionately on short-term speculation, "probably eliminates it much more effectively than complex layers of new regulation" (Fullerton 2014). The recent financial regulation measures referred to in Chapter 2 – the Dodd-Frank Act in the United States and the Markets in Financial Instruments Directive adopted by the EU – are also positive signs. Human rights–based campaigns aimed at establishing binding regimes of obligations on TNCs have won some significant successes. The Extraterritorial Obligations (ETO) Consortium contributed to the definition in 2011 of the "Maastricht Principles", which detail the obligations of states to ensure that businesses and corporations based in their territories respect economic, social, and cultural human rights standards when they operate abroad. This principle was incorporated in the Tenure Guidelines adopted in the CFS in 2012. The Global Campaign to Dismantle Corporate Power and End Impunity advocates the development of a People's Treaty for Binding Obligations on TNCs. It has succeeded in having its main demands incorporated in an official Submission made by the Ecuador Government to the UN Human Rights Council (UNHCR) in September 2013 with the support of eighty-five other countries and some six hundred organizations from around the world.[3] On 26 June 2014, the Council adopted a resolution establishing "an open-ended intergovernmental working group on a legally binding instrument on transnational corporations and other business enterprises with respect to human rights, the mandate of which shall be to elaborate an international legally binding instrument to regulate, in international human rights law, the activities of transnational corporations and other business enterprises" (A/HRC/26/L.1). Twenty governments favored the resolution, fourteen voted against, and thirteen abstained, with the United States and the EU leading the opposition (Krishna 2014).

Equally important is strategizing on how to do a better job of transiting from global "soft" normative law to national "hard" enforceable regulation. Nonbinding, voluntary codes are not all the same. The quality of their content, the legitimacy of their process, and the effectiveness of their follow-up mechanisms make a big difference. Instruments like the CFS tenure guidelines are potentially suited to being

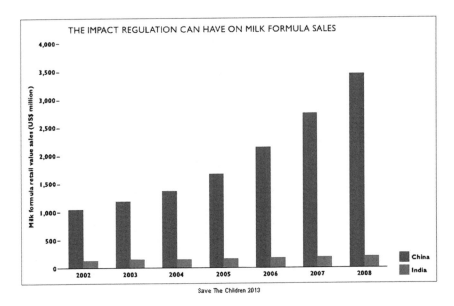

FIGURE 7.1 Milk formula sales in China and India

Source: Save the Children (2013). *Superfood for Babies*. Reproduced with permission.

transformed into strong, enforceable regulations at the national level since they result from inclusive, decentralized consultation and serious negotiation, which has incorporated many of the concerns of those most affected. As we have seen in Chapter 6, efforts to "take them home" are underway in all regions. Examples of the difference that national regulation can make even in our globalized world abound. We looked at some in Chapter 5. Figure 7.1 documents the contrast between the increase in export of baby formula from New Zealand to China, where marketing has few restrictions and breastfeeding rates are falling, and India where marketing is regulated and sales are static.

Combining negotiation of equitable – even if nonbinding – normative regulation at the global level with its transformation into enforceable legislation at national and local levels is a key area for forward looking "what's next" strategic reflection. In the end it is not so much an issue of hard versus soft law per se, but rather of the dynamics of power and law in developing effective ways to control the powerful (Monsalve Suárez and Aubry *op.cit.*)

Accountability – by whom to whom, and for what?

More stringent regulation needs to be accompanied by measures to improve – or introduce – accountability and to clarify who should be held accountable to whom and by what means. We have seen during our discussions of the CFS that the very word is a red flag to most governments. Here the outcome of an alliance between pussyfooting governments and blinder-wearing technicians is an attempt, resisted by civil society, to transform the political function of accountability into a sanitized exercise in measuring "effectiveness".

The unpromising etymology of "accountability" conjures up Dickensian images of emaciated gray-faced clerks perched on high stools and bent over dusty ledgers. According to the Oxford English Dictionary, it stems from late Latin *accomptare* (to account), a prefixed form of *comutare* (to calculate), which in turn derived from *putare* (to reckon). In the Western world the term went on from its Latin origins to build itself a relatively straightforward pedigree in the world of representative political life (vertical accountability of the elected to the electors) and administration (horizontal accountability among different organs) within the context of the modern nation-state. As we have seen, however, the advent of neoliberal structural adjustment policies and globalization from the mid-1980s on brought with it severe reductions of the policy space of nation-states and heralded the entry onto the scene of other important actors. These evolutions shot holes in accountability as previously theorized and practiced. In the absence of an infrastructure for global accountability both vertical and horizontal accountability are difficult to attain. "Powerful non-state actors act with impunity across borders and can evade the reach of conventional state-based accountability systems" (Goetz and Jenkins 2004, p. 1). At the same time, the functioning of conventional domestic nation-state accountability itself is compromised since local conflicts are "increasingly embedded in global politics in a context in which relations between public/state and private/market actors are undergoing change" (Newell and Wheeler 2006, p. 14).

A revised approach to governance and accountability in a context of globalization began to take shape within the international community in the 1990s as the World Bank and other architects of structural adjustment progressively realized that markets can't operate in the absence of governments and public policies. The "good governance" approach to accountability places the emphasis squarely on promoting financial responsibility and efficient performance, measured in ways that are generally aimed at enhancing productivity rather than outcomes (Dubnick and Frederickson 2011, p. 23). It is essentially apolitical. It aims at promoting accountability through measures such as law reform and capacity building, ignoring the structural economic, social, and political barriers that marginalize those sectors of the population who most need to be able to seek redress (Newell and Wheeler *op. cit.*, p. 16). The neoliberal bias of institutions that apply this approach leads them to marketize the concept of accountability, equating citizens with consumers and state functions with service delivery, and to ignore the anti-poor bias that such an approach introduces (*ibid.*, p. 26). It is essentially about creating an "enabling environment" for outside investors.

The good governance version of accountability places considerable emphasis on transparency but ignores the fact that being aware of injustice or corruption is hardly sufficient if there is no possibility of righting the wrong. Such discourse is right up the alley of the business world, and corporations have adopted it with alacrity and transformed it into the voluntary social responsibility codes discussed above. Having contributed for a couple of decades to annulling public policy space in the Global South, the proponents of good governance now place the onus for achieving accountability on the shoulders of weakened national governments. This allows them to evade the responsibilities of international institutions and the extra-territorial responsibilities of rich countries taken both individually and collectively in informal groups such as the G8. Despite their distaste for such responsibility-shrugging on the part of the international community, national governments in the Global South often find themselves taking the same line on the issue of where to situate accountability. They prefer that it be dealt with at the national level, where they have more control over the game, than globally, where they risk being subjected to accusations from outsiders or boomerang effects launched by their own civil society.

How does civil society fare in the context of good governance–driven, effectiveness-oriented accountability discourse? Experience indicates that CSOs forfeit their capacity to make meaningful accountability claims when they conform to the dominant approach. A case study of civil society engagement with the International Monetary Fund concludes that "the Fund has mainly become more transparent for English-speaking elite specialists in the global north. . . . Arguably, the types of greater information that the IMF has released, and the forms and channels through which this disclosure has occurred, have mainly served to advance already dominant policy paradigms" (Scholte 2011, pp. 86–87). Civil society advocacy, conducted essentially by Northern-based NGOs, has contributed to marginalizing social movements that seek accountability through a structural transformation beyond capitalism and has reinforced the power of rationalism to keep truly alternative paradigms outside the room (*ibid.*, p. 339). In such conditions, exercising accountability can be a way of disciplining dissent and promoting false institutional legitimacy. The hegemony of Northern-based NGOs in global policy engagement applies across a broad range of international forums, as we have seen in Chapter 4, and this is one reason why the CFS is such a fertile terrain for experimentation in the field of accountability as elsewhere.

The human rights (HR) framework, with its identification of duty-bearers and rights-bearers and the relationship between the two, is a major reference point for alternative accountability discourse that seeks to get to structural issues and political responsibility. "Rights frame the possibilities for making claims, and accountability frames the relationships between actors and institutions that are necessary for these rights to be realized" (Newell and Wheeler 2006, p. 28). We have noted that civil society actors and social movements fought hard to place the reformed CFS within a human rights framework. They succeeded in incorporating HR principles and practices in language about monitoring in the Global Strategic Framework and are now seeking to draw on HR practices in designing the "innovative monitoring mechanism" that the CFS reform document calls for. Human rights reporting mechanisms and institutions, they feel, constitute best practices on which efforts to call for accountability should build.

The human rights approach fits well with a range of experiences underway in all regions that approach the question of accountability essentially from the viewpoint of mobilization and advocacy by communities and people's movements (Newell and Wheeler 2006; Ebrahim and Weisband 2007; Scholte 2011). Accountability as it is claimed from below seeks to constrain power and make it responsive to the people that it affects. Reaching toward the global, it seeks to turn the encounter between local struggles and supra-national spaces and authorities to the advantage of the former. As contrasted with the good governance approach, accountability claiming from below places the issue of power at the center. The idea that fiddling with procedures or introducing better accounting and reporting and greater transparency can have any effect on the structural causes of marginalization and socio-economic injustice is roundly and unanimously dismissed. Accountability claiming from below asks questions like: "*what* is accountability for? (what broader political ends does it serve?); *who* is it for? (who benefits, who articulates the claims, who bears the rights to accountability?); *how* is it practiced? (through what means and processes?); *where* is it practiced? (in which sites and across what levels of political decision making?)" (Newell and Wheeler 2006, pp. 37–38).

Human rights frameworks as they emerged in the post–WWII era tended to concentrate on national governments as the main holders of obligations to respect, protect, and fulfill their citizens' rights. The perspective of accountability is becoming broader and more complex in an era in which governance sites have multiplied and sovereign states are often accomplices of corporate rights abuses. The requirement to call governments to account regarding their commitments to put in place and enforce the necessary legislative frameworks and binding regulations continues to be fundamental, and we have seen that social movements engaged in the CFS place strong emphasis on "bringing back the state". The state, in this vision, is not a monolithic leviathan but "a contested space in which the agendas and interests of the marginalized and the excluded can and must be actively advocated" (Akram-Lodhi 2013, p. 165). At the same time, the multiscalar nature of governance today offers new possibilities for developing strategies for regulation and accountability. This is without doubt one of the fruitful areas for "what next" reflection and action. We had a taste in Chapter 5 of ways in which regulation and accountability may be built from subnational levels, and we evoked above the weight that national regulation can have in a globalized world. The juxtaposition of authority and society at and between these different levels can be seen less in terms of boundaries and more in terms of relationships, as was suggested in Chapter 5. These relationships can and often do operate top-down in ways that are destructive of local rights and autonomy. Too often a "paradox of sovereignty" is created when the state system internalizes the dictates of global market rule, as in the case of Ethiopia or Tanzania (McMichael 2014, p. 13). But they can also stimulate dynamic interaction leading, as in the case of Venezuela, in the direction of a shift both from food dependency to food sovereignty and from representative to participatory democracy (Schiavoni 2014, p. 6). The idea of conceiving territory in terms of regionally organized ecologically resilient agrifood systems that we encountered in Chapter 5 is a visionary one, capable of overriding un-useful oppositions like producer/consumer and rural/urban. Work is underway in all regions to construct it in concrete terms and to see how it can "fit" with and dynamize more traditional institutional personifications of territory and authority.

Mobilization from below can open spaces for change and liberate constructive possibilities in systems. When dynamics like this from below meet a site of governance experimentation like the CFS, a transforming dialectic could be reinforced. The CFS could function as a global space in which to defend diversities, an institutional signpost of a post-corporation food regime approach to food governance.

Can we move step by step to big change?

What kind of scenario is likely to unfold over the coming period? Will we prove so tragically inept in addressing the ecological, social, economic, and political impacts of our iniquitous and unsustainable food system that it blows up in our faces in one or multiple big bangs? Or is it likely, or at least possible, that food sovereignty alternatives will continue to build up within the dominant regime and to interact dialectically with it until, step by step, "something radically new" emerges?

This book has presented considerable evidence that the dominant food system – at the same time as it seeks to marginalize ways of food provision that challenge its logic – creates conditions, spaces, and motivations for alternatives to develop. These include agro-ecological approaches to food production, nested markets, peasant initiatives to save their seeds, and many more. A common characteristic of these alternatives is their place-based nature, as contrasted with the homogenized, globalized "food from nowhere" and from no one that the corporate food system serves up. As an attentive analyst of current evolutions in agro-food systems has put it, in order to profit from opportunities and potentials for adaptive changes, "agriculture will have to return to being what it was: a more embedded, connected and localized activity largely serving and being served by its city regions" (Marsden 2012, p. 259). We have seen, too, that these locally situated experiences are generating, from the bottom up, alternative rules and ways of applying them that prefigure alternative modes of food governance. The nested markets that van der Ploeg describes owe their resilience to common-pool resources, using the terminology of Elinor Ostrom. These, he underlines, are not the physical assets themselves but rather the set of rules that regulate their governance and management. "These rules differ from the logic of capital [and] reflect, instead, the interests and perspectives of the involved producers, ecological cycles and/or principles such as social justice, solidarity or the containment of (potential) conflicts" (van der Ploeg et al. 2012, p. 164). The local food councils and similar initiatives reviewed in Chapter 5 are decentralized laboratories in institution building and governance based on principles other than those that animate the corporate food system, and they liberate citizen energies on which the dominant system has a soporific effect.

What is necessary for such initiatives to survive the efforts of the dominant system to marginalize them? What does it take for them to scale up and continue to engage, step by step? In the course of this book – particularly in Chapter 5 and in this concluding chapter – a number of factors that can contribute to this end have been identified. The importance of preserving the autonomy of sustainable, family-based peasant food production and local food systems from the dominant value chain market logic has been highlighted. There is a need to build solidarity among different components of the food sovereignty movement and transcend what might seem to be conflicts of interest among different sectors of the marginalized. Public sensitization is required, and progressively broader alliances have to be built in order to widen the ranks of those who are willing to envisage transformation and not just fiddle with the existent. Making progress with the agenda of regulation, monitoring, and accountability outlined above is essential. In order to successfully take a tactical, step-by-step approach to big change, it is indispensable to build up a systemic and prospective understanding of how the currently dominant system functions, where the entry points for change are situated, what options for action are present, and what their consequences are likely to be. This kind of requirement has been expressed in terms of a food utopia, understood as a means of "thinking the unthinkable, but in a way that provides a unified explanation with obtainable targets" and allows us to learn as we go along (Rosin, Stock and Campbell, 2012, p. 228). From the perspective of a San Franciscan food activist, the food sovereignty movement needn't and probably can't know with certainty how to make radical changes to the structure of food systems. Rather, it "can know values that might direct that future food system; it can know the tactics that can begin to instill those values into citizens, eaters, producers and politics; it can know the structural failures of its market and government systems and how these limit the solutions that can be expected from them; and it can know how to question itself enough to gauge if its efforts are bearing the desired fruits" (Roman-Alcala 2013, p. 37).

Values, public goods, human rights, and a touch of desire

Values are a solid ground to start from. In Chapter 2 the issue of what is and isn't being valued in a "value chain" was raised. We've heard praise, from peasant movements in realities as distant from one another as West Africa and Palau, of food systems that incorporate values like solidarity, social peace, and relatedness. Working on freeing ourselves from capital's obsession with profit and getting other values back into the heart of food provision is one promising way forward. Doing so does not imply ignoring the significance of the material side of life, since we've seen that food sovereignty alternatives win out over what the dominant food system has to offer even in terms of productivity and economic viability. Dethroning the modernization scenario is another. Instead of fretting about improving on the past, we could learn to do a better job of managing the future, for ourselves and our children and grandchildren.[4]

Putting a bit of order into our ideas about what constitutes public and private goods and what are our rights and responsibilities as we pursue them would merit attention. Do we really think that doing away with limits on the amount of money that corporations can contribute to election campaigns, as the US Supreme Court did in April 2014, is a victory in the name of the human right to freedom of speech? We could critique the emphasis that has been placed, in the modern era, "on the maximization of the freedom of the individual as consumer and property owner, discovering that freedom in the private domain of liberalized markets rather than as citizens achieving the common good in the public domain" (Lee 2007). We could, instead, join Olivier De Schutter in celebrating the CFS's acknowledgment of food security as a global public good (De Schutter 2014a, p. 220) and agrarian movements in "increasingly resorting to human rights as an alternative international legal framework to the *lex mercatoria*" (Monsalve Suárez 2012a, p. 244). In the end, in the CFS the food sovereignty movement is fighting for public policies that defend its autonomous spaces and strengthen the alternatives that populate them. They are fighting to reclaim the public sphere and to reiterate the separation between market and politics. Exactly the opposite direction from the privatization of the UN agenda that is envisaged in the push to put corporations in the driver's seat of the post-2015 Global Partnership for Development (Holland 2014).

In what he is said to have considered the book he most enjoyed writing, economist Albert Hirschman shed light on a fascinating aspect of the passage from a pre-capitalist to a capitalist order: the elevation of the pursuit of commerce and profit making as exemplified in the work of merchants and bankers – previously considered a mortal sin – to the moral function of taming unruly human passions (Hirschman 1977). Perhaps it is time to dethrone profit from the role of peacekeeper that it has failed so miserably to fulfill and to liberate passions along with values and rights. In the words of human rights advocate Richard Falk, we may need to embrace the politics of desire in order to bridge the gap between the politics of the feasible and the politics of the needed.[5]

West African peasant leader Mamadou Cissokho, whom I have cited on various occasions, has been a companion-in-arms for more than three decades of the experience I have drawn on in writing this text. The last time we were together I asked him whether or not he felt hopeful about the possibility of achieving the kind of change we have been fighting for. "You know, Nora", he replied, "sometimes when we lose a battle I wonder if we shouldn't just give up, but it doesn't last long. I think about how far we've come and all that is moving today and I'd like to live for another one hundred years!" If this book has done anything to infuse readers with a sense of hope and a desire to engage, it will have fulfilled its purpose.

Notes

1. See Brem-Wilson (2012) for a detailed application of the concept of public sphere to the reformed CFS.
2. Some pro–food sovereignty authors propend in this direction, for example, in proposing a pro-poor redistributive global institution (Akram-Lodhi 2013, p. 167), while others remind us that "transferring too much regulatory powers to the international level would undoubtedly entail trade-offs for people's self-determination" (Monsalve Suárez and Aubry 2014).
3. See www.stopcorporateimpunity.org/?p=3830.
4. Remark by Philip McMichael at the International Studies Association, 2014.
5. Remark at the International Studies Association, 2013.

BIBLIOGRAPHY

ACRA (2013). *Farmers' Rights in Practice: Synthesis of the Case Studies on Sustainable Use of Biodiversity. Focus on European Experiences.* http://issuu.com/fondazioneacra/docs/farmers_rights [Accessed 12 November 2014]

Africa Group and PAFO (2011). *Africa Can Feed Itself!* www.europafrica.info/en/cfs/africa-can-feed-itself-the-summary-report [Accessed 12 November 2014]

African Center for Biosafety (2009). *Patents, Climate Change and African Agriculture: Dire Predictions.* www.acbio.org.za/images/stories/dmdocuments/ACB-Brief_Patent_Climate_African_Agric_Sep-2009.pdf [Accessed 12 November 2014]

African Trade Network (2013). *Statement on the Bali Package Adopted at the End of the 9th Ministerial Conference of the WTO in Bali.* 7 December 2013. www.scribd.com/doc/190167010/ATN-Statement-on-WTO-MC9 [Accessed 12 November 2014]

Agrawal, Arun (2010). "Local Institutions and Adaptation to Climate Change", in Robin Mearns and Andrew Norton (eds), *Social Dimensions of Climate Change: Equity and Vulnerability in a Warming World*, Ch. 7, pp. 173–198. Washington, DC: The World Bank.

Agricultural Transition. http://ag-transition.org [Accessed 12 November 2014]

Agricultures (2012). *Installation of Brazil's Agroecology Policy Commission.* www.agriculturesnetwork.org/news/brazilian-national-commission-of-agroecology-policy-has-been-installed [Accessed 12 November 2014]

Ahn, Christine and Andres Riel Muller (2013). "South Korea: Ground Zero for Food Sovereignty and Community Resilience". *The Nation* 14 November 2013. www.thenation.com/blog/177159/south-korea-ground-zero-food-sovereignty-and-community-resilience [Accessed 12 November 2014]

Akram-Lodhi, A. Haroon (2013). *Hungry for Change. Farmers, Food Justice and the Agrarian Question.* Halifax: Fernwood Publishing.

Alcock, Rupert (2009). *Speaking Food: A Discourse Analytic Study of Food Insecurity.* University of Bristol School of Sociology, Politics and International Studies Working Paper 07–09. www.bristol.ac.uk/spais/research/workingpapers/wpspaisfiles/alcock0709.pdf [Accessed 12 November 2014]

Ali, Nosheen (2010). "Re-Imagining the Nature of Development: Biodiversity Conservation and Pastoral Visions in the Northern Areas, Pakistan", in Philip McMichael (ed.), *Contesting Development*, pp. 64–80. New York and London: Routledge.

Alternative World Water Forum (2012). *Declaration of Participants at the Alternative World Water Forum in Marseille, 14–17 March 2012.* www.fame2012.org/files/declaration-finale-en.pdf [Accessed 12 November 2014]

Anderson, Molly D. (2013). "Working toward the Right to Food in the USA". *Right to Food and Nutrition Watch 2013*, pp. 89–91. www.rtfn-watch.org/fileadmin/media/rtfn-watch.org/ENGLISH/pdf/Watch_2012/R_t_F_a_N_Watch_2012_eng_web_rz.pdf [Accessed 12 November 2014]

Anseeuw, Ward, Liz Walden Wily, Lorenzo Cotulo and Michael Taylor (2012). *Land Right and the Rush for Land.* www.landcoalition.org/sites/default/files/publication/1205/ILC%20GSR%20report_ENG.pdf [Accessed 12 November 2014]

Araujo, Saulo (2010). "The promise and challenges of food sovereignty policies in Latin America". *Yale Human Rights and Development Law Journal*, 13: 493–506.

Arial, Anni, David Palmer, Margret Vidar, Juan Carlos Garcia Cebolla, Francesca Romano and Leila Shamsaifar (2012). "Governance of tenure. Making it happen". *Land Tenure Journal*, 1. Rome: FAO. www.fao.org/nr/tenure/land-tenure-journal/index.php/LTJ/article/view/51/91 [Accessed 12 November 2014]

Avant, Deborah, Marthan Finnemore and Susan K. Sell (eds) (2010). *Who Governs the Globe.* Cambridge: Cambridge U. Press.

Ayres, Jeffrey and Michael J. Bosia (2011). "Beyond global summitry: food sovereignty as localized resistance to globalization", *Globalizations*, 8:1, 47–63.

Aziz, Sartaj, ed. (1975). *Hunger, Politics and Markets: The Real Issues in the Food Crisis.* New York: New York University Press.

Badgley, Catherine, Jeremy Moghtader, Eileen Quintero, Emily Zakem, M. Jahi Chappell, Katia Avilés-Vazquez, Andrea Samulon and Ivette Perfecto (2007). "Organic agriculture and the global food supply". *Renewable Agriculture and Food Systems*: 22:2, 86–108. www.stopogm.net/sites/stopogm.net/files/Orgsupply.pdf [Accessed 12 November 2014]

Baker, Lauren (2012). *Food Agriculture and CETA.* www.cban.ca/Resources/Topics/Trade/Food-Agriculture-and-CETA [Accessed 12 November 2014]

Banana Link (n.d.). *Monoculture and High Input Production.* www.bananalink.org.uk/environmental-problems [Accessed 12 November 2014]

Bangkok Post (2013). "Organic Food Goes through the Roof". 16 June 2013. www.bangkokpost.com/lite/topstories/355332/organic-food-goes-through-the-roof [Accessed 12 November 2014]

Bauman, Zygmunt (2011). "On glocalization coming of age". *Social Europe Journal.* 29 August 2011. www.social-europe.eu/2011/08/on-glocalization-coming-of-age/ [Accessed 12 November 2014]

Bell, Beverly (2013). "A Penny a Pound, Plus Power: The Coalition of Immokalee Workers Changes History". *Huffington Post.* 15 May 2013. www.huffingtonpost.com/beverly-bell/a-penny-a-pound-plus-power_b_3274169.html [Accessed 12 November 2014]

Benbrook, Charles M. (2012). "Impacts of genetically engineered crops on pesticide use in the U.S. – the first sixteen years". *Environmental Sciences Europe*, 24:24. www.enveurope.com/content/24/1/24 [Accessed 12 November 2014].

Bernstein, Henry (2013). "Food Sovereignty: A Skeptical View". *Food Sovereignty: A Critical Dialogue.* International Conference. Yale University. September 14–15, 2013. www.yale.edu/agrarianstudies/foodsovereignty/pprs/1_Bernstein_2013.pdf [Accessed 12 November 2014]

Berrón, Gonzalo, Jenina Joy Chavez, Cecilia Olivet and Graciela Rodríguez (eds) (2013). *Rethinking Regionalisms in Times of Crises: A Collection of Activists' Perspectives from Latin America, Asia, Africa and Europe.* Rio de Janeiro: Instituto Equit Gênero, Economia e Cidadania Global.

Bhutan, Royal Government of (2013). *The New Development Paradigm.* www.newdevelopment paradigm.bt/[Accessed 12 November 2014]

Bishop, Robert V. (2013). "The Mother of Our Breath. Pride, Power and Income". *Farming Matters* December 2013. www.agriculturesnetwork.org/magazines/global/family-farming/palau-family-values [Accessed 12 November 2014]

Bittman, Mark (2013). "How to Feed the World". *The New York Times* 14 October 2013. www.nytimes.com/2013/10/15/opinion/how-to-feed-the-world.html?pagewanted=1&_r=0 [Accessed 12 November 2014]

Bob (2011). "Why McDonalds Favors Schenzen in China". www.szcchina.com/blog/why-mcdonalds-favors-shenzhen-in-china.html [Accessed 12 November 2014]

Boiral, P., J. F. Lantieri and J. P. Olivier de Sardan (eds) (1985). *Paysans, experts et chercheurs en Afrique Noire: Sciences sociales et développement rural.* Paris: Karthala.

Borras, Saturnino M. (2008.) "La Via Campesina and its Global Campaign for Agrarian Reform", *Journal of Agrarian Change*, 8:2–3 (April and July), 258–289.

Borras, S. and J. Franco (2010) *From Threat to Opportunity? Problems with the Idea of a "Code of Conduct" for Land-Grabbing.* www.tni.org/sites/www.tni.org/files/Yale%20April%20 2010%20Borras_Franco%20CoC%20paper.pdf [Accessed 12 November 2014]

———— (2012). *A 'Land Sovereignty Alternative? Towards a Peoples' Counter-Enclosure.* TNI Agrarian Justice Programme Discussion Paper. www.tni.org/sites/www.tni.org/files/a_land_sovereignty_alternative_.pdf [Accessed 12 November 2014]

Borras, Saturnino M. Jr., Jennifer C. Franco and Chunyu Wang (2013). "The challenge of global governance of land grabbing: changing international agricultural context and competing political views and strategies". *Globalizations*, 10:1 (February), 161–180.

Brem-Wilson, J. W. (2012). *La Via Campesina and the Committee on World Food Security: A Transnational Public Sphere?* Unpublished doctoral thesis.

———— (2013). "Towards Food Sovereignty: Interrogating Peasant Voice in the UN Committee on World Food Security". *Food Sovereignty: A Critical Dialogue.* 24 January 2013. Conference Paper no. 87. International Institute of Social Studies. The Hague, the Netherlands. www.iss.nl/fileadmin/ASSETS/iss/Research_and_projects/Research_networks/ICAS/87_Brem-Wilson.pdf [Accessed 12 November 2014]

Brennan, Brid (2014). *The State of Corporate Power-Insights into the Power of Corporations.* www.tni.org/article/state-corporate-power [Accessed 12 November 2014]

Brown, Lester (2012). *Full Planet, Empty Plates. The New Geopolitics of Food Scarcity.* New York: Norton.

Brunori, Gianluca (2011). *Nested Markets.* http://pianodelcibo.ning.com/page/strategie-urbane [Accessed 12 November 2014]

Burgan, Michael and Mark Winne (2012). *Doing Food Policy Council Right: A Guide to Development and Action.* Mark Winne Associates. www.markwinne.com/wp-content/uploads/2012/09/FPC-manual.pdf [Accessed 12 November 2014]

Buczynsk, Beth (2010). *The Gates Foundation Invests Millions in Monsanto.* Care2, 11 October 2010. www.care2.com/causes/gates-invests-millions-in-monsanto.html [Accessed 12 November 2014]

Buffet, Warren (2002). "Chairman's Letter". *Berkshire Hathaway Inc 2002 Annual Report*, pp. 3–23. www.berkshirehathaway.com/2002ar/2002ar.pdf [Accessed 12 November 2014]

Bury, J. B. (1960). *The Idea of Progress.* New York: Dover Publications.

Bush, Ray (2010). "Food riots: poverty, power and protest". *J. of Agrarian Change*, 10:1 (January), 119–129.

Campbell, Hugh (2009). "Breaking new ground in food regime theory: corporate environmentalism, ecological feedbacks and the "food from somewhere" regime?". *Agriculture and Human Values*, 26, 309–310.

Cargill (n.d.). *Food security. One of the World's Most Pressing Issues.* www.cargill.com/corporate-responsibility/food-security/[Accessed 12 November 2014]

Carson, Rachel (1962). *Silent Spring.* Boston: Houghton Mifflin.

Cépède, Michel. (1984). "The fight against hunger. Its history on the international agenda". *Food Policy*, 9:4 (November), 282–290.

CFS/FAO (2012). *Voluntary Guidelines on the Responsible Governance of Tenure of Land, Fisheries and Forests in the Context of National Food Security.* Rome: FAO.

Cheru, Fantu (2000). "Transforming our common future: local dimensions of global reform". *Review of International Political Economy*, 7:2 (Summer), 353–368.

CIDSE, IUF, La Via Campesina and FIAN International (2013). *Using the Global Strategic Framework for Food Security and Nutrition to Promote and Defend the Peoples' Right to Adequate Food. A Manual for Social Movements and Civil Society Organizations.* http://viacampesina.org/downloads/pdf/en/GSF-Manual_en.pdf [Accessed 12 November 2014]

Cissokho, Mamadou (2012). *Letter to His Excellence Yayi Boni, President of the African Union.* www.europafrica.info/en/news/foos-security-a-letter-to-the-president-of-the-african-union

Civil Society Mechanism (2011a). *Civil Society Work on Agricultural Investment in the 37th Session of the CFS.* www.csm4cfs.org/files/SottoPagine/59/cso_assessment_on_cfs_37_ag._investment_rt_en.pdf [Accessed 12 November 2014]

——— (2011b). *Committee on World Food Security (CFS) 2011 Food Price Volatility Roundtable.* www.csm4cfs.org/files/SottoPagine/30/cso_37_assessment_fpv_en.pdf [Accessed 12 November 2014]

——— (2014). *Actions and Policies on Investment in Agriculture.* www.csm4cfs.org/files/SottoPagine/118/actions_and_policies_proposals_from_csm_en.pdf [Accessed 12 November 2014]

Claeys, Priscilla (2013). "From Food Sovereignty to Peasants' Rights: an Overview of La Via Campesina's Rights-Based Claims over the Last 20 Years". *Food Sovereignty: A Critical Dialogue.* Yale University, September 14–15 2013. Conference Paper no. 24. www.tni.org/sites/www.tni.org/files/download/24_claeys_2013-1.pdf [Accessed 12 November 2014]

Claeys, Priscilla and N. P. Lambert (2014). "Introduction: In Search of Better Options: Food Sovereignty, the Right to Food and Legal Tools for Transforming Food Systems", in N.P. Lambert, P. Claeys, A. Wong and L. Brilmayer (eds) (2014). *Rethinking Food Systems. Structural Challenges, New Strategies and the Law*, pp 1–15. New York: Springer.

Clapp, Jennifer (2012). *Food.* Cambridge, UK: Polity.

——— (2013). "Financialization, Distance and Global Food Politics". *Food Sovereignty: A Critical Dialogue.* International Conference Yale University 14–15 September 2013. Conference Paper no. 5.

——— (2014). "Responsibility to the Rescue? Governing Private Financial Investment in Global Agriculture". Paper prepared for presentation at the International Studies Association Annual Meeting, Toronto, March 26–29, 2014.

Clapp, J. and Marc J. Cohen, eds. (2009). The *Global Food Crisis. Governance Challenges and Opportunities.* Waterloo: Wilfred Laurier University Press.

Clapp, J. and Doris Fuchs (eds) (2009). *Corporate Power in Global Agrifood Governance.* Cambridge, MA: MIT Press.

Clapp, Jennifer, and Jason Thistlethwaite (2012). "Private Voluntary Programs in Environmental Governance: Climate Change and the Financial Sector", in Ronit Schneider (ed.), *Business and Climate Policy: The Potentials and Pitfalls of Private Voluntary Programs*, pp. 43–47. New York: United Nations University Press.

Collier, Paul (2008). "The Politics of Hunger. How Illusion and Greed Fan the Food Crisis". *Foreign Affairs* November/December 2008. www.foreignaffairs.com/articles/64607/paul-collier/the-politics-of-hunger [Accessed 12 November 2014]

Colombo, Luca and Antonio Onorati (2013). *Food. Riots and Rights*. IIED, CIC, FIRAB. www. firab.it/site/wp-content/uploads/2013/09/foodrights_aw.pdf [Accessed 12 November 2014]

Commission on Global Governance (1995). *Towards the Global Neighbourhood. The Report of the Commission on Global Governance*. Oxford: Oxford University Press.

Committee on World Food Security (2009). *Reform of the Committee on World Food Security*. Final Version. CFS: 2009/2 Rev.2. Rome: FAO.

———— (2010a). *Proposal for an International Food Security and Nutrition Civil Society Mechanism for Relations with CFS (Committee on World Food Security) – Status Report*. CFS/2010/INF/14.

———— (2010b). *Final Report on the Thirty-Sixth Session*. Rome, 11–14 and 16 October 2010. CFS: 2010/Final Report. Rome: FAO.

———— (2011). *Final Report on the Thirty-Seventh Session*. Rome, 17–22 October 2011. CFS:2011/Final Report. Rome: FAO.

———— (2013a). *Final Report on the Fortieth Session*. Rome, 7–11 October, 2013. CFS: 2013/40 Report. www.fao.org/docrep/meeting/029/mi744e.pdf [Accessed 12 November 2014]

———— (2013b). *Global Strategic Framework for Food Security and Nutrition*. www.fao.org/ fileadmin/templates/cfs/Docs1213/gsf/GSF_Version_2_EN.pdf [Accessed 12 November 2014]

CNCR and FONGS (2010). *Comment les exploitations familiales peuvent nourrir le Sénégal ?* www.inter-reseaux.org/IMG/pdf_brochure_recap_Forum.pdf [Accessed 12 November 2014]

Corporate Watch (2004). *A Rough Guide to the UK Farming Crisis*. www.corporatewatch. org/?lid=2624 [Accessed 12 November 2014]

———— (2011). *Corporate Organics*. www.corporatewatch.org/?lid=412 [Accessed 12 November 2014]

———— (n.d.). *Corporate Control of the Food System*. www.corporatewatch.org/sites/default/ files/corporateorganics.pdf [Accessed 12 November 2014]

Couibaly, Ibrahima (2006). "Historique et évolution du concept de Souveraineté alimentaire dans le monde." *Forum sur la Souveraineté Alimentaire, Niamey, 7–10 Novembre 2006*. ROPPA.

Cranbrook, Caroline (2006). *The Real Choice*. London: CPRE. Available at www.cpre.org. uk/resources/farming-and-food/local-foods/item/1912-[Accessed 12 November 2014]

Critical Agrarian Studies (2014). *Food Sovereignty: A Critical Dialogue*. 24 January 2014 Colloquium. www.iss.nl/research/research_programmes/political_economy_of_resources_ environment_and_population_per/networks/critical_agrarian_studies_icas/food_ sovereignty_a_critical_dialogue/[Accessed 12 November 2014]

CSOPVGN (2012). *Joint Political Statement of Civil Society Organizations which Have Actively Participated in the Process of Developing the Voluntary Guidelines*. www.csm4cfs.org/policy_ working_groups-6/land_tenure-6/[Accessed 12 November 2014]

Cush, Jonathan (1995). *Power of Development*. New York: Routledge.

Daniel, S. (2010) *(Mis)Investment in Agriculture. The Role of the International Finance Corporation in Global Land Grabs*. Oakland, CA: The Oakland Institute.

Davis, M. (2001). *Late Victorian Holocausts: El Nino Famines and the Making of the Third World*. London: Verso.

———— (2006). *Planet of Slums*. London: Verso.

Demeke, Mulat, Adriano Spinelli, Stefania Croce, Valentina Pernechele, Eugenia Stefanelli, Areej Jafari, Guendalina Pangrazio, Giovanni Carrasco, Barthelemy Lanos and Camille Roux (2014). *Food and Agriculture Policy Decisions. Trends, Emerging Issues and Policy Alignments since the 2007/08 Food Security Crisis*. Rome: FAO. www.fao.org/docrep/019/ i3514e/i3514e.pdf [Accessed 12 November 2014]

De Schutter, Oliver (2008). *Mission to the World Trade Organization.* A/HRC/10/5/Add.2. 4 February. Geneva: Human Rights Council.

———— (2009a). *Crisis into Opportunity: Reinforcing Multilateralism.* Report of the Special Rapporteur on the Right to Food to the Twelfth Session of the Human Rights Council. 21 July.

———— (2009b). *Large-Scale Land Acquisitions and Leases: A Set of Minimum Principles and Measures to Address the Human Rights Challenge.* A/HRC/13/33/Add.2. 28 December.

———— (2009c). *International Trade and the Right to Food.* Dialogue on Globalization. Occasional Paper no. 46/November. Geneva: Friedrich Ebert Stiftung.

———— (2009d). *The Right to Food and the Political Economy of Hunger.* Twenty-Sixth McDougall Memorial Lecture. Opening of the Thirty-Sixth Session of the FAO Conference. 18 November. www.pfsa.be/IMG/pdf_DeSchutterSRRTFMcDougall 18November20091.pdf [Accessed 12 November 2014]

———— (2009e). *Agribusiness and the Right to Food.* Report of the Special Rapporteur on the Right to Food to the Thirteenth Session of the Human Rights Council. 22 December. A/HRC/13/33.

———— (2009f). *Contribution of Mr. Olivier De Schutter, Special Rapporteur on the Right to Food, to the 2nd Meeting of the Contact Group to Support the Committee on World Food Security.* Rome, 22 May. www2.ohchr.org/english/issues/food/docs/CFS_reform_note22 May09.pdf [Accessed 12 November 2014]

De Schutter, Olivier (2009g). *Summary. Agribusiness and the Right to Food. Report of the Special Rapporteur on the Right to Food, Olivier De Schutter.* www.srfood.org/en/agribusiness-and-the-right-to-food

———— (2010a). *Responsibly Destroying the World's Peasantry.* Project Syndicate, 6 April. www.project-syndicate.org/commentary/responsibly-destroying-the-world-s-peasantry [Accessed 12 November 2014]

———— (2010b). *Access to Land and the Right to Food.* Report of the Special Rapporteur on the Right to Food presented at the 65th General Assembly of the United Nations [A/65/281], 21 October.

———— (2010c). *Addressing Concentration in Food Supply Chains.* Briefing Note no. 3, December.

———— (2010d). *Agroecology and the Right to Food.* Report of the Special Rapporteur on the Right to Food to the 16th Session of the Human Rights Council. A/HRC/16/49/ Add.1. March. Geneva: Human Rights Council. www.srfood.org/images/stories/pdf/ officialreports/20110308_a-hrc-16-49_agroecology_en.pdf [Accessed 12 November 2014]

———— (2011a). "The green rush: The global race for farmland and the right of land users". *Harvard International Law Journal,* 52:2 (Summer), 504–559.

———— (2011b). *The Right to Food.* Interim report to the General Assembly. 4 August. A/66/262.

———— (2013). *Interim Report to the UN General Assembly of the Special Rapporteur on the Right to Food.* A/68/288. www.srfood.org/images/stories/pdf/officialreports/20131025_rtf_ en.pdf [Accessed 12 November 2014]

———— (2014a). "The Reform of the Committee on World Food Security: The Quest for Coherence in Global Governance", in N. Lambert, P. Claeys, A. Wong and L. Brilmayer (eds) (2014). *Rethinking Food Systems. Structural Challenges, New Strategies and the Law,* pp. 219–238. New York: Springer.

———— (2014b). *Final Report: The Transformative Potential of the Right to Food.* UN General Assembly, A/HRC/25/57, 24 January.

———— (2014c). *The Power of Procurement. Public Purchasing in the Service of Realizing the Right to Food.* Briefing Note no. 8. www.srfood.org/images/stories/pdf/otherdocuments/ 20140514_procurement_en.pdf [Accessed 12 November 2014]

De Schutter, Olivier and Kaitlin Y Cordes (2011). *Accounting for Hunger. The Right to Food in the Era of Globalisation*. Oxford: Hart Publishing.

De Schutter, Olivier and Gaetan Vanloqueren (2011). "The new Green Revolution: how twenty-first century science can feed the world". *Solutions*, 2:4, 33–44. www.thesolutions journal.com/node/971 [Accessed 12 November 2014]

Desmarais, Annette Aurélie (2007). *La Via Campesina*. London: Pluto Press.

Desmarais, Annette and Paul Nicholson (2013). "La Via Campesina: An Historical and Political Analysis". *La Via Campesina's Open Book: Celebrating 20 Years of Struggle and Hope*. http://viacampesina.org/downloads/pdf/openbooks/EN-10.pdf [Accessed 12 November 2014]

Desmarais, Annette and Hannah Wittman (2013). "Farmers, Foodies and First Nations: Getting to Food Sovereignty in Canada". *Food Sovereignty: A Critical Dialogue*. International Conference. Yale University. September 14–15. www.yale.edu/agrarianstudies/foodsovereignty/pprs/3_Desmarais_Wittman_2013.pdf [Accessed 12 November 2014]

Detroit Black Community Food Security Network (n.d.). *About Us*. http://detroitblackfood security.org/about.html [Accessed 12 November 2014]

Dubnick, Melvin J. and H. George Frederickson (2011). *Public Accountability. Performance Measurement, the Extended State and the Search for Trust*. Dayton, Ohio: The Kettering Foundation.

Duncan, Jessica and David Barling (2012). "Renewal through Participation in Global Food Security Governance: Implementing the International Food Security and Nutrition Civil Society Mechanism to the Committee on World Food Security". *International Journal of Sociology and Agriculture & Food*, 19:2, 143–161.

EAFF, PROPAC and ROPPA (2011). *Agricultural Investment Strengthening Family Farming and Sustainable Food Systems in Africa*. African farmer workshop, 4 and 5 May, Mfou, Yaoundé, Cameroun. www.europafrica.info/en/publications/agricultural-investment-strengthening-family-farming-and-sustainable-food-systems-in-africa [Accessed 12 November 2014]

———— (2013). *Family Farmers for Sustainable Food Systems. A Synthesis of Reports by African Farmers' Regional Networks on Models of Food Production, Consumption and Markets*. Rome: EuropAfrica. www.europafrica.info/en/publications/family-farmers-for-sustainable-food-systems [Accessed 12 November 2014]

Ebrahim, A. and E. Weisband (eds) (2007). *Global Accountabilities: Participation, Pluralism and Public Ethics*. Cambridge: Cambridge University Press.

ECOWAS Peoples' Summit (2013). *West African Civil Society Declaration on the Economic Partnership Agreements and Common External Tariff*. www.wacsi.org/en/site/newsroom/2199/West-African-Civil-Society-Declaration-on-the-Economic-Partnership-Agreements-and-Common-External-Tariff [Accessed 12 November 2014]

Ecumenical Advocacy Alliance (2012). *Nourishing the World Sustainably: Scaling up Agroecology*. Geneva: EAA. www.e-alliance.ch/typo3conf/ext/naw_securedl/secure.php?u=0&file=fileadmin/user_upload/docs/All_Food/2012/AgroEcology/2012_10_ScalingUp Agroecology_WEB_.pdf&t=1354049219&hash=f3ab6025a46c1edd27152b1ce9da99f0 [Accessed 12 November 2014]

Edelman, Marc (2003). "Transnational Peasant and Farmer Movements and Networks", in *Global Civil Society 2003*, 185–220. London: Centre for the Study of Global Governance, London School of Economics and Political Science.

———— (2013). "Food Sovereignty: Forgotten Genealogies and Future Regulatory Challenges". *Food Sovereignty: A Critical Dialogue. International Conference*. Yale University. September 14–15. Conference Paper no. 72. www.yale.edu/agrarianstudies/foodsovereignty/pprs/72_Edelman_2013.pdf [Accessed 12 November 2014]

ENDA (1987). *Pour une recherché-formation action sur la fertilité des sols. Un étude de cas en milieu sahelien*. Dakar : ENDA.

Engler, Yves (2013). *Canada-European Union Free Trade Agreement (CETA): A "Corporate Bill of Rights"*. Global Research. 12 November. www.globalresearch.ca/canada-european-union-free-trade-agreement-ceta-a-corporate-bill-of-rights/5357807 [Accessed 12 November 2014]

Epstein, Gerald (ed.) (2005). *Financialization and the World Economy*. Cheltenham, UK: Edward Elgar.

Escobar, Arturo (1995). *Encountering Development. The Making and Unmaking of the Third World*. Princeton: Princeton University Press.

Essential Information and Consumer Education Foundation (2009). *Sold Out. How Wall Street and Washington Betrayed America*. www.wallstreetwatch.org/reports/sold_out.pdf [Accessed 12 November 2014]

ETC Group (2008). *Who Owns Nature?* www.etcgroup.org/content/who-owns-nature [Accessed 12 November 2014].

———— (2009). *Who Will Govern?* Communiqué no. 103. December. www.etcgroup.org

———— (2010). *Gene Giants Stockpile Patents on "Climate-Ready" Crops in Bid to Become "Biomasters"*. Issue 106. October 2010. www.etcgroup.org/node/522 [Accessed 12 November 2014]

———— (2011a). *Who Will Control the Green Economy?* www.etcgroup.org/content/who-will-control-green-economy-0 [Accessed 12 November 2014]

———— (2011b). *Capturing "Climate Genes"*. www.etcgroup.org/sites/www.etcgroup.org/files/publication/pdf_file/Genegiants2011_0.pdf [Accessed 12 November 2014]

———— (2013). *With Climate Chaos . . . Who Will Feed Us? The Industrial Food Chain or the Peasant Food Web?* www.etcgroup.org/content/poster-who-will-feed-us-industrial-food-chain-or-peasant-food-webs [Accessed 12 November 2014]

EuropAfrica (2010). *Advancing African Agriculture. CSO Monitoring 2009–2010: The Impact of Europe's Policies and Practices on African Agriculture and Food Security*. www.europafrica.info/en/themes/advancing-african-agriculture [Accessed 12 November 2014]

———— (2012). *(Bio)Fueling Injustice*. www.europafrica.info/en/publications/biofueling-injustice [Accessed 12 November 2014]

FANN – Facilitating Alternative Agro-Food Networks (2010). *Local Food Systems in Europe*. IFZ Graz. www.faanweb.eu/sites/faanweb.eu/files/FAAN_Booklet_PRINT.pdf [Accessed 12 November 2014]

Food and Agriculture Organization of the United Nations – FAO (1958). *Marketing Problems and Improvement Programmes. FAO Marketing Guide no. 1*. Rome: FAO.

———— (1970). *Report of the Second World Food Congress*. Rome: FAO.

———— (1983). *World Food Security: A Reappraisal of the Concepts and Approaches. Director General's Report*. Rome: FAO.

———— (1996). *Rome Declaration on World Food Security*. World Food Summit, Rome 13–17 November. www.fao.org/docrep/003/w3613e/w3613e00.HTM [Accessed 12 November 2014]

———— (1997). *Agriculture, Food and Nutrition for Africa. A Resource Book for Teachers*. www.fao.org/docrep/w0078e/w0078e00.HTM [Accessed 12 November 2014]

———— (2002). *Declaration of the World Food Summit: Five Years Later*. Rome: FAO. www.fao.org/docrep/MEETING/005/Y7106E/Y7106E09.htm#TopOfPage [Accessed 12 November 2014]

———— (2003). *Trade Reforms and Food Security: Conceptualizing the Linkages*. Rome: FAO. www.fao.org/docrep/005/y4671e/y4671e00.htm#Contents [Accessed 12 November 2014]

———— (2004) *What Is Agrobiodiversity?* ftp://ftp.fao.org/docrep/fao/007/y5609e/y5609e00.pdf [Accessed 12 November 2014]

———— (2006). *Trade Reforms and Food Security: Country Case Studies and Synthesis*. Rome: FAO.

———— (2008a). *Declaration of the High-Level Conference on World Food Security: The Challenges of Climate Change and Bioenergy.* www.fao.org/fileadmin/user_upload/foodclimate/HLCdocs/declaration-E.pdf [Accessed 12 November 2014]

———— (2008b). *The State of Food Insecurity in the World 2008: High Food Prices and Food Security – Threats and Opportunities.* Rome: FAO.

———— (2009a). *The Special Challenge for sub-Saharan Africa.* High Level Expert Forum: How to Feed the World 2050. Rome: FAO. www.fao.org/fileadmin/templates/wsfs/docs/Issues_papers/HLEF2050_Africa.pdf [Accessed 12 November 2014]

———— (2009b). *Declaration of the World Summit on Food Security.* 16–18 November. WSFS2009/2. Rome. www.fao.org/fileadmin/templates/wsfs/Summit/Docs/Final_Declaration/WSFS09_Declaration.pdf [Accessed 12 November 2014]

———— (2011a). *Save and Grow. A Policymaker's Guide to the Sustainable Intensification of Smallholder Crop Production.* Rome: FAO.

———— (2011b). *The State of Food Insecurity in the World 2011. How Does International Price Volatility Affect Domestic Economies and Food Security?* Rome: FAO.

———— (2011c). *Why Has Africa Become a Net Food Importer?* www.fao.org/docrep/015/i2497e/i2497e00.pdf [Accessed 12 November 2014]

———— (2012a). *The State of Food Insecurity in the World. Economic Growth Is Necessary but Not Sufficient to Accelerate Reduction of Hunger and Malnutrition.* Rome: FAO

———— (2012b). *Trends and Impacts of Foreign Investment in Developing Country Agriculture. Evidence from Case Studies.* Rome: FAO.

———— (2012c). *The State of Food and Agriculture 2012. Investing in Agriculture for a Better Future.* Rome: FAO.

———— (2013a). *Organic Agriculture: African Experiences in Resilience and Sustainability.* Rome: FAO.

———— (2013b). *The State of Food and Agriculture 2013: Food Systems for Better Nutrition.* Rome: FAO.

———— (2014a). *FAO Food Price Index.* www.fao.org/worldfoodsituation/foodprices index/en/ [Accessed 12 November 2014]

———— (2014b). *The International Year of Family Farming.* www.fao.org/family-farming-2014/en/ [Accessed 12 November 2014]

———— (n.d.a). *How Does FAO Define the Private Sector?* www.fao.org/partnerships/private-sector/en/ [Accessed 12 November 2014]

———— (n.d.b). *Voices of the Hungry.* www.fao.org/fileadmin/user_upload/newsroom/docs/VOH_final_COLOR.pdf [Accessed 12 November 2014]

FAO Investment Centre (2012). *Outgrower Schemes: Advantages of Different Business Models for Sustainable Crop Intensification. Ghana Case Studies.* Rome: FAO.

FAO Rural Infrastructure and Agro-industries Division (2012). *Guiding Principles for Responsible Contract Farming Operations.* Rome: FAO.

FAO, IFAD, OECD, UNCTAD, WFP, World Bank, WTO, IFPRI and UN HLTF (2011). *Price Volatility in Food and Agricultural Markets: Policy Responses.* www.worldbank.org/foodcrisis/pdf/Interagency_Report_to_the_G20_on_Food_Price_Volatility.pdf [Accessed 12 November 2014]

Farming Online (2014). *USDA Rice Breakthrough.* 16 January. www.farming.co.uk/news/article/9412 [Accessed 12 November 2014]

Faye, Jacques (1999). *L'exploitation familiale du terroir à l'environnement international: éléments de stratégie.* Dakar: CNCR/FONGS/FAO.

Fern (2010). *Designed to Fail. The Concepts, Practices and Controversies behind Carbon Trading.* www.fern.org/sites/fern.org/files/FERN_designedtofail_internet_0.pdf [Accessed 12 November 2014]

FFTC (2011). *Strengthening Local Food Systems for Small-Scale Farmers in the Asian and Pacific Region.* www.fftc.agnet.org/files/lib_articles/20120621160523/ac2011e.pdf [Accessed 12 November 2014]

Fiedler, Doreen (2013). "Bhutan Looks to Become the World's First 100% Organic Country". *Gulf Times* 9 September. www.gulf-times.com/environment/231/details/365266/bhutan-looks-to-become-world%E2%80%99s-first-100%25-organic-country [Accessed 12 November 2014]

Focus on the Global South (2013). *From Latin America to Asia. Learning from our Roots. A Conversation on Vivir Bien.* http://focusweb.org/sites/www.focusweb.org/files/Viver Bien_EN.pdf [Accessed 12 November 2014]

Food & Water Watch (2013). *Biotech Ambassadors. How the U.S. State Department Promotes the Seed Industry's Global Agenda.* www.foodandwaterwatch.org/reports/biotech-ambassadors/[Accessed 12 November 2014]

Food Mythbusters (2013). *Hunger & Food Security Myth No 1. We Need Industrial Agriculture to Feed the World.* http://foodmyths.org/wp-content/uploads/2012/08/Hunger_Companion Guide_FINAL1.pdf [Accessed 12 November 2014]

Food Think Tank (2013). *Farming in the Bay. Ten Urban Agriculture Projects in San Francisco.* http://foodtank.com/news/2013/12/farming-in-the-bay-10-urban-agriculture-projects-san-Francisco [Accessed 12 November 2014]

———— (2014). *Family Farmers. Food Tank by Numbers.* www.scribd.com/doc/210989966/Food-Tank-by-the-Numbers [Accessed 12 November 2014]

Foucault, Michel (1980). *Power/Knowledge: Selected Interviews and Other Writings. 1972–1977.* New York: Vintage.

Fraser, Nancy (2007) "Transnationalizing the public sphere: on the legitimacy and efficacy of public opinion in a post-Westphalian world". *Theory, Culture & Society*, 24:4, 7–30.

Friedmann, Harriet (1987). "International Regimes of Food and Agriculture since 1870", in T. Shanin (ed.), *Peasants and Peasant Societies*, pp. 247–258. Oxford: Basil Blackwell.

———— (1993). "The political economy of food: a global crisis". *New Left Review*, I/197 (January–February), 29–57.

———— (2005). "From Colonialism to Green Capitalism: Social Movements and Emergence of Food Regimes", in Frederick H. Buttel and Philip McMichael (eds) *New Directions in the Sociology of Global Development*, pp. 227–264. Bingley, UK: Emerald Group Publishing Limited.

———— (2009). "Discussion: moving food regimes forward: reflections on symposium essays". *Agriculture and Human Values*, 26:4, 335–44.

———— (2010) "Scaling Up: Bringing Public Institutions and Food Service Corporations into the Project for a Local Sustainable Food System in Ontario", in A. Blay-Palmer (ed.) *Imagining Sustainable Food Systems: Theory and Practice*, pp. 157–172. Farnham, UK: Ashgate.

———— (2013). "Beyond the Price Paradox: Towards Deepening the Ecological/Material Foundations of Alliances Across the Food System". Abstract for *Food Sovereignty: A Critical Dialogue.* International Conference, Yale University. September 14–17. www.yale.edu/agrarianstudies/foodsovereignty/abstracts.html [Accessed 12 November 2014]

Friends of the Earth International (2014). *Who Benefits from GM Crops? An Industry Built on Myths.* https://www.foeeurope.org/sites/default/files/publications/foei_who_benefits_from_gm_crops_2014.pdf [Accessed 12 November 2014]

Fuchs, Doris and Agni Kalfagianni (2010). "The causes and consequences of private food governance". *Business and Politics*, 12:3, 1–36.

Fullerton, John (2014). "High-Frequency Trading Is a Blight on Markets that the Tobin Tax Can Cure". *The Guardian* 4 April. www.theguardian.com/business/economics-blog/

2014/apr/04/high-frequency-trading-markets-tobin-tax-financial-transactions-algorithms [Accessed 12 November 2014]

Gaia Foundation (2014). "UN Climate Experts: Green Revolution Leaves Food Systems Vulnerable to Climate Change". 1 April. www.gaiafoundation.org/news/un-climate-experts-green-revolution-leaves-food-systems-vulnerable-to-climate-change [Accessed 12 November 2014]

Gates, Bill (2013). *Agricultural Productivity Is Key to Reducing World Poverty*. Farmers Feeding the World, 9 May. www.agweb.com/article/bill_gates_agricultural_productivity_is_key_to_reducing_world_poverty/[Accessed 12 November 2014]

Gaventa, J. and R. Tandon (eds) (2010). *Globalizing Citizens: New Dynamics of Inclusion and Exclusion*. London: Zed.

Ghosh, Jayati (2010). "The unnatural coupling: food and global finance". *Journal of Agrarian Change*, 10:1 (January), 72–86.

Gibbon, Peter (2004). "Value-Chain Governance, Pubic Regulation and Entry Barriers in the Global Fresh Fruit and Vegetable Chain into the EU", in Simon Maxwell and Rachel Slater (eds), *Food Policy Old and New*, pp. 71–80. Oxford: ODI and Blackwell Publishing.

Global Campaign for Agrarian Reform and Land Research Action Network (2010). *Why We Oppose the Principles for Responsible Agricultural Investment (RAI)*. www.viacampesina.org/en/images/stories/pdf/whyweopposerai.pdf [Accessed 12 November 2014]

Global Harvest (2011). *A Private-Sector Voice for Productivity Growth through the Agricultural Value Chain to Sustainably Meet the Demands of a Growing World*. www.globalharvestinitiative.org/index.php/policy-center/removing-barriers-to-global-and-regional-trade-in-agriculture/[Accessed 12 November 2014]

Goetz, A. M. and R. Jenkins (2004). *Reinventing Accountability: Making Democracy Work for Human Development*. Basingstroke: Palgrave.

Goldenberg, Suzanne (2014). "Climate Change a Threat to Security, Food and Humankind – IPCC Report". *The Guardian* 31 March. www.theguardian.com/environment/2014/mar/31/climate-change-threat-food-security-humankind [Accessed 12 November 2014]

Gordillo, Gustavo (2013). *Seguridad y Soberania Alimentarias. Documento base para discussion*. Santiago, Chile: FAO, RLAC.

GRAIN (2008). *Seized! The 2008 Land Grab for Food and Financial Security*. Grain Briefing, October. www.grain.org [Accessed 12 November 2014]

—— (2011). "Food and Climate Change: The Forgotten Link". *Against the Grain* 28 September. www.grain.org/article/entries/4357-food-and-climate-change-the-forgotten-link

—— (2013). "Seed Laws in Latin America: The Offensive Continues, So Does Popular Resistance. *Against the Grain* 30 October. www.grain.org/article/entries/4808-seed-laws-in-latin-america-the-offensive-continues-so-does-popular-resistance [Accessed 12 November 2014]

Gramsci, Antonio (1971). *Selections from the Prison Notebooks*. New York: International Publishers.

Green, Jessica F. (2014). *Rethinking Private Authority. Agents and Entrepreneurs in Global Environmental Governance*. Princeton: Princeton University Press.

GRET (n.d.). *Factsheet no. 10 – How to Take Action*. http://catalogue.gret.org/publications/ouvrages/infoomc/en/F10en.html [Accessed 15 April 2013]

Gunders, Dana (2012). *Wasted: How America Is Losing Up to 40 Percent of Its Food from Farm to Fork to Landfill*. Natural Resources Defence Council. www.nrdc.org/food/files/wasted-food-IP.pdf [Accessed 12 November 2014]

Gustafson, Daniel J. and John Markie (2009). "A Stronger Global Architecture for Food and Agriculture: Some Lessons from FAO's History and Recent Evaluation", in Jennifer

Clapp and Marc J. Cohen (eds), *The Global Food Crisis. Governance Challenges and Opportunities*, pp. 179–192. Waterloo, CA: Wilfred Laurier University Press.

Gustavsson, Jenny, Ulf Sonesson, Robert van Otterdijk and Alexandre Meybeck (2011). *Food Losses and Wastes: Extent, Causes and Prevention.* Rome: FAO.

Habermas, Jürgen (1989). "The Public Sphere", in Steven Seidan (ed.), *Jürgen Habermans on Society and Politics. A Reader*, pp. 231–236. Boston: Beacon Press.

Hall, Bud (1981). "Participatory research, popular knowledge and power". *Convergence*, 14:3, 6–19.

Handy, Jim (2013). "The 'Non-Economy' and the Radical Dreams of Food Sovereignty". *Food Sovereignty: A Critical Dialogue*, International Conference, Yale University. September 14–17. Conference Paper no. 26. www.yale.edu/agrarianstudies/foodsovereignty/pprs/26_Handy_2013.pdf [Accessed 12 November 2014]

Harvey, David (2014). *Seventeen Contradictions and the End of Capitalism.* Oxford: Oxford University Press.

Headey, Derek and Shenggen Fan (2010). *Reflections on the Global Food Crisis – How Did It Happen? How Has It Hurt? And How Can We Prevent the Next One?* Research Monograph. Washington, DC: IFPRI.

Held, David and Mathias Koening-Archibugi (2005). *Global Governance and Public Accountability.* Oxford: Blackwell.

High-Level Panel of Experts on Food Security and Nutrition – HLPE (2011). *Land Tenure and International Investments in Agriculture.* Rome: Committee on World Food Security. www.fao.org/3/a-mb766e.pdf [Accessed 12 November 2014]

———— (2013). *Investing in Smallholder Agriculture for Food Security.* Rome: Committee on World Food Security. www.fao.org/3/a-i2953e.pdf [Accessed 12 November 2014]

Higgot, Richard (2001). "Economic Globalization and Global Governance: Towards a Post-Washington Consensus?", in Volker Rittberger (ed.), *Global Governance and the United Nations System*, pp. 127–157. Tokyo, New York, Paris: United Nations University Press.

Hirschman, Albert Otto (1977). *The Passions and the Interests: Political Arguments for Capitalism Before its Triumph.* Princeton, NJ: Princeton University Press.

Hoddinott, John and Marc J. Cohen (2007). *Renegotiating the Food Aid Convention: Background, Context and Issues.* IFPRI Discussion Paper 00690. February 2007.

Holland, Luke (2014). "Civil Society Rallies to Prevent Privatization of Post-2015 Process". *Center for Economic and Social Rights.* http://cesr.org/article.php?id=1576 [Accessed 12 November 2014]

Holmes, Marisa (2013). "Why We Occupied the World Social Forum". *Waging Nonviolence*, April 23. http://wagingnonviolence.org/feature/why-we-occupied-the-world-social-forum/[Accessed 12 November 2014]

Holt-Giminez, Eric (2002). "Measuring farmers' agroecological resistance after Hurricane Mitch in Nicaragua: a case study in participatory, sustainable land management impact monitoring". *Agriculture, Ecosystems and the Environment*, 93:1–2, 87–105.

———— (2006). *Campesino A Campesino: Voices from Latin America's Farmer to Farmer Movement for Sustainable Agriculture.* Oakland, CA: Food First.

———— (ed.) (2011). *Food Movements Unite!* Oakland, CA: Food First.

Holt-Giminez, Eric and Annie Shattuck (2011). "Food crises, food regimes and food movements: rumblings of reform or tides of transformation?". *Journal of Peasant Studies*, 38:1, 109–144.

House of Lords. European Union Committee (2014). *Counting the Cost of Food Waste: EU Food Waste Preventions Today.* www.parliament.uk/documents/lords-committees/eu-sub-com-d/food-waste-prevention/154.pdf [Accessed 12 November 2014]

Howard, Phil (2006). "Consolidation in food and agriculture". *The Natural Farmer*, 2:68. Northeast Organic Farmers Association. www.organicconsumers.org/articles/article_416.cfm [Accessed 12 November 2014]

Humanitarian News and Analysis (2008). *Burkina Faso: Food Riot Shuts Down main Towns.* 22 February. www.irinnews.org/Report/76905/BURKINA-FASO-Food-riots-shut-down-main-towns [Accessed 12 November 2014]

Hydén, Gören (1980). *Beyond Ujamaa in Tanzania: Underdevelopment and an Uncaptured Peasantry.* Berkeley: University of California Press.

IAASTD – International Assessment of Agricultural Knowledge, Science and Technology for Development (2009). *Agriculture at a Crossroads. Synthesis Report.* Washington, D.C.: Island Press. www.unep.org/dewa/agassessment/reports/IAASTD/EN/Agriculture%20at%20 a%20Crossroads_Synthesis%20Report%20%28English%29.pdf [Accessed 12 November 2014]

IBGE (2006). *Censo Agropecuario 2006. Agricultura Familiar.* www.ibge.gov.br/home/estatistica/ economia/agropecuaria/censoagro/agri_familiar_2006/familia_censoagro2006.pdf [Accessed 12 November 2014]

Ingram, John, Polly Ericksen and Diana Liverman (eds) (2010). *Food Security and Global Environmental Change.* London: Earthscan.

Inter-réseaux (2012). *Brazil's Zero Hunger Strategy.* Rural Development Briefing, September. www.inter-reseaux.org/IMG/pdf/Note_FaimZe_ro_Sept2012_EN_vp.pdf [Accessed 12 November 2014]

International Civil Society Planning Committee for Food Sovereignty – IPC (2002). *NGO/ CSO Forum for Food Sovereignty: A Right for All. Acts of the Forum Held in Parallel to the World Food Summit: Five Years Later.* Rome. 8–13 June.

—— (2008). *No More Failures as Usual.* https://www.swissaid.ch/sites/default/files/FAO_ Gipfel_Rom_statement_foodemergency.pdf

—— (2010). *Call to Civil Society to Participate in the Process towards the Adoption of Voluntary Guidelines for Land and Natural Resource Tenure by FAO.* www.foodsovereignty.org [Accessed 30 March 2012]

—— (2014). *Critical Comments on "The Land Indicators Initiative".* 20–22 February. Rome.

—— (forthcoming). *Popular Manual to Discuss and Apply the Voluntary Guidelines on Responsible Governance of the Tenure of Land, Fisheries and Forests.*

ICARRD – International Conference on Agrarian Reform and Rural Development (2006). *Final Declaration.* Rome: FAO.

Jacobs, Ryan (2013). "Charts: The Top 5 Land-Grabbing Countries". *Mother Jones* 6 February. www.motherjones.com/blue-marble/2013/01/top-land-grabbing-countries [Accessed 12 November 2014]

Jacolin, Pierre, Hugues Dupriez, Pape Maissa Fall, Joséphone Ndione, Mamadou Sow, Mor Diaw, Astou Ndong, Andala Diop, Maimouna Diouf and Cheikh Ndiaye (1991). *Diobass: les paysans et leurs terroirs. Guide pédagogique.* Dakar: FONGS, ENDA, Terres et Vie, CTA.

Jarosz, Lucy (2009). "The political economy of global governance and the world food crisis. The case of the FAO". *Review,* 32:1, 37–60.

Johns, Timothy (2012). *Traditional and Local Food Systems: Nutritional, Social and Sustainable Balance to Global Supply Chains.* Presentation to Traditional Food International Conference, Cesena, Italy. 2 October.

Juma, Calestous (2011). *The New Harvest. Agricultural Innovation in Africa.* Oxford: Oxford University Press.

Kastler, Guy, Antonio Onorati and Bob Brac (2013). "Seeds and Peasant Autonomy". *Right to Food and Nutrition Watch.* www.fian.org/fileadmin/media/publications/Watch_2013_ eng_WEB_final.pdf [Accessed 12 November 2014]

Kay, Sylvia (2012). *Positive Investment Alternatives to Large-Scale Land Acquisitions or Leases.* Amsterdam: Transnational Institute.

——— (2014). *Reclaiming Agricultural Investment: Towards Public-Peasant Investment Synergies.* Transnational Institute Agrarian Justice Programme Policy Paper. Amsterdam, Transnational Institute.

Kay, Sylvia and Jenny Franco (2012). *The Global Water Grab: A Primer.* Amsterdam: Transnational Institute.

Keats, Sharada and Steve Wiggins (2014). *Future Diets. Implications for Agriculture and Food Prices.* Overseas Development Institute. www.odi.org.uk/sites/odi.org.uk/files/odi-assets/publications-opinion-files/8776.pdf [Accessed 12 November 2014]

Keck, Margaret E. and Kathryn Sikkink (1998). *Activists beyond Borders.* Ithaca, NY: Cornell University Press.

Kingdom of Bhutan (2013). *Happiness: Toward a New Development Paradigm.* www.newdevelopmentparadigm.bt/wp-content/uploads/2013/12/NDP_Report_Bhutan_2013.pdf [Accessed 12 November 2014]

Kissinger, Henry (1974). *Implications of Worldwide Population Growth for U.S. Overseas Interests.* National Security Memorandum. http://pdf.usaid.gov/pdf_docs/PCAAB500.pdf [Accessed 12 November 2014]

Kouras, Colin K., Anne D. Bjorkman, Hanes Dempewolf, Julian Ramirez-Villegas, Luigi Guarino, Andy Jarvis, Loren H. Riesberg and Paul C. Struik (2014). "Increasing homogeneity in global food supplies and the implications for food security". *Proceedings of the National Academy of Sciences of the United States of America,* 111:11 (18 March). www.pnas.org/content/111/11/4001 [Accessed 12 November 2014]

Krishna, Gopal (2014). "India supported historic resolution adopted for a legally binding instrument on TNCs." *Toxic Watch Alliance.* 2 July 2014. www.toxicswatch.org/2014/07/india-supported-historic-resolution.html [Accessed 12 November 2014]

Kurtz, Hilda E. in collaboration with Heather Retberg and Bonnie Preston (2013). *Scaling Biopolitics: Enacting Food Sovereignty in Maine (USA).* Food Sovereignty: A Critical Dialogue. International Conference. Yale University. September 14–15. www.yale.edu/agrarianstudies/foodsovereignty/pprs/40_Kurtz_2013.pdf [Accessed 12 November 2014]

Lang, T. (2011). "Conclusions – Big Choices about the Food System", in Geoffrey Lawrence, Kristen Lyons and Tabatha Allington (eds), *Food Security, Nutrition and Sustainability,* pp. 271–287. London: Earthscan.

Lang, Tim, David Barling and Martin Caraher (2009). *Food Policy. Integrating Health, Environment and Society.* Oxford: Oxford University Press.

Lang, T. and M. Heasman (2004). *The Food Wars: The Global Battle for Mouths, Minds, and Markets.* London: Earthscan.

Lappe, Francis Moore et al. (2013). *Framing Hunger. A Response to the State of Food Insecurity in the World 2012.* http://smallplanet.org/sites/smallplanet.org/files/Framing-Hunger-SOFI12-12-2.pdf [Accessed 12 November 2014]

Lathan, Jonathan and Alison Wilson (2008). "Roundup Ready 2 Yield as Much as Conventional Soybeans?". *Independent Science News* 19 November. www.independentsciencenews.org/commentaries/roundup-ready-2-soybeans/[Accessed 12 November 2014]

Latouche, Serge (2009). *Farewell to Growth.* Cambridge, UK: Polity.

La Via Campesina – LVC (1996a). *II International Conference of the Via Campesina Tlaxcala, Mexico, April 18–21.* http://viacampesina.org/en/index.php/our-conferences-main-menu-28/2-tlaxcala-1996-mainmenu-48/425-ii-international-conference-of-the-via-campesina-tlaxcala-mexico-april-18–21 [Accessed 12 November 2014]

——— (1996b). *Food Sovereignty: A Future without Hunger.* www.voiceoftheturtle.org/library/1996%20Declaration%20of%20Food%20Sovereignty.pdf [Accessed 12 November 2014]

——— (2008). *La Via Campesina and the Global Food Crisis: Adequate Food Is Simple Justice.* 25 July. http://viacampesina.org/en/index.php/main-issues-mainmenu-27/foodsovereignty-and-trade-mainmenu-38/568-la-vcampesina-and-the-global-food-crisis-adequate-food-is-simple-justice [Accessed 12 November 2014]

—— (2010). *Sustainable Peasant and Family Farm Agriculture Can Feed the World*. Djakarta, Indonesia: La Via Campesina.

—— (2011). *Thematic Debate on the Green Economy*. http://viacampesina.org/en/index. php/actions-and-events-mainmenu-26/-climate-change-and-agrofuels-mainmenu-75/1057-thematic-debate-on-the-green-economy [Accessed 12 November 2014]

—— (2012). *The Committee on World Food Security (CFS): A New Space for the Food Policies of the World, Opportunities and Limitations*. http://viacampesina.org/downloads/pdf/en/report-no.4-EN-2012-comp.pdf [Accessed 12 November 2014]

—— (2013a). *Our Seeds, Our Future*. http://viacampesina.org/downloads/pdf/en/EN-notebook6.pdf [Accessed 12 November 2014]

—— (2013b). *The WTO Pushes through Bad Deal in the Final Hours; Developed Countries and TNCs Are the Big Winners*. www.viacampesina.org/en/index.php/actions-and-events-mainmenu-26/10-years-of-wto-is-enough-mainmenu-35 [Accessed 12 November 2014]

—— (2014). *La Via Campesina's Position on the International Year of Family Farming – 2014*. http://viacampesina.org/en/index.php/main-issues-mainmenu-27/sustainable-peasants-agriculture-mainmenu-42/1625-la-via-campesina-s-position-on-the-international-year-of-family-farming-2014 [Accessed 12 November 2014]

Lawrence, Geoffrey, Kristen Lyons and Tabatha Wallington (eds) (2010). *Food Security, Nutrition and Sustainability*. London: Earthscan.

Leathers, Howard D. and Philips Foster (2009). *The World Food Problem. Toward Ending Undernutrition in the Third World*. Fourth Edition. Boulder, Colorado: Lynne Rienner Publishers.

Lee, Simon (2007). "Common Good", in Mark Bevir (ed.), *Encyclopedia of Governance*, vol. 1, pp. 116–117. Thousand Oaks, CA: Sage.

Lin, Brenda et al. (2011). "Effects of industrial agriculture on climate change and the mitigation potential of small-scale agro-ecological farms". *Perspectives in Agriculture, Veterinary Science, Nutrition and Natural Resources*, 6:020. www.academia.edu/2462012/Effects_of_industrial_agriculture_on_climate_change_and_the_mitigation_potential_of_small-scale_agro-ecological_farms [Accessed 12 November 2014]

Livingston, Geoffrey, Steven Schonberger and Sara Delaney (2011). *Sub-Saharan Africa: The State of Smallholders in Agriculture*. Rome: IFAD. www.ifad.org/events/agriculture/doc/papers/livingston.pdf [Accessed 12 November 2014]

Lowder, S., B. Carisma and J. Skoet (2012). *Who Invests in Agriculture and How Much? An Empirical Review of the Relative Size of Various Investments in Low- and Middle-Income Countries*. ESA Working Paper no.12–09. Rome, FAO.

Lynn, Matthew (2013). "Food Prices May Be Catalysts for 2013 Revolutions". *The Wall Street Journal* 16 January. www.marketwatch.com/story/food-prices-may-be-catalyst-for-2013-revolutions-2013-01-16 [Accessed 12 November 2014]

MacKenzie, Debora (2013). "Brazil Uprising Points to Rise of Leaderless Networks". *New Scientist* 26 June. www.newscientist.com/article/mg21829234.300-brazil-uprising-points-to-rise-of-leaderless-networks.html#.Us-yxrTShjI [Accessed 12 November 2014]

MacMillan, Tom (2005). *Power in the Food System: Understanding Trends and Improving Accountability*. Background Paper. London: Food Ethics Council.

Maetz, Materne (2014). "Trends in Food and Agricultural Policies: Short Term Decisions Likely to Jeopardise Transition to Sustainable Agriculture and Hunger Eradication". *Hunger Explained* 26 February. www.hungerexplained.org/Hungerexplained/News_26_February_2014.html [Accessed 12 November 2014]

Margulis, Matias E., Nora McKeon and Saturnino M. Borras Jr. (2013). "Introduction: land grabbing and global governance: critical perspectives". *Globalizations*, 10:1 (February), 1–24.

Marsden, Terry (2012). "Third natures? recasting space through place-making strategies for sustainability". *Int. Jrnl. of Soc. of Agr. & Food*, 19:2, 257–274.

Martiniello, Giuliano (2013). "Food Sovereignty as a Weapon of the Weak? Rethinking the Food Question in Uganda". *Food Sovereignty: A Critical Dialogue*. Yale University and ISS. www.iss.nl/fileadmin/ASSETS/iss/Research_and_projects/Research_networks/ICAS/41_Martiniello_2013.pdf [Accessed 12 November 2014]

Mastrandrea, Angelo (2013). "Agricoltura: ritorno alla terra". *Rassegna.it*. www.rassegna.it/articoli/2013/07/23/103055/agricoltura-ritorno-alla-terra [Accessed 12 November 2014]

Maxwell, Simon and Marisol Smith (1992). *Household Food Security: A Conceptual Review.* www.ifad.org/hfs/tools/hfs/hfspub/hfs_1.pdf [Accessed 12 November 2014]

Mazoyer, Marcel and Laurence Roudart (2002). *Histoire des agricultures du monde: Du néolitique à la crise contemporaine*. Paris: Le Seuil. English edition Earthscan 2006.

McCoy, Kevin (2013). "Dodd-Frank Action: After 3 Years a Long To-Do List". *USA Today* 12 September. www.usatoday.com/story/money/business/2013/06/03/dodd-frank-financial-reform-progress/2377603/[Accessed 12 November 2014]

McCullough, Ellen B., Prabhu L. Pingali and Kostas G. Stamoulis (eds) (2008). *The Transformation of Agri-Food Systems. Globalization, Supply Chains and Smallholder Farmers.* Oxford and Rome: Earthscan and FAO.

McDonald, Bryan L. (2010). *Food Security: Addressing Challenges from Malnutrition, Food Safety and Environmental Change*. Cambridge, UK: Polity Press.

McKay, Ben (2012). *A Socially-Inclusive Pathway to Food Security: The Agroecological Alternative.* International Policy Centre for Inclusive Growth. Research Brief no. 23. June. www.ipc-undp.org/pub/IPCPolicyResearchBrief23.pdf [Accessed 12 November 2014]

McKeon, Michael (2005). *The Secret History of Domesticity. Public, Private and the Division of Knowledge*. Baltimore: The Johns Hopkins Press.

McKeon, Nora (1988). *Synthesis of the African National Reports*. Rome: The Image of Africa Project.

——— (2005). "Poverty Reduction in the Sahel: What Do Farmers Have to Say?", in Nicola Bocella and Andrea Billi (eds), *Distribution des révenues, inégalités et politiques de réduction de la pauvreté*, pp. 173–202. Paris: Karthala.

——— (2008). "ACP farmers' organisations and EPAs: from a whisper to a roar in two short years". *Trade Negotiation Insights*, 7:1 (February), 16.

——— (2009a). *The United Nations and Civil Society: Legitimating Global Governance – Whose Voice?* London: Zed.

——— (2009b). *A Food Battle Won*. www.csm4cfs.org/files/Pagine/16/a_food_battle_won_nora_mckeon_en.pdf [Accessed 12 November 2014]

——— (2011a). *Global Governance for World Food Security: A Scorecard Four Years after the Eruption of the "Food Crisis"*. Heinrich Boll Foundation. www.boell.de/sites/default/files/Global-Governance-for-World-Food-Security.pdf [Accessed 12 November 2014]

——— (2011b). "Now's the Time to Make It Happen: The UN's Committee on Food Security", in Eric Holt-Giminez (ed.), *Food Movements Unite!*, pp. 257–273. Oakland, CA: Food First Books.

——— (2012). "Including the Excluded in Global Politics: The Case of Peasants", in Jan Aart Scholte (ed.), *Building Global Democracy: Including the Excluded in Global Politics*, forthcoming.

——— (2013a). "'One does not sell the land upon which the people walk': Land grabbing, transnational rural social movements and global governance". *Globalizations*, 10:1 (February), 105–122.

———— (2013b). "African Peasants Have Their Own Ideas about How to Meet the Growing Food Demand". *Right to Food and Nutrition Watch 2013*, pp. 17–19. www.rtfn-watch.org/fileadmin/media/rtfn-watch.org/ENGLISH/pdf/Watch_2013/Watch_2013_PDFs/Watch_2013_eng_WEB_final.pdf [Accessed 12 November 2014]

———— (2013c). *Investing in Smallholders and Food Security in Africa: What Do Small-Scale Food Producers Themselves Have to Say?* www.europafrica.info/en/themes/investing-in-smallholders-and-food-security-in-africa-what-do-small-scale-producers-themselves-have-to-say [Accessed 12 November 2014]

———— (2014). *The New Alliance for Food and Nutrition Security: A Coup for Corporate Capital?* Transnational Institute and Terra Nuova. www.tni.org/briefing/new-alliance-food-security-and-nutrition [Accessed 12 November 2014]

McKeon, Nora and Carol Kalafatic (2009). *Strengthening Dialogue: UN Experience with Small Farmer Organizations and Indigenous Peoples*. New York: UN NGO Liaison Service. www.un-ngls.org/spip.php?article1702 [Accessed 12 November 2014]

McKeon, Nora, Michael Watts and Wendy Wolford (2004). *Peasant Associations in Theory and Practice*. Geneva: UNRISD.

McMichael, Philip (2005). "Global Development and the Corporate Food Regime", in Frederick H. Buttel and Philip McMichael (eds), *New Directions in the Sociology of Global Development*, pp. 269–303. Oxford: Elsevier.

———— (2009). "A food regime analysis of neo-liberalism's food crisis". *Agriculture and Human Values*, 14, 281–295.

———— (2009). "A food regime genealogy". *Journal of Peasant Studies*, 36:1, 139–169.

———— (ed.) (2010). *Contesting Development. Critical Struggles for Social Change*. London: Routledge.

———— (2012a). "The land grab and corporate food regime restructuring". *The Journal of Peasant Studies*, 29:3–4, 681–701.

———— (2012b). "Biofuels and the financialization of the global food system", in Christopher Rosin, Paul Stock and Hugh Campbell (eds), *Food Systems Failure*, pp. 60–82. Oxford: Earthscan.

———— (2013a). "Value-chain agriculture and debt relations: contradictory outcomes". *Third World Quarterly*, 34:4, 671–690.

———— (2013b). *Food Regimes and Agrarian Questions*. Halifax & Winnipeg: Fernwood Publishing.

———— (2014). "Historicizing food sovereignty". *Journal of Peasant Studies*, Vol. 41, Issue 6, 2014, pp. 933–957.

McNamara, Robert (1973). *Address to the World Bank Board of Governors*. http://siteresources.worldbank.org/EXTARCHIVES/Resources/Robert_McNamara_Address_Nairobi_1973.pdf [Accessed 12 November 2014]

Mehta, L., G. J. Veldwisch, and J. Franco (2012). "Introduction to the special issue: water grabbing? Focus on the (re)appropriation of finite water resources". *Water Alternatives*, 5:2, 193–207.

Millennium Ecosystem Assessment (2005). *Ecosystems and Human Well-Being: Synthesis*. Washington, DC: Island Press.

Mills, Frederick B. and William Camacaro (2013). "Venezuela and the Battle against Transgenic Seeds". *Venezuelanalysis.com*, 11 December. http://venezuelanalysis.com/analysis/10236 [Accessed 12 November 2014]

Monbiot, George (2012). "Putting a price on the rivers and rain diminishes us all". *The Guardian* 6 August. www.theguardian.com/commentisfree/2012/aug/06/price-rivers-rain-greatest-privatisation [Accessed 12 November 2014]

Monsalve Suárez, Sofia (2012a). "The human rights framework in contemporary agrarian struggles", *The Journal of Peasant Studies*, 40:1, 239–290.

—— (2012b). "The Recently Adopted Guidelines on the Responsible Governance of Tenure of Land, Fisheries and Forests: A Turning Point in the Global Governance of Natural Resources?". *Right to Food and Nutrition Watch 2012: Who Decides About Global Food and Nutrition?*, pp. 37–41. Heidelberg: FIAN.

Monsalve Suárez, Sofia and Fabienne Aubry (2014). "Rethinking the Voluntary vs Binding Divide: A Reflection after 10 Years of the *Voluntary* Guidelines on the Right to Food", *Right to Food and Nutrition Watch* 2014. www.rttn-watch.org/uploads/media/watch_2014_Article_3_Voluntary_vs_Binding_Instrument_ENG.pdf [Accessed 12 November 2014]

Mulvany, Patrick (2007). "Food Sovereignty comes of age". *Food Ethics*, 2:3 (Autumn). www.ukfg.org.uk/docs/FoodSov17Dec2007.pdf [Accessed 12 November 2014]

—— (2013). Governments Renew Commitment to Implement Farmers' Rights! http://agrariancrisis.in/wp-content/uploads/2013/10/GB5-CSOreflection_PatrickMulvany.pdf [Accessed 12 November 2014]

Mulvany, P. M. and M.A. Moreira (2008). "Food Sovereignty: A Farmer Led Policy Framework". www.future-agricultures.org/farmerfirst/files/T3b_Arce_Mulvany.pdf [Accessed 12 November 2014]

Mulvany, Patrick and Jonathan Ensor (2011). "Changing a Dysfunctional Food System. Towards Ecological Food Provision in the Framework of Food Sovereignty". *Food Chain*, 1:1 (May), 34–51. Practical Action Publishing.

Murphy, Sofia and Timothy A. Wise (2013). *A Year of Squandered Opportunities to Resolve the Food Crisis*. IATP. http://ase.tufts.edu/gdae/Pubs/rp/IATPFoodCrisisJan2013.pdf [Accessed 12 November 2014]

Nambek N., P. Claeys, A. Wong and K. Brilmayer (eds) (2014). *Rethinking Food Systems. Structures, Challenges, New Strategies and the Law*. New York: Springer.

National Family Farm Coalition (n.d.). *Food Sovereignty*. www.nffc.net/Issues/Trade%20and%20Food%20Sovereignty/NFFCFoodSovBrochure.pdf [Accessed 12 November 2014]

Nestle, Marion (2007). *Food Politics. How the Food Industry Influences Nutrition and Health*. Oakland: University of California Press.

—— (2013). "Annals of Nutrition Science: Coca-Cola 1, NHANES 0". www.foodpolitics.com/2013/10/annals-of-nutrition-science-coca-cola-1-nhanes-0/ [Accessed 12 November 2014]

Newell, P. and J. Wheeler (eds) (2006) *Rights, Resources and the Politics of Accountability*. London: Zed.

Nicholson, Paul (2011). "Food Sovereignty: Alliances and Transformation", in Eric Holt-Giminez (ed.), *Food Movements Unite!*, pp. 9–19. Oakland, CA: Food First Books.

—— (2012). "Food Sovereignty, a Basis for Transforming the Dominant Economic and Social Model". Extract from *Terre et liberté! A la conquête de la souveraineté alimentaire*, PubliCetim no. 36, CETIM edition, Geneva. www.cetim.ch/documents/food_sovereignty-Paul_Nicholson_interview.pdf [Accessed 12 November 2014]

NGO Forum (1996). Supplement to *Volontari e Terzo Mondo*, XXV(1–2) January–June 1997. Rome: Volontari nel Mondo-FOCSIV.

NoREDD Make Noise (2010). *No REDD! A Reader*. http://noredd.makenoise.org/wp-content/uploads/2010/REDDreaderEN.pdf [Accessed 12 November 2014]

Nyéléni 2007 – Forum for Food Sovereignty (2007). *Synthesis Report*. www.nyeleni.org/spip.php?article334 [Accessed 12 November 2014]

—— (2013). "Peasant Farmers' Markets in Colombia". *Nyéléni Newsletter No. 13*. www.nyeleni.org/DOWNLOADS/newsletters/Nyeleni_Newsletter_Num_13_EN.pdf [Accessed 12 November 2014]

———— (2014). "Young People in Action: Struggles and Visions for Food Sovereignty". *Nyéleni Newsletter No. 17.* March, p. 2. www.nyeleni.org/DOWNLOADS/newsletters/Nyeleni_Newsletter_Num_17_EN.pdf [Accessed 12 November 2014]

Oakland Institute (2014). *Down on the Farm. Wall Street: America's New Farmer.* www.oakland institute.org/down-on-the-farm [Accessed 12 November 2014]

Onorati, Antonio (2014). "Can Small-Scale Food Producers Feed Shanghai? The Autonomy of Peasant Agriculture and the Market". Communication to Critical Dialogue on Food Sovereignty, ISS, February.

Organization for Economic Cooperation and Development – OECD (n.d.). *Paris Declaration and Accra Agenda for Action.* www.oecd.org/dac/effectiveness/parisdeclaration andaccraagendaforaction.htm [Accessed 12 November 2014]

Our Water Commons (n.d.). "Case 5: 'Social Control' and Public-Collective Partnerships with Country-Run Systems in Cochabamba, Bolivia". http://ourwatercommons.org/water-solutions/case-5-%E2%80%9Csocial-control%E2%80%9D-and-public-collective -partnerships-community-run-systems-coc [Accessed 12 November 2014]

Overbeek, Henk, Klaus Dingwerth, Philipp Pattberg and Daniel Compagnon (2010). "Forum: Global Governance: Decline or Maturation of an Academic Concept?" *International Studies Review,* 12, 696–719.

OXFAM (2013). *The New Alliance: A New Direction Needed.* www.oxfam.org/en/grow/"policy/new-alliance-new-direction-needed [Accessed 12 November 2014]

Oya, C. (2012). "Contract farming in sub-Saharan Africa: A survey of approaches, debates and issues". *Journal of Agrarian Change,* 12:1, 1–33.

Paarlberg, R. L. (2008). *Starved for Science. How Biotechnology Is Being Kept out of Africa.* Cambridge: Harvard University Press.

———— (2010). *Food Politics. What Everyone Needs to Know.* Oxford: Oxford University Press.

Paffetti, Maurizio and Eleonora Amelio (2013). *Mercato interno e agricoltura contadina. I contratti di coltivazione: spetti giuridici ed economici. Un caso emblematico: l'Italia.* www.cro ceviaterra.it/index.php/cosa-facciamo/progetti/13-mercati/140-mercato-interno-e-agricoltura-contadina-il-caso-studio [Accessed 12 November 2014]

PANAP (2010). *Communities in Peril: Global Report on Health Impacts of Pesticide Use in Agriculture.* www.panap.net/sites/default/files/PAN-Global-Report.pdf [Accessed 12 November 2014]

———— (2013). *Building Community Resistance against Land Grabbing.* Penang, Malaysia: PANP.

Patel, Raj (2005). "Global fascism, revolutionary humanism and the ethics of food sovereignty". *Development,* 48:2, 79–83.

———— (2009). "Food sovereignty". *Journal of Peasant Studies,* 36:3, 663–706.

———— (2012). "The long green revolution". *The Journal of Peasant Studies,* 40:1, 1–63.

Patel, Raj and Philip McMichael. (2010). "A political economy of the food riot". *Review – A Journal of the Fernand Braudel Center,* 32:1, 9–36.

Pattberg, P. (2006). *Global Governance: Reconstructing a Contested Social Science Concept.* Garnet Working Paper 04/06, March. London: London School of Economics and Political Science.

Paul, Helena (2010). *Carbon Markets – A Distraction from the Real Priority: Immediate Emission Reductions.* EcoNexus. www.econexus.info/publication/carbon-markets-distraction-from-real-priority [Accessed 12 November 2014]

Petersen, Paulo, Eros Marion Mussoi and Fabio Dal Soglio (2013). "Institutionalization of the agroecological approach in Brazil. Advances and challenges". *Agroecology and Sustainable Food Systems,* 37:1, 103–114.

Pianta, Mario (2005). *UN World Summits and Civil Society. The State of the Art.* UNRISD. www.unrisd.org/80256B3C005BCCF9/%28httpAuxPages%29/5709F9C06F40FDBA C12570A1002DC4D2/$file/pianta.pdf [Accessed 12 November 2014]

Piketty, Thomas (2013). *Capitalism in the Twenty-First Century.* Cambridge, MA: Harvard University Press.

Pimbert, Michel (2009). *Towards Food Sovereignty.* London: IIED.

Pimbert, Michel, Boukary Barry, Anne Berson and Khanh Tran-Thanh (2010). *Democratising Agricultural Research for Food Sovereignty in West Africa.* Bamako and London: IIED, CNOP, Centre Djoliba, IRPAD, Kene Conseils and URTEL.

Polanyi, Karl (1936). "The Essence of Fascism", in J. Lewis, K. Polanyi and D. K. Kitchen (eds), *Christianity and the Social Revolution*, pp. 359–394. New York: Charles Scribner's.

——— (1957). *The Great Transformation.* Boston: Beacon Press.

Polis (2010). "The Right to Urban Agriculture in Rosario, Argentina". www.thepolisblog. org/2010/09/right-to-urban-agriculture-in-rosario.html [Accessed 12 November 2014]

Pretty, J.N., A. D. Noble, D. Bossio, J. Dixon, R. E. Hine, F.W.T. Penning de Vries and J.I.L. Morison (2006). "Resource-conserving agriculture increases yields in developing countries", *Environmental Science and Technology*, 40:4, 1114–1119.

PROCASUR Corporation (2012). *Keekenyoike Market and Slaughterhouse.* www.cop-ppld. net/cop_knowledge_base/detail/?dyna_fef[uid]=3440 [Accessed 12 November 2014]

Rahmanian, Maryam and Michel Pimbert (2014). "Creating Knowledge for Food Sovereignty". *Nyéléni Newsletter No. 18.* Jun. www.nyeleni.org/DOWNLOADS/newsletters/ Nyeleni_Newsletter_Num_18_EN.pdf [Accessed 12 November 2014]

Ramdoo, Isabelle (2013). "9th WTO Ministerial in Bali: Trade Deal Struck but What Implications for Geopolitics?". *ECDPM Talking Points* 11 December. www.ecdpm. org/talking-points/wto-ministerial-bali-trade-deal-implications-geopolitics [Accessed 12 November 2014]

Resilient Urban Food Systems: Opportunities, Challenges and Solutions. Outcomes of the Resilient Urban Food Systems Forum (2013). Bonn, Germany, 1 June. http:// resilient-cities.iclei.org/fileadmin/sites/resilient-cities/files/Resilient_Cities_2013/ RUFS/RUFS_2013_Report.pdf [Accessed 12 November 2014]

Richards, Paul (1985). *Indigenous Agricultural Revolution.* New York: Harper Collins.

Right to Food and Nutrition Watch (2012). *Who Decides about Global Food and Nutrition? Strategies to Regain Control.* Heidelberg: FIAN. www.rtfn-watch.org/fileadmin/media/rtfn-watch.org/ENGLISH/pdf/Watch_2012/R_t_F_a_N_Watch_2012_eng_web_rz.pdf [Accessed 12 November 2014]

——— (2013). *Alternatives and Resistance to Policies that Generate Hunger.* Heidelberg: FIAN. www.fian.org/fileadmin/media/publications/Watch_2013_eng_WEB_final.pdf [Accessed 12 November 2014]

Robinson, Joanna L. (2013). *Contested Water. The Struggle against Water Privatization in the United States and Canada.* Boston: MIT Press.

Roffe, Pedro (2008). "Bringing Minimum Global Intellectual Property Standards into Agriculture: The Agreement on Trade-Related Aspects of Intellectual Property Rights (TRIPS)", in Geoff Tansey and Tasmin Rajtte (eds), *The Future Control of Food*, pp. 48–68. London: Earthscan.

Rojo, Javier and Manuel Perez-Rocha (2013). "NAFTA at 20: The New Spin". *Foreign Policy in Focus.* 14 March. http://fpif.org/nafta_at_20_the_new_spin/ [Accessed 12 November 2014]

Roman-Alcala, Antonio (2013). *Food Sovereignty: A Critical Dialogue.* International Conference, Yale University. September 14–15. www.iss.nl/fileadmin/ASSETS/iss/Research_ and_projects/Research_networks/ICAS/75_Roman_Alcala_2013.pdf [Accessed 12 November 2014]

ROPPA (2004). *Final Declaration. Synthesis Workshop of Farmer Organization Reflection on "The Farmers' Vision of What Agriculture for NEPAD?"* Ouagadougou, Burkina Faso: ROPPA.

—— (2012a). *La cohérence régionale et nationale des politiques agricoles et commerciales mises en œuvre. Vision de ROPPA.* Ouagadougou, Burkina Faso: ROPPA.

—— (2012b). *Les politiques régionales de souveraineté alimentaire en Afrique de l'Ouest dans le contexte du changement climatique.* www.roppa.info/IMG/pdf/TDR_Forum_Niamey_Changements_climatiques.pdf [Accessed 12 November 2014]

Rosin, Christopher, Paul Stock and Hugh Campbell (eds) (2012). *Food Systems Failure. The Global Food Crisis and the Future of Agriculture.* London: Earthscan.

Rosset, Peter M. and Maria Elena Martinez-Torres (2012). "Rural Social Movements and Agroecology: Context, Theory and Process". *Ecology and Society*, 17:3, 17, 1–12.

Rosset, Peter, B. M. Sosa, A. M. Jaime and D. R. Lozano (2011). "The Campesino-to-Campesino agroecology movement of ANAP in Cuba: social process methodology in the construction of sustainable peasant agriculture and food sovereignty". *Journal of Peasant Studies*, 38:1, 161–191.

Rostow, W. W. (1960). *The Stages of Economic Growth: A Non-Communist Manifesto.* Cambridge: Cambridge University Press.

Rulli, Maria Cristina, Antonio Saviori and Paolo D'Odorico (2013). "Global land and food grabbing". *PNAS (Proceedings of the National Academy of Sciences of the United States of America)*, 110:3 (January 15), 892–897.

Sachs, Wolfang (ed.) (1992). *The Development Dictionary. A Guide to Knowledge as Power.* London: Zed.

Saez, Catherine (2013). "Farmers' Groups Warn ARIPO about Implementing UPOV 91 in Africa". *Intellectual Property Watch* 30 October. www.ip-watch.org/2013/10/30/farmers-groups-warn-aripo-about-implementing-upov-91-in-africa/[Accessed 12 November 2014]

Samsel, Anthony and Stephanie Senef (2013). "Glyphosate, pathways to modern diseases II: celiac sprue and gluten intolerance". *Interdisciplinary Toxicology*, 6:4, 159–184. http://nhrighttoknowgmo.org/BreakingNews/Glyphosate_II_Samsel-Seneff.pdf [Accessed 12 November 2014]

Sassan, Saskia (2003). "Globalization or denationalization?". *Journal of International Political Economy*, 10:10 (February), 1–11.

Sarkozy, Nicholas (2011). *Le discours du Président Nicolas Sarkozy sur le G20 et G8.* www.ambafrance-is.org/Le-discours-du-President-Nicolas [Accessed 12 November 2014]

Save the Children (2013). *Superfood for Babies.* www.savethechildren.org.uk/sites/default/files/images/Superfood_for_Babies_UK_version.pdf [Accessed 12 November 2014]

Schanbacher, William D. (2010). *The Politics of Food. The Global Conflict between Food Security and Food Sovereignty.* Santa Barbara, CA: Praeger Security International.

Schiavoni, Christina (2014). "Competing Sovereignties in the Political Construction of Food Sovereignty". *Food Sovereignty: A Critical Dialogue.* www.iss.nl/fileadmin/ASSETS/iss/Research_and_projects/Research_networks/ICAS/90_Schiavoni.pdf [Accessed 12 November 2014]

Schneider, Mindi (2008). *We Are Hungry! Summary Report of Food Riots, Government Response and State of Democracy in 2008.* http://cornell.academia.edu/MindiSchneider/Papers/175793/_We_are_Hungry_A_Summary_Report_of_Food_Riots_Government_Responses_and_State_of_Democracy_in_2008 [Accessed 12 November 2014]

Scholte, Jan Aart (ed.) (2011). *Building Global Democracy? Civil Society and Accountable Global Governance.* Cambridge: Cambridge University Press.

—— (2013). "Civil society and financial markets: what is not happening and why", *Journal of Civil Society*, 9:2 (June), 129–147.

Scott, James C. (1998). *Seeing Like a State*. New Haven: Yale University Press.

Seattle to Brussels (2013). *A Brave New Transatlantic Partnership*. http://corporateeurope.org/sites/default/files/attachments/brave_new_transatlantic_partnership.pdf [Accessed 12 November 2014]

Seidman, Steven (ed.) (1989). *Jurgen Habermas on Society and Politics. A Reader*. Boston: Beacon Press.

Sen, Amartya (1981). *Poverty and Famines. An Essay on Entitlement and Deprivation*. Oxford: Clarendon Press.

——— (2013). *Why Is There So Much Hunger in the World?* Twenty-Eighth McDougall Memorial Lecture. FAO Conference Thirty-Eighth Session. C2013/INF/11/FAO. www.fao.org/docrep/meeting/028/mg856e.pdf [Accessed 12 November 2014]

Seufert, Philip (2013). "The FAO Voluntary Guidelines on the Responsible Governance of Tenure of Land, Fisheries and Forests". *Globalizations*, 10:1 (February), 181–186.

Shah, Anup (2010). *A Primer on Neoliberalism*. www.globalissues.org/article/39/a-primer-on-neoliberalism [Accessed 12 November 2014]

Shaw, D. John (2007). *World Food Security. A History since 1945*. London/New York: Palgrave Macmillan.

Sinclair, Timothy J. (2012). *Global Governance*. Cambridge: Polity.

Slaughter, Anne-Marie (2004). *A New World Order*. Princeton: Princeton University Press.

Slow Food. *About Us*. www.slowfood.com/international/1/about-us [Accessed 12 November 2014]

Smith M., J. Pointing, S. Maxwell et al. (1993). *Household Food Security: A Conceptual Review*. www.ifad.org/hfs/tools/hfs/hfspub/hfs_1.pdf [Accessed 12 November 2014]

Sogge, David (2014). "State of Davos – The Camel's Nose in the Tents of Global Governance". *The State of Corporate Power*. Transnational Institute. www.tni.org/sites/www.tni.org/files/download/state_of_davos_chapter.pdf [Accessed 12 November 2014]

SOS – Faim (2013). *Finding Funding Solutions for Rural Activities: FONGS of Senegal Has Some Answers*. Zoom microfinance no. 38. Brussels: SOS-Faim.

——— (2014). "Senegalese Family Farms Are Investing and Modernizing". *Farming Dynamics*, 32 (March). www.sosfaim.org/be/publication/les-exploitations-familiales-senegalaises-investissent-et-se-modernisent/[Accessed 12 November 2014]

Spitznagel, Eric (2012). "Rise of the Barter Market". *Bloomberg Business Week*. 26 April. www.businessweek.com/aticles/2012–04–26/rise-of-the-barter-economy [Accessed 12 November 2014]

Stiglitz, Joseph E. (2013). *The Price of Inequality: How Today's Divided Society Endangers Our Future*. New York: W. W. Norton.

Surprise Ending in Madrid! (2009). La Via Campesina. http://viacampesina.org/en/index.php/main-issues-mainmenu-27/food-sovereignty-and-trade-mainmenu-38/649-surprise-ending-in-madrid-no-consensus-on-a-g8-driven-partnership-for-now [Accessed 12 November 2014]

Sustainable Development (2015). www.sustainabledevelopment2015.org/index.php/intergovernmental-processes/[Accessed 12 November 2014]

Swanston, Linda, Kim Burnett and Christopher Rompre (2009). "People's Food Sovereignty Forum: Civil Society's Role in Global Food Governance." *CIGI online*. http://www.cigionline.org/articles/2009/12/people%E2%80%99s-food-sovereignty-forum-civil-society%E2%80%99s-role-global-food-governance [Accessed 2 December 2014]

Tansey, Geoff and Tasmin Rajotte (eds) (2008). *The Future Control of Food. A Guide to International Negotiations and Rule on Intellectual Property, Biodiversity and Food Security*. Oxford: Earthscan.

TEEB (2009). The Economics of Ecosystems & Biodiversity. TEEB for National and International Policy Makers. Summary: Responding to the Value of Nature. www.teebweb. org/wp-content/uploads/Study%20and%20Reports/Reports/National%20and%20 International%20Policy%20Making/Executive%20Summary/National%20Executive% 20Summary_%20English.pdf [Accessed 12 November 2014]

Thakurta, Paranjoy Guha (2008). "Trade-India: Mixed Feelings Over WTO Failure in Geneva". *Inter Press Service* 2 August. www.ipsnews.net/2008/08/trade-india-mixed-feelings-over-wto-failure-in-geneva/[Accessed 12 November 2014]

Thapa, Ganesh and Raghav Gaiha (2011). *Smallholder Farming in Asia and the Pacific: Challenges and Opportunities*. Rome: IFAD. www.ifad.org/events/agriculture/doc/papers/ganesh. pdf [Accessed 12 November 2014]

The Guardian (2013). *Food Waste: Tesco Reveals Most Bagged Salad and Half Its Bread Is Thrown Out.* 21 October. www.theguardian.com/business/2013/oct/21/food-waste-tesco-reveals-most-bagged-salad-and-half-its-bread-is-thrown-out [Accessed 12 November 2014]

Thompson, E. P (1991). "The Moral Economy of the English Crowd in the Eighteenth Century", in *Customs in Common*, pp. 185–258. Pontypool, Wales: The Merlin Press.

——— (1991). "The Patrician and the Plebs", in *Customs in Common*, pp. 16–96. Pontypool, Wales: The Merlin Press.

Tran, Mark, Claire Provost and Liz Ford (2014). "Aid to Africa: Private Sector Becomes the New Priority". *The Guardian* 18 February. www.theguardian.com/global-development/2014/ feb/18/aid-africa-private-sector-investment-priority-new-alliance [Accessed 12 November 2014]

Transnational Institute (2013). *The Global Land Grab. A Primer.* The Hague: Transnational Institute, Agrarian Justice Programme. www.tni.org/sites/www.tni.org/files/download/ landgrabbingprimer-feb2013.pdf [Accessed 12 November 2014]

——— (2014). *The State of Corporate Power – Insights into the Power of Corporations.* www.tni.org/sites/www.tni.org/files/download/state_of_power-6feb14.pdf [Accessed 12 November 2014]

Transnational Institute and Serikat Petani Indonesia – SPI (2013). *Tailored for Sharks: How Rules Are Tailored and Public Interest Surrendered to Suit Corporate Interests in the WTO, FTAs and BITs Trade and Investment Regime".* www.tni.org/briefing/tailored-sharks [Accessed 12 November 2014]

Trent, Ashley (2011). "Unhappy Meals". *Inside Counsel* March, p. 21. www.insidecounsel digital.com/insidecounsel/201103?pg=21#pg21 [Accessed 12 November 2014]

Truman, Harry (1949). *Inaugural Address.* www.trumanlibrary.org/whistlestop/50yr_archive/ inagural20jan1949.htm [Accessed 12 November 2014]

Tudge, Colin (2013). "The Founding Fables of Industrialized Agriculture". *Independent Science News* 30 October. www.independentsciencenews.org/un-sustainable-farming/the-founding-fables-of-industrialised-agriculture/[Accessed 12 November 2014]

Tuta, I. (2014). ISA. "'Translating' Human Rights to International Markets – The Emergence of a Private Human Rights Regime?". Paper presented at the International Studies Association 55th Annual Convention, 26–29 March, Toronto, Canada.

UN (1975). *Report of the World Food Conference.* Rome, 5–16 November 1974. New York: United Nations.

——— (n.d.). Zero Hunger. www.un.org/en/zerohunger/#&panel1–1 [Accessed 12 November 2014]

UN Committee on Economic, Social, and Cultural Rights – CESCR (1999). *General Comment No. 12: The Right to Adequate Food (Art. 11 of the Covenant).* www.refworld.org/ docid/4538838c11.html [Accessed 12 November 2014]

UN Conference on Trade and Development – UNCTAD (2013). *Wake Up Before It Is Too Late. Make Agriculture Truly Sustainable Now for Food Security in a Changing Climate.* Trade and Environment Review 2013. Geneva: UNCTAD. http://unctad.org/en/PublicationsLibrary/ditcted2012d3_en.pdf [Accessed 12 November 2014]

UN Development Programme – UNDP (1994). *Human Development Report 1994.* Oxford: Oxford University Press. http://hdr.undp.org/sites/default/files/reports/255/hdr_1994_en_complete_nostats.pdf [Accessed 12 November 2014]

UN Environment Programme – UNEP (2010), *Agriculture: A Catalyst for Transitioning to a Green Economy. A UNEP Brief.* www.unep.ch/etb/publications/Agriculture/UNEP_Agriculture.pdf [Accessed 12 November 2014]

——— (2012). Avoiding Future Famines: Strengthening the Ecological Foundation of Food Security through Sustainable Food Systems. Nairobi: UNEP.

——— (2013). *Report of the Independent Group of Experts on New Mechanism for Stakeholder Engagement at UNEP. Final Report.* 24 October 2013.

——— (n.d.). *What Is the Green Economy?* www.unep.org/greeneconomy/AboutGEI/WhatisGEI/tabid/29784/Default.aspx [Accessed 12 November 2014]

United Nations High-Level Task Force on the Global Food Security Crisis – HLTF (2008). *Comprehensive Framework for Action.* New York: United Nations.

Ungoed-Thomas, Jon and Kate Mansey (2013). "World Health Experts Want to Halve Sugar Consumption". *The Sunday Times* 29 December. www.thesundaytimes.co.uk/sto/news/uk_news/Health/article1357556.ece [Accessed 12 November 2014]

UK Food Group (2010). *Securing Future Food: Towards Ecological Food Provision.* London: UK Food Group.

USAID (2009). *Global Food Security Response. West Africa Value Chain Analysis Protocol.* Microreport no. 153. http://pdf.usaid.gov/pdf_docs/PNADP052.pdf [Accessed 12 November 2014]

US Department of Agriculture (2010). *Local Food Systems: Concepts, Impacts and Issues.* www.ers.usda.gov/media/122868/err97_1_.pdf [Accessed 12 November 2014]

US Food Aid and Security (n.d.). "The History of Food Aid". http://foodaid.org/resources/the-history-of-food-aid/[Accessed 12 November 2014]

Utting, Peter and Jennifer Clapp (2008). *Corporate Responsibility and Sustainable Development.* Oxford: Oxford University Press.

Van der Ploeg, J. D. (2008) *The New Peasantries: Struggle for Autonomy and Sustainability in an Era of Empire and Globalization.* London: Earthscan.

——— (2010) "The food crisis, industrialized farming and the imperial regime", *Journal of Agrarian Change,* 10:1, 98–106.

——— (2013). "Ten qualities of family farming". *Farming Matters.* AgriCultures Network. December. www.agriculturesnetwork.org/magazines/global/family-farming/theme-overview [Accessed 12 November 2014]

Van der Ploeg, Jan Douwe, Ye Jingzhong and Sergio Schneider (2012). "Rural development through the construction of new, nested markets: comparative perspectives from China, Brazil and the European Union". *Journal of Peasant Studies,* 39:1, 133–173.

Vanloqueren, Gaetan and Philippe V. Baret (2009). "How agricultural research systems shape a technological regime that develops genetic engineering but locks out agroecological innovations". *Research Policy,* 38, 971–983.

Vidal, John (2013). "India's Rice Revolution". *The Guardian.* www.theguardian.com/global-development/2013/feb/16/india-rice-farmers-revolution?view=mobile [Accessed 12 November 2014]

Vorley, Bill, Ethel de Pozo-Bergnes and Anna Barnett (2012). *Small Producer Agency in the Globalized Market.* HIVOS, IIED, Mainumby Nakuratu. http://pubs.iied.org/pdfs/16521IIED.pdf [Accessed 12 November 2014]

Wallerstein, Immanuel, Randall Collins, Michael Mann, Georgi Derluguian and Craig Calhoun (2013). *Does Capitalism Have a Future?* Oxford: Oxford University Press.

Weis, Tony (2007). *The Global Food Economy. The Battle for the Future of Farming.* London: Zed.

Weiss, Thomas G and Leon Gordenker (eds) (1996). *NGOs, the UN & Global Governance.* London: Lynne Rienner Publishers, Inc.

Windfuhr, M. and J. Jonsén (2005). *Food Sovereignty: Towards Democracy in Localized Food Systems.* Rugby, Warwickshire: ITDG Publishing.

Wise, T. (2013a). *Can We Feed the World in 2050? A Scoping Paper to Assess the Evidence.* Tufts University. http://ase.tufts.edu/gdae/Pubs/wp/13-04WiseFeedWorld2050.pdf [Accessed 12 November 2014]

—— (2013b). "US Opposition to Ambitious Indian Program a 'Direct Attack on the Right to Food'". *Pulse* 3 December. www.globalpost.com/dispatches/globalpost-blogs/global-pulse/obama-administration-food-security-act?utm_source=GDAE+Subscribers&utm_campaign=42f790e623-TW_WTOBaliRights_12_9_2013&utm_medium=email&utm_term=0_72d4918ff9–42f790e623–52154177 [Accessed 12 November 2014]

—— (2014). "Monsanto Meets Its Match in the Birthplace of Maize". *Triple Crisis* 12 May. http://triplecrisis.com/?p=9713 [Accessed 12 November 2014]

Wise, Timothy A. and Sophia Murphy (2012). *Resolving the Food Crisis. Assessing Global Policy Reforms since 2007.* Global Development and Environment Institute and Institute for Agriculture and Trade Policy. www.ase.tufts.edu/gdae/Pubs/rp/ResolvingFoodCrisis. pdf [Accessed 12 November 2014]

Wittman, Hannah, Annette Desmarais and Nettie Wiebe (eds) (2010). *Food Sovereignty: Reconnecting Food, Nature and Community.* Halifax and Oakland: Fernwood Publishing and FoodFirst Books.

Wood, Ellen Meiksins (1991). *The Pristine Culture of Capitalism.* London: Verso.

World Bank (1986). *Poverty and Hunger.* Washington, DC: World Bank.

—— (1998). *The Initiative on Defining, Monitoring and Measuring Social Capital. Overview and Programme Description.* Social Capital Initiative Working Paper No. 1.

—— (2007a). *World Bank Assistance to Agriculture in Sub-Saharan Africa: An IEG Review.* Washington, DC: World Bank.

—— (2007b). *Agriculture for Development. World Development Report 2008.* Washington, DC: World Bank.

—— (2008). "Value Chains and Small Farmer Integration". *Agriculture for Development,* LCSAR Agriculture and Rural Development. www-wds.worldbank.org/external/default/WDSContentServer/WDSP/IB/2012/06/07/000333037_20120607010752/Rendered/PDF/693840BRI0P1100sed06060201200Agri05.pdf [Accessed 12 November 2014]

—— (2012). "World Bank Warns Against Complacency Amid High Food Prices and Hunger". Press Release. 29 November. www.worldbank.org/en/news/press-release/2012/11/29/world-bank-warns-against-complacency-amid-high-food-prices-hunger [Accessed 12 November 2014]

—— (2013). *Growing Africa: Unlocking the Potential of Agribusiness.* Washington DC: World Bank.

—— (n.d.). *Worldwide Governance Indicators.* http://info.worldbank.org/governance/wgi/index.aspx#home [Accessed 12 November 2014]

World Development Movement (2011). *Broken Markets. How Financial Regulation Can Help Prevent Another Global Food Crisis.* www.wdm.org.uk/sites/default/files/Broken-markets. pdf [Accessed 12 November 2014]

World Economic Forum (2010). *Everybody's Business: Strengthening International Cooperation in a More Interdependent World.* www3.weforum.org/docs/WEF_GRI_Everybodys Business_Report_2010.pdf [Accessed 12 November 2014]

World Trade Organization (n.d.). *Uruguay Round Agreement. Agreement on Agriculture.* www. wto.org/english/docs_e/legal_e/14-ag_01_e.htm [Accessed 12 November 2014]

——— (2001). *Ministerial Declaration.* 20 November. WT/MIN(01)/DEC1. www.wto.org/english/thewto_e/minist_e/min01_e/mindecl_e.htm [Accessed 12 November 2014]

——— (2014). *What Are Intellectual Property Rights?* www.wto.org/english/tratop_e/trips_e/intel1_e.htm [Accessed 12 November 2014]

Xcroc (2009). "AGRA & Monsanto & Gates, Green Washing & Poor Washing". *Crossed Crocodiles* April 6. http://crossedcrocodiles.wordpress.com/2009/04/06/agra-monsanto-gates-green-washing-poor-washing/[Accessed 12 November 2014]

Zhou,Y.(2010). *Smallholder Agriculture, Sustainability and the Syngenta Foundation.* Syngenta Foundation for Sustainable Development. www.syngentafoundation.org/__temp/Smallholder_Agriculture__Sustainability_and_the_Syngenta_Foundation.pdf [Accessed 12 November 2014]

INDEX

Printed by PGSTL